CLASSIFYING BY RACE

PRINCETON STUDIES IN AMERICAN POLITICS:
HISTORICAL, INTERNATIONAL, AND COMPARATIVE
PERSPECTIVES

SERIES EDITORS

IRA KATZNELSON, MARTIN SHEFTER, THEDA SKOCPOL

Labor Visions and State Power: The Origins of Business Unionism in the United States by Victoria Hattam

The Lincoln Persuasion: Remaking American Liberalism by J. David Greenstone

Politics and Industrialization: Early Railroads in the United States and Prussia by Colleen A. Dunlavy

Political Parties and the State: The American Historical Experience by Martin Shefter

Prisoners of Myth: The Leadership of the Tennessee Valley Authority, 1933–1990 by Erwin C. Hargrove

Bound by Our Constitution: Women, Workers, and the Minimum Wage by Vivien Hart

Experts and Politicians: Reform Challenges to Machine Politics in New York, Cleveland, and Chicago by Kenneth Finegold

Social Policy in the United States: Future Possibilities in Historical Perspective by Theda Skocpol

Political Organizations by James Q. Wilson

Facing Up to the American Dream: Race, Class, and the Soul of the Nation by Jennifer L. Hochschild

Classifying by Race edited by Paul E. Peterson

CLASSIFYING BY RACE

Edited by Paul E. Peterson

PRINCETON UNIVERSITY PRESS   PRINCETON, NEW JERSEY

Library of Congress Cataloging-in-Publication Data
Classifying by race / edited by Paul E. Peterson.
p.   cm.—(Princeton studies in American politics)
Includes bibliographical references and index.
ISBN 0-691-03796-5 (cl : alk. paper).—ISBN 0-691-00176-6 (pbk. : alk. paper)
1. Minorities—United States—Political activity.
2. Representative government and representation—United States.
3. Election districts—United States.   4. Apportionment
Election law—United States.   5. United States—Race relations.
I. Peterson, Paul E.   II. Series.
JF1063.U6C53   1995
324'.08—dc20   95-13494   CIP

This book has been composed in Times Roman

Princeton University Press books are printed
on acid-free paper and meet the guidelines
for permanence and durability of the Committee
on Production Guidelines for Book Longevity
of the Council on Library Resources

Printed in the United States of America by Princeton Academic Press

10   9   8   7   6   5   4   3   2   1

10   9   8   7   6   5   4   3   2   1

(Pbk.)

Contents

Figures

Tables

Preface and Acknowledgments

RACIAL classification has haunted American politics from its beginning. The Constitution dodges the issue by making no reference to race but allowing states to count slaves as "three-fifths" of a person. The Civil War transformed the Constitution, making it, in Lincoln's words, a document "dedicated to the proposition that all men are created equal." But the Constitution was not made color-blind over night. The moral passion unleashed by the Civil War quickly evaporated, leaving behind a legacy of segregation and disenfranchisement that has not yet been erased. Racial distinctions have torn the American political fabric ever since, causing repeated instances of civil violence.

The contemporary debate over racial classification has been dominated by fringe voices in American society. Cries from the right say history should be abrogated and public policy made color-blind, though conservatives once defended racial classification in the name of traditional practice and states' rights. "Advozealots" of the left insist that all customs, language, institutions, and practices are racially tinged. Only aggressive, color-conscious programs can reverse the course of American history.

These proclamations make for strident talk shows and frenzied media commentary. Moderate expressions do not have the same newsworthiness. But racial classification is an issue that cuts too deeply, pervades too many institutions, divides too many people into separate geographical spaces, and poses too many constitutional questions to be resolved by slogans of either the right or the left. The Constitution may now be color-blind, but public policy cannot fulfill its purposes without taking into account the country's past. Racial classification may be deeply entrenched, but it hardly helps to give a racist label to all people, institutions, and practices.

The following essays explore the question of racial classification in many of its political dimensions. The volume begins in part I by examining one of the most contentious of contemporary questions: the self-conscious creation of election districts in which minorities are a majority of the electorate. Part II places this debate in historical context by examining the way in which race has shaped the development of key political institutions. The way in which racial issues fashion electoral politics provides the subject of part III. The last part identifies similarities and differences in the opinions and political resources of racial and ethnic groups.

The essays in this volume were originally presented at a series of seminars that formed the Workshop on Race, Ethnicity, Governance, and Participation in the Center for American Political Studies at Harvard University, which began in the summer of 1992 and concluded in the summer of 1994. The workshop was made possible by a grant from the Ford Foundation. The Joseph B. Grossman Fund and the Center for American Political Studies provided additional funding. Further support for the research for one or more essays included in the collection came from the Hewlett Foundation, John Simon Guggenheim Memorial Foundation, National Science Foundation for research grants SBR-93-07924, SBR-9321212, and SBR-9223637, Aspen Institute for Non-Profit Sector Research, grant 93-NSRF-6, Nuffield College at Oxford University, Rockefeller Foundation, Social Policy and Citizenship Study Group at the Center for European Studies at Harvard University, Spencer Foundation, Tinker Foundation, German Marshall Fund, and the Social Science Research Council.

Many people assisted with the preparation of one or more essays. Research assistance was provided by Jeff Beatty, Ray Joseph, Jr., Paulette Kamenecka, Sarah Laurence, Tamara Lyn, Chris Martin, Kira Sanbonmatsu, and Greg Strizek. Alison Kommer and Sarah Peterson provided staff assistance.

The contributors would also like to thank the following individuals for their helpful comments and suggestions on one or more essays: Edward L. Ayers, James Blacksher, Gary Cox, Dayna Cunningham, Chandler Davidson, Martha Derthick, Angelo Falcon, Catherine Grémion, Bernard Grofman, Jerome Hernandez, Christopher Howard, Pamela Karlan, Ira Katznelson, Desmond King, Morgan Kousser, Jean Leca, Steve Macedo, Cathie Jo Martin, Ken McCue, James Morone, Gary Orfield, Paul Pierson, H. Douglas Price, Doug Rivers, Rogers Smith, Charles Steward, Nanette Tobin, Hilary Silver, James Snyder, Loic Wacquant, Xi Wang, Nick Ziegler, and participants in seminars held by the Cardozo Law Review and at the University of Virginia seminar on April 7, 1994.

An earlier version of the essay by Lani Guinier was published in the *Cardozo Law Review* 14 (5) (1993) as part of a special symposium issue; an earlier version of the essay by Sidney Verba, Kay Schlozman, and Henry Brady appeared in the *British Journal of Political Science* 23 (1993): 453–97.

CLASSIFYING BY RACE

1

A Politically Correct Solution to Racial Classification

PAUL E. PETERSON

WHETHER OR NOT to classify by race is a political, not a moral or ethical, question. Put more exactly, the politically correct answer in a pluralist democracy is also likely to be ethically correct. Those who first attempt to work out a moral position and then devise ways of imposing their answers on their fellow citizens are unlikely to have discerned the correct moral position in the first place. Paradoxically, those who first attempt to find a politically satisfactory resolution to racial classification and only then place it within a moral or legal framework are the more likely to have found an ethically satisfying answer.

"Politically correct" has acquired a derogatory connotation in contemporary social discourse. But if one adheres to its grammatically correct meaning, then one can say that on matters of race and ethnicity one should, indeed, be politically correct. Those on the political right who relentlessly charge their opponents with political correctness are unlikely to agree with the proposition I am advancing. They have recently discovered that classifying by race is contrary to the equal protection clause of the Fourteenth Amendment, conveniently ignoring the fact that in the past many conservatives defended the constitutionality of racial classifications.

The proposition I am advancing may not necessarily appeal to everyone on the political left either. Many liberals have insisted that classifying by race is essential if past patterns of discrimination are to be reversed—despite the fact that liberals have in the past rejected any and all classifications based on race. As Justice John M. Harlan said in his famous dissent in *Plessy v. Ferguson*, the Constitution is color-blind.

The Historical Case for Racial Classification

Both conservatives and liberals make compelling arguments for their newly acquired ethical positions. Conservatives point out that classifying individuals by race introduces a suspect category into public policy. If used as a criterion for allocating educational and occupational opportunities, it confers advantages on members of some racial groups to the disadvantage of members of others. It creates a suspicion that individuals in the advantaged group have acquired their position for reasons other than their individual merit. In so doing, it perpetuates racial antagonisms as well as feelings of racial superiority and inferiority. In the end, racial classification is self-defeating. If it is difficult to fire minorities, they will not be hired in the first place.

To these normative arguments, liberals have an equally powerful reply. Racially blind public policies are a myth, they say. The Constitution is not color-blind: it permitted the slave trade; it counted black slaves as only three-fifths of a person; it gave the white population from slave states disproportionate representation in the Senate. Though a Civil War ended slavery, the country allowed racial segregation to continue virtually unabated for over a century after the Emancipation Proclamation was issued. Racism permeates institutions and practices so thoroughly that the only way discrimination can be alleviated is through explicitly race-conscious policies designed to reverse past practices. The equal protection clause of the Fourteenth Amendment does not preclude classification by race. The clause requires only that race classifications not harm those minorities against whom discrimination has historically been practiced.

The essays in the second part of this volume substantiate and elaborate many of these claims. Richard Valelly's essay, "National Parties and Racial Disenfranchisement," tells us that in the period after the Civil War, African Americans contested southern efforts to reconstruct the antebellum world through segregation and disenfranchisement. But as their Republican allies in the North abandoned Reconstruction, the elaboration of color lines accelerated. Theda Skocpol's analysis, "African Americans in U.S. Social Policy," describes the extent to which social policy has been shaped by racial considerations. Robert Lieberman extends this argument in his essay, "Race and the Organization of Welfare Policy." He shows the way in which even the Social Security Act, the essential core of New Deal liberalism, was designed in ways that would safeguard existing patterns of racial discrimination. By excluding agricultural and domestic laborers, the legislation denied Social Security to most black workers. By leaving the implementation of federal welfare policy to state and local governments, state and local officials were given opportunities to classify by race (which they were most sincerely willing to do).

Some may dismiss these essays as reports from the past, historic examples of racial classification utterly removed from contemporary political and social life. I learned about such predispositions when an influential policy analyst mentioned to me one day that he opposed using historical approaches to the study of public policy. He felt such studies dredged up the dead hand of the past and ignored all that has since been done in recent years to bring past patterns of racial discrimination to an end. But Margaret

Weir's comparative analysis, "The Politics of Racial Isolation in Europe and America," suggests that the past is not easily exorcised. She shows that the geography of American cities, when viewed in comparative perspective, has been defined as much by racial conflict as by technological innovation. As late as 1980, 70 percent of the black or white population would have had to have moved in order to eliminate racial segregation in the residential neighborhoods of our metropolitan areas.[1] When public schools are as racially segregated in 1995 as they were in 1972, one can hardly conclude that the *Brown* decision brought an end to discriminatory practices rooted in two hundred years of slavery.[2]

Lincoln's Politically Correct Solution

The historic and contemporary patterns of racial segregation and classification cannot be denied. But the mere citation of past discriminatory practices does not by itself justify any and all policies designed to rectify them. Progress in race relations cannot be realized unless forward steps are politically viable. The best way out of a racial dilemma does not require a fixed course without regard to wind or wave but a route that allows the political process to sort alternatives until the country finds policies with which it can live.

Abraham Lincoln was the first great American statesman to articulate a politically derived ethic for resolving racial conflict. Lincoln, of course, had to address the far more difficult question of slavery, which he knew to be fundamentally evil. Yet as certain of slavery's inherent immorality as Lincoln was, his political ethic differed from that of the abolitionists. Lincoln opposed only the extension of slavery into the federal territories; he did not oppose its continuation within the slave states for the foreseeable future, nor did he publicly claim that blacks and whites were social equals.[3]

Lincoln tolerated slavery within its existing boundaries because of his fundamental commitment to preserving the experiment in liberty and democracy unfolding within the United States. To preserve the Union, slavery could not yet be abolished. To restore the Union, a Civil War was initiated without calling it a war against slavery. To win the war, slaves were eventually emancipated in the rebellious parts of the Union, though not within those states loyal to the Union. It is easy to condemn these examples of Lincoln's politically correct toleration of what he perceived to be a fundamental evil. But Lincoln's commitment to the Union was not simply a desire to keep intact the compact among the several states. Lincoln understood the Union to be a country dedicated to the proposition that all men are created equal, a country with a government "of the people, by the people, for the people."[4]

This Union had to continue to be one that was worth preserving, and, therefore, any new actions that it took, any additions that it made to its territory, had to enhance the cause of freedom, not of slavery. If slavery could not yet be abolished, it certainly could not be extended into the Mexican territories. If such an extension could be prohibited, than the United States would eventually find a solution to the slave question.[5]

If Lincoln's politically correct answer to the question of racial enslavement is morally acceptable, then perhaps one can also find a politically correct answer to racial classification. If the United States was by 1860 a democratic experiment worth preserving, then today it is worth keeping secure the much further progress the country has since made toward realizing political unity out of people from diverse linguistic, ethnic, and racial traditions. In his analysis, "The Effects of Ethnicity on Political Culture," Rodolfo O. de la Garza provides ample evidence that democratic values are deeply entrenched and widely shared. His findings help make credible the belief that racial classification will some day disappear, provided the democratic experiment is preserved. In the meantime, it is necessary to search for ambiguous solutions not unlike those Lincoln constructed.

The *Bakke* Case

Politically correct solutions are likely to be imprecise, inconsistent, pragmatic, logically indefensible. That does not make them any less ethical. The reasoning of Justice Lewis Powell in the 1978 *Bakke* case is a relevant case in point.

Allen Bakke, a Norwegian American, sued for admission to the medical school of the University of California at Davis.[6] He had been denied a place among the eighty-four positions open to all applicants, despite the fact that his grade point average, his aptitude test, and his overall evaluation scores exceeded those of the average admitted applicant. Bakke's scores exceeded by an even larger amount the average of the sixteen students admitted under a special program reserved for economically or educationally disadvantaged minority students. The Supreme Court allowed Bakke to enter Davis, and he eventually became a medical doctor.

Powell cast the decisive vote in favor of Bakke on the grounds that quotas were unconstitutional unless used to rectify the defendant's past discriminatory practices. Since Davis had never been found to have discriminated against minorities, its use of racial and ethnic distinctions was constitutionally impermissible. Powell went on to say that even though the quotas at Davis were unconstitutional, Harvard's diversity program (which admitted students only after taking into account a variety of personal characteristics, including race and ethnicity) did not violate the equal protection clause. A university had a legitimate interest in having a diverse group of students, and classifications that insured such diversity were reasonable as long as specific racial quotas were not established.[7]

Every single one of Powell's colleagues disagreed with the position he had taken. Though four justices voted with Powell, they did so for different reasons. In concurring opinions, they said Bakke should be admitted because racial quotas, diversity programs, and other distinctions based on race were in violation of the Civil Rights Act of 1964, unless the racial category was needed to apply a remedy for specific grievances against a particular institution. Distinguishing between quotas and diversity was drawing a distinction without a difference.

Four other justices dissented from the *Bakke* decision altogether. In their opinion, quotas were constitutionally acceptable because the purpose of "remedying the effects of past societal discrimination is sufficiently important to justify the use of race-conscious admission programs where there is a sound basis for concluding that . . . the handicap of past discrimination is impeding access of minorities to Medical School." Justice Harry Blackmun noted that "the difference between the Davis program and the one employed by Harvard is [neither] profound nor constitutionally significant." Indeed, he observed that "the cynical . . . may say that under a program such as Harvard's one may accomplish covertly what Davis concedes it does openly."[8]

Blackmun's comments are perceptive. Powell came very close to giving constitutional sanction to public hypocrisy as a policy. He said that one could classify by race as long as no specific numbers were established and racial classifications were not called as such by name. Classifying by race, it seems, was constitutionally acceptable as long as it did not appear as such. But as questionable as Powell's opinion seemed to the other justices, his reasoning has never been explicitly overturned. In 1978 the Supreme Court approved quotas used by a company to overcome past societal discrimination. But the court distinguished the case from *Bakke* because racial classification was undertaken by a private party, not by the state.

Bakke remains a controlling precedent, in large part because it strikes a balanced position on racial issues that the public seems to support. In 1991 Congress passed and George Bush signed civil rights legislation requiring businesses to take affirmative steps to avoid racial and gender discrimination—but forbidding firms from establishing quotas. When Bill Clinton campaigned in favor of affirmative action but against quotas, he, too, adopted a position as ambiguous—but as politically correct—as the one taken by Powell. The wisdom, if not the logic, of such a policy is presumably related to the fact that white public opinion has supported affirmative action policies—as long as these policies do not involve quotas (see table 1.1).

TABLE 1.1

Public Opinion on Quotas and Diversity (Percentage Saying Yes)

	Whites	Blacks
Do you favor or oppose affirmative action programs that promote black employment by requiring businesses to hire a specific number or quota of blacks?	27	69
Do you favor affirmative action programs that promote black employment but do not contain quotas?	69	65

Source: Opinion Research Service, *American Public Opinion Date,* 1991.

Stephen Macedo has made the intriguing suggestion that Powell's position may be both substantively coherent and politically correct. He says that inasmuch as laws have educative effects, they should not have a prima facie racial content even when their practical effect is to give minority groups an advantage.[9] To this argument, it may be replied that one cannot fool the public so easily; policies with a disguised racial content have as educative an effect as those with a prima facie racial content—with the additional consequence that citizens are educated to the art of hypocrisy. Despite Macedo's intriguing effort to give coherence to Powell's position, its only defense is its political acceptability.

The Representation Debate

If in the 1980s the question of racial classification was debated in the language of quotas and diversity, in the 1990s the question has come to focus on issues of political representation. Are states legally required to draw the boundaries of congressional and legislative districts in such a way as to insure the election of the maximum feasible number of minority legislators? Or does the intentional creation of racially homogeneous congressional districts constitute a classification by race that violates the equal protection clause?

The logically coherent answers to these questions come from opposite ends of the political spectrum. Those who oppose racial redistricting argue that the use of racial criteria in the creation of congressional districts cannot be tolerated by a color-blind Constitution. As long as the population of each district is essentially the same and as long as boundaries are not intentionally drawn in order to discriminate against minorities, courts should remain aloof from the political thicket. Certainly, the court should not order states to put all other considerations to one side in order to draw districts with the sole purpose of maximizing minority representation in Congress and state legislatures.[10]

Proponents of racial redistricting argue that the only way that racial minorities can have a political voice is through the creation of districts in which they cast a majority of the votes.[11] They argue that race consciousness is so pervasive a part of American politics that whenever black candidates run against white candidates, racial bloc voting occurs: very large percentage of white voters vote for the white candidate, while a very large percentage of black voters vote for the black candidate. Thus, the only way in which African American and Latino candidates can win elections is by running in districts in which minorities constitute a voting majority. Because voters classify by race, the courts must also ask states to use racial categories. Proponents of racial redistricting disparage the concern for geographical contiguity and compactness. Nearly all political districts are shaped "like animal crackers," Jessie Jackson has claimed. "Democracy is not defined by the symmetry of political district lines—it is determined by function."[12]

The Voting Rights Act and Reapportionment

The roots of the reapportionment debate lie in the Voting Rights Act (VRA) of 1965. The legislation effectively eliminated many mechanisms white southerners had used to deny blacks access to the ballot box. As a result, blacks began voting in record numbers, a process facilitated in important ways, Fredrick Harris tells us in "Religious Institutions and African American Political Mobilization," by politically active black churches. But despite the role of black churches, differences between black and white voter participation rates closed only gradually. James Alt points out in his analysis, "Race and Voter Registration in the South," that a racial gap in voter turnout remains even twenty-five years after the passage of the VRA. Minorities have even less access to other politically relevant resources, as Sidney Verba, Kay Schlozman, and Henry Brady demonstrate in their survey, "Race, Ethnicity, and Political Participation."

Not only did the VRA fail to achieve full equality in rates of political participation, but it raised an entirely new range of questions having to do with the way in which votes were counted. To avoid sharing power with African Americans and Latinos, whites in many cities and counties changed the jurisdictional boundaries of candidates running for public office. Ward elections in municipal elections were eliminated in favor of city-wide elections, making it more difficult for minority candidates to win office. City boundaries were altered to remove minorities and incorporate more whites. Bullet voting in multiple candidate races was eliminated so that minority voters could no longer concentrate all their voting power on a single candidate.[13]

To address these new forms of racial discrimination, Congress in 1982 gave the Department of Justice new authority. In amendments to the VRA, Congress declared that no "practice or procedure shall be . . . applied by any State . . . which results in a denial or *abridgement* of the right of any citizen of the United States to vote on account of race or color [my emphasis]."[14] Denial of the right to vote seems clear enough. But what does it mean to say that a state may not "abridge" the right to vote? Presumably it refers to situations in which a vote is cast but the way in which votes are counted reduces its value. Congress seemed to clarify what it meant by abridgement by saying that members of a minority group may not "have less opportunity than other members of the electorate . . . to elect representatives of their choice." Congress became even more specific when it said that "the extent to which members of a protected class have been elected to office in the State . . . is one circumstance which may be considered" in ascertaining whether an abridgement of the right to vote has occurred. But Congress then came close to contradicting itself when it qualified this requirement with a clause saying that "nothing in this section establishes a right to have members of a protected class elected in numbers equal to their proportion in the population."[15] The VRA thus requires that states must make sure minorities are elected to office and tells them that such minority representation need not be proportional. But if it is not proportional, then how much is enough? Is token representation sufficient? Or must every effort be made to maximize minority representation?

The Department of Justice initially used its new authority to challenge clear instances of racial discrimination, such as the substitution of at-large for ward elections. Then the department sought to extend the meaning of the VRA by challenging the drawing of district boundaries that seemed to deny minorities opportunities to elect candidates of their choice, and lower courts agreed that the VRA required states to increase the number of opportunities for electing minority representatives.[16] Flush with these court victories, the Department of Justice encouraged (without ever explicitly requiring) states to draw new boundaries required by the 1990 census in such a way as to maximize the number of districts in which minority voters could elect a candidate of their choice. In Louisiana, for example, the department refused to approve a plan under which only one district had a majority of black voters on the grounds that another apportionment plan could be designed "in a manner that would more effectively provide to black voters an equal opportunity . . . to elect candidates of their choice."[17] It advised the State of Louisiana that it could give black voters the ability to elect a second candidate of their choice if it combined "significant concentrations of black voters in northeastern Louisiana and in the parishes bordering the State of Mississippi, both along the river and the state's southern border." When the State of Louisiana took this advice and created a district in which the population was 63 percent black, it drew the district boundaries in the shape of a flaming Z, fetching it the nom de guerre "Zorro district." By telling Louisiana and many other states that they could avoid a court suit only if they created new minority districts, the Department of Justice helped increase the number of districts in which African Americans were a majority from seventeen in 1990 to thirty-two in 1992. The number of districts in which Latinos were in the majority increased from nine to nineteen.[18]

Some may think it ironic that a Department of Justice under Presidents Ronald Reagan and George Bush interpreted the VRA as requiring racial redistricting. Both Reagan and Bush condemned racial quotas and other classifications by race. Why then did their appointees in the Justice Department pursue an apparently contradictory set of policies by telling states they had to use racial criteria when redistricting? The department said that racial classifications were required by the VRA, but, as we have seen, the legislation itself was internally contradictory and open to a variety of interpretations. Cynics had a nonlegal explanation for the department's enthusiasm for racial redistricting: it helped Republicans, hurt Democrats.

Before 1994 Republicans generally did poorly in state legislative and congressional elections. More than 60 percent of state legislative seats were won by Democrats.[19] Republicans also chafed at their inability after 1952 to capture control of the House of Representatives. During the 1980s Republicans began a prolonged campaign with the objective of capturing control of the House in 1992. They picked that year because it would be the first election year after the redistricting required by the 1990 census. To win control of the House in 1992 required drawing boundaries in 1991 that were favorable to Republican interests. Their success came just two years later, in 1994.

Racial redistricting was a key component of this strategy. African Americans are much more likely to vote for Democrats than for Republicans.[20] Latinos are less one-sided in their voting preferences, but, except for Cubans, they too are inclined to vote for Democratic candidates. Democratic representatives serve every single member of Congress elected from a district in which minorities constitute more than 40 percent of the population.[21]

At first glance, it would seem that creation of districts in which the minority population constitutes a majority of the electorate would favor the Democratic Party. But the creation of minority districts typically implies the creation of districts that have Democratic supermajorities. The Justice Department advised (but never exactly required) states that to insure the election of a candidate that was the choice of minorities, the minority proportion of the population living in a district should approach 65 percent. This figure was based on the assumptions that an extra 15 percentage points were needed to take into account the fact that minority populations were younger, less likely to register, and less likely to vote if registered. Because of this rule, most minority districts are supra-Democratic districts. Not only are they often 65 percent or more minority, but they also include a significant percentage of whites inclined to vote for Democratic candidates. African Americans elected to the House of Representatives in 1992 won, on average, 78 percent of the vote cast in the general election, 12 percentage points better than did the average Democrat.[22] It takes only a minor arithmetic calculation to demonstrate that the creation of supra-Democratic districts leaves fewer Democratic voters elsewhere, giving Republicans better opportunities to win in more closely contested elections elsewhere in the state.

Republican hopes for control of the House after the 1992 elections were not realized—they gained only ten additional seats—mainly because the Republican presidential ticket ran poorly. Also, the creation of African American and Latino districts did not cost white Democratic officeholders as many seats as Republican strategists had anticipated and Democratic strategists had feared. Racial redistricting resulted in only a few additional Republican seats in the House of Representatives. In states where Democrats controlled the redistricting process, they were able to design minority districts without adversely affecting Democratic success in 1992. But in states where Democrats were not in control of both the state legislature and the gubernatorial chair, racial redistricting did help Republicans win additional seats in the 1992 elections.

Though the effects of racial redistricting in 1992 were modest, the full partisan consequences of racial redistricting were not yet fully apparent. As David Lublin shows in "Race, Representation, and Reapportionment," racial redistricting resulted in still additional Republican gains in 1994, an election year favorable to the Republican Party.

Republican Party strategists anticipated three other benefits from racial redistricting. First, the election of minority candidates from supra-Democratic districts is likely to result in the election of minorities that have little appeal to the political mainstream. As Kenneth Benoit and Kenneth Shepsle demonstrate in their essay, "Electoral Systems and Minority Representation," winners of elections in supra-Democratic districts can be expected to be well to the left of voters in the middle of the political spectrum. To the extent that election boundaries dictate the election of left-leaning minority representatives, minority political leaders will have little appeal to the electorate as a whole, posing difficulties for a Democratic Party attempting to maintain a biracial coalition.[23]

Second, the election of left-leaning minority political leaders reinforces the appearance of race-related voting. As Gary King, John Bruce, and Andrew Gelman show in their essay, "Racial Fairness in Legislative Redistricting," whenever candidates of different races differ on public issues, voters may appear to be choosing on the basis of race or ethnicity even when they are issue oriented. To the extent that election boundaries are drawn so that candidates must appeal only to minority votes, minority candidates may take extreme positions on issues that make them unattractive to white voters. Even when voters are not classifying by race, they may seem to be. If Republicans benefit from persistent racial conflict, and careful research suggests that they do,[24] then Republicans once again benefit from racial redistricting.

Third, interracial conflicts within the Democratic Party are intensified by the competing electoral interests of minority and white Democratic politicians. White Democratic legislators suffer from racial redistricting; minority Democratic legislators benefit from it. The tensions between these two wings of the Democratic Party induced by the reapportionment controversy were in no small measure responsible for the withdrawal by President Clinton of his nomination of Lani Guinier as Assistant Attorney General for Civil Rights.[25]

Racial Bloc Voting

If a Republican-controlled Justice Department may have promoted racial redistricting for partisan rather than public-spirited reasons, this would not be the first time that steps toward racial equality were taken mainly for political reasons. Nothing less than the first presidential civil rights address was in no small part motivated by the advice given Harry Truman by an astute political strategist in February 1948. "The northern Negro vote today," James Rowe wrote in a confidential memorandum that Clark Clifford laid on the president's desk, "holds the balance of power in Presidential elections for the simple arithmetical reason that the Negroes not only vote in a block but are geographically concentrated in the pivotal, large and closely contested electoral states such as New York, Illinois, Pennsylvania, Ohio and Michigan."[26] If Truman's call for civil rights legislation was inspired as much by the fierce election contest upon which he was about to embark as by his desire to improve race relations, this hardly makes his action any less laudable or significant. The same may be said for the Justice Department's position on racial redistricting.

If such redistricting is justified as a response to racial bloc voting, then certainly there is a strong case for the department's policy. In "The Color of Urban Campaigns," David Metz and Katherine Tate show that racial themes pervade mayoral campaigns in which black candidates run against whites. In "Racial Group Competition in Urban Elections," Lublin and Tate demonstrate that the outcome of mayoral elections in which black candidates are participating is extremely dependent upon the number of votes cast by the minority population. Nor is racial bloc voting confined to local politics. Lublin's analysis in "Race, Representation, and Reapportionment" indicates that black congressional candidates are very unlikely to win unless they are running in a district that is at least 40 percent black.

But if racial bloc voting cannot be denied, is this sufficient grounds for requiring that courts draw election districts in such a way as to maximize black representation? Gary King, John Bruce, and Andrew Gelman try to resolve the problem by justifying a degree of racial redistricting that falls at a point short of maximum racial redistricting. They point out that blacks and whites differ in their political opinions (a fact documented in the essay by Verba, Schlozman, and Brady). King, Bruce, and Gelman then note that what appears to be racial bloc voting may be at least in part voting based on nothing other than differences in political opinion. But if blacks vote for black candidates and whites vote for white candidates because the two groups have different political opinions, then is it appropriate to label such bloc voting as racial? Racial redistricting is needed only to the extent that bloc voting is due to electoral choices based solely on the color of the candidate. King, Bruce, and Gelman conclude by suggesting there is good reason to believe that the degree of racial redistricting currently practiced is just about enough to offset the current level of racial bloc voting, as they have defined it.

Lani Guinier's discussion of these issues in her essay, "The Representation of Minority Interests," provides a quite different but equally thought-provoking answer. Although she suggests that racial redistricting may be necessary to rectify past patterns of discrimination, she notes that the policy has important drawbacks. She points out that the first-past-the-post, winner-take-all characteristic of most electoral contests in the United States discriminates against all minorities. The adverse effects of this electoral system is especially great when reinforced by racial bloc voting. Even the most dramatic efforts to maximize minority representation are unlikely to secure proportional representation for minorities.

Guinier recommends that a system of proportional representation be explored as an alternative to the first-past-the-post system characteristic of most U.S. elections. She makes the persuasive argument that proportional representation, unlike racial redistricting, avoids the assumption that political interests are defined solely by racial considerations. But if there are differences of opinion within racial and ethnic groups, then something other than race should become the basis for political representation. In Guinier's view, the answer lies in a system of proportional representation.

Shaw v. Reno

In the summer of 1993 the Supreme Court, in *Shaw v. Reno*, finally gave its own answer to the racial redistricting question. Justice Sandra O'Connor, writing for a five-member majority, rejected both defenders and critics of racial redistricting. Just as Powell came close to endorsing quotas if they were called by another name, so O'Connor and her fellow justices adopted a muddled, middle position in *Shaw v. Reno* that came close to saying that racial redistricting is permissible as long as it is disguised as something else. If racial redistricting is open, apparent, and blatant, the Court will reject it as an unconstitutional classification by race.

The Court agreed to consider the constitutionality of the reapportionment of North Carolina's congressional delegation necessitated by the 1992 census. To conform with guidelines issued by the Department of Justice, the state drew election boundaries in such a way as to create two minority districts. The Twelfth District looked like a snake about to eject its venom; the minority First District appeared as if it were a desperate but one-legged man vainly trying to escape the viper's bite (see figure 5.2). These strange shapes seem to have provoked the Court to apply constitutional scrutiny to the question of racial redistricting. The Court decided that the shape of North Carolina's congressional districts was "so bizarre on its face," "irrational on its face," and so "extremely irregular on its face" that it "rationally cannot be understood as anything other than an effort to segregate citizens into separate voting districts on the basis of race."[27] The Court took pains to say that nothing in its decision should be understood as saying that the Constitution required that congressional districts be compact, contiguous, or respectful of existing political boundaries. It was saying only that the absence of these characteristics revealed an unconstitutional motivation to classify voters on the basis of their race. Yet it also claimed that its decision was perfectly consistent with an earlier decision in which the Supreme Court upheld the right of states "to attempt to prevent racial minorities from being repeatedly outvoted by creating districts that will afford fair representation to the members of . . . racial groups."[28] The Court apparently reasoned that the state can take race into account if it can disguise its intention, but if the results are so geographically bizarre that it cannot disguise its racial intention, the racial gerrymander becomes unconstitutional. Much as Powell had decided in the *Bakke* case that diversity plans were constitutional because the racial motive could be disguised, so O'Connor argued that racially motivated redistricting is permissible only when the intention can be masked.

Four justices dissented from the majority decision. Justice David Souter reasoned that "as long as racial bloc voting takes place, legislators will have to take race into account in order to avoid dilution of minority voting strength." Justice Byron White questioned "the logic" of the majority's "theory," which "appears to be that race-conscious redistricting that 'segregates' by drawing odd-shaped lines is qualitatively different from race-conscious redistricting that affects groups in some other way. The distinction is without foundation."[29]

White's criticism seems to the point. The reasoning used by O'Connor and the Court majority is logically incoherent. Had the Court majority agreed that race can never be taken into account in drawing electoral district lines, it would have taken the straightforward position that classification by race is unconstitutional. Had the Court said that the state must classify by race because only by so doing can it deliberately offset the effects of racial bloc voting, that, too, would have been logically consistent.

But if White wins the logical argument, it is not so clear that he has a persuasive political case. If the Court in *Shaw v. Reno* took an incoherent position along the lines taken by Powell in *Bakke*, such a position may be more politically correct than the logically more consistent policies recommended by Court critics. Ignoring race hardly makes sense in a society where racial distinctions have long loomed large. But making racial considerations the one and only factor to be considered in drawing election boundaries elevates race to the center stage of American politics, a focal point that led to a Civil War in the mid-nineteenth century and civil violence in the mid-twentieth. It is better that the significance of race in governmental decisions be disguised than made explicit. The more obviously governmental actions are motivated by race, the more government intensifies the racial divisions in our society. The more government can take actions that assist minorities without explicitly challenging the individualistic, liberal tradition upon which the country's democratic experiment is founded, the more likely it is that the need to classify by race will eventually disappear.

Classification by race should help achieve racial progress without endangering the country's political stability. Some racial classification is necessary to facilitate the continued incorporation of racial minorities within the fabric of the American economic, social, and political order. But racial classification carried to an extreme will only retard that progress by intensifying hostilities among racial groups. The distinction between some and too much cannot be drawn logically; the line can be politically calculated only by experienced politicians and jurists who have a sense of the appropriate balance. What emerges from an open political process is likely to be the appropriate balance—at least as long as ideologues of both the right and left are kept at the margins of power.

These conclusions are my own, though I reached them only after thinking about the issues posed by the papers in the collection that follows. They are not necessarily shared by each and every author of the essays in this book nor compelled by the findings they report. Ethical judgments are informed, not dictated, by empirical research. Readers are invited to draw their own conclusions after taking into account the arguments and analyses that follow.

Notes

1. Farley 1991, p. 280.
2. Orfield et al. 1993.
3. Neither did the Apostle Paul specifically condemn the practice of slavery, though he said, "In Christ, there is no East nor West, . . . no slave nor free," a phrase that later served as a guide for the abolitionist movement.
4. G. Wills 1992.
5. Greenstone 1993.
6. *Regents of the University of California v. Bakke*, 700–717.
7. Ibid.
8. Ibid., 716.
9. Discussion before the Workshop on Race, Ethnicity, Participation and, Governance, June 20, 1994.
10. Thernstrom 1987.
11. Grofman and Davidson 1992; Grofman, Handley, and Niemi 1992.
12. Smothers 1994, 24.
13. Davidson 1984.
14. Grofman, Handley, and Niemi 1992.
15. Ibid., chap. 2.
16. Ibid.
17. *Hayes v. Louisiana*, 17.
18. Lublin 1994.
19. Fiorina 1992, 26.
20. Tate 1993.
21. Lublin 1994.
22. Lublin 1994, chap. 4.
23. See also the discussion of this issue in Swain 1993.
24. Carmines and Stimson 1989.
25. Guinier 1994.
26. McCullough 1992, 590.
27. *Shaw v. Reno*, 10, 12 and 21.
28. *United Jewish Organizations of Williamsburgh v. Carey*.
29. *Shaw v. Reno*, 88, 67.

Part I

RACE AND REPRESENTATION

2

The Representation of Minority Interests

LANI GUINIER

MAJORITY BLACK electoral districts are the remedy of choice in most voting rights cases brought by black plaintiffs. This preference is consistent with the particular bias toward winner-take-all single-member electoral districts common in the United States. This article focuses on the limits of districting as a method for representing minority interests.

Elections based on multimember districts and proportional or semiproportional representation may work better than districting as a remedy for vote dilution.[1] These alternatives would assure fair minority representation and would better reflect all voters' true preferences. Semiproportional, multimember electoral systems do not rely on territorial or residential location as a fixed proxy for interests. Instead, these alternative electoral systems allow voters to establish their own communities of interest at each election. Unlike race-conscious districting,[2] which predetermines voting options based on a concept of group representation, these alternative electoral systems allow contenders to win representation based on their proportion of the votes actually cast.

For example, in an at-large system with cumulative voting, voters can cast multiple votes for one candidate. Although each voter possesses the same total number of votes, a voter has the option of plumping or cumulating her votes to express the intensity of her preferences. Instead of creating one majority black single-member district in a jurisdiction with a black electoral minority of 30 percent and three county commissioners, each voter would create her own election district by the way she distributed her votes. If voting for a black candidate was important to her, she could give the black candidate all three of her votes. If the 30 percent black voting minority all felt this way and was therefore politically cohesive, it could not be denied at least one representative of its choice.[3]

By juggling the number of legislative positions within each multimember district, a jurisdiction can set a community-specific threshold of exclusion—something less than 50 percent but more than 5 percent—to approximate the actual population percentage of minority voters in the locality.

The threshold of exclusion can be set high enough to eliminate real fringe groups or marginal claims, yet low enough to empower many other politically cohesive minorities, including white liberals who live in Republican-dominated suburbs, white women who are not geographically concentrated, and Latinos who live in small, dispersed concentrations.

By contrast, winner-take-all districting gives those who get the most votes all the power. Thus, votes cast for "losers" are wasted. This submerges the voting strength of all voters who do not support the winning candidate. Given the preference of incumbents for safe districts, even some of the votes cast for winners may be wasted. Moreover, the decennial process of districting, in which incumbents enjoy inordinate control, often produces voter disinterest in noncompetitive election contests.

Because they remove the power of districting from self-interested incumbents, multimember districts with cumulative voting may generate greater voter interest in competitive election contests. In addition, negative campaigning is less effective in elections with multiple winners than in elections with only one opponent. As a result, candidates may have to offer more than name recognition, thereby reducing the incentive for contests based solely on television advertising and negative campaigning.

Candidates may turn to political parties to assist them in identifying interest constituencies. The lowered exclusion threshold gives third political parties a real chance to win representation. This might revive community-based, local political organizations, which could play an important role in educating and mobilizing grass-roots support for ideas rather than just for career politicians. If so, these alternatives would accomplish many of the objectives of term limitations.

Even if they are not actually implemented as remedies in vote dilution cases, semiproportional election systems also serve as a baseline for measuring the political fairness of existing systems. As such, they focus our attention on the value of direct rather than virtual representation of interests. They also redirect the responsibility for establishing interest constituencies away from incumbent politicians and back to the voters themselves. They introduce, without the immutable and separatist nature of its contemporary stigma, the concept of proportionality. By at least raising some of these ideas, a discussion of alternative election systems may inject new meaning into the debate about political fairness.

The goal of this article is ultimately to revive our political imagination. "Change the way people think," said South African civil rights martyr Steven Biko, "and things will never be the same."[4] Developing the perspective of minority interest representation, emphasizing voter participation and voter choice, and reintroducing proportionality into the lexicon of political fairness enriches the debate about how to increase the legitimacy of our political system.

I

In this part, this article reexamines, from the perspective of a racially distinct, insular minority, one of the critical aspects of political equality: the
question of political fairness. The concept of political fairness is helpful in
determining the inclusion of all participants in the American political process. Here, the interest is specifically in whether our political system's emphasis on winner-take-all single-member districts is *legitimate* from the
perspective of a previously disenfranchised group.[5]

Political legitimacy raises the procedural question of whether officials
have a reason for "implementing a certain decision after the votes are
counted," not whether the decision itself is justified on the merits.[6] Political
legitimacy, as defined here, is a process-oriented standard. It does not ex-
haust, nor necessarily implicate, the substantive possibilities of legitimacy.

In other words, political fairness or legitimacy is defined as a form of
procedural justice. Procedural justice for black voters has three interrelated
goals: to give dignity and satisfaction to many of the strongly held sentiments of minorities, to make black representatives necessary participants
in the governing process, and to disaggregate a majority faction that is
permanently self-constituted based on prejudice.

Procedural justice challenges the entitlement of a 51 percent majority
exercising 100 percent of the power. It focuses on requirements of structured election and legislative decisional mechanisms to enforce fairness in
policy making. Outcomes are not considered, however, in order to judge
the rightness of particular substantive policy choices. Outcomes are relevant in a procedural justice sense only to the extent they enable us to measure degrees of participation of all eligible voters in the decision-making
process. Interest group participation in governance is critical, even without
a substantive standard for invalidating legislative outcomes.

Some political scientists have measured political legitimacy by the extent to which a system establishes the opportunity for public participation
and ensures procedural regularity.[7] They have focused on provisions dealing with majority rule, minority rights, and accountability in regular and
frequent elections. The traditional approach to procedural legitimacy emphasizes four attributes:

1. *Accountability* (whether leaders are accountable to their constituents via a
process that permits wide, effective participation)

2. *Efficiency* (whether government avoids undue waste of time or resources;
sometimes described in terms of stability)

3. *Procedural fairness* (whether issues are resolved in a regular, predictable, and open way that provides citizens *equal access to the decision-making
process*)

   4. *Distributive fairness* (whether advantages and costs are distributed equally
   or, if not, whether deviations from presumptive equality are justified)[8]

   The discussion in this part focuses on procedural fairness, emphasizing
in particular equal access to the process of decision making. It assumes that
the legitimacy of our system depends on providing all citizens meaningful
access to the "forum where public policy is finally fashioned."[9] In a representative democracy, the right to be represented contemplates the right to
be heard, not just the right to be "present." In other words, the assumption
inherent in a system of self-government based on election of representatives is that political fairness involves legislative influence, not just legislative presence.

   Empowerment should be measured not just by degrees of physical inclusion or representative presence but by structures that reinforce a sense that
one's contribution is valued, that choice is possible, and that outcomes may
be different because of one's participation. Autonomy and mechanisms to
ensure direct accountability are critical to empowerment. Without such
structural mechanisms to shape participation, representative presence may
be used simply to ratify or legitimate preexisting consensus.

   Equal access to decision making is therefore defined as an equal opportunity to influence the policy-making process. Such a situation has two
elements: a realistic opportunity to participate on the basis of self-defined
interests and a continuous opportunity to hold representatives accountable
to community-based interests. Attributes of accountability and distributive
fairness are directly incorporated into a discussion of procedural fairness.

   Accountability and distributional equality help define "equal access to
decision making."[10] Accountability is essentially a delegate conception of
representation in which the representative's primary role is to transmit and
interpret constituency views. For minority interests to be represented fairly,
the interests must be defined primarily by the voters and not by the representatives. Distributional equality refers to the distribution of procedural
resources such as equally weighted votes or proportional influence.

   The goal is to develop a political fairness standard for procedural moni-
toring of the political process. I begin by formulating a standard of procedural fairness that measures the degree to which a system avoids *structural
impediments* to minority participation, influence, and confidence in decision making. Stated differently, procedural fairness means that minorities
enjoy a "fair share" of procedural resources such as votes, opportunities for
participation, and mechanisms to persuade and influence.

   As part of this project, I use a concept I have termed *proportionate interest representation.*[11] Under proportionate interest representation, the relevant unit of participation is the "interest group" or the interest constituency.
Interests are those self-identified voluntary constituencies who choose to

combine because of like minds, not like bodies. Minority interests include those smaller constituencies who, because of polarization, are permanently consigned to a numerically inferior status. An interest's identity may be self-defined in racial terms either because it is racially apparent or racially derived, and its choice to self-define is partly a function of historical treatment by the numerically superior racial majority.[12] Blacks in the United States are an obvious minority interest group, despite the presence of a range of ideologies and class status. Whites in South Africa are also a minority interest, although their choice to self-define is a function of their historical treatment of, not by, the numerically superior racial majority.

Another major premise of proportionate interest representation is that political fairness has an equal influence component, that is, an equal opportunity to influence legislative outcomes.[13] The term *influence* is used to include opportunities to exchange information about, as well as capacities to reward or punish compliance with, preferences and intentions. For those at the bottom, it is not enough that a representation system give everyone an equal chance of having policy preferences physically represented. A fair system of political representation should include mechanisms to ensure that a disadvantaged and stigmatized minority group also has a fair chance of having its needs and desires satisfied.

I assume here that each voter should enjoy the same opportunity to influence political outcomes. No one is entitled to absolutely equal influence; by the same token, no one is entitled to grossly disproportionate influence or a monopoly on control. The majority should enjoy a majority of the power, but the minority should also enjoy some power too. Thus, proportionate interest representation measures opportunities for fair participation using a baseline of proportional power or proportional influence.

The concept of proportional power is not new. Others have recognized it as an important barometer of political fairness. Its absence often spurs movements to reform the political system.[14] This was certainly part of the impetus behind the reapportionment revolution of *Baker v. Carr* and *Reynolds v. Sims*. Population shifts over the preceding fifty years had not been accompanied by population-based reapportionments. Indeed, many legislatures had refused to reapportion at all. As Justice Brennan noted in *Baker v. Carr*, since 1901 "all proposals in both Houses of the [Tennessee] General Assembly for reapportionment have failed to pass."[15] As a result, several southern legislatures were dominated by rural interests who represented a population minority yet controlled a majority of the legislative seats.

Incumbent politicians in these legislatures were riveted to their seats by legislative gridlock and the absence of a legislative will to change. The failure of will was associated with the failure of the legislature to represent fairly the majority. This disproportionate concentration of power prompted federal judicial intervention in the early 1960s into areas that had traditionally been classified as off-limits "political questions."

In response to the disproportionate power exercised by a political minority, the Supreme Court developed its "one-person, one-vote" jurisprudence. The Court found a constitutional right to population-based apportionment on the theory that the majority of the population should have a majority voice in the legislature.

The Court recognized that the growing urban population majority would never command its fair share of legislative power unless the Court intervened. A recent essay makes the same point. "When disproportionality is great and when attitudes and interests differ radically across groups—as with rural/urban differences of the 1950s or current racial/ethnic differences—corrective steps must be taken if our system is to be regarded as fair."[16]

As I use the term, a *fair share* or a *fair opportunity* to influence is a principle of proportional power designed to maintain legitimacy primarily from the perspective of minority interests. Some argue, however, that the one-person, one-vote principle was designed primarily to restore a competing principle: the principle of majority legislative power. In this understanding, the Court's fair share rule was limited to the majority. In order to give a fair share of power to the majority, the Court (perhaps unwittingly) devised a one-person, one-vote rule that actually gives the majority disproportionate power in winner-take-all districts. The majority—in a now equally populous district—gets all the power.

Yet, the fair opportunity to influence principle constrains both the majority and the minority. By definition majority rule need not mean that a simple majority controls *all* the legislative power. A simple majority exercising most, but not all, the power is also majority rule. Indeed, I have argued elsewhere that winner-take-all majority rule can be fundamentally at odds with traditional notions of democracy.[17]

In fact, the proportional power principle is consistent with the core concept of the one-person, one-vote cases, meaning that each voter should get to cast an equally weighted vote.[18] In this sense, the one-person, one-vote cases are not about winner-take-all majority rule at all. Arguably, they can be better understood as simply voiding minority rule (that is, a system in which a minority actually decides all, or even a majority, of the decisions). Although the Supreme Court found minority domination unconstitutional, it did not necessarily constitutionalize a particular decision-making or aggregating alternative.

For example, in considering a 60 percent vote requirement, the Supreme Court recognized that "any departure from strict majority rule gives disproportionate power to the minority." Yet, the Court found nothing unconstitutional per se in the 60 percent decisional rule that gave a minority temporary political leverage: "There is nothing in the language of the Constitution, our history, or our cases that requires that the majority always prevail on every issue."[19]

To a great extent, the norm of proportional influence and the idea of interest constituencies already shape our views regarding political participation. For example, in the same reapportionment cases that voided minority rule, the Supreme Court declared that representative government provides "each and every citizen ... [with] an inalienable right to full and effective representation."[20] The notion of full and effective representation has two components. First, full and effective representation envisions an equality norm—that is, the right of all citizens to equal treatment as citizens in a democracy. The equality norm was based upon the Supreme Court view of legislative reapportionment, in particular, the aforementioned constitutional principle of one person, one vote. The equality norm provides that every citizen has the right to vote and every citizen has the right to an equally weighted vote.[21] Additionally, the equality norm supports an equal right to government services for every person.

The right to "full and effective representation" thus subsumes concerns about equal voting and equal access. As the Court stated in one of its early reapportionment cases, "Equal representation for equal numbers of people is a principle designed to prevent debasement of voting power and diminution of access to elected representatives."[22] I would also argue that implicit in the equality norm is the moral proposition that every citizen should enjoy the opportunity to exercise equal legislative influence.[23]

The second component of the one-person, one-vote vision is the empowerment norm, explicated in the Voting Rights Act of 1965, as amended in 1982.[24] As such, it is informed by the goals and strategies of the Civil Rights movement that led to the act's passage in 1965 and that has been successful in extending and amending the act in 1970, 1975, and 1982. The empowerment norm views political participation and the right to participate throughout the political process as critical to democratic legitimacy. In other words, it is not enough that people receive certain formal or symbolic rights; it is critical that citizens be given the opportunity and incentive to exercise those rights in order to promote their interests. What legitimizes representative government is the fact that citizens knowingly *choose* those who represent them and that citizens have the opportunity not only to elect but to remove those who do not represent them effectively.

Both norms are expressed in the act's 1982 amendments, which afford all citizens the same or "equal opportunity to participate in the political process and to elect representatives of their choice."[25] Both norms are also suggested in the Court's treatment of other areas of the political process, and in its recognition of the importance of meaningful participation to advance ideas, not just candidates.

Voting is not just about winning elections. The reason people participate in competitive elections is not simply *to win* a contested seat in the legislature, but to have their ideas and interests represented in the public debate as well as in deliberation of the legislature. Voting is about representing interests throughout the process of governing. The notion of "one interest, one vote" has been explicitly discussed in cases dealing with special-function elections.[26] The importance of influencing the governing process based on one's self-defined interests has also implicitly permeated constitutional cases involving the right of blacks to vote in white primaries,[27] and the right of minor political parties to gain access to the ballot.[28]

As a numerical minority, black voters are unlikely to win elections. The Court nevertheless has insisted that blacks not be denied any effective voice in their government.[29] Black votes should be more than "empty vote[s] cast after [or before] the real decisions are made."[30] Likewise, the contribution of minor political parties to "diversity and competition in the marketplace of ideas" does not depend upon their ability to win elections.[31] Minor political party candidates do not seek only to get elected; minor political parties participate to "expand and affect political debate." Indeed, the contribution of minor political parties cannot be realized "if they are unable to participate meaningfully" in the phase of the political process "in which policy choices are most seriously considered."[32]

Even in its discussion of the rights of the two major political parties, the Court has recognized the value of a forum in which to voice one's ideas in order to persuade and influence. Where the state has attempted to regulate the internal structure of a major political party, the Court has generally deferred to that party's interest in self-determination and autonomy—its right to define its own associational boundaries, to determine the content of its message, and to engage in effective political association at the point where it is most likely to be influential.[33] In both the equal protection and the First Amendment context, participation on behalf of one's self-defined interests is an important value that the Court has protected in the political process.

In this part I have attempted to develop two critical assumptions that underlie a political fairness standard. The first is the importance of representing interest constituencies and the second is the importance of insuring these constituencies opportunities to exercise proportional influence. These assumptions are very different from electoral quotas or the peculiarly American notion of proportional representation. Proportional descriptive representation, or head counting the number of black elected officials, does not necessarily address either of these aspects of political fairness.

On the one hand, it is certainly true that race in this country has defined individual identities, opportunities, frames of reference, and relationships. Where race has and continues to play a significant role in determining historical outcomes, racial group membership often serves as a political proxy for shared experience and common interests. At least to the extent that an overwhelming majority of group members experiences a common "group identity," those who are group members are more likely to represent similar interests.[34] Group members *may* also share common cultural styles or operating assumptions.

A racial group is also more likely to perceive that representatives from their own group will best represent them. This definition of representative as descriptive likeness or racial compatriot has a psychological component. Just as the flag stands for the nation, the presence of racial group members symbolizes inclusion of a previously excluded group. This symbolic role results from both the personal characteristics of the racial group member and the assumption that, because of those characteristics, the racial group member has had experiences in common with her constituents. As Hanna Pitkin writes, "We tend to assume that people's characteristics are a guide to the actions they will take, and we are concerned with the characteristics of our legislators for just this reason."[35] Thus, many racial minorities report that they do not feel represented unless members of their racial group are physically present in the legislature.

As a result, traditional voting rights advocates comfortably rely on race as a proxy for interests. For example, in traditional voting rights litigation, it is election contests between black and white candidates that help define the degree of racial polarization, that is, the degree to which blacks and whites vote differently. The idea is that the outcome would be different if elections were held in either one community or the other. The assumption of racial polarization extends explicitly to the specific candidate elected and implicitly to the issues that the candidate, once elected, would emphasize.

The implicit inference of difference in the degree of candidate responsiveness rests in part on the claim that where black candidates enjoy protection from electoral competition with whites, black voters can easily ratify their choices to hold their representatives accountable. In this way, the association between race and interests is a function of the degree to which voters are given a meaningful choice. Voting rights advocates assume that minority group sponsorship is critical. It is only where minority voters exercise electoral control, or have a meaningful opportunity to choose their representative, that race functions as a representative proxy. Thus, majority black single-member districts take advantage of segregated housing patterns to use geography as a proxy for racial choice, racial control, and racial representation.

On the other hand, some commentators challenge proportional descriptive representation (that is, representation of racial groups by racial group members) on the grounds that special protection throughout the political process for the rights of minority groups is unnecessary as long as individual minority group members have a fair chance to participate formally by casting a ballot in an election. For these commentators, "race-conscious" districting is illegitimate because the right to vote is individual, not group based. These observers challenge the right of minority groups to representative *or* responsive government.[36]

Given the prominence of racial group identities, I am not persuaded by this criticism, and disagree with those critics of race-conscious districting who object on moral grounds to the drawing of districts along racial lines.[37] One cannot define political fairness as merely electoral fairness that guarantees impartial conditions of voting eligibility and equally counted votes. Yet, the critics are right in suggesting the need to rephrase the question more broadly. The critical issue is not whether blacks have special claims for protection or whether whites can or should represent blacks.

Rather, the critical issue is whether *all* voters can exercise a fair choice in selecting and retaining representatives. As stated by a white Democratic congressperson who represents a largely minority constituency: "I'm torn about it. I do not believe you have to be of the exact same ethnic group to do a good job in representing that community. But, in the end, I think it's that community's choice."[38] Thus, proportionate interest representation emphasizes the connection between choice, accountability, and influence. Whoever represents minority interests, just as whoever represents majority interests, should enjoy proportionate influence and should be directly, not merely virtually, accountable to those interests as defined by the voters themselves.[39]

Thus, empowerment strategies that are designed primarily to increase the proportion of minority group legislators may ignore the issues of influence and accountability. I argue that empowerment requires that voters directly receive the opportunity and the information necessary to define their interests for themselves. I also suggest that race and geography are useful but limited proxies for defining interests. I will attempt to show that unlike some aspects of race-conscious districting, proportionate interest representation is not rigidly essentialist or presumptuously isolating. Proportionate interest representation encourages all voters to make informed and active choice in identifying their interests.

Proportionate interest representation uses procedural rules to consider issues of influence, rather than just initial access. The procedural rules also measure sustained accountability to minority expressions of interest based on continuous opportunities to make informed choices and to voice opinions. In this sense, Professor Kathryn Abrams's "extended political process" view of participation is accurate.[40] Opportunities for participation should not stop after one-time election-day voting. Minority voters, just like all other voters, should enjoy incentives to become informed and opportunities to exercise their political choices throughout the entire process of governing.

In sum, proportionate interest representation reflects an attempt to develop a standard of procedural fairness based on the importance of representing interests, giving those interests proportional influence, and allowing *all* voters the choice and the incentive to assert their interests directly and continuously. Electoral and representational structures will be measured by the extent to which they mobilize broad-based voter participation, foster substantive debate from a range of viewpoints, provide and reinforce opportunities for minority interests to exercise meaningful choice throughout the process of decision making and governance, and allow genuine, community-based leaders to emerge.

II

Elsewhere, in order to explore issues of political fairness, I have reviewed current remedial strategies and enforcement mechanisms by first asking the question: How do we measure success? The argument in brief is that strategies to maximize minority voting strength that concentrate on creating majority black districts may fail to achieve political fairness as defined herein. To the extent that segregated residential patterns permit the formation of majority black districts, the voting rights strategy has been successful in increasing the number of blacks elected to office. But it has been less successful in reinvigorating black political participation or in getting blacks a fair share of influence on policy outcomes.

There have been three generations of voting rights issues. The first generation approach focused directly on access to the ballot on the assumption that the right to vote by itself was "preservative of all other rights."[41] As is evident in the current debate over motor-voter registration, problems remain regarding definitions of universal suffrage and the extent of government prevoting registration obligations. Nevertheless, first generation issues do not now dominate the voting rights political terrain.

Access issues, for the most part, have been replaced by the second generation approach to voting rights, increasing the number of minority group members elected to office. Second generation cases assume that the right to vote is meaningful only to the extent that minority group members enjoy the right to elect candidates of their choice. This approach, using the theory of black electoral success, measures the political fairness of a system by purely electoral standards. It relies on the physical integration of the elected body to effectuate representational fairness.

The second generation of voting litigation has attempted to realize the influence and the accountability aspects of the political equality and political empowerment norms through what I term Black Electoral Success Theory (BEST). BEST chooses as its enforcement mechanism majority black single-member districts. It aims to create majority black single-member districts based on the following assumptions:

> **1.** It is important to elect authentic representatives, that is, representatives chosen by black voters who are community based and physically, culturally, and psychologically connected to their constituency base. The key aspect of authenticity is the fact that black voters *choose* who represents them.
> **2.** Electing authentic representatives mobilizes black voters to participate. Voter mobilization is a valued part of democratic legitimacy.
> **3.** Electing authentic representatives is necessary to overcome racially polarized voting; and electoral systems that allow the majority to select government officials are unfair *if* the majority is racially homogenous, permanent, and votes as a racial bloc against minority-sponsored representatives.
> **4.** By electing authentic representatives, black voters will experience greater governmental responsiveness; in other words, authentic representation yields functional or substantive representation.

BEST's four assumptions involve claims about authenticity, mobilization, polarization, and responsiveness. Through BEST, the equality norm and the empowerment norm find partial expression in second generation voting rights litigation strategies. However, BEST's assumptions are flawed. Consequently, BEST is inadequate to realize fully political fairness for several reasons I discuss elsewhere. Here I focus on one failing: BEST fails to anticipate the third generation claim.[42]

In the third generation, the marginalization of minority group interests is reproduced in the newly integrated legislature. With the Supreme Court's 1992 decision in *Presley v. Etowah County*, we have witnessed the official arrival of this new generation of voting discrimination. In *Presley*, the first black county commissioners were elected to two Alabama county governing bodies from majority black electoral districts. These districts were created to settle a second generation vote dilution case. The holdover white incumbents redistributed the commission's power immediately upon the black commissioners' election. Power that had traditionally been exercised by each commissioner individually was given in one county to an appointed administrator; in the other county, that same decision-making power was redistributed to the commission as a whole.

The Supreme Court ruled that the erection of structural impediments to meaningful black participation in governance was *not* covered by the Voting Rights Act.[43] According to Justice Kennedy's majority opinion, "the Voting Rights Act is not an all purpose antidiscrimination statute." Most importantly, according to Justice Kennedy the statute merely said blacks may vote, not that blacks should govern.[44]

The Kennedy majority's cramped view of participation, and its effort to detach voting from governing, represents a major setback to contemporary efforts to legitimize our political system. I have argued that political fairness requires proportionate influence to claim the allegiance of minority group members and to legitimate, from their perspective, a system that previously disenfranchised them. It follows from this that closer attention to the concept of political fairness may help one understand vote-aggregating and decision-making procedures as a third generational conflict. Using the proportionate interest representation standard, in the next section I will assess the political fairness of single-member district electoral arrangements in light of the three generations of voting rights issues.

III

The single-member district is the predominant system of electoral representation in the United States. It is, therefore, not surprising that voting rights cases have traditionally measured minority representational potential by reference to electoral control of single-member districts. Justice William Brennan explained as follows in one of three U.S. Supreme Court cases in the 1980s that considered the actual standards for proving political inequality:

> The single-member district is generally the appropriate standard against which to measure minority group potential to elect because it is the smallest political unit from which representatives are elected. Thus . . . if the minority group is so small in relation to the surrounding white population that it could not constitute a majority in a single-member district, these minority voters cannot maintain that they would have been able to elect representatives of their choice.[45]

Several explanations have been offered to justify the American bias toward winner-take-all single-member districts, in addition to the absence of European-type proportional representation systems in the United States. These explanations include the importance of the individual voter as the preferred unit of representation, the assumption that geography works as a proxy for that voter's interests, especially where there is residential segregation, the constitutionalization of one person, one vote as the Court's jurisprudential answer to making government more responsive to the people, and the Voting Rights Act's explicit disclaimer against proportional election of minority members.[46]

In this section, I evaluate the single-member district in terms of the three generations of voting rights claims. I question the extent to which winner-take-all districts evenhandedly distribute power throughout the political process. I assess the winner-take-all single-member district using the standard of political fairness I have articulated thus far, which emphasizes participation, influence, and accountability. I examine the extent to which single-member districts mobilize broad-based voter participation; reinforce a sense of genuine inclusion as opposed to token representation; and foster substantive, issue-oriented debate in which minority representatives advocate effectively the interests of their constituents.

I focus here on single-member districts in the particular enforcement context of local county and city government because these types of government have a tradition of experimentation and innovation; they are usually not monitored by intermediaries; bottom-up approaches to empowerment are more desirable than top-down; and there are plenty of actual examples as a result of contemporary voting rights litigation. I will argue that districting imperfectly allocates power at the local level. Because of the limits of any winner-take-all district that elects only one representative, even race-conscious districting does not reasonably achieve the objectives I posit for measuring political fairness from the perspective of minority interests.

While it may be true that no election structure alone completely accomplishes my goals, modified multimember alternatives to single-member districts should at least be considered. Because semiproportional alternatives such as cumulative voting give minority voters, based on their political cohesiveness, the potential to enjoy electoral success and proportionate influence throughout the extended political process, they may offer a better chance for meaningful participation. Even from the perspective of those who do not share my view of political equality, semiproportional election systems may provide a more politically fair route to participation and political representation for all voters. Since semiproportional election systems represent *voluntary interest constituencies*, they potentially empower all politically cohesive interests.

Winner-Take-All Districting Has Failed to Mobilize Sustained Voter Participation

Districting systems rely on geography as a tool for identifying voter interests. Based on principles of equal population, districting uses a decennial process in which voters are assigned to a fixed territorial constituency. Because of rules regarding compactness and contiguity, the territorial constituency presumably represents a community of interest.

Districting assumes that smaller political units best fulfill the political empowerment and equality norms of American constitutional jurisprudence. The main benefits of smaller units include increased identification with political leaders by their constituents, recognition of communities of

interest at the local or neighborhood level, and increased political participation by the citizenry. Local districts are presumed to heighten citizen
awareness of, and their reasons for, participating in electoral activity. Also,
safe black districts enable blacks to get elected and then reelected, leading
to positions of seniority and status within the elected body.[47]

Yet, by emphasizing individual candidacies, winner-take-all single-
member district structures may demobilize poor black and Latino voters.
Turnout generally goes up in response to first-time election opportunities
for candidates of the minority community's choice. The mobilization efforts for these breakthrough elections, however, are generally not repeated.
As a consequence, turnout tends to go down in subsequent elections after
the first black pioneer becomes the incumbent.

The incumbent's core constituency may then become alienated, given
the absence of local, alternative community organizations to educate and
mobilize constituent participation outside of elections. Indeed, once
elected, incumbents may demobilize constituents by not maintaining a
genuine, community-based political organization to provide feedback,
ideas, and reinforcement to the elected official while in office.

In addition, the districting process arbitrarily limits electoral choice
based on decisions made *for* voters by commissions, by the incumbents
themselves, or in some situations by federal judges whose political allegiances may dominate their judgment.[48] The process is often arbitrary because of the self-interest of incumbent legislators and because the process,
which occurs within artificial time constraints, shapes voter choice for a
decade.

Incumbents usually enjoy tremendous power over the districting process, through which they frequently attempt to create safe districts to make
their reelection margins even more comfortable. Within the legislature,
pitched redistricting battles often disregard issues of community interests
or voter representation. One concern expressed by some elected officials is
whether they will represent the same voters as they did in the past, not
whether those voters continue to have something in common other than an
elected official.[49] To maximize their chance of reelection, those in control
of districting may promote noncompetitive election contests that further
reduce voter participation and interest.

Moreover, given polarized voting, single-member districts improve the
prospects of minority representation only to the extent that there is substantial residential segregation at the appropriate geographic scale. Thus, for
Latinos who live in barrios that are dispersed throughout a jurisdiction,
districting does not capture either their real or potential power.[50] Further,
the districting process may exacerbate intergroup conflict, as minorities are
pitted against each other in what one New York commentator described as
a "political landgrab."[51]

Single-member districts also tend to underrepresent minority voters, even where some race-conscious districts are created. Unless minority voters are both numerous enough and concentrated just right, they will not enjoy even proportional descriptive representation as evidenced by the fact that blacks are not proportionately represented in any of the southern legislatures, even after a decade of race-conscious districting.[52]

Empowerment strategies, premised on the value of participation and the importance of choice, abound in contemporary discourse. Districting, however, denies the connection between empowerment and participation in two critical ways. First, voters are not directly involved in districting because districts are drawn by professionals. The voters' interests are presumed to be represented by their indirect, preexisting choice of residence.

Second, districting assumes that even where voters' interests are not represented by the ultimate district winner, the winner will indirectly represent those interests. In this way, districting relies on the concept of virtual representation (that is, that winners will represent the losers' interests or that losers may experience defeat in one district but will be represented by winners in another district). The Supreme Court in *Davis v. Bandemer, Gaffney v. Cummings*, and *United Jewish Organizations of Williamsburgh v. Carey*, endorsed this concept.[53] Virtual representation, as viewed by the Court, involves two critical assumptions: first, certain voters are fungible; and second, the minority loser is not so permanent, isolated, or stigmatized as to negate any future political threat.

Virtual representation, however, is fundamentally at odds with the idea behind empowerment. The process of physically confecting districts, which may be accompanied by extensive but perfunctory public hearings, is one dominated by incumbent self-interest and court-appointed experts with no particular ties to grass-roots concerns. By removing the issue from the voter, the districting process is antithetical to empowerment strategies based on voter participation and voter choice.

Districting Has Failed to Foster Genuine, Accountable Debate about Issues

Districting fosters the politics of individualism. In geographic districts, the threshold of representation is close to 50 percent because the winning candidate must demonstrate significant support to justify gaining *all* the power. Districts, therefore, push candidates toward the middle of the political spectrum, where they can find most of the votes. The focus on developing consensus *prior to the election* means that issues are frequently not fully articulated or debated. Positions on controversial issues are often eschewed for palliatives designed to offend no one.[54]

Each district essentially creates a single-person office with a majoritarian bias. It is this bias that dooms third political parties to perpetual defeat. Interests within the district are represented only to the extent they garner majority support. It is also the winner-take-all quality of single-member districts that tends to submerge minority political interests.

By promoting only two real choices, winner-take-all districting has created an environment conducive to negative campaigning. A system that fosters two-way races is the "basis for such tried-and-true strategies as driving up the negatives of [an opponent] without worrying that the defecting voters will turn to a relatively unsullied third candidate," a common occurrence in three-way races.[55] Negative campaign tactics contribute to voter alienation and apathy.[56]

Districting Has Sometimes Failed to Promote Opportunities for More Than Token Inclusion

Proponents of race-conscious districting believe that separate can be made equal, or at least that poor blacks are empowered when provided a choice to elect a representative accountable only to them. Thus, they assume that geography works as a proxy for both identifying and promoting minority interests.

Creating majority black, predominantly poor districts is one alternative to ensure at least symbolic representation of black interests. Symbolic representation is important even where it does not insure accountability and influence. Moreover, where black voters have electoral control over their representatives, it is assumed the voters will hold those representatives accountable. But where black voters are concentrated in majority black districts, it must also be assumed that those voters have no influence over white representatives.

Because majority black districts free black candidates from electoral competition with whites, white legislators may enjoy electoral success in white districts that are not dependent on black votes. For this reason, some conservative critics of race-conscious districting argue that majority minority districts quarantine poor blacks in inner-city ghettos. For example, critics of newly drawn majority black districts claim that the districts ultimately benefit white Republicans. In Alabama, one critic claims such a district "yokes together by violence" areas as geographically different but racially similar as a large section of industrial Birmingham and vast expanses of the rural Black Belt, thus leaving other districts whiter and more Republican.[57]

The direct consequence of majority black districts is that fewer white legislators are directly accountable to black interests. In this way, districting may reproduce within the legislature the polarization experienced at the polls. If so, the third generation *Presley* problem of token legislative presence then follows.

Where blacks and whites are geographically separate, race-conscious districting by definition isolates blacks from potential white allies such as white women who are not geographically concentrated. It "wastes" the votes of white liberals who may be submerged within white, conservative districts. Thus, it suppresses the potential development of issue-based campaigning and cross-racial coalitions.

In these ways, race-conscious districting may not ensure that blacks enjoy proportional legislative influence. Because majority black districts are necessarily accompanied by majority white districts, black representatives may become isolated in the governing body.

Remedial Alternatives to Majority Black Districts

MINORITY INFLUENCE DISTRICTS

One alternative to creating majority black districts is to disperse the black voting population, creating pockets of electoral influence. A few courts, commentators, and litigators have urged the adoption of districting plans in which blacks are an electoral minority in several districts rather than an electoral majority in just a few. These critics of majority black districts claim that minority influence districts would better integrate minorities into the political process.[58]

In its strongest version, an influence district is a district in which minority voters enjoy electoral influence and legislative clout despite the fact they are a numerical minority and voting is racially polarized. For example, an electoral minority may have influence where it can determine the outcome of an election contest between competing majority preferred candidates. Although the minority voters cannot sponsor their own representative, they may influence which majority candidate gets elected.

At the legislative decision-making stage, the strong minority influence claim would be that the power of minority voters is superior because minority voters enjoy influence over multiple representatives rather than concentrated control over one or two. Because minority voters must work with other groups in order to enjoy either electoral or legislative power, influence districts arguably mobilize cross-racial alliances in particular and political participation throughout the extended political process in general.

There is also a weak influence claim in which influence occurs only *under the right combination of circumstances.* The weak influence claim is based on three alternative assumptions. First, the minority may be influen-

tial despite its numerical scarcity *where voting is not racially polarized.*
Second, even where the electorate is racially polarized, the racial minority
may be influential if there are multiple racial groups that coalesce around
a single minority sponsored candidate. Third, even where voting is racially
polarized, the racial minority might be influential where there is unusual
fragmentation within the white community and the aggregating decisional
rule is a plurality, not a majority, vote threshold.

The first and second assumptions rely on the existence *within the district*
of a functional electoral majority to which the jurisdiction's racial minority
belongs. But while these assumptions require a functional electoral majority, the third assumption does not. The third assumption is that a black-
supported candidate may squeak through with less than a majority before
the white community reunites. This might also happen where a sizable
minority plays a role in competitive two-person elections. In such elections, blacks may be the swing vote.

All three assumptions, however, hold a single idea in common: they all
require a district in which whites do not function as a monolithic majority.
In other words, in its weak version, influence districts depend on some
fragmentation within the white community because whites are politically
divided or simply outnumbered, albeit not by a single racial majority.

In this sense, the weak version of influence districts is consistent with at
least one aspect of the political fairness standard posited earlier. Since there
is no majority monopoly of *all* the power, racial minorities potentially exercise a fair share of procedural resources. These minorities might have an
equal opportunity to influence decisions at the election stage, exchanging
information about their preferences as well as enjoying the capacity to reward or punish candidates.

But where whites function as a cohesive district majority, a numerical
racial minority simply cannot be influential. Within the dilution paradigm,
the racial minority does *not* have equal access to relevant decision-making
processes because the white majority exercises disproportionate power.

For this reason, I am not persuaded that the strong version of so-called
influence districts achieves political fairness as defined herein. The idea
that a racial minority *in a polarized district electorate* has influence or clout
is simply inconsistent with the very definition of minority vote dilution.

The strong version of influence districts is therefore incoherent within
the dilution paradigm. At the electoral stage, the number of blacks in a
minority influence district will simply make no difference. If voting is racially polarized, those elected by the racial majority can ignore the interests
of minority voters, even those who supported them, without suffering any
electoral consequences.

Where voting is racially polarized, those blacks who support the winning candidate enjoy minimal influence as a swing vote. Black voters may

help determine which candidate gets elected, but the successful candidate must first be one who started out with white support. Moreover, once in office, black voters' influence on that candidate's performance is questionable. In a racially polarized environment, white officials are often unaware of black voters' decisive impact or deliberately ignore it because of even more decisive white support. As a consequence, it is hard to imagine a racially stigmatized minority, whatever its size, exercising genuine influence in a racially polarized winner-take-all district.

Even the weak version of influence claims portends a practical difficulty; the number of minority voters needed to exercise influence needs to be defined: What number or percentage of minorities is enough to be influential? The term is used to suggest a point of reference based on some population threshold short of a numerical majority. At what point are blacks better off? Should a jurisdiction create two 25 percent influence districts rather than one 40 percent influence district and one 10 percent district? Who should choose, and based on what factors? Demonstrating electoral influence within winner-take-all districting is thus problematic as a pragmatic question.

Of course, the answer to this question may itself be pragmatic. One could approach each situation with an intensely factual, local appraisal on a case-by-case basis. The case-by-case approach attempts to discover locally contextualized answers rather than universalizing theories. This is consistent with the empowerment norm, which strives to let voters themselves define their political interests at the local level. It is also consistent with the "functional approach" to the Voting Rights Act taken by Congress and the Court, requiring intensely local appraisal of relevant political realities.[59]

If the empowerment norm attempts to enable voters to articulate their own political interests, one method to determine the influence baseline is simply to ask the voters themselves. At what level of population do voting rights plaintiffs consider themselves influential? What benchmark or indicia of influence are the plaintiffs themselves using? To some extent this is what the district court did in *Upham v. Seamon* when it determined that because voting was not racially polarized, minority voters in the Dallas area were better off, in light of local circumstances, with two minority influence districts.

Another approach, still framed conceptually in terms of empowerment, is to ask political scientists what constitutes a competitive district in nonracial terms. If a 60 percent vote is considered a landslide, then a district in which a minority political party is less than forty percent is a safe district for the majority party. Stated in racial terms, a 65 percent minority population district has been used as a rule-of-thumb threshold for effective voting equality (defined as the realistic potential to elect).[60] If a 65 percent black district is a safe seat for blacks, then a 65 percent white district is not an influence district, but probably a safe seat for whites.

Given both these propositions, an influence district may be defined as a district with less than 65 percent but more than 35 percent minority population. In such a district, it may make sense to give black plaintiffs the opportunity to prove that they enjoy a realistic potential to influence. This, of course, would depend on the totality of relevant circumstances.

To resolve the practical question of influence thresholds, it is also necessary to define influence. Thus far the term *influence* has meant electoral or legislative control, or at least the ability to affect electoral or legislative outcomes. In all of the influence claims, however, minority influence generally means either minority support for a white candidate or minority support for a black candidate who is more directly accountable to the larger white electorate. This is because winner-take-all districting has such a high threshold of exclusion.

Yet, a minority that merely supports, rather than sponsors or elects, its own candidate is still not necessarily influential in the extended political process. Genuine influence requires that the minority voters have the ability at least occasionally to sponsor their own candidates or to punish unresponsive officials whose election depended on minority support. Without this ability, the minority may have limited influence in determining election outcomes, but it does not have any real influence over legislative performance. That kind of extended influence, which depends on reciprocity and mutuality, generally requires a lower exclusion threshold than is permitted by winner-take-all districting.

MULTIMEMBER DISTRICTS THAT ARE NOT WINNER-TAKE-ALL

Alternative election systems, which lower the threshold of exclusion to less than 50 percent, may be preferable to minority influence districts. For example, cumulative voting systems enable a minority of less than 50 percent to exercise electoral control *and* legislative influence.

Under cumulative voting, voters cast multiple votes up to the number of open seats. Voters may choose to express the intensity of their preferences by aggregating all of their votes for a single candidate. If voting is polarized along racial lines, as voting rights litigation cases hypothesize, semi-proportional systems of representation, such as cumulative voting, generally operate to provide at least a minimal level of minority representation. Unlike districting, however, they allow minority group members to self-identify their allegiance and their preferences based on their strategic use of multiple voting possibilities. In this sense, they allow voluntary interest constituencies to form at each election. Voters "district" themselves every election.

Because of concerns with procedural fairness, a cumulative voting system that relies on voluntary districting by each voter is a reasonable, and in many cases, preferable alternative to geographic districting. Cumulative voting would abandon districting altogether to represent fairly minority voters who do not enjoy either the numerical strength to become an electoral majority within a district or who are geographically dispersed within a large area such that their strength cannot be maximized within one or more single-member districts.[61]

Political boundaries traditionally define a community of interest.[62] However, structures for fairly representing divergent interests within a large, heterogenous body are necessary, especially to the extent local government structures become more regionally based. To meet the increasing suburbanization of America, demands are growing for metropolitan government and interdistrict planning.[63] Unless voting rights advocates are preoccupied by the importance of black control of increasingly poor, isolated urban areas, they too may begin to seek representational strategies within a metropolitan, not simply a citywide, area.

Alternatives such as cumulative voting are one such strategy. Cumulative voting lowers the threshold of representation to encourage local political organizations to form. Minority political organizations or third political parties might then reclaim, at a newly invigorated grass-roots level, the traditional party role of mobilizing voter participation. Additionally, locally based political parties might then organize around issues or issue-based coalitions. Since the potential support for the minority political party is not confined to a geographic or racial base, cross-racial and pan-geographic coalitions are possible.

The interjection of an issue-oriented dimension might potentially transform what has essentially become the celebrity politics of candidate-centered campaigns.[64] As a spokesperson for the Ross Perot petition campaign put it: "Back in the 70s, the parties lost to television advertising their role as the main source of the nation's political information. Reaching voters through emotion-based image-making became far more efficient than trying to enlist them as party members."[65]

I propose these alternative election systems as a substitute for term limits because they allow for greater turnover among incumbents who no longer enjoy exclusive control over the districting process.[66] Incumbent politicians, who fear that term limits will prematurely shorten their careers, may be persuaded to support alternative election systems, which also promote accountable citizen legislators as a preferable and less arbitrary election reform.[67]

IV

Based on the same view of political fairness posited earlier, cumulative voting systems define representational fairness by reference to standards of proportionality based on interests, not physiognomy. They measure political fairness by procedural, not substantive, notions of justice. Proportionate interest representation takes the idea of democracy by consensus and compromise and structures it in a deliberative, collective decision-making body in which a prejudiced white majority is disaggregated.

It begins with the proposition that a consensus model of power sharing is preferable to a majoritarian model of centralized, winner-take-all accountability and popular sovereignty. By definition, majority preferences enjoy greater popular support; yet, from the minority perspective, centralized authority is neither legitimate nor stabilizing if the majority is permanent and racially fixed. Where this occurs, American majoritarianism, including the tradition of direct election of single executives, unnecessarily marginalizes the minority perspective in a society deeply cloven by race.[68]

Proportionate interest representation disaggregates the white majority by minimizing the threshold of exclusion. It lowers the threshold for participation and representation to something less than 51 percent to neutralize existing prejudice. In this sense, proportionate influence requires a threshold of exclusion comparable to the size of the minority population. Winner-take-all districts simply cannot provide this to a numerically weak minority.

Proportionate interest representation attempts to change the process of governmental decision making away from a rigidly majoritarian model toward one of proportional power. As a remedial measure, efforts to centralize authority in a single executive might be discouraged in favor of power-sharing alternatives that emphasize collective decision making. Within the legislature itself, rules would be preferred that force the majority to bargain with minority groups and include them in any winning coalition. Other fair and legitimate electoral and legislative decision-making alternatives exist, such as legislative cumulative voting. These alternatives preserve representational accountability, yet they are more likely than current practices to promote just results.[69] Because electoral cumulative voting may disaggregate the majority, cross-racial legislative coalitions and logrolling may result even without special legislative rules.

The concept of proportionate interest representation is molded by the hope that a more cooperative political style of deliberation and a more equal basis for preference satisfaction are possible when accountable minority representatives are reinforced by structures to empower them at every stage of the political process.[70] In this sense, proportionate interest representation is a liberal view of strategic political interaction, framed and modified by fair procedural rules.[71]

Ultimately, however, proportionate interest representation is also an attempt to hypothesize about the reconstruction of political equality. This task, though relatively easy to describe, may be harder to implement, especially in a context in which a strategy based on litigation heads the agenda. But I remain confident in its objective: to reorient voting litigation away from the chimera of achieving a physically integrated legislature in a color-blind society toward a clearer vision of a fair and just society for all voters.

Conclusion

The idea of fairness should be used to monitor all aspects of the political process, challenging the right of the majority to a monopoly of power at the executive and legislative, not just the electoral, level. This idea should also be used to challenge the right of the majority to wield its power on the basis of its prejudices. To do so, we must use a meaningful standard of political fairness, not merely a token measure of minority group election and access.

In the debate over competing claims to democratic legitimacy based on the value of minority group representation, I side with the advocates of an integrated, diverse legislature. A homogeneous legislature in a heterogeneous society is simply not legitimate. Black legislative visibility, however, while it is an important measure of electoral fairness, by itself represents an anemic approach to political fairness and justice.

As Senator Bill Bradley observed on the Senate floor following the recent events in Los Angeles, "We must reform the political process so that the powerless have a voice more powerful than violence." A vision of fairness and justice must begin to recognize a full and effective voice for disadvantaged minorities, a voice that is accountable to self-identified community interests, a voice that persuades, and a voice that resonates throughout the political process.

Notes

1. Vote dilution "refers to the practice of limiting the ability of blacks to convert their voting strength into the control of, or at least influence with, elected public officials." Engstrom 1985, 14.

2. I use the term *race-conscious districting* with some trepidation to describe the practice of maximizing or consolidating the number of minority group members in

a single, or a few winner-take-all subdistricts. In this sense, race-conscious district-ing takes advantage of the practice of districting to avoid majority monopoly over *all* seats elected in the jurisdiction. By creating some subdistricts in which the mi-nority group predominates, the jurisdiction majority does not get to control the election of *all* representatives as they might if elections were conducted winner-take-all and at-large.

On the one hand, then, race-conscious districting, as I use the term, refers to the *goal* of creating majority minority districts. On the other hand, the term misleads to the extent it implies that there is a *process* of race-conscious districting and, by extension, "non-race-conscious," districting. To the extent it is used to refer to dis-tricting as a process, the term may convey the idea that the antithesis of maximizing or consolidating the number of minority group members *is not* itself race-conscious districting. It possibly implies, for example, that a choice to disperse minority group members—thus maximizing the number of majority white districts—is somehow not race-conscious districting.

The problem is that all districts—even those carefully drawn to assure a fifty-fifty split—will ultimately enable one group or another to dominate. In other words, there is a racial consequence to the demographic construction of all districts. This is because districting is a winner-take-all process. Only one person represents the en-tire district constituency, and consequently only one "group" wins all the power at any given election. In this way, in a racially polarized environment, the process of districting is inevitably race-conscious.

Just as the one-person, one-vote rule requires an accounting of the number of people within each district, the process of districting in a racially polarized commu-nity also requires an accounting of the race of all voters in that community. To say otherwise suggests that only minority group members have a race.

3. The threshold of exclusion would be 25 percent. The threshold of exclusion is the number of votes that cannot be denied representation under the most ad-verse conditions. It is calculated by a formula of one divided by one plus the number of seats.

4. Myers 1992, A19.

5. The term *legitimate* is defined here in a limited, procedural sense to refer to the extent to which a process follows valid rules to produce results that are acceptable because of the perceived fairness of the process, even from the perspective of ad-versely affected parties.

6. Waldron 1990, 45.

7. See Dahl 1956.

8. For further discussion of these attributes, see Weatherford 1992, 150.

9. *Whitcomb v. Chavis*, 159. (Justice White wrote the opinion.)

10. Weatherford 1992, p. 150.

11. The term *interest* refers to self-identified interests, meaning those highly sali-ent needs and wants articulated by any politically cohesive group of voters. Inter-ests, however, are *not* necessarily descriptive of an essentialist concept of group identity but are fluid and dynamic articulations of group preferences.

12. An interest constituency need not be racially homogenous from a physiolog-ical standpoint. In other words, interests may be racially identifiable for a particular racial group because members are more likely to hold certain views. But not all

members of the group are assumed to agree on all issues in order for the group to form an interest constituency. In addition, nongroup members in a "racial" sense may be part of the interest group to the extent they identify with the group's primary agenda. In this way, an interest constituency is defined by its racial identification, not its racial origin.

13. The implicit influence claim is further developed in Guinier 1991a.

14. See Weatherford 1992, 149.

15. *Baker v. Carr*, 191.

16. Grofman, Handley, and Niemi 1992, 133.

17. See Guinier 1991a, 1477–84.

18. It is also consistent with one person, one vote because each voter casts the same number of ballots or votes on the same number of choices. In addition, it is consistent with the disclaimer against "proportional election" in the 1982 amendments to the Voting Rights Act. See Squires 1992, A20. See also, Lani Guinier "[E]rasing Democracy: The Voting Rights Cases," *Harvard Law Review* 108: 109, 128, and nn. 122–24.

19. *Gordon v. Lance*, 6.

20. *Reynolds v. Sims*, 565.

21. Howard and Howard 1983, 1633, 1636.

22. *Kirkpatrick v. Preisler*, 531.

23. See Yanos 1993.

24. 42 U.S.C. sec. 1973 (1982), *amended by* 42 U.S.C. sec. 1973(b) (1988) (providing that all citizens have the right to "participate in the political process and to elect representatives of their choice").

25. 42 U.S.C. sec. 1973(b) (1988).

26. See *Salyer Land Company v. Tulare Lake Basin Water Storage District* (upholding election scheme in which votes were apportioned according to the assessed valuation of land).

27. See, e.g., *Terry v. Adams*, 484 (Clark, J., concurring).

28. See *Illinois Board of Elections v. Socialist Workers Party*, 185–86.

29. The 1992 decision in *Presley v. Etowah County* represents a significant departure from this view.

30. *Terry v. Adams*, 484.

31. *Anderson v. Celebrezze*, 794. See also *Williams v. Rhodes*, 32.

32. See *Munro v. Socialist Workers Party*, 202 (Marshall, J., dissenting).

33. See, e.g., *Tashjian v. Republican Party of Conn.* (1986).

34. Studies of black and female elected officials do show that these officials have somewhat different agendas than do white male elected officials. See Browning, Marshall, and Tabb 1990; Dodson and Carroll 1991.

35. Pitkin 1967.

36. See Brownstein 1991, Al. See also *Jeffers v. Clinton*, 227 (Eisele, J., dissenting).

37. See Guinier 1993.

38. Brownstein 1991, A1.

39. The concept of virtual representation is developed further in Guinier 1993. See also Minow 1991.

40. Abrams 1988.
41. *Yick Wo v. Hopkins*, 370.
42. See Guinier 1991b for an extensive criticism of these four assumptions.
43. *Presley v. Etowah County*.
44. Ibid., 829–30.
45. *Thornburg v. Gingles*, 50 n. 17.
46. With regard to the explanation based on the statutory disclaimer in the Voting Rights Act, 42 U.S.C. sec. 1973(b) (1988), I note here that the statute disavows only the right to elect *members* of the protected group in proportion to their numbers. This means there is no right to proportional, *descriptive* representation. The disclaimer does *not* disavow a principle of proportional representation that measures proportionality by an empowerment norm.
47. See Gay 1993.
48. See Karlan 1993. See also Suro 1992, A15.
49. See Verhovek 1992a, B1; Verhovek 1992b, B1.; Sack 1992, A1.
50. Bernard Grofman has pointed out, however, that under some circumstances districts may be effective in compensating for the large number of noncitizens in the Latino community. See, e.g., *Garza v. United States*, 778 (Kozinski, J., concurring and dissenting in part).
51. Reed 1992, 759.
52. Single-member districts cannot be expected to yield proportional representation. See Taagapera and Shugart 1989; Tufte 1973. For example, in 1994, a majority of blacks in the South still lived in majority white congressional districts.
53. In *United Jewish Organizations of Williamsburgh v. Carey*, for example, the Court denied the claim brought by Hasidic Jews in Brooklyn challenging a legislative plan on the grounds that it employed race-conscious districting. The Court measured disadvantage using the concept of virtual representation, treating the Hasidim as white voters. *United Jewish Organizations of Williamsburgh v. Carey*, 161–65.
54. See Wines 1992, A18.
55. Toner 1992, A22.
56. See, e.g., Kolbert 1992b, A18.
57. Smothers 1992, A8, (quoting William D. Barnard, a history professor at the University of Alabama).
58. See, e.g., Abrams 1989 (advocating "strong plurality districts" to remedy vote dilution); *Armour v. Ohio* (1990), *rev'd and remanded on other grounds*, (6th Cir. 1991); *Voinovich v. Quilter* (N.D. Ohio 1992) (three-judge court).
59. *Thornburg v. Gingles*.
60. See Grofman, Handley, and Niemi 1992.
61. Some multimember subdistricts may be necessary in large jurisdictions with sizable legislative bodies.
62. See, e.g., *Holt Civic Club v. City of Tuscaloosa*. In special function elections, however, the Court has approved community of interest tied to land ownership. See *Salyer Land Company v. Tulare Lake Basin Water Storage District*.
63. See Rusk 1992, A29.
64. See Huckfeldt and Sprague 1992, 71.

65. Squires 1992, A20.

66. I assume that turnout would be higher in elections that used cumulative voting. Thus, elections would be more competitive even though each candidate would need a lower percentage of the available votes in order to win.

67. Cumulative voting, to the extent it may reinvigorate grass-roots mobilization efforts and political party formation, has the potential to create more churn in the system. While some may fear balkanization as a result, I fear ossification. To the extent that the fear of excessive fragmentation is justified, techniques, including raising the threshold of exclusion, are available to moderate it.

68. See Lijphart et al., "Separation of Powers and the Management of Political Cleavages," manuscript on file with the author.

69. See Guinier 1991a, 1502–8.

70. In a subsequent article, I hope to explore more fully the legitimacy of a proportionality principle as an alternative to winner-take-all majority rule and respond to criticisms that proportional influence is no less balkanizing than race-conscious districting. Although proportionate interest representation does not directly rely on the concept of group representation, it implicitly adopts a view of interests that are fragmented and potentially divisive.

In brief, the argument might proceed as follows: Multiple cleavages are preferable to a single deep cleavage in a racially diverse society; moreover, proportionality does not destroy a preexisting general, common perspective. For members of a racial minority who have been, and continue to be, victimized as a result of their racial identity, a deep consensus that does not acknowledge the pervasiveness of the oppression that some, and the indignity that most, have suffered on account of their race is impossible. In this way multiple cleavages may be more stabilizing from the minority perspective than one deep cleavage that serves only to silence. Unlike some approaches to group rights, proportionate interest representation does not fix power exogenously or mechanically, and therefore should not alienate those who strongly believe in individual autonomy.

I will suggest that the assumption behind multiple cleavages is similar to the pluralist assumption that shifting alliances operate as a check against tyranny; that distributing preference satisfaction more widely gives groups presently alienated a reason for participating; and that the decision-making process can be empowering to the extent it gives participants a stake in the outcome or at least a meaningful opportunity to present their views.

I will attempt to develop analogies to the therapeutic model in which airing grievances is important to negotiation and conflict resolution—that surfacing antecedent conflict need not be dysfunctional but may foster a cooperative approach to gaining and exercising power. In this sense, a consensus, deliberative model is consistent with the American tradition of dispersed power through checks and balances.

In response to the argument that proportionality may simply make the country ungovernable, I concede that an equilibrium point is necessary between dispersing power and direct, simple accountability and centralized responsibility and power. In the latter view, participation depends on direct lines of authority, not on attempts to set the equilibrium point a little differently or continually to reset it. But this is not a reason to embrace the centralized, uniform perspective on accountability.

Finally, I agree that a substantive justice approach is ultimately necessary. My concept of political fairness, even if implemented, is not alone sufficient to overcome vastly disproportionate economic and personal resource differences. It is still a valuable improvement over existing access-based approaches to political participation.

71. Cf. Michelman 1989, 449.

3

Electoral Systems and Minority Representation

KENNETH BENOIT AND KENNETH A. SHEPSLE

Minority Empowerment and Electoral Market Failure

Minority political enfranchisement in America is a subject of great complexity, forcing students of democratic practice to wrap their minds around the subtle relationships between broad philosophical purpose, on the one hand, and the practical details of democratic machinery, on the other. At the *philosophical level* there are controversies concerning which public purposes among the many possible involving minority empowerment should be served—participation, promotion of indigenous leaders, representation, influence, satisfaction with outcomes. At the *practical level* there are mysteries surrounding the operating characteristics of specific democratic design features—Does plurality voting deny representation to supporters of losing candidates? Will at-large or racially gerrymandered districting best guarantee minority representation? What are the arguments for single-member or multimember districts, single-vote or multiple-vote electors, the option to cumulate multiple votes or not? Finally, at the *policy level* there is the matter of linking mechanical practicalities and philosophical purpose—once the objectives to pursue have been stipulated and the mechanical principles associated with alternative designs of the democratic machinery have been mastered, which design features should one select and how might one implement them to achieve the chosen objectives?

Each new generation of activists, legislators, judges, lawyers, and philosophers slices into these issues in a manner heavily conditioned by historical experience. For much of this century, attention focused on the basic *enfranchisement* of minorities. Philosophical and political agitation, legislation (the Voting Rights Act of 1965), and litigation were successful in securing the right to vote for minority citizens. While all issues of enfranchisement have not disappeared (reducing the costs of voter registration, for example, is a mildly salient political issue at present, toward which the recently passed "motor voter" legislation is aimed), priorities clearly shifted during the 1970s from enfranchisement per se to *representation* and to the issue of *vote dilution*, in which the electoral rules are manipulated to reduce the effectiveness of minority enfranchisement.[1] When a group's votes are diluted, writes Chandler Davidson, it "implies that the ineffectiveness of its ballots is beyond its control, and that the causes are in the larger political structure."[2]

Debates currently revolve around alternative formulas and mechanical features—racial gerrymandering, multimember districting, the casting of multiple votes—some of which we examine in this paper. Reformers express distinctive views on these formulas and mechanical features based on anticipations concerning their consequences; these, in effect, are *equilibrium claims*. Yet, these claims are rarely accompanied by either of the two forms of support that make such claims scientifically persuasive—theoretical argument and empirical evidence (perhaps a result of the fact that the advocates are often lawyers, not social scientists).

Even as strategies of litigation and legislation are pursued to secure greater minority representation in elected bodies, a third priority, that of *influence*, is already being anticipated by activists and academics alike. Here the issue is whether minorities, having secured the vote and a presence—even a roughly proportionate presence—in representative bodies, have any effect on collective choices. Lani Guinier, for example, arguing against the major remedy for vote dilution—the creation of majority-black electoral districts—contends that they have limited benefits: "The main beneficiaries have been individual candidates and the middle-class blacks occasionally included in white-dominated governing coalitions. Such victories too often are little more than political and psychological symbols for poor and working-class blacks." For her, in contrast, "empowerment means the ability to make government more responsive to minority interests, not just the ability to integrate legislative bodies."[3]

Although voter disenfranchisement, malrepresentation, and disempowerment may all constitute instances of electoral market failure, the first has been more or less satisfactorily dealt with by thirty years of civil rights legislation and litigation, while the third constitutes an issue that has not fully ripened.[4] In this paper we focus on representational imperfections and proposed solutions, focusing on arguments and assessments about the modification of electoral law to enhance minority political power in the United States.

Our purpose in the next two sections is to assess several bodies of literature in order to see whether there are scientifically persuasive equilibrium claims about alternative electoral arrangements. We first examine equilibrium theories of single-member district systems, since this is the arrangement according to which most popular legislative bodies are elected in the United States. We then turn to some alternatives to the single-member-district plurality system (SMP) that put greater emphasis on proportionality. These are multimember-district systems, in which voters may cast one or more votes. Single nontransferable voting (SNTV), limited voting (LV), and cumulative voting (CV) are the alternatives reformers most frequently suggest for the United States. The next section turns to more empirical matters, examining comparative evidence of minority representation in different electoral contexts. What we learn from these theoretical and empirical surveys is that at present compelling evidence is unavailable to warrant much faith in strong equilibrium claims: This is not so much a rejection of any reform agenda as it is a practical admission of scientific ignorance. In the concluding section we return to some of the substantive issues involving electoral reform in the United States.

A Theoretical Assessment of Plurality Systems

First Past the Post

The SMP system, also known as "first past the post," awards a single prize to the contestant who obtains the most votes. The prize is singular and indivisible, which means that, with m candidates, there will always be $m-1$ "losers." Only relative position in the vote outcome matters, and a miss is as good as a mile. Second, the winner is popular only in the narrow sense that he or she obtains more votes than any other. But in at least two other senses, this winner may not be very popular at all. On the one hand, he or she may be the beneficiary of strategic preference revelation by voters; as such, the winner's votes are given only grudgingly by at least some of his or her nominal supporters. On the other hand, even putting strategic behavior to one side, it is entirely possible that some other candidate is more popular in the sense that the latter could defeat every other candidate in a pairwise contest. This so-called Condorcet winner may not fare well in a plurality contest, because he or she may lack a large number of top-preference evaluations from voters, yet nevertheless be preferred by majorities to each other candidate. Thus, a plurality winner has a relatively weak popular claim to victory; getting more votes than someone else may be trumped by some other standard or desideratum.

This property has led critics to claim that SMP systems are disempowering. In a two-candidate race for a single seat, for instance, it is possible for just under 50 percent of the constituency to be "without representation." In a three-candidate race, it is possible for nearly 67 percent of the voters to back a loser. Generally, in an m-candidate race, as much as $100 \left(1 - 1/m\right)$ percent of the electorate may not have elected a representative. In these circumstances it is often argued that many voters waste their votes, where "waste" means "not voting for the winner." These voters, moreover, are thought to be effectively disempowered and without influence as a result of having wasted their votes in this sense. Normative disapproval follows: "Procedural justice challenges the entitlement of . . . a 51 percent majority to exercise 100 percent of the power. . . . The majority should enjoy a majority of the power; but the minority should also enjoy some power too."[5]

Such normative claims and the issues that underlie them deserve more rigorous treatment. Here we introduce a formal structure—incredibly simple, to be sure—to enable us to think analytically about electoral-system effects on minority representation. This structure is the Hotelling-Downs spatial model. Consider a one-dimensional issue space, say the bounded interval [0, 100]. This may be a dimension of general ideology, with 0 constituting the extreme left and 100 the extreme right; or it may represent a singularly salient policy—say, the appropriate "proportion" of economic activity that remains outside of governmental regulation—with 0 constituting a fully socialized economy and 100 the free-market apex. This issue space serves the dual purpose of representing both voter tastes and candidate strategies.

Each voter is associated with an ideal point—the voter's most-preferred policy in the [0, 100] interval—and single-peaked preferences. The latter reflects the assumption that voter preferences for policy decline monotonically in either direction from her ideal policy. Under these circumstances, Duncan Black's famous Median Voter Theorem informs us that when the number of voters is odd and each voter votes, there is a unique policy in the [0, 100] interval that can command a simple majority over every other policy. That point is the ideal policy of the median voter. If one labeled voters numerically, with voter 1 possessing the left-most ideal point and voter n the right-most, then voter $(n + 1)/2$ is in the catbird seat. If, for example, voters are evenly distributed in the interval [10, 100]—forming a slightly "right-leaning" constituency—then the median ideal point, located at 55, is the policy position that can defeat any other by a simple majority in a pairwise contest.

The important substantive point of this theorem is the *centripetal tendency* of pure majority rule.[6] Thus, if two candidates were to compete for one legislative seat in this constituency, with each voter supporting the candidate whose announced policy is closest to his or her ideal, there would be strong electoral pressures on the candidates to converge in their announcements toward the median voter ideal. This conclusion holds whether candidates are *office seeking* (the classic Downsian politician) or *policy seeking*.[7]

In equilibrium, then, the two candidates will converge toward the median. In practice, of course, one may be slightly to its left and the other slightly to its right. The winner will be the one closest to it. And, as is claimed by some, those who did not vote for the winning candidate go unrepresented; indeed, it might even be alleged that only those with preferences very much like the median voter are represented at all, with those in the tails of the ideal point distribution unrepresented. This, at least, is the flavor of indictments of SMP referred to at the beginning of this section.

Now suppose that, in the spirit of 1965, a voting rights act is passed enfranchising m additional voters. (Assume m is even, a harmless assumption that simplifies the exposition.) Suppose all these voters possess ideal points on the left-hand side of [0, 100], between 0 and 10 on the dimension. What happens now? The electorate is now $m + n$ in size. Let us renumber the voters in this new electorate so that voters numbered 1 to m are the new voters (and are left-most) and voters numbered $m + 1$ to $m + n$ are the original voters (and are right-most). The Median Voter Theorem again applies, suggesting that through political competition, the two candidate announcements will converge on the ideal policy of voter $(m + n + 1)/2$. It is easy to show that this outcome is to the left of the outcome in the electorate of size n—the median of the expanded electorate has been shifted leftward.[8] If, for instance, the $m + n$ voters of the new electorate are now evenly distributed in [0, 100], the new median is at 50 instead of 55.

This exercise demonstrates that assessing claims of nonrepresentation, ineffectuality, and wasted votes frequently leveled at SMP is not a simple matter. The application of the most basic model of electoral competition— the Hotelling-Downs spatial model—suggests that a newly enfranchised group of voters may influence candidate positions even when that group elects no representative from its own ranks. The inclusion of the new voters altered the equilibrium location *in the direction of their own preferences.* Put slightly differently, the pivotal voter in the new constituency is someone whose ideal policy the new voters *prefer* to the ideal policy of the "old" pivot. More generally, since this applies to almost any equilibrium situation, the outcome responds to the preferences of all voters in the sense that they pull the equilibrium toward them or prevent it from drifting farther from them; in equilibrium, there is balance, and each voter is influential in sustaining it.[9]

More Equilibrium Results for SMP

Nevertheless, the inventor of this spatial model, Harold Hotelling, worried about the apparent lack of choice electoral incentives provide.[10] It turns out, however, that equilibrium convergence—what Hotelling termed an "excessive sameness"—is in many respects a peculiarity of the two-candidate world only (with qualifications to be mentioned below). With $k \geq 4$, k candidates will evenly locate themselves throughout the voter distribution.[11]

To see this, define an *electoral equilibrium* as a set of k locations in [0, 100], one for each of k candidates, such that no candidate has any incentive to alter her location. Let x_i be the location of the ith candidate. Candidate i

is *interior* if she has candidate neighbors on either side; otherwise she is *peripheral*. She is said to be *paired* if another candidate occupies the same electoral position. Call candidate *i*'s *electoral support* the set of voter ideal points closer to x_i than to any other candidate location, and partition this support into *left-hand* and *right-hand support* (generically, *half-support*). A theorem by Eaton and Lipsey provides the necessary and sufficient conditions for an electoral equilibrium:[12]

> *Theorem (Eaton and Lipsey):* If voter ideals are uniformly distributed in the interval [0, 100] and if each voter votes for the candidate closest to his or her ideal, then $(x_1, x_2, \ldots x_k)$ is an electoral equilibrium of electoral-support-maximizing candidates if and only if (1) no candidate's electoral support is smaller than any other candidate's half-support and (2) peripheral candidates are paired.

The intuition here is that, first, if any candidate's electoral support were smaller than some other's half-support, the former could relocate to the position of the latter, share equally in the latter's support, and still do better than if he or she had stayed put; and, second, if a peripheral candidate were unpaired, then there would be nothing preventing him from converging to his (only) neighbor.[13]

This theorem subsumes the two-candidate Median Voter Theorem. When $k = 2$, both candidates are peripheral and thus must be paired (condition 2 above). The only location for this pairing for which no incentives to change apply is at the median voter's ideal. In addition, the theorem provides equilibrium locations for other values of k. For $k = 3$, as noted, no configuration of candidate locations satisfies the conditions of the theorem. For $k = 4$, $(x_1, x_2, x_3, x_4) = (25, 25, 75, 75)$ is the equilibrium. For five candidates, (16.67, 16.67, 50, 83.67, 83.67) is the equilibrium. For $k \geq 6$, equilibrium is no longer unique. In all these cases, however, except $k = 2$, an equilibrium consists of candidates spreading themselves throughout the policy interval. Voters are not confronted by an "excessive sameness."

There are three premises in the Eaton-Lipsey theorem that, though stated above, nevertheless may require some elaboration. We have already noted that, first, the theorem assumes a *uniform distribution of voter ideal points*. Relaxation of this restriction does not significantly alter the theorem's conclusion. The conditions in the theorem are still necessary but are no longer sufficient; Eaton and Lipsey provide the additional conditions for sufficiency.

The second premise of significance is that of *voter sincerity*. Each voter is assumed to vote for the candidate whose announced policy position is closest to her ideal policy. One of the contributing causes of Duverger's Law, however, is a "psychological effect" in which voters are alleged to be averse to wasting their votes on hopeless candidacies.[14] Voters, that is, may vote *strategically*, thereby abandoning the candidate closest to them. A theorem by Feddersen, Sened, and Wright shows that, with strategic voting, the "uniform spread" of candidate locations in the Eaton-Lipsey equilibrium no longer holds.[15] Indeed, dramatically to the contrary, *all* candidates will locate at the median voter's ideal, reinstating Hotelling's "excessive sameness."

Third, candidates in the Eaton-Lipsey theorem were assumed to be *maximizers of electoral support*. But, it might reasonably be claimed, candidates are not interested in votes per se; they are interested in winning an office or in implementing specific policies. At best, votes are intermediate objectives. Cox addresses this issue (though he retains the assumption of sincere voting) by suggesting alternatives to the vote-maximizing objective.[16] Suppose each candidate is interested in maximizing the *difference* between her vote total and that of her most serious competitor; among the candidate locations that do this, she is interested in maximizing the difference between her vote total and that of her second most serious competitor; and so on. That is, a candidate is interested in her *plurality* since, under SMP, only the locational strategy that yields a positive plurality against each and every competitor assures office. Cox calls this lexicographic decision rule for strategy selection *complete plurality maximization*, and seeks equilibrium spatial distributions of candidate policy positions. He proves the following:

> *Theorem (Cox)*: If the distribution of voter ideals is uniform on [0, 100], if voters cast sincere ballots, and if $k \geq 3$ candidates are complete plurality maximizers in a SMP election, then (1) if k is odd there is no equilibrium and (2) if k is even, then the equilibrium has candidates paired at equally spaced points, $100/k$, $300/k, \ldots ,100(k-1)/k$.

In this case, then, there is not always an equilibrium, but when one exists, it covers the whole spectrum. If, for example, there were ten candidates, then there would be five equilibrium locations—10, 30, 50, 70, and 90—each occupied by two candidates.

The reader's eyes may be glazing over by this point. We do not wish to put too fine a point on the details of the various theorems we have reviewed above (and there are many more where those come from). What we hope the preceding discussion has served to illustrate is that a significant body of formal literature exists on electoral implications for representation. At the very least, this literature indicates that representation is more than a matter of a group electing its own candidates. Our discussion shows that even with so straightforward and well known an electoral arrangement as the one-winner/plurality-rule system, equilibrium situations are neither robust nor unconditional.

Equilibriums in electoral models depend on candidate objectives and behavioral principles in addition to the mechanical features of electoral law, and these vary from specification to specification. Hence, any equilibrium claim relies heavily on contextual detail. Finally, theory indicates that for some specifications there are simply *no* equilibriums. Together these lessons from the formal literature indicate that caution is warranted in advancing equilibrium claims—arguments that proponents of electoral reform are implicitly making.

Unfortunately for the issue of racial representation, the vast majority of the formal literature we have been discussing on electoral properties deals with standard Downsian issue dimensions, and not race. There is strong evidence that the issue of race is different in kind than the policy-oriented issues which the Hotelling-Downs model assumes.[17] If voters of different races cast their ballots in self-contained blocs, for instance, then the equilibrium influences suggested by our exposition of spatial models may be undermined. This is why the issue of racial bloc voting deserves special attention.

Equilibrium Results with Racial Bloc Voting

The experience with vote dilution suggests that a straightforward application of the Hotelling-Downs model is inappropriate. In county after county, especially in the deep South, white politicians and electors have managed to maintain an *electoral cartel*, effectively diluting minority votes; minority voters go un- or underrepresented on numerous school boards, city councils, and county planning bodies. These instances constitute more than racial bloc voting; they evidence a degree of coordination on the candidate supply side as well.

To accommodate these factors we return to our one-dimensional world with n "majority" voters with ideals in the $[10, 100]$ interval and m "minority" voters with ideals in $[0, 10]$, where $m < n$. In the expanded $(m + n)$–person electorate, the median is voter $(m + n + 1)/2$, whereas in the original electorate, the median is voter $[m + (n + 1)/2]$, according to the $(m + n)$–electorate counting convention. The new median is to the left of the old. Now we add:

> *Bloc Voting Stipulation:* No (majority or minority) elector votes for a candidate of the other group.

If there were two candidates only, one from each group, then the majority candidate would clearly triumph and, with no further contextual detail, her spatial position could be anywhere in $[0, 100]$. The bloc voting stipulation guarantees victory for the majority candidate, whatever her spatial position. If the two candidates were the representatives of group political parties, on the other hand, each of whom had triumphed in a primary or other party selection process, then it is likely that they would be located at the respective group medians, the ideal points of voters $(m + 1)/2$ and $[m + (n + 1)/2]$, respectively, of the full $(m + n)$–person electorate. The majority candidate at the latter position would then win.

It is easy to see that this location is to the right of voter $(m + n + 1)/2$— the winning location in the non-bloc-voting scenario—and is identical to the winning position in the pre–Voting Rights Act expansion of the electorate from n to $m + n$. So, in a world of bloc voting, with one candidate per bloc, the minority is completely shut out. Not only can it not elect one of its own; it cannot even influence whom the majority elects.

This example, however, is extreme in at least two respects. First, at the candidate level, the restriction to exactly one candidate per group suggests a degree of group control over entry and of group regulation of political competition that is inordinate. Second, at the voter level, the bloc voting stipulation is extreme. Even with group candidates located at the respective group median ideal points given above, it is surely imaginable that some left-leaning majority group members and right-leaning minority group members might desert the candidacy of their respective group nominees. That is, even though group members are disposed to support the group candidate, they may desert him or her if the opposing candidate is sufficiently more attractive in policy terms.

These factors, in turn, would affect (or at least could affect) the spatial positions of the nominees. Even if we retain for the moment the assumption of group control over candidate entry (one per group), ex post group cohesiveness and candidate locations are interdependent. In equilibrium, an interesting result may transpire. Sophisticated voters in the majority group nominate a candidate to the left of its group median to reduce the potential for majority defections, and sophisticated voters in the minority group nominate a candidate to the right of its group median to encourage majority crossovers. The majority candidate nevertheless prevails *with almost perfect bloc voting*. That is, as long as bloc voting is not absolutely binding, the actual extent of bloc voting should be seen as a *consequence* of group politics (especially entry control), not as a rigid sociological law.

There is an interesting legal implication of this last development. Notice that the winning candidate is from the majority group and that there is nearly perfect bloc voting. But also notice that the winning candidate's position is to the left of ideal point $[m + (n + 1)/2]$, the winning location if the majority shuts the minority out completely. Less than perfectly binding group cohesiveness has pulled the position of the winning majority candidate toward the ideal points of the minority group. This is now an "influence district," even though conventional court criteria (in U.S. civil rights litigation) would regard the extensive bloc voting as an impermissible instance of group polarization. In short, polarized voting and the group identity of the winning candidate are *part of an equilibrium*. They reflect the potential of individuals to break free of group criteria, if only slightly (since we have relaxed the bloc voting stipulation), and it would be misleading to confuse bloc voting *in equilibrium* with bloc voting as an exogenous constraint. From a legal point of view, the voting polarization evident in this example is the *wrong* dependent variable on which to focus; the position of the winning candidate is the appropriate one.[18]

U.S. Senate elections in southern states display this electoral dynamic. Minority enfranchisement has, in the nearly thirty years since the passage of the Voting Rights Act, significantly influenced candidacies, strategies, and ultimate winners in Senate contests. One of the strong conclusions of the modern literature on the U.S. Congress is the degree to which floor-voting differences between southern Democrats and northern Democrats have virtually disappeared, a phenomenon attributed to the changing racial composition of southern constituencies.[19] Trent Lott (R-Miss.) is not Theodore Bilbo (D-Miss.); Strom Thurmond (R-S.C.), 1993 version, is not Strom Thurmond (D-S.C.), 1963 version.[20]

This has hardly been a systematic examination of the problem of bloc voting. But it does suggest the kinds of analysis that formal modeling permits. Our own extension of spatial analysis to accommodate racial phenomena like bloc voting has been casual. Such analyses must be performed when considering the representational ramifications of electoral law. We encourage more rigorous extension of the models reviewed here to racial issues, under the complicated conditions found in real politics. At the same time, we discourage the facile embrace of electoral reform proposals claiming implicitly to have resolved these formal issues.

Theoretical Alternatives to SMP

Bruce Cain recently noted that the Supreme Court "has steadfastly denied . . . a right to proportional representation, even while accepting a disproportionality between population and representation as an indicator of voting rights violation."[21] This position does not mandate departures from SMP, but it surely opens the door to this possibility. Moreover, as Cain observes, it is hard to get away from some aspect of proportionality or symmetry or monotonicity in constructing "fair" electoral machinery. The issue of electoral proportionality arises because minority voting rights are often diluted by majority manipulation of the electoral machinery. This is alleged to disempower minorities even if it does not disenfranchise them. Voting rights are preserved, but voter influence is diminished.

One solution to disproportionality is the creation of minority districts—preserving SMP, but drawing district boundaries to assure minorities the capacity to elect "representatives of choice." There are, however, many critics of this solution. Some feel it violates the spirit, if not the letter, of the Voting Rights Act of 1965 by providing for minority legislative quotas.[22] Others charge minority districts are a form of tokenism, doing little more than subsidizing the careers of a small number of minority politicians.[23] Still others wonder about the wisdom of trading off some influence in many districts for complete influence in considerably fewer, and about the impracticalities of creating districts secure for minorities even if the trade-off were worth it.[24]

Students of voting rights have, as a consequence, turned their attention to alternatives. The electoral target drawing much of their attention is the *single-member district*. The unitary and indivisible nature of political prizes under single-seat plurality contests, it is alleged, ill serves minority populations, at best providing them with a modest amount of influence and, perhaps, a small handful of tokens. Guinier exemplifies this view. She claims that SMP arrangements fail to "(1) mobilize broad based voter participation, (2) foster substantive, issue oriented debate, (3) reinforce a sense of genuine inclusion as opposed to token representation, and (4) allow authentic leaders to emerge."[25] While Guinier's desiderata are both vague and contestable—indeed, nearly fifty years of social-choice theory suggests that such criteria are often jointly unattainable under *any* arrangements—she does underscore the need for systemically examining alternative electoral institutions.

Generalizing Electoral Institutions

The categories of electoral system that have been devised or proposed stand as monuments to the human capacity for inventiveness. The sheer variety of ways to assign, cast, and count votes, on the one hand, and translate the results into an allocation of seats in an elected body, on the other, boggles the mind.[26] Cutting through this variety is no mean feat, and it is small wonder that both theoretical and empirical literatures on electoral systems tend to be disjointed and unorganized.

A body of work by Gary Cox, however, has sought to bring some of the issues into focus.[27] Cox, while consciously oversimplifying, defines an *electoral system* in terms of five bits of information—a five-tuple (v, p, c, k, f).[28] The first parameter, v, is the number of *votes* each elector may cast. Parameter p is a dummy variable equal to 1 if $v > 1$ and *partial abstention* (casting fewer than v but more than 0 votes) is permitted; $p = 0$ otherwise. Parameter c is also a dummy variable equal to 1 if $v > 1$ and electors are allowed to *cumulate* their votes (cast more than one vote for a candidate); $c = 0$ otherwise. Parameter k is a measure of *district magnitude* (the number of seats at stake in the district). Finally, f describes the *formula* by which votes cast are translated into seat allocations.

To illustrate, SMP allows each elector to cast one vote; he or she can, as a consequence, neither partially abstain nor cumulate votes; exactly one seat is at stake; and the winner is the candidate with the most votes. That is, SMP is described by the five-tuple ($v = 1$, $p = 0$, $c = 0$, $k = 1$, $f =$ plurality). With this notation we can also describe a number of alternative electoral systems that have been proposed by voting rights scholars. All seek a more proportional outcome by rejecting single-member districts.

The *single nontransferable vote* (SNTV), a system used in Taiwan and in Japan until 1994, elects a legislature from multimember districts (in Japan the district magnitude is 3, 4, or 5). Each elector casts a single vote. The top k vote getters are elected. Thus, as practiced in Japan, for example, SNTV = ($v = 1$, $p = 0$, $c = 0$, $k = 3$, 4, or 5, $f =$ plurality). Thus, SNTV is seen as a straightforward generalization of SMP. The only difference is a larger district magnitude (which might be called MMP, for multimember plurality, in which the winners are first k candidates past the post).

The *limited vote* (LV) generalizes SNTV in the sense that it allows electors to cast multiple votes; but they may neither partially abstain nor cumulate votes. Thus, LV = ($1 < v < k$, $p = 0$, $c = 0$, k, $f =$ plurality).

The *cumulative vote* (CV) gives each voter as many votes as there are seats to be filled and allows cumulation (but typically not partial abstention): CV = ($v = k$, $p = 0$, $c = 1$, k, $f =$ plurality). Illinois, for a century after 1870, elected its lower house by cumulative voting. Each district elected three representatives. Each elector cast three votes in any one of the following ways: one vote for each of three candidates; one and a half votes for each of two candidates; or three votes for a single candidate.[29]

In addition to the variations on SMP just reviewed, all of which retain the plurality formula, there is a large family of explicitly proportional electoral systems. These systems are party-oriented rather than candidate oriented, and are referred to as *party list systems*. Each party presents electors with a list of candidates. Electors cast a single vote for a party (some systems provide the means for electors to reveal a candidate preference within a party list). Each party whose popular vote percentage exceeds an exogenously specified *threshold* qualifies for seats. The formula for proportionally allocating these seats among qualifying parties varies from system to system (mostly depending upon arithmetical details concerning how fractional seats are allocated). We will not devote further attention to these strict proportional representation systems, since they are less relevant to minority representation in the United States.[30]

Electoral System Influence on Group Success

Under SMP, a group with 50 percent + 1 of the vote can guarantee itself a seat by coordinating on a single candidate and voting cohesively. A smaller group *may* win, but this will depend upon within-group coordination and cohesion as well as malcoordination and fractionalization among those not in the group.[31]

More generally, suppose there are n electors, each with v votes, and seats to be allocated to the first k candidates past the post. The number of votes sufficient to guarantee a candidate election is sometimes called the *threshold of exclusion*, or T; any candidate whose vote total exceeds T is assured a seat. It may be seen that $T = nv/(k + 1)$ as follows. Suppose that k candidates each exceeded T. We show that no other candidate could finish among the top k vote-getters. For the k candidates exceeding the threshold, their combined vote is greater than kT, or $k[nv/(k + 1)]$. The total vote remaining, then, is less than $nv - k[nv/(k + 1)]$, or $[(k + 1) - k][nv/(k + 1)]$. Simplifying, the total vote remaining is less than $nv/(k + 1)$. That is, the remaining vote is less than T, and thus no other candidate could obtain as many votes as the k candidates who exceeded T.[32]

This means that a group of electors can guarantee itself representation as a function of its size and the district magnitude. For SNTV and CV, if the group size exceeds $T/v = n/(k + 1)$, then that group can guarantee itself a seat.[33] Table 3.1 gives this sufficient group size as a function of district magnitude. The minimum sufficient size under LV depends upon whether electors can cumulate or not. The results given in table 3.1 apply to LV *with* cumulation.

If electors cannot cumulate, then some additional analysis of LV is required. Suppose the electorate is size n, the district magnitude is k, and each elector is given v votes. Consider a group G of size g. Though G controls gv votes in total, it may not cast more than g of these votes for any one candidate because of the prohibition against cumulation. So, the question is: When will g votes be sufficient under LV? In the worst case, the $n - g$ other electors spread their $(n - g)v$ votes evenly among k candidates, each of whom obtains $(n - g)v/k$ votes. In order for G to succeed, g must exceed this number: $g > (n - g)v/k$, or $g > nv/(k + v)$. Put in a slightly different form, $g > n/[(k/v) + 1]$. In contrast, SNTV, CV, and LV *with* cumulation require $g > n/(k + 1)$. The right-hand side of this latter inequality is smaller than the right-hand side of the former inequality. Hence, group G must be *larger* under LV if it cannot cumulate. Table 3.2 gives values for g sufficient to guarantee group success under LV for various values of k and v (and the noncumulation restriction).

Several features of this display are worth noting. First, whenever each

TABLE 3.1
Group Size and District Magnitude (SNTV, CV, LV with Cumulation)

District Magnitude (k)	Sufficient Group Size (g)
1	$n/2$
2	$n/3$
3	$n/4$
4	$n/5$

TABLE 3.2
Group Size and District Magnitude (LV without Cumulation)

District Magnitude (k)	Number of Votes (v)	Group Size (g) Must Exceed
1	1	$n/2$
2	1	$n/3$
	2	$n/2$
3	1	$n/4$
	2	$2n/5$
	3	$n/2$
4	1	$n/5$
	2	$n/3$
	3	$3n/7$
	4	$n/2$

elector has as many votes as there are seats—$v = k$—then only groups of majority size are assured a seat under LV without cumulation. Indeed, in this case a majority is assured *all* the seats, and any minority is shut out absolutely, as long as the majority electors can agree on the k candidates to support. Second, without cumulation, LV is most propitious for a minority when v/k is small: the larger this ratio, the bigger g must be. Third, comparing the two tables, a group must be larger to assure a seat when it cannot cumulate its votes than when it can (except in the degenerate case, $v = 1$, in which LV with and without cumulation, CV, and SNTV are identical).[34]

As this initial analysis suggests, with exceptions as noted, alternatives to single-member districts do permit cohesive minorities to organize to secure representation.[35] Additionally, these alternatives render moot most issues of *districting*, and the shenanigans associated with gerrymandering. Given exogenously established political units like states, counties, and cities, representative bodies (state legislatures, county planning boards, city councils, respectively) may be elected at-large under one of these alternative electoral systems in a manner that preserves the representative preferences of sufficiently large and well-organized groups (as given in the tables above).

It should also be noted that groups that secure representation satisfy the principle of free association.[36] If spatially dispersed left-handed Lithuanian Americans want common representation, then so long as they are a large enough minority, and so long as they explicitly or implicitly coordinate sufficiently, this representational preference can be accommodated.

Finally, let us emphasize again that what we have described are conditions on group size *sufficient* to assure the group of *one* representative. A group may do better—even a relatively small group—if its opposition is disorganized. The strategic issue facing the group in this case is the matter of *how many* representatives to support (or how many to nominate).[37] Of course, a group that tries to improve on what it could *guarantee* itself engages in a risky course of action, since it may overestimate or be strategically deceived by (apparent but not real) disorganization in the opposition.

Electoral System Influence on Group Incentives

Any theoretical investigation of multimember electoral systems would be incomplete without examining the incentives these electoral systems provide for individuals and groups. For this purpose, it is useful to return to our one-dimensional spatial formulation and some explicit models of political competition.

Cox's model of double-member plurality districts is especially simple.[38] This electoral system, which Cox reports was the most common in England from the thirteenth through most of the nineteenth century (and at least through the 1970s was common in a number of U.S. state legislative electoral systems), is described by $(v = 2, p = 0, c = 0, k = 2, f = \text{plurality})$. Each elector is endowed with two votes, which she must cast for two distinct candidates; the top two vote getters win.

Each of the n electors is assumed to have an ideal point in the [0, 100] interval and to vote *sincerely*—that is, for the two candidates whose spatial locations are closest to her ideal point. Each candidate maximizes its *vote margin*, defined as follows. Let v_j denote the total vote received by candidate j. If j is among the top two, define j's margin as $M_j = v_j - v_3$, where v_3 is the vote total of the candidate finishing just out of the running; in this case, M_j is j's margin of victory. If, on the other hand, j is not among the top two, then define j's margin as $M_j = v_j - v_2$, where v_2 is the vote total of the second-place finisher; in this case, M_j, which is negative, is a measure of how far short j falls of winning. Candidates are assumed to want to maximize their vote margin.

With this setup, which does no great injustice to a historically common multimember district electoral system, we may now determine the electoral incentives for candidates. They are surprising. Cox proves that if there are three candidates, their respective locations in equilibrium are given by $x_1 = x_2 = x_3$—that is, all candidates *converge* to a common electoral location.[39] Thus, even though, as we saw above, a minority group may be sufficiently large to elect a "candidate of choice," *there may not be a whole lot of choice* since candidates, interested in securing their electoral base, have strong incentives to converge toward one another.

Cox reports a second, similar result for the case where there are four candidates. The four, in equilibrium, converge to the ideal point of the median voter. Here, his result holds only for electorates where n is odd. He concludes that "the centrist bias of single-member districts is not unique."[40]

Although the results are limited in a variety of ways—to only three- and four-candidate contests, unidimensional voter preferences, and sincere voting—they are quite important because they lucidly demonstrate that incentives for groups of voters and candidates are not at all transparent. Tinkering with electoral systems is a complicated matter. Moreover, Cox generalizes these results substantially in a subsequent paper.[41] In doing so, he suggests that there is a quite subtle relationship among the number of votes per elector (v), district magnitude (k), and number of candidates (m).

First, he shows, for *all* multimember-district/plurality electoral systems that disallow cumulation or partial abstention, the central-clustering-of-candidates result reported above holds whenever the number of candidates is bounded from below by district magnitude and from above by twice the number of votes per elector—that is, whenever $k \leq m \leq 2v$. Thus, in an eleven-seat ($k = 11$) county planning commission elected at-large, where each elector votes for nine candidates ($v = 9$), convergence occurs whenever the number of candidates (m) is between eleven and eighteen.

Second, Cox proves that if the number of candidates is larger than $2v$, then there will be some dispersion of candidate positions. Specifically, he shows that, in equilibrium, the farthest left candidate must be at or below the $(v/m)^{\text{th}}$ percentile of the voter-ideal point distribution, while the farthest right candidate must be at or above the $(1 - v/m)^{\text{th}}$ percentile. Thus in the example in the previous paragraph, if there were twenty candidates for the eleven planning board seats, then the farthest left candidate must be at or below the 45th percentile and the farthest right candidate at or above the 55th percentile. Cox is unable to be more specific so that it is entirely possible that there will be even more dispersion than this; but it is also quite conceivable that all twenty candidates will be bunched between the 45th and 55th percentiles of the distribution of elector ideal points.

In this same paper, Cox also examines multimember district/plurality systems that permit partial abstention (e.g., Arizona state legislative elections) and those that permit cumulation of votes (e.g., board of director elections in many American corporations). The theorems, which the interested reader should consult in the original source, are remarkably similar. Some configurations of m, k, and v yield a median converging equilibrium, while others provide incentives for dispersion.[42]

The theoretical operating characteristics of electoral arrangements depend upon mechanical features, to be sure, but also on voter and candidate behavioral adaptations (strategic interaction). Whether such arrangements yield equilibriums, and the properties of equilbriums when they exist are anything but straightforward. In summary, equilibrium claims like those made by Guinier and other reformers need to be scrutinized with caution— not because the claims are radical or because they are inspired by normative concerns, but because the claims are about very subtle social systems. Merely asserting a claim does not make it persuasive. *Theory* sustaining the claim is required. So, too, is *evidence* drawn from empirical experience, which is our next topic.

Alternatives to SMP in Practice: Empirical Evidence

Electoral systems in practice yield a multitude of ingenious and often quite complicated arrangements. While the basic goal of an electoral system is to fill decision-making bodies with elected representatives, the rules transforming the expression of voter preferences into election outcomes can be of almost any variety. The most robust empirical regularity across all this electoral experience is the positive relationship between large-district, proportional-representation systems and success by electoral minorities in gaining seats. In this regard, advocates of alternatives to SMP as a means of enhancing minority representation appear to have the bulk of evidence on their side. The translation of votes into seats, however, is far from a simple, linear process; many institutional, cultural, and informal practices also affect seat outcomes. Often a system designed to serve one purpose results in consequences unforeseen by its designers, consequences that may even be counterproductive for the objectives of the electoral reform. This section examines electoral law in practice, looks at how minority groups have fared under various electoral arrangements, and discusses some of the practical issues involved in shaping governmental institutions to provide greater minority inclusion.

While the ultimate focus of our discussion is minority representation, the presentation that follows is oriented primarily toward minority seat gains. Gaining seats for one's group is sufficient for representation, but we hope the preceding section makes it clear that it is not necessary for representation. Minorities may influence representatives, even those who are not members of their group. Our examination in this section of the effects of electoral law on the seats-votes relationship and the ability of minority groups to gain seats in representative bodies, however, limits the discussion to more comparable and familiar terrain.

The target of the electoral reforms discussed in this paper is the African American minority in the United States. Looking for comparative evidence of minority representation in other countries, therefore, must account for the inevitable differences between American blacks and electoral minorities in other nations. An ideal minority group for comparison would be one with a similar historical background, not separated from the majority group by linguistic differences, not segregated geographically, and not distinguished by additional cleavages beyond race (such as religion or nationality). For the most part, however, such ideal comparison groups do not exist. Racial minorities in other systems are frequently defined by a multiplicity of cleavages, sometimes owing to an imperial or colonial heritage but also to migrations, war settlements, religious patterns, the socioeconomic legacies of modernization, or subnational tribal or clan allegiances; matters are further complicated in that many of these cleavages may be cross-cutting. In addition, the demographic characteristics of other minority groups vary widely, from their geographical distributions to the population proportions they constitute.

Despite the numerous differences of ethnic minorities across the globe, we believe that fruitful comparisons are possible where electoral consequences are concerned. Even the most basic feature of ethnic minorities—social designation by an identifiable characteristic such as skin color or ethnicity— may be relaxed for the purposes of electoral comparisons. Hence, for present purposes we interpret *electoral minorities* broadly to include any relatively unified voting group seeking to gain seats by fielding its own candidates in elections. Concentration on electoral minorities instead of on racial minorities moves the discussion away from many of the important characteristics unique to individual minority groups, but at the gain of greater understanding of the general problems and possibilities faced by minority groups that compete against majorities in the electoral process. What follows is a selective look at how other minorities have fared under alternative electoral arrangements. The cases are selected to illustrate the possibilities for minority representation through institutional design, and to point out minority groups that might warrant more intensive comparative study.

SMP Alternatives and Minority Representation in Other Countries

The proposition that large-district, proportional representation (PR) systems are conducive to seat gains by electoral minorities is widely confirmed in practice. This contrasts with the majoritarian tendencies of first-past-the-post systems such as those found in Great Britain, the United

States, and (until recently) New Zealand. In a majority system, 51 percent of the voters can elect the candidate or candidates of their choice; in a plurality election, this threshold may be even lower. Under a system of proportional representation, however, a group's seat share will be more or less proportional to its poll of the vote share, permitting groups with small vote shares to win seats. A party with 20 percent of the votes, for instance, would be expected to gain approximately two seats in a ten-seat district.[43]

Numerous examples of the low barriers to entry and associated seat gains by minorities in PR systems may be found. We alert the reader that the survey of PR is chosen to illustrate the effect of lowered "thresholds of exclusion," not to explore any of the other properties of PR. As we have mentioned previously, list-PR has so few proponents in the American context that its consideration as an electoral alternative is not really warranted here. Nevertheless, for illustrative reasons we do draw some of our examples from this system.

Northern Europe holds many examples of minority parties with small vote shares gaining seats. In Iceland, small parties with vote shares under 10 percent have demonstrated their ability to form and capture seats in the list-PR elections to the sixty-three-member national assembly (the Althing). Three new parties formed in the 1980s, two as breakaway factions from larger parties (the Citizens' Party, formed in 1987, and the New Social Democrats, formed in 1983) and one as an independent political movement (the Women's Alliance Party, formed in 1983). The Women's Alliance Party polled 5.5 percent of the vote in its first election, and because of electoral rules gained three seats, almost 5 percent of the Althing. In the 1987 election the Women's Alliance Party doubled its seats, roughly proportional to its 10.1 percent vote share. The other new parties experienced similar electoral success: the New Social Democrats won four seats in 1983 with a 7.3 percent vote share; in 1987 the newly formed Citizens' Party captured a 10.9 percent vote share to win seven seats.[44]

Similar seat gains have been realized by small parties in Finnish elections. One minority interest that has maintained a repeated parliamentary presence in Finland's two hundred-member Eduskunta (elected by list-PR, but with a 4 percent legal threshold) is the Swedish People's Party, formed in 1906 to protect the rights and interests of Finland's 6 percent (350,000) population of Swedish descent. With a consistent 4.5 to 5.5 percent vote share, the Swedish People's Party has held from ten to twelve seats throughout the 1970s and 1980s.[45]

Regionally based minority parties in southern Europe have also managed to win seats despite their numerically inferior status. Two Spanish regions that have traditionally sought autonomy or even independence, Basque and Catalonia, are both represented in the 350-member House of

Deputies by multiple regional parties. With between 4 and 6 percent of the national vote throughout the 1980s, in list-PR elections, Catalan parties managed to win 13, 18, and 18 seats in the 1982, 1986, and 1989 elections, respectively. Likewise, the Basque parties gained over 10 seats in each election, with between 3 and 4 percent of the vote.[46] Another regionally defined electoral minority that has benefited from its country's extreme PR electoral system is Italy's Northern League. In Italy's 1992 elections, the populist Lombard League drew an 8.7 percent national vote share to capture over 50 seats; in local elections in the main northern cities later that year, they polled over 30 percent of the vote to become a major force in government.

Italy's large district magnitudes and large parliamentary size—630 members—made its pre-1994 system extremely proportional, benefiting small parties of all kinds. Of the fifty-four parties contesting the 1992 Italian national election, many small parties winning 5 percent or even less of the vote won seats. These included the Liberals, the Radicals, and the Greens, in addition to the regional parties. But it also includes the neo-Fascist Italian Social Movement, which has held 35-40 seats throughout the 1980s. The presence of many other parties in electoral competition suggests they thought seat gains a possibility, despite small support. These included the Party of Love, whose ticket was headed by a pornography star (another pornography star had won a seat in the 1987 election).

No pornography stars competed in Poland's 1991 national election, but many small parties winning less than 1 percent of the vote share managed to gain seats in the 460-seat Polish Sejm. The Polish political scene, traditionally occupied by numerous parties, was especially crowded on the eve of the first fully democratic election. Struggling to become new parliamentary forces, some sixty-seven parties contested the election. Because of large districts and the absence of threshold requirements, twenty-nine parties won seats in the new parliament, eleven holding only one seat apiece. The variety of parties admitted ranged from traditional, large-issue parties to single-issue and ethnic-national parties, including the Polish Beer-Lovers Party, which won 3.5 percent of the seats (16) with 3.3 percent of the vote. Other parties winning seats polled less than 1 percent of the vote. This contrasts with the electoral laws adopted by Hungary. Its first election in 1990 was contested by approximately forty-five parties, yet only seven were awarded seats. Likewise, Romania's parliamentary election of 1990 saw seventy-four parties competing for votes with only seven awarded seats. The differences are explained almost entirely by electoral rules: Romania imposed a minimum vote threshold that increased progressively according to the number of parties entering the election. Hungary used a mixed-system where half of the seats were decided in single-member majority-system districts, but national-level seats were allocated according to proportions from the single-member election results, subject to a threshold that affected many of the seats.[47]

Many other examples exist showing how proportional representation electoral rules permit small parties—electoral minorities—to maintain a parliamentary presence. These small groups may be ideological parties, single-issue parties, or nationalist, ethnic, or regional minority parties. Nearly all they have in common is their minority status. One electoral minority, however, that is similar across countries—and electoral systems— is the environmentalists, represented by various Green and ecological parties.

Green parties arose in many advanced industrial democracies in the 1970s and 1980s to focus attention on environmental concerns, nuclear dangers, and general alternatives to traditional politics. Although many differences exist among national Green parties (and many "Green" parties within countries are in fact alliances of smaller ecological parties), Greens provide an interesting comparative case of the fate of electoral minorities under different electoral laws.

Figure 3.1 compares the deviations from proportionality experienced by European Green parties throughout the 1980s. The comparison is between the percentage of votes won by an ecological party in a particular election, and what Taagepera and Shugart have termed the "advantage ratio" (A), the percentage of seats won by a particular party divided by its percentage of votes.[48] When $A = 0$, the party has obtained no seats. If the party obtains fewer seats than its proportional share, then $A < 1$; and if a party receives a seat proportion greater than its vote share, then $A > 1$. The graph shows how nations with different electoral systems yielded different advantage ratios according to whether their vote-counting rules were proportional or plurality/majority. France, with its majoritarian system, maintained an advantage ratio of 0, even in 1993, when the Greens polled around 8 percent of the vote. The same result occurred in Great Britain for all of the elections shown.[49] The middle group of Switzerland (1983), and Belgium, Luxembourg, and Finland experienced advantage ratios between 0.5 and 0.7. Finally, the most proportional countries (Italy, Germany, Sweden) were close to the proportional advantage ratio (1.0) once their vote shares had exceeded around 3 percent. Note the different advantage ratios at different levels of the Green vote share in Sweden and Germany, attributable to the minimum vote thresholds imposed by each country's electoral law. Both Sweden and Germany have a mixture of district seats and national at-large seats; Germany imposes a 5 percent threshold on national seats (districts use SMP), and Sweden uses a 4 percent threshold (with 12 percent at the district level). This explains why the German Greens attained proportional results in 1983 and 1987, but not in 1980, when they had less

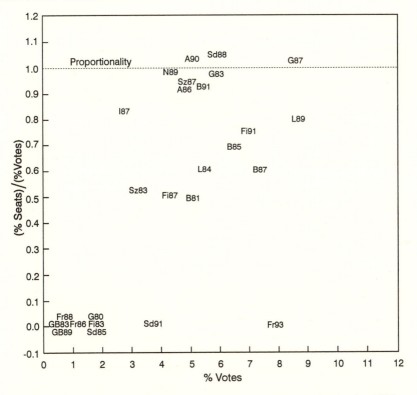

Figure 3.1. Seats-Votes Relationship of European Green Parties in the 1980s. A = Austria, B = Belgium, Fr = France, Fi = Finland, G = Germany, GB = Great Britain, L = Luxembourg, I = Italy, N = Netherlands, Sd = Sweden, Sz = Switzerland.

than a 2 percent vote share, and why the Swedish Green's advantage ratio was near 1.0 in 1988 but (with under 4 percent of the vote) was 0 in 1980 and 1991. Legal minimum thresholds are a common feature in many PR systems.

One European country—France—presents a rare single-country contrast of the differences between proportional representation and single-member majoritarian electoral systems. For many years using a single-member, majoritarian system to elect its 577-member National Assembly, France switched in 1986 to a system of proportional representation. (After one election, France returned to its majoritarian system for the elections of 1988.) Comparisons of the election in 1986 with other French elections therefore permits a unique opportunity for the study of the political consequences of electoral law. Unfortunately, French ecological parties have never been a major force, and the 5 percent threshold France used for the 1986 election kept the Green alliance from gaining any seats. Even in 1993, with 7.6 percent of the votes, the ecologist alliance failed to win any seats. In the proportional representation elections to the eighty-one French seats in the European Parliament, however, the Greens gained nine seats with a 10.6 percent vote share in 1989. Another small French party that formed in the 1980s—the National Front—illustrates quite clearly the consequences electoral law can have for the fortunes of electoral minorities.

The electoral vicissitudes of the National Front illustrate not only the differences that institutions make, but also the fact that lowered exclusion thresholds open the possibility of seat gains by *any* well-organized electoral minority, including racist opponents of ethnic minority groups. The National Front is a populist, anti-immigration, extreme right party formed in the early 1980s. It entered the political scene in 1984 by garnering a 10.9 percent vote share in the European Parliament elections, winning ten of France's eighty-one seats. In the 1986 national elections held under PR, the National Front won 35 seats in the National Assembly, with a 9.7 percent vote share. When the electoral law reverted to single-member-district rules for the 1988 national elections, the National Front captured an identical 9.7 percent of the vote, yet won only a single seat. And although it gained 12.5 percent of the votes in the 1993 national elections, the National Front won no seats. The success in 1986 of the National Front, such data suggest, was entirely caused by the use of PR in allocating seats.

The theme common to these numerous examples is that non-single-member, nonplurality, or nonmajority electoral rules enable political groups in the minority to capture seats with small vote shares, but that such access is available to all electoral minorities. Racial minority groups thus have the potential to gain increased representation insofar as they constitute self-contained electoral minorities, although lowering the threshold of exclusion by adopting more proportional electoral laws grants exclusive access to no particular group. The evidence from minorities in other systems conclusively supports the proposition that alternatives to SMP may effectively remove the penalties imposed by winner-take-all systems on minority electoral groups.

Plurality Alternatives in the United States

Although plurality methods predominate in the United States, alternative electoral arrangements have been tried on a limited scale.[50] Cumulative voting was used until 1980 in Illinois to elect the lower house of the state legislature, and is used currently in some Alabama county elections. Recently, a federal court judge ordered cumulative voting for the Worcester

County, Maryland, county commission. CV is also widely used in corporate elections in the United States. Currently, thirteen states permit CV to elect corporate boards of directors, and approximately twenty require it. Experience indicates that cumulative voting in corporate elections prevents a simple majority of the shareholders from electing the entire board, and in at least one well-known instance gave a minority interest control when the majority miscalculated its nomination strategy.[51] Edward Still's examination of CV to elect the county commission, the board of education, and three town councils in Chilton County, Alabama, indicates that blacks were able to use the ability to cumulate their votes for minority candidates to their advantage, breaking the white Democratic monopoly.[52] Other empirical studies of cumulative voting have shown a similar propensity for minorities to use strategic vote cumulation to achieve more proportional outcomes.[53]

Limited voting has received somewhat less application but has been tried in at least twenty-one municipal elections in Alabama and several in Pennsylvania county commissioner elections. The results indicate that LV was conducive to greater black electoral success, although the successes were less marked than those under cumulative voting, perhaps due to the greater exigencies of strategy under LV.[54] These results are consistent with experience in other systems that have used the limited vote. Between 1867 and 1885, for instance, Britain used LV in thirteen three-member constituencies with two votes for each elector; in all but two districts no party won all three seats.[55] Evidence from other countries indicates similar results. In Spain, upper chamber elections have used the limited vote since 1977. In elections to Japan's national assembly (both houses), voters have a single vote in three-, four-, or five-member districts. The results indicate that the LV disadvantages large majorities and achieves results that are increasingly proportional as the votes are more limited.[56]

The single-transferable vote (STV) has received the widest application of alternative electoral methods in the United States. STV has been used in approximately two dozen cities to elect city councils and school boards.[57] In New York City in 1970, blacks comprised more than 20 percent of the population and Puerto Ricans made up approximately 12 percent. On the thirty-seven-member city council, elected by SMP, there were no Puerto Ricans and only two blacks. By contrast, on the newly established 279-member community school boards elected that year by STV, nearly 28 percent (77) of the officials were black or Puerto Rican.[58]

Alternative electoral methods are found in the United States, then, although not on a wide scale. The American flavor of democracy is decidedly plurality, usually (and increasingly) associated with single- or small-magnitude districts. Of the two dozen municipalities using STV, in fact, only Cambridge, Massachusetts, has not changed to plurality elections.

Alternative Representational Structures and Minority Inclusion

Electoral rules (according to the typology we have borrowed from Cox) are but one set of variables in the institutional settings that are designed to represent minorities. Many countries accommodate minority representation by including them in governing by legal means other than lowering the electoral threshold of exclusion. Although PR rules may be part of the representational system, the representational framework is often structured so that various groups are guaranteed seats and offices alongside, or perhaps in spite of, the electoral law.

Many varieties of "workarounds" to the Duverger's Law tendencies of SMP are found in systems that attempt to combine minority representation with the stabilizing influences of single-member districts. These solutions are designed to mitigate the winner-take-all, single-prize character of SMP. Such designs include majoritarian rules, where the top vote getters from the first round of voting face off in a second round if none receives an initial majority (France, 1988–present); special overlapping districts for ethnic minority groups (used to ensure Maori seats in combination with New Zealand's pre-1994 SMP system); national-level PR-determined seats in combination with district-based single-member elections (used in Germany, Sweden, Hungary, and Romania); or districts drawn around populations whose representation is desired, so that majorities are manufactured at the district level (race-based reapportionment in the United States).

Another modification to the single-member district structure involves changing the structure of the ballot to permit an ordinal preference expression. This system is known as the alternative vote (AV), used to elect Australia's lower house, and proposed by Donald Horowitz for use in single-member districts in South Africa.[59] The alternative vote permits each voter to rank candidates, rather than expressing a single first preference. When no candidate receives more than 50 percent of the first preferences cast, the candidate with the least number of first preferences is dropped, and the alternative preferences from his or her ballots are distributed to other candidates, and so on until a candidate has original and transferred first preferences equal to at least 50 percent of the ballots cast. This system "wastes" fewer votes and permits minorities to vote for their first choice while casting an effective preference expression for an alternative candidate in case the first is not elected. Its appropriateness in South Africa was suggested because the use of ordinal preferences is thought to encourage centripetal appeals and discourage ethnic extremism. "Under alternative voting with a majority threshold for victory, many elections will turn on second and third preferences. Parties that succeed in negotiating for second and third preferences will be rewarded. The price of a successful negotiation is inter-group accommodation and compromise."[60]

Thus, proportional results can be accomplished in a system largely based on SMP, and ethnic representation or centrist appeals can be engineered through means other than sweeping changes of district size and vote-counting rules. Such solutions accomplish specific objectives of representation while preserving the general political characteristics produced by an electoral design constructed according to a particular nation's ideas of governing. These specific solutions, however, are often controversial insofar as they endow the target groups with privileged status.

Such controversy is evident in the decennial redistricting process that occurs in the United States, designed to correct partisan and racial imbalances due to demographic patterns that have changed since the previous census. The practice of drawing districts around concentrations of minority voters, while predominant among current strategies to remedy vote dilution, draws criticism precisely for its fixed nature. African American representation in the United States has seen remarkable gains, but this achievement is owed almost entirely to the deliberate drawing of districts around areas of minority concentration, a form of "affirmative gerrymandering."[61] Hence, proportionality in legislative composition with a single-member district system requires active judicial reapportionment. Once state or local jurisdictions have been found guilty of diluting minority voting strength, courts can order the jurisdiction to create districts of sufficient nonwhite majorities to enforce compliance with the Voting Rights Act. The result is that minority electoral gains become dependent on a form of gerrymandering. Single-member districts have been popular in the black community largely because of the association of multimember districts with the discriminatory at-large plurality elections adopted in the twentieth century to dilute minority votes. The switch to single-member districts by many states in the 1970s and 1980s, in fact, has been associated with gains in minority representation (table 3.3).

One disadvantage of racially based reapportionment is that the solution breaks down when the minority group is geographically dispersed or when multiple minority groups coexist in the same area. Hispanics, for instance, who are less geographically concentrated, have been less successful in gaining seats through the single-member-district approach. Generally, minorities have representation closer to their population strengths in municipal elections, where populations are more identifiable and more concentrated, than in state legislative elections, where more dispersion exists.[62] In addition, redistricting for one minority often has negative consequences for other ethnic constituencies. A frequently cited example of this occurred in 1974 when a court-ordered plan to create minority districts divided the Williamsburgh section of Brooklyn. The Hasidic Jews formerly constitut-

TABLE 3.3
Blacks in State Assemblies under At-large and Single-Member
District Systems (Percentages)

State	Black Population (% of total) (1980)	MMD (1971)	SMD (1981)
Alabama	24.5	1.9	12.4
Georgia	26.2	7.2	11.7
Louisiana	29.6	1.0	9.5
Mississippi	35.1	0.8	12.3
South Carolina	31.0	2.4	12.1
Texas	12.5	1.3	8.7

Source: Joint Center for Political Study, *National Roster of Black Elected Officials*, vol. 1 (1976), vol. 6 (1976), and vol. 11 (1981). In Amy 1993.

ing a majority in their district suddenly became minorities in districts that were predominantly black and Hispanic.[63] The electoral success of the latter groups came at the expense of the former, because of the zero-sum nature of representing subinterests through districts.

How districts are drawn, in fact, has tremendous implications for racial representation and general race relations in society. Two nations with sharp ethnic divisions, Sri Lanka and Malaysia, both adopted SMP electoral systems, yet each produced different ethnic tendencies. The Malaysian districts, drawn around ethnically heterogeneous populations, encouraged "vote pooling," where candidates had incentives to make moderate and transethnic appeals to maximize their support. In Sri Lanka, where districts were more ethnically homogenous, the result was a more divisive series of ethnic parties competing with one another.[64]

One much-debated extra-electoral representational structure is known as *consociationalism.* Consociational democracies accomplish representation of various segments in a divided society by devices designed to mitigate the effects of pure majority rule. Consociational features have been implemented in Belgium, Switzerland, Austria, and Malaysia and have been proposed for a democratic South Africa.[65]

Especially in plural societies—societies that are sharply divided along religious, ideological, linguistic, cultural, ethnic, or racial lines into virtually separate subsocieties with their own political parties, interest groups, and media of communication—the flexibility necessary for majoritarian democracy is absent. Under these conditions, majority rule is not only undemocratic but also dangerous, because minorities that are continually denied access to power will feel excluded and discriminated against and will lose their allegiance to the regime.[66]

Features of these "consensus democracies" include executive power sharing, separation of powers, proportionate minority representation in legislatures and civil service posts, federalism and decentralization, and a minority veto over important matters affecting the minority interest. In nations like Belgium, where the country is divided between French and Flemish speakers, institutional arrangements exist to guarantee representation for each segment. The Belgian constitution was amended in 1970 to recognize the linguistic cleavage formally, dividing members of parliament into two separate Cultural Councils that serve as "parliaments" in the domain of cultural and educational autonomy granted to each linguistic community. Laws affecting cultural autonomy must be passed with a two-thirds majority including the concurrent majority of each language group. In addition, the French-speaking minority can appeal any bill that threatens its interests to the cabinet, which is composed of equal numbers of Flemish and French speakers. Bilingual Brussels is governed by a similar arrangement.[67] Even the three major political parties, differentiated along issue and religious lines, are divided into separate camps for the French and Flemish-speaking constituents.[68]

Switzerland has a similar arrangement in the form of its Federal Council, the seven-member executive that since 1959 has been divided among the Radical Democrats, the Christian Democrats, and the Social Democrats, with two members apiece, and one member supplied from the Swiss People's Party. In addition, the seven members are also selected to represent Switzerland's multiple linguistic groups proportionally, four or five German speakers, one or two French speakers, and frequently an Italian speaker. Both the party and the linguistic rule are informal but are strictly obeyed.[69]

Consociationalism, like list-PR, is virtually absent from the discourse of political reform in the United States. This is no doubt due to its anti-majoritarian character, which strikes many Americans as "undemocratic" or "un-American." The storm of opposition to Lani Guinier's nomination as Assistant Attorney General for Civil Rights shows just how strong the sentiments against minority vetoes and other power-sharing arrangements that tamper with majoritarian principles are felt by American political elites. It is therefore ironic that the current paradigm of racial reapportionment to achieve greater black representation, basically a circumvention of the majoritarian tendencies of SMP that turns racial minorities into electoral majorities, has characteristics so similar to some of the consociational structures just reviewed.

Comparative evidence suggests that many factors influence minority representation. If the goal is to enable minority groups in the electorate to gain seats, then empirical evidence indicates that lowered thresholds of exclusion accomplished through alternatives to SMP can be effective in awarding seats to groups with small vote shares. This process applies to groups by virtue of their size, and not according to their political views or cultural and ethnic characteristics. Small right-wing parties are provided the same electoral access as previously excluded minority groups of the same support size, as are any other small parties that can muster the minimum vote requirements to gain a seat. These contrast with more rigid representational solutions where electoral minorities are represented by legal guarantees or other workarounds of the electoral law. Such solutions guarantee representation for minority groups but raise additional normative and political issues. Rigid solutions may guarantee representation for targeted minority groups, but bring disadvantages from their inflexible nature. Without such workarounds, however, experience indicates that the single-member plurality system is ill-suited for providing seats to electoral minorities.

Concluding Remarks

Our substantive attention has focused on the relationship between electoral system characteristics and the resolution of representation and influence claims by electoral minorities in popularly elected assemblies. While we have examined such properties in the context of numerous electoral systems, we have not necessarily advocated any particular institutional arrangement or reform. Our purpose has been rather to explore their operating characteristics to see what lessons the last twenty years of political science have to offer concerning electoral structures and minority representation.

A principal conclusion we draw from our survey is that while questions of equilibriums and electoral incentives are fundamental to the issue of representation and electoral systems, these questions have yet to be fully engaged by the substantive literature on minority representation. Our brief examination of formal electoral theory has highlighted the complex nature of the issues underlying claims of representation and minority empowerment. It points unequivocally to the need for systematic extension of theory on such issues as electoral incentives, candidate convergence, and group strategy and coordination. This should precede, and inform, consideration of electoral reform proposals based on such concepts as "vote wasting," "disempowerment," and "procedural justice." Unfortunately, many advocates employing such claims tend to offer neither rigorous argument nor empirical evidence. Furthermore, the largely distinct theoretical and empirical scholarly literatures on electoral systems tend to address issues of minority representation only indirectly. As a consequence, we find at present little firm basis for unambiguous claims about electoral system properties and minority representation.

Evidence does indicate that multimember districts combined with voting rules like limited voting, cumulative voting, or SNTV make it possible for electoral minorities to secure a representative of their choosing, more so than under a single-member, plurality electoral system. Yet the equilibrium properties of these systems as they pertain to minority representation, and the consequences of the structural incentives they exert on parties, issues, and voters, have yet to be given a rigorous and systematic treatment.

Experience also makes it plain that electoral design in practice serves multiple and often conflicting purposes. At the heart of electoral design is the question of which normative concerns the system should promote. Inevitably, the normative desiderata linked with electoral systems are mutually competitive or even exclusive. The issue of representation versus governance, for instance, is a basic consideration underlying any electoral design. The fact that proponents of radical reforms in the United States have looked only at one side of this conflict—representation—further underscores the differences between advocacy and scientific research.

Another disconcerting tension is the trade-off between minority access and minority guarantees. Minority representation guaranteed by specific legal provision may conflict with the representational claims of other minority groups. Likewise, electoral rules that lower the threshold of exclusion to permit numerically smaller groups to gain seats may empower minorities, but without distinguishing among them. African Americans in Mississippi are not the only voters empowered by more proportionate vote-counting rules—so are the Louisiana supporters of David Duke. In other words, what's sauce for the goose is sauce for the gander.

We hope that our analysis will further stimulate the growing scientific interest in the effects of electoral system properties on minority representation. Formal theory has tremendous potential to inform the debate on electoral reform as a means of minority empowerment, but existing models need to be extended to racial issues. Comparative empirical evidence, we have shown, also holds many lessons for those considering reform. Any comparative study, however, should carefully consider which contextual factors are most relevant to the American experience. Finally, we hope that political scientists can inject a healthy measure of scholarly skepticism into the policy debate surrounding alternative electoral arrangements, joining advocacy with theory and evidence and combining salient experience with critical knowledge.

Notes

1. For a general discussion of post–Civil War electoral discrimination against African Americans see Kousser 1984 and Davidson 1992.
2. Davidson 1984, 4–5.
3. Guinier 1992, 283, 285.

4. Although we will not focus in this paper on this third instance of electoral market failure, it has received a good deal of recent scrutiny owing to the nomination (subsequently withdrawn) of one of its stongest proponents, Professor Lani Guiner. To resolve problems of disempowerment—minority representatives effectively shut out of actual governing—she advocates "proportionate interest representation," the current label for moving beyond guaranteeing the *presence* of minority representatives to guaranteeing their *influence* in elected bodies. Guinier (1991b, 1136) put it thus: "A system that gives everyone an equal chance of having their political preferences *physically represented* is inadequate. A fair system of political representation would provide mechanisms to ensure that disadvantaged and stigmatized minority groups also have a fair chance to have their policy preferences *satisfied.*" Elsewhere, she points to problems of "minority marginalization" and "interest submersion" in legislative bodies, and thus claims that "legislative seats alone do not enfranchise" (Guinier 1991a, 1462, 1436, and 1416, respectively).

5. Guinier, this volume. As is evident, we rely heavily throughout this essay on the writings of Guinier for a number of reasons. First, she is an extremely clear and outspoken critic of SMP and advocate for scrapping it in favor of a proportional representation (PR) system. Second, she is a prolific writer. Third, Guinier has probably gone farther than any other critic of the current electoral system in advocating not only radical electoral reform, but significant interventions into the conventional operations of elected bodies as well. Fourth, she appeared at an earlier incarnation of the conference for which our own paper has been prepared; indeed, the invitation to write this paper from the conference convenor, Professor Paul Peterson, encouraged us to respond to some of the issues Guinier so lucidly raised in her paper (Guinier, this volume). In doing so, we should add, we are not suggesting that Guinier is the only advocate of PR and other institutional reforms; nor are we particularly interested in rebutting her advocacy or sparring with her as an intellectual exercise. Rather, we are most interested in seeing whether there is anything in the scientific literature—either theoretical or empirical—that might shed light on the performance of the PR alternatives Guinier advocates in place of SMP to empower minorities.

6. Moreover, only the mildest of additional qualification is required if we relax the strictures stipulated in the last paragraph (odd-numbered electorate, full participation).

7. See Calvert 1985 for a formal proof of this result.

8. *Informal proof.* If $m = 0$, then the original median obtains. If $m = n - 1$, then the first of the "old" voters is the new median. If $m \geq n$, then one of the new voters is median. In all of these instances, the new median is equal to or to the left of the old median. In the typical case, where $0 < m < n$, the median will be one of the old voters to the left of old voter $(n + 1)/2$.

9. In fact, some reformers disenchanted with (nonracially gerrymandered) single-member districts acknowledge the "influencing" effects of minority voters on candidate strategies. They simply reject that form of representation, preferring racially gerrymandered districts instead, for example. See Guinier, this volume, for a discussion of this point of view.

10. Hotelling 1929.

11. There is *no* equilibrium for $k = 3$. For any distribution of the three candidates, the outermost candidates have incentives to converge toward the intermediate candidate, thereby increasing their vote totals. The intermediate candidate then has the incentive to leapfrog to the outside. This pattern of jockeying has no stopping point.

12. Eaton and Lipsey 1975. Their theorem is stated in terms of spatial locations for firms seeking to maximize market share.

13. Eaton and Lipsey generalize this theorem to the case in which voter ideals are not restricted to a uniform distribution; essentially the same result holds. For a fuller discussion of this theorem and various elaborations, see Shepsle 1991, chap. 3.

14. For systematic work on Duverger's Law, see Riker 1982; Palfrey 1989; and Feddersen 1993.

15. Feddersen, Sened, and Wright 1990.

16. Cox 1987.

17. Hagen 1993.

18. If the winning candidate locates at the *majority* group's median, then the minority is without influence.

19. Rohde 1991; Shepsle 1989.

20. The question arises, Is the pattern of vote dilution and electoral cartels at the *local* level compatible with the pattern of minority group influence at the *congressional district* and *state* levels? Or is one of these a transitional, out-of-equilibrium situation? Based on the common experience with cartels—namely, that they are unstable in the long run (though the long run may be quite long)—we speculate that local white politicians will not be able to maintain majority bloc voting. (Harvey Gantt, it will be recalled, was popularly elected at the local level, with considerable white support, as mayor in Charlotte, North Carolina, before he nearly toppled, again with considerable white support, the incumbent U.S. senator, Jesse Helms [R-N.C.].) More significantly, the demise of cartels will be hastened by the inability of cartel managers to check the ambitions of politicians, ambitions that provide incentives for politicians to seek crossover votes. As this becomes the case, the spatial analysis offered above becomes increasingly relevant to the electoral dynamics of minority representation.

21. Cain 1992, 262.

22. Thernstrom 1987.

23. Guinier 1991b, 1992.

24. Kousser 1993.

25. Guinier, this volume.

26. While we draw on both bodies of work in this essay, the formal and empirical literatures are too immense to be comprehensively reviewed here. Both literatures are, for the most part, scattered in a variety of journals. This is especially true of the theoretical literature, though a monographic review is found in Shepsle 1991. The classic of the empirical literature is Rae 1967, updated recently by Lijphart 1990. Taagepera and Shugart 1989, Grofman and Lijphart 1986, and Lijphart and Grofman 1984 arbitrage across the boundaries of these literatures.

27. Cox 1990 and other papers of his cited there provide a good starting point for the theoretically interested reader.

28. Cox 1990.

29. An Illinois Supreme Court decision in 1928 provided for a fourth manner of casting votes: two votes for one candidate and one vote for another. On cumulative voting in Illinois, see Blair 1960; and Sawyer and MacRae 1962.

30. While multimember districting schemes have historical precedent in the United States (and are in use today in limited jurisdictions), list proportional representation presumes a strong party system and would constitute a much more radical departure from Americam political traditions. It turns out, however, that at least some of the PR systems bear a close relationship to those plurality systems we list in the text. Cox 1991, for example, proves that one prominent method of allocating seats by PR—the d'Hondt method—is strategically equivalent to SNTV in the sense that, holding district magnitude and votes for (candidates of) parties fixed, both methods yield identical seat allocations.

31. This possibility is nicely illustrated in the special election in the Second District of Mississippi to fill the uncompleted term of Congressman Mike Espy (who had joined the Clinton administration as Secretary of Agriculture). A nonpartisan primary was held in this majority-black district to choose two candidates for a subsequent runoff election. The lone white Republican, who was pitted against nearly a dozen black aspirants, finished first in the primary and, owing to a considerable falloff in participation, nearly won the runoff. The large number of black entrants made the job of coordinating on one especially difficult, sapping the strength and draining the resources of the eventual runoff qualifier to the point that he nearly lost the runoff election.

32. Recall that, as in the preceding paragraph, T is *sufficient* for election, but is not necessary. If the number of candidates is large enough and the vote sufficiently fractionalized, then it is entirely possible for a candidate to win election with fewer than T votes.

33. With SNTV, where $v = 1$, the threshold to insure a candidate's election, T, is exactly the same as the size a group must exceed, T/v, to insure its capacity to elect a representative of its own choosing. With CV, T/v electors (where, presumably, $v > 1$), among themselves, control the T votes necessary to elect a candidate (on the assumption that all these electors cumulate their votes).

34. For a general introduction to these issues, and the simple mathematics of electoral systems, see Still 1984.

35. This confirms Guinier's (this volume) observation that, in comparison to the alternatives we have been considering, "single-member districts tend to underrepresent minority votes."

36. Sugden 1984. As Guinier (this volume) puts it, "Interests are those *self-identified voluntary constituencies* who choose to combine because of like minds, not like bodies."

37. See Brams 1975, chap. 3, for an analysis along these lines of minority representation on the governing board of the American Political Science Association.

38. Cox 1984.

39. Cox 1984, theorem 1. That position need not be the median of the voter distribution. It may be any point between the quantiles of order 1/3 and 2/3 of the distribution of voter ideals. But the median does have special attractions, a point developed in greater detail by Cox (1984, 447).

40. Cox 1984, 447–48.

41. Cox 1990, theorems 1a and 1b.

42. Additional theoretical results on cumulative voting may be found in Glazer, Glazer, and Grofman 1984; and Felsenthal 1990, chap. 4.

43. In a k-seat district the threshold of exclusion (the minimum vote share required to gain a seat, as a proportion) is normally $1/(k + 1)$ of the vote. Thus, about 9.1 percent of the vote will yield one seat in a ten-seat district. There are many different ways to deal with electoral remainders, which affect how small parties are awarded seats, but this discussion is merely intended to point out the general tendencies of PR and plurality systems.

44. Cossolotto 1991.

45. Ibid., 279.

46. Urwin and Paterson 1990, 280.

47. McGregor 1993.

48. Taagapera and Shugart 1989. Portraying the seats-votes relationship using the advantage ratio instead of a straightforward plot of seat and vote percentages highlights deviations from proportionality, according to the percentage of votes. This more clearly depicts how large parties may be overrepresented and how small parties may be underrepresented, although here only small parties are depicted. See ibid., 67–68.

49. We do not suggest that the levels of small party vote shares are exogenous to incentives provided by electoral law. To the contrary, Duverger's Law suggests that voters will hesitate to "waste" their votes on small parties in majority/plurality systems. But for this example the low levels of voter support are equally revealing.

50. Leon Weaver estimates that proportional representation systems (of various types) have constituted "a fraction of 1%" of all electoral systems in the United States, and these are usually found only at the local level (1986, 140).

51. Glazer, Glazer, and Grofman 1984, 295, 297. The case was the 1883 Sharpsville Railroad Company's election of its board of directors, upheld by the Pennsylvania Supreme Court in *Pierce v. Commonwealth*, 104 Pa. 150 (1883).

52. Still 1984, 189.

53. Engstrom, Taebel, and Cole 1989, 469; Engstrom and Barilleaux 1991; Weaver 1984, 191.

54. Still 1984, 190–91; Featherman 1992, 882–84.

55. Still 1984, 253.

56. Lijphart, Pintor, and Sone 1986.

57. Weaver 1986.

58. Zimmerman 1992, 216.

59. Horowitz 1991, chap. 5.

60. Ibid., 189.

61. It is generally believed that a "safe" population proportion for ethnic minorities is around 65 percent, to compensate for lack of voter turnout (Grofman and Handley 1992, 34; Parker 1984, 112). But see Kousser 1993 for an alternative point of view.

62. Amy 1993.

63. Wells 1982.

64. Horowitz 1989.

65. Lijphart 1985.

66. Lijphart 1984, 22–23.

67. Lijphart 1977, 97.

68. Cossolotto 1991, 79.

69. Lijphart 1984, 24.

4

Racial Fairness in Legislative Redistricting

GARY KING, JOHN BRUCE, AND ANDREW GELMAN

1. The Search for a Standard of Racial Fairness

In this chapter, we study standards of racial fairness in legislative redistricting—a field that has been the subject of considerable legislation, jurisprudence, and advocacy, but very little serious academic scholarship. We attempt to elucidate how basic concepts about "color-blind" societies, and similar normative preferences, can generate specific practical standards for racial fairness in representation and redistricting. We also provide the normative and theoretical foundations on which concepts such as *proportional representation* rest, in order to give existing preferences of many in the literature a firmer analytical foundation.

Our work also addresses a troubling discrepancy between partisan and racial standards of fairness in the redistricting of American legislatures. Scholars have reached near consensus on *partisan symmetry* as a standard of partisan fairness and have made great progress on developing measures that can be used to see whether electoral systems and redistricting plans meet this standard. Perhaps appropriately, the law has lagged well behind, with the Supreme Court recognizing only in 1986 that political gerrymandering was justiciable (*Davis v. Bandemer*) but not yet adopting either a standard or measure of partisan unfairness.[1] Unfortunately, almost the reverse applies to standards of racial fairness: scholars have hardly begun to discuss appropriate absolute standards of fairness in racial redistricting, but we now have a long list of legislation (largely the Voting Rights Act and its amendments), constitutional and statutory interpretation (through a long series of Supreme Court cases), and Justice Department activism.[2] With all this activity, it is remarkable that there presently exists no agreed upon absolute standard of racial fairness in redistricting, and there is even relatively little discussion about such a standard in public law or the academic literature. We begin to address this problem here.[3]

Considerable scholarship in recent years has been devoted to issues of representation of ethnic minority groups in various American electoral systems. Scholars contributing to this literature consistently have identified the basic "problem" as *under*-representation of these groups in Congress, state and county legislatures, city councils, and other legislative bodies. In this paper, we study the *question* of what constitutes fairness in minority legislative representation rather than assume the *answer*—that minorities have too few or too many representatives than they deserve based on their numbers in the population. We therefore ask: What is the appropriate level of representation of a given racial minority group in an American legislature? Our search is for an absolute standard of racial fairness, not merely for a relative answer such as "minorities have too much or too little." The possible answers to our question may be normative, but at least our question does not presuppose a particular normative answer.[4]

We begin our analysis in section 2 by asking a somewhat stylized version of a question about standards: How many legislative seats should be allocated to minority groups? We discuss previous answers to this question in section 2.1 and then offer three new approaches in sections 2.2 and 2.3. Section 3 then addresses the issue of comparative standards—comparing a minority group's representation with that of other groups in the population. We conclude in section 4.

2. Theoretical Standards: What Is a Fair Seat Proportion for the Representation of Protected Minorities?

We focus our question about racial fairness in four ways. First, one can concentrate generally on a minority group's "candidate of choice" or specifically on the election of a member of that group. The former is supported by many scholars who prefer to focus on the wishes rather than characteristics of the minority population.[5] The latter can be justified by appealing to concepts of *descriptive representation* and the desirability of role models.[6] Since the two frequently coincide in practice, we use the criteria interchangeably in this section, usually focusing on election of members of the minority group.[7] Although the distinctions between these standards are important, our analysis is relevant to both.

Second, for further simplicity, we will usually focus on African Americans. They constitute the group to which the literature has been primarily addressed, and their more uniform voting behavior makes theoretical and empirical analyses easier.

Third, our question can be focused even further by asking directly about the number of legislative seats that African Americans should be allocated. This is possible since it is often easy in practice to draw legislative districts that have extremely high probabilities of electing minority legislators. These majority-minority districts may be oddly shaped and of dubious contiguity, they may violate many other desirable criteria in redistricting, but they have been and can be drawn by legislative mapmakers. Alternative choices—ignoring minorities when redistricting, using "neutral" redistricting criteria, or using something other than minority-based rules—also have immediate and predictable consequences for racial representation. In the practice of drawing districts, one can ignore the issue, but one cannot avoid it. Our decision to recognize this fact of American redistricting should not be taken as an endorsement or criticism; other approaches could be taken.

Fourth, we clarify the relation between racial fairness and affirmative action. Proponents of affirmative action in redistricting suggest that redistricting be used to "affirmatively gerrymander" in the interests of racial minorities. Some of these affirmative steps would only correct the situation to one of "fairness" (as yet undefined by any existing consensus), while others would explicitly go beyond some definition of fairness in order to redress *and* compensate for years of district lines drawn to prevent blacks from being elected to legislative posts. We view the question of whether to go beyond some absolute standard of fairness to compensate for past discrimination as very important but outside the scope of this paper. Our only present concern is defining this standard of fairness in the first place. Regardless of whether one is interested in reaching a level of absolute fairness or something beyond, one first needs a clear, absolute definition of fairness, a definition that has not been provided by the literature.

To pose our question about standards of racial fairness directly: What proportion of legislative seats should be held by blacks? Some may be uncomfortable with this formulation (as are we) since it seems to ignore the role of the electoral process entirely. This certainly is true, and a complete policy choice must address the electoral *process* as well. However, the question of results is straightforward and, even in the extreme form posed here, is relevant to the policy of drawing majority-minority districts, in which it is possible, in practice, for redistricters to decide on the number of seats that will be won by blacks.[8] Possible answers to the question include "zero," "as many as possible," "use other criteria and ignore the number of black districts," "the number proportional to their percentage in the general population (proportional representation)," or others. We explore several of these possible answers to this question and offer some new approaches.

At least until recently, the explicit or implicit normative judgment that racial minority groups were *under*-represented was not the subject of much controversy, since in many areas there were significant proportions of the population composed of these minorities but zero legislators from this group. Few would argue that this situation occurred by chance alone rather than by an intentional strategy of racial gerrymandering. In South Carolina,

30 percent of the population is black, blacks vote with a very high degree of unity for Democratic candidates and almost unanimously for black candidates, but from Reconstruction until 1992, South Carolina's congressional delegation included no black members. The 1992 election not only saw the first African Americans since Reconstruction elected to the U.S. House from South Carolina, but also from Alabama, Florida, and Virginia, and the first black elected from North Carolina since 1898—all states with significant black populations. Regardless of one's ideological position or preference for a normative standard, it is not difficult to see at least the possibility of inequity here. Of course, this "inequity," even if agreed upon, is a *relative* standard, and therefore does not answer our call for an absolute standard of racial fairness.

We believe the question about the right absolute standards of minority representation we have posed is relevant regardless of the existing level of minority representation. The question is also of special relevance currently, since the number of minorities elected to legislatures around the country has been increasing rapidly. Nationwide, the number of African Americans elected in U.S. state legislatures more than doubled between 1970 and 1990, increasing from 179 to 440, with additional increases in 1992. The number of Hispanics holding state legislative and executive offices increased from 110 in 1984 to 133 in 1990. In the U.S. Congress, the number of blacks increased from 10 in 1970 to 25 in 1990 and 38 in 1992, while Hispanic representation in the U.S. Congress increased from 5 to 11 between 1977 and 1992. The actual levels are still far below what some advocates consider desirable, but the trend is unambiguous.

In figure 4.1, we give a summary of the current situation for black representation in the lower houses of American state legislatures, as of 1990.[9] The horizontal axis is the percentage of the voting age population that is black. The vertical axis is the percentage black in the legislature. States that fall on the diagonal line have blacks proportionally represented in the legislature. The few states that are plotted above the line have a (slightly) higher proportion of blacks in the legislature than in the voting age population. States below the line have a smaller proportion of blacks in the legislature than among those of voting age.

Several features of figure 4.1 are of importance. First, states with fewer than about 7–10 percent of the voting age population are represented approximately proportionally. However, states with larger black voting age populations are disproportionally farther from proportional legislative representation (since they are farther below the line). The latter may reflect V.O. Key's finding that political discrimination against blacks is strongest when they become threatening, that is, when they come closer to forming a majority and winning political office.[10] Additionally, states with higher

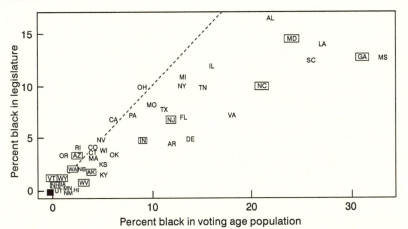

Figure 4.1. State Legislatures in 1990. States with at least one multimember district are in boxes. States falling on the diagonal line have proportional representation of blacks in their legislatures. The square at the origin corresponds to the states Maine, Montana, Idaho, North Dakota, and South Dakota. All had zero blacks in the legislature and less than 0.5 percent blacks in the voting age population. Several states (Colorado, Connecticut, Hawaii, Iowa, Minnesota, Nebraska, New Mexico, Vermont, Washington, and Wyoming) were moved by small amounts (always less than 0.5 percent on each scale) to make the figure more legible.

proportions of blacks are more likely to have had a history of slavery, discrimination, and disenfranchisement. Finally, states with at least one multimember district have boxes around their names in figure 4.1. Since the boxed states appear randomly spread out on this graph, the type of district appears unrelated to the proportion black in the population and the legislature and to the degree of disproportionality. Of course, different types of multimember districts, and differences in the extent to which they are used in a state, might have very different consequences for minority representation.

2.1 Previous Answers

Previous research on fairness to protected minorities in redistricting has been either advocacy, empirical research, or both. Very little theoretical work has been devoted to developing absolute standards of fairness. Advocates have made philosophical arguments, proposed remedies, and outlined legislative and judicial strategies to increase the representation of protected minorities.[11] Empirical researchers have studied general trends in minority representation,[12] the way certain electoral arrangements lead to "low" levels of minority representation,[13] and the consequences of different levels of representation for voter efficacy.[14]

Although, as we have indicated, most scholars do not usually discuss theoretical *absolute* standards for racial fairness, at least six answers are implied in the literature. We discuss each in turn.

2.1.1 USE NEUTRAL REDISTRICTING CRITERIA

Some scholars believe that districts should not be drawn on the basis of race at all.[15] Race should be irrelevant and, the argument goes, should not be used in deciding where to draw district lines. One version of this argument would require districts only to have equal numbers of voters, with other factors entirely under the control of the redistricters. Another version would require district lines to be drawn without reference to the racial characteristics of voters, perhaps even making it illegal to include this information in the same computer used to draw districts. Similar arguments have also been made about political gerrymandering.

Although requiring ignorance is an attractive position to many justices, it is not realistic: good politicians, with or without computers and electronic data, know where their voters are. Moreover, ignorance of race is probably not desirable either, because unintended consequences of redistricting can be as large as the intended consequences. Ignoring race and focusing only on compactness will almost guarantee that no blacks will be elected in many areas. Only very rare areas will elect many African Americans.

Using neutral redistricting criteria is a process-oriented approach to what unfortunately remains a results-oriented problem. In most areas of democratic theory, it is desirable to define a process and let the results fall where they may. However, this is appropriate only when one defines the process sufficiently carefully so that any result which follows the rules is normatively acceptable. Such has not been the case in redistricting, since within the rules one can produce partisan gerrymanders or virtually guarantee that members of a racial minority will never be elected to the legislature.

Indeed, this is one of the few areas of American democracy where the rules of the game remain open to regular manipulation as a "legitimate" part of the political process. As one of the features of a representative democracy that one might think should have been resolved at the founding of the republic, redistricting produces regular abuses of the system and enormous political conflicts. Indeed, redistricting battles are one of the most intense forms of regular political conflict in the country. From George Washington's first presidential veto, to some of the worst abuses of due process even today, to many of the most colorful political stories of blatant partisanship and even fraud among the judiciary, the rules of the game do not guarantee that the results of racially motivated redistricting will be held within acceptable ranges.[16]

Not only is the definition of *acceptable outcomes* of a redistricting process not yet formulated, but exactly what process-oriented rules would produce which range of acceptable outcomes remains largely an open question. Indeed, this is one of the most important topics for future scholarly research. Ignoring racial representation and requiring adherence only to certain "neutral" redistricting criteria is an appropriate ultimate goal, and one that we entirely support, but scholarship is not nearly to the point of identifying these rules. "Neutral" redistricting criteria, as presently conceived, are not always neutral in their effects.

2.1.2 MAXIMIZE MINORITY REPRESENTATION

According to this approach, any change in an electoral system, such as in redistricting, should be accompanied by attempts to maximize the influence of the minority community on the elective process. In redistricting, this means drawing as many districts that are likely to elect blacks as possible. This approach might be reasonable if one takes the position that fair racial representation requires some, perhaps as yet undefined, level of minority representation higher than now exists. Those who drew the lines in the 1992 redistricting process acted as if the U.S. Justice Department took this position in their Voting Rights Act preclearance decisions, but Justice Department personnel almost unanimously deny that maximization is their standard in theory or practice.

Maximization is a position for an advocate to adopt, but without justification or the explicit constraints we describe in section 2.1.4, it is insufficient for present purposes. At best it provides a direction to move, a relative standard, but beyond that it does not help characterize an *absolute* standard of fairness.

2.1.3 NO RETROGRESSION

"No retrogression" is the language used by the Supreme Court in *Beer v. United States* (1976), a case on preclearance under section 5 of the Voting Rights Act. In this case, the justices ruled that a change in an electoral system need not produce an increase in minority representation, but it must not represent a decline from the status quo. The rule allows the possibility of a considerably slower path to maximization, since redistricting will not always be accompanied by a change in the electoral system. However, the degree of minority representation must be either the same or higher. And once this higher level of minority representation is in place, it automatically becomes the new minimum. Thus, in the long run, the ultimate fairness standard underlying a no-retrogression rule is essentially the same as maximization. It thus also suffers from the same weaknesses for present purposes: no-retrogression might be a useful policy and relative standard, but it does not help us define an absolute standard of fairness in racial representation.

2.1.4 MAXIMIZE SUBJECT TO CERTAIN CONSTRAINTS

A slight modification of the maximize and no-retrogression rules is to require that redistricting plans be subject to the constraints of compactness, maintaining communities of interest (other than minorities), breaking a minimum number of county lines or other local political subdivisions, and others. This rule helps narrow in on a standard of fairness that is absolute, rather than relative, but it does not provide a definition except by saying what fairness is not. Just as with ignoring race and drawing districts according to neutral redistricting criteria, scholarship has not yet progressed to the point where we know the precise effects of each of the alternative constraints on redistricting plans. In a state with considerable discrimination, this criterion, although not absolute and therefore not useful for our theoretical purposes, define a reasonable operating rule from a practical perspective.

2.1.5 PROPORTIONAL REPRESENTATION

To some, proportional representation is not only a logical possibility; it *defines* fair representation. The idea is that the legislature should reflect the public: the proportion of blacks in the legislature should be the same as the proportion of blacks in the general public (or perhaps the proportion of blacks in the voting age population, or some other number). Proportionality is a standard for fairness that is defined independently of the current level of representation and has great intuitive appeal.

However, we have some skepticism about the universal appropriateness of proportional representation, based on its known limitations as a criterion for partisan fairness. What is wrong with proportional representation as a standard of fairness for Democrats and Republicans? For one thing, no solely *district-based* electoral system in the world has ever consistently produced proportional representation of parties. Meeting a proportionality standard would be easy if we were willing to give up district-based electoral systems and move to some form of national- (or state-) level party list or single transferable vote system. This would be possible, but it does not take into account the advantages of having districts in the first place—notably, geographic representation of local communities. Indeed, all electoral systems represent compromises between some type of national representation (proportional or other) and the representation of local areas and groups. American-style district-based electoral systems place large weight on local representation. An appropriate standard of fairness should take into account the inherent advantages and characteristics of the system of representation now in place.

Another way to see why proportionality is widely regarded as unacceptable as a standard of representation in district-based electoral systems is by comparing it to the standard of partisan fairness that is widely accepted in the academic community—partisan symmetry.[17] This and most other standards of fairness apply after votes are cast to the translation of votes statewide into an allocation of seats in the legislature. The standard of partisan symmetry requires that all political parties receive the same proportion of seats for a given vote proportion. For example, if the Democrats receive 55 percent of the votes statewide and are able to translate this into 75 percent of the seats in the state legislature, this is fair only if the Republicans, in some other election under the same districting scheme, receive 55 percent of the statewide votes and are also able to translate them into 75 percent of the seats. Proportional representation is a special case of partisan symmetry, but not the only case. Thus, partisan symmetry is a way of treating the parties equally on a statewide basis and still recognizing the unique advantages of American-style district-based elections.

Although proportionality seemed reasonable at first, more careful reflection has convinced most of the scholarly community that it is not a reasonable standard of *partisan* fairness to be used in redistricting, at least in district-based electoral systems. It seems to us the scholarly community is in a very similar situation with respect to racial redistricting: Can proportionality be justified for reasons other than the direct feature of "reflection"? Do deeper principles of fairness lead to proportional representation or to some other standard for racial group representation? We suggest one possibility in section 2.2, which indicates that proportionality may have more of a role to play in racial fairness than in partisan fairness, and demonstrate in section 2.3 conditions under which it would be especially appropriate for racial redistricting. In either case, it should be clear that proportionality will never be sufficient as a first principle in deriving a standard of racial fairness.[18]

2.1.6 RACIAL SYMMETRY

A final standard occasionally suggested is modifying the partisan symmetry standard as directly as possible: a racially fair electoral system would be one that treats the racial groups equally. That is, if blacks comprise 20 percent of the population but only 15 percent of the legislature, this system is fair only if whites, if they were to comprise 20 percent of the population, would also receive 15 percent of the legislative seats.[19]

This standard is internally consistent and reasonably compatible with the idea of partisan symmetry. However, its disadvantages are as obvious. At least during any single ten-year redistricting period, the black population will almost never grow from 20 percent to 80 percent of the population. This might be a reasonable counterfactual assumption over extremely long periods of time, but the question is what is fair in the present redistricting period; a standard that is fair only on average over many centuries will not be fair during the lifetimes of people now in the electorate and is probably not generally appropriate.[20] Another problem with a racial, as opposed to a partisan, symmetry standard is that the necessary condition for black election is black nomination, and blacks do not get nominated in most districts. This is not usually a problem in evaluating partisan symmetry, since both parties are usually on the ballot.[21]

2.2 Color-blind Voters and Candidates, Nondistinctive Ideology

In this section, we develop one perspective on a standard of fairness in redistricting based on deeper concepts of political fairness. *Under this standard, blacks would be allocated the proportion of seats in the legislature they would get if voters and candidates were color-blind, and if ideology and party were independent of race.* The color blindness assumptions are obviously unrealistic, but that is intentional: the idea is to draw districts that would have been drawn naturally if the world were different in these ways. We develop a mathematical model that formalizes our theoretical notions of fairness so that it can be compared with—not automatically match—current empirical circumstances. The assumption that ideology and partisanship are uncorrelated with race will be generalized in section 2.3. The normative idea underlying this model is to impose (presumably through drawing majority-minority districts, but possibly through other procedures) a level of representation that would exist if the conditions that cause us to make blacks a protected minority did not exist.

2.2.1 A MATHEMATICAL MODEL FOR COMPLETE COLOR-BLINDNESS

Our first theoretical model makes three specific assumptions:

1. *Color-blind Voters.* Label as "black" a group of randomly selected voters composed of $\alpha < 0.5$ proportion of all voters.
2. *Color-blind Nominations.* Nominees for each party are chosen without regard to race. That is, for each party and each seat in the legislature the probability of nominating a black candidate is α.

3. *Color-blind Election.* The probability that the Democrat wins is π_j and that the Republican wins is $1 - \pi_j$, and these probabilities are independent of the race of the candidate. This assumption implies that ideology, party, and other electorally relevant characteristics of candidates and voters do not differ by race.

Our goal is to calculate the probability of a black candidate being elected under these ideal circumstances, since this will give the fraction of blacks that should comprise the legislature if this standard is to be followed. The unconditional probability that a black candidate is elected is the sum of the probabilities that a black Democrat is elected or a black Republican is elected:

$$
\begin{aligned}
\text{P (winner is black)} &= \text{P (winner is a black Democrat)} \qquad (1) \\
&+ \text{P (winner is a black Republican)} \\
&= \text{P (Democrat is black) P (Democrat} \\
&\quad \text{wins} \mid \text{Democrat is black)} \\
&+ \text{P (Republican is black) P (Republican} \\
&\quad \text{wins} \mid \text{Republican is black)} \\
&= \alpha\pi_j + \alpha(1 - \pi_j) \\
&= \alpha.
\end{aligned}
$$

The simplicity of the result derives from assumption 3, color-blind elections, which requires that

$$
\text{P (Democrat wins} \mid \text{Democrat is black)} = \text{P (Democrat wins)}, \qquad (2)
$$

and similarly for Republicans.

2.2.2 INTERPRETATION

Under this model, the probability of electing a member of a minority group to the legislature is equal to α, their proportion in the population. Thus, we have derived a different and perhaps more fundamental justification for proportional representation in racial redistricting: minorities would be represented proportionally if voters, nominations, and elections were all color-blind. Certainly, no one would desire a political system in which voters could not discriminate on the basis of party or ideology, so it is also easy to see why this justification for proportional representation would not apply to partisan fairness.

The standard for racial fairness this model formalizes includes color-blind voters and nominations. Since the odds of election are independent of the racial characteristics of the candidates, we are also in the hypothetical situation where funding of minority campaigns is about the same as for other candidates (a situation that could be made realistic with a strong campaign-financing law). These are reasonable characterizations of an ideal standard for racial fairness. Allocating legislative seats on the basis of these aspects of this model seems like a reasonable standard to impose.

However, the assumption of color-blind elections, where minority groups do not have distinctive political positions, is quite extreme.[22] The assumption could perhaps be justified if one were willing to assume that all social, cultural, economic, and therefore political differences between minorities and everyone else resulted only from racism.

Certainly, some of the political positions of minority groups are generated by the racist status of the society in which they live, but it would be difficult to argue that the *only* reason their political positions differ is due to racism. Indeed, nonminorities hold many different ideological positions, and so there generally is reason to think that minorities would have social, cultural, or economic reasons not based on race for divergent political opinions. Although we might want our ideal political system, and therefore our standard of racial fairness, to fix some aspects of the current problem, it need not correct for everything in the world that makes minority groups different from majorities. If it did, then we would be in the situation where fairness would lead to proportional representation, but minority representation would not be an issue because minorities would not be politically distinctive. Some will argue that a society in which racial minorities are politically indistinct from others is the appropriate ultimate goal; if so, then proportional representation is the appropriate standard.

2.3 Color-blind Voters and Candidates, Actual Ideology

In this section, we characterize a second standard for racial fairness, now allowing minorities to have distinctive voting preferences. That is, we construct a hypothetical world in which voters and nominations are color-blind as a standard, but elections depend in part on the degree to which candidates are ideologically moderate.

We begin by portraying the distinctive ideological preferences of blacks and nonblacks. Table 4.1 reports the self-identified ideology of black and nonblack citizens. The original scale is the traditional Likert scale, which ranges from 1 for very liberal to 7 for very conservative. For the nation as a whole, for data pooled for 1988 and 1990, nonblacks respond to the question with an average score of 4.3, and blacks are somewhat more liberal at 3.9. In California, the nation's largest state (a state we chose so that we would have a reasonably large N), the range is about the same. In both cases, there is considerable variability within racial groups, but there still

TABLE 4.1
Conservatism of Racial Groups in the Population

	Nonblack Citizens	Black Citizens
United States	4.3	3.9
	(1.3)	(1.5)
N	2,362	301
California	4.4	3.7
	(1.3)	(1.3)
N	299	25

Note: Self reported mean conservatism is reported for blacks and nonblacks (with standard deviations, not standard errors, in parentheses). This is the average of all respondents in a group in the 1988 and 1990 pooled National Election Study public opinion polls. Responses to this survey question are from 1 (very liberal) to 7 (very conservative). Blacks view themselves as more liberal than nonblacks do.

TABLE 4.2
Conservatism of Racial Groups in Congress

Interest Group	Nonblack Legislators		Black Legislators	
	(Average)	(Stand. Dev.)	(Average)	(Stand. Dev.)
ADA*	52.0	(32.4)	7.2	(8.2)
ACLU*	57.0	(31.5)	7.8	(8.4)
COPE*	44.8	(33.3)	3.6	(3.0)
ACU	43.3	(32.3)	5.1	(3.8)
NTLC	61.4	(29.1)	17.1	(16.0)
NSI	57.3	(58.5)	3.4	(6.8)

Note: Interest groups scores of legislators were coded by the authors of the *Almanac of American Politics*, 1991, and abbreviated as: ADA = Americans for Democratic Action; ACLU = American Civil Liberties Union; COPE = Committee on Political Education (of the AFL-CIO); ACU = American Conservative Union; NTLC = National Tax Limitation Committee; and NSI = National Security Index (of the American Security Council). In order to arrange the table so all scores are from 0 (most liberal) to 100 (most conservative), the liberal groups (those marked with an asterisk) were subtracted from 100.

remains a distinctive difference: blacks in the nation and in California are more liberal the others.

Another way to examine the relative ideological groupings of different racial groups is by studying legislators, and examining the scores assigned to them by various interest groups. We do this for the U.S. House of Representatives and for the lower house of the Massachusetts and California legislatures, the only two state legislatures for which we could obtain voting scores. Table 4.2 compares the average interest-group rating, along with the standard deviations, of black and nonblack legislators in the U.S.

TABLE 4.3
Conservatism of Racial Groups in Massachusetts

Interest Group	Nonblack Legislators		Black Legislators				
	Average	(Stand. Dev.)	(Individual Scores)				
CLT	58.9	(30.6)	10	15	15	21	26
CLUM*	59.2	(35.8)	0	0	0	17	17
CPPAX*	57.9	(34.2)	0	9	9	18	27
NOW*	62.4	(38.9)	0	0	0	0	40

Note: Interest groups scores of legislators were coded in the *Massachusetts Political Almanac* and abbreviated as: CLT = Citizens for Limited Taxation; CLUM = Civil Liberties Union of Massachusetts; CPPAX = Citizens for Participation in Political America; NOW = National Organization for Women. In order to arrange the table so all scores are from 0 (most liberal) to 100 (most conservative), the liberal groups (those marked with an asterisk) were subtracted from 100. The small number of black legislators enabled us to present the more detailed information here and in table 4.4, as compared to just means and standard deviations in table 4.2 for Congress.

TABLE 4.4
Conservatism of Racial Groups in California

Interest Group	Nonblack Legislators		Black Legislators			
	Average	(Stand. Dev.)	(Individual Scores)			
NRA	46.3	(43.8)	0	0	0	97
AFL*	41.2	(41.0)	0	5	6	7
PIRG*	33.9	(33.0)	0	9	9	14
NOW*	32.9	(31.4)	0	0	0	0

Note: Interest groups scores of legislators were coded in the *California Political Almanac* and abbreviated as: NRA = National Rifle Association; AFL = California AFL-CIO; PIRG = California Public Interest Research Group; NOW = National Organization for Women. In order to arrange the table so all scores are from 0 (most liberal) to 100 (most conservative), the liberal groups (those marked with an asterisk) wre subtracted from 100.

House. For each interest group, this rating is an agreement score constructed so that the most liberal score is 0 and the most conservative is 100. As can be seen, the difference between black and nonblack legislators is quite substantial: for every interest group, blacks are very much closer to the liberal end of the ideological continuum.

Finally, the results from the lower house of the Massachusetts and California legislatures appear in tables 4.3 and 4.4. Because of the smaller numbers of blacks, along with the averages and standard deviations for nonblacks we list the score for each black legislator. Again, the scores range from 0 (most liberal) to 100 (most conservative), and again the black legislators are near the liberal end of the continuum.

It should not be surprising that blacks look more extreme in these three legislatures than in the general public, since the measures used depend on the judgment of these interest groups. Interest groups are often focused on a single issue or just a few issues, and it is well known that they tend to view the world in more either/or terms. Thus, it would be difficult to use these data to see whether black legislators are more or less liberal than black citizens. However, the results unambiguously demonstrate that black citizens and legislators are more liberal than are their nonblack counterparts.

2.3.1 A MATHEMATICAL MODEL FOR COLOR-BLIND ELECTIONS WITH IDEOLOGICALLY DISTINCT RACIAL GROUPS

We now generalize the model in section 2.2 to develop a standard in which a minority group may be ideologically distinct from the majority. In our simplified model, each district is represented by a legislator whose ideology is that of the median voter in the district. To begin, let y_i be a continuous variable representing the ideology of voter i, where $y_i = 0$ is moderate, $y_i < 0$ is liberal, and $y_i > 0$ is conservative. We define ideology so that the distribution of the ideologies of all the voters within any district is a normal distribution. This is a useful simplification, but our results are not heavily dependent on this particular distributional choice. The distribution of *the ideology of a voter chosen at random* from district J is normal with mean θ_J and common variance $(1 - \gamma^2)$, with $0 < \gamma^2 < 1$; that is,

$$f(y_i, i \in J) = N(y_i \mid \theta_J, 1 - \gamma^2). \tag{3}$$

The subscript J appears in the notation for the mean but not the variance, indicating that average ideology may differ across districts, but the variance of voter ideology is the same in every district. The parameter γ indexes the degree of ideological homogeneity of voters within each district; larger values of γ model electoral systems with more ideologically homogeneous districts. We further assume that the legislator elected in district J has an ideology equal to θ, the mean ideology among voters in that district.[23] We discuss complications of this basic model later in this section.

In addition, we assume the mean ideologies θ_J of the districts follow a normal distribution with mean 0 and variance γ^2

$$f(\theta_J) = N(\theta_J \mid 0, \gamma^2) \tag{4}$$

As a result of our median voter assumption, the distribution of *the ideology of legislators across districts* is normal with mean 0 and variance γ^2 as well. From equations 3 and 4, we can derive the ideology of a voter chosen at random from the entire state. This distribution will have a mean of 0 and variance of 1 (the scale being arbitrary) and be a mixture of distributions. In states with a large number of districts, the distribution is approximately standard normal.

We can now model representation by comparing the distribution of legislator ideology in equation 4 to the distribution of voter ideology. When districts are perfectly homogeneous and $\gamma = 1$, nothing is changed in the aggregation process: the distribution of legislator ideology is identical to the statewide distribution of voter ideology; this is equivalent to proportional representation of ideological groupings. Smaller values of γ refer to progressively more ideologically heterogeneous districts; with each district becoming more of a microcosm of the entire state, centrist candidates are favored, and centrist ideological groups of voters are disproportionately represented in the legislature. Since γ cannot exceed 1.0, this model requires that centrist ideological groupings receive relatively more representatives than more extreme groups, as seems to be the case in the U.S. Congress and many other legislatures.

Another way to compare the ideological distributions of voters and legislators is to take the ratio of the latter to the former, which we call the *representation function, R(·)*:

$$R(y) = \frac{P \text{ (representative has ideology } y)}{P \text{ (voter has ideology } y)} \qquad (5)$$

$$= \frac{N(y \mid 0, \gamma^2)}{N(y \mid 0, 1)}$$

$$= \frac{1}{\gamma} \exp\left(-\frac{1}{2}\left[\frac{1}{\gamma^2} - 1\right] y^2\right)$$

For any given voter, $R(y)$ tells us how well the voter's ideology, y, is represented in the legislature, with $R(y) = 1$ being proportional representation. If $R(y) > 1$, then the ideology y has a larger proportion of legislators than its proportion in the population. For example, a value of $R(y) = 2.0$ for a group indicates that this group receives twice as large a proportion of legislators than their proportion in the population. Similarly, values of $R(y)$ less than 1.0 indicate a level of representation below proportionality; if $R(y) = 0.5$ for a group, then this group has half the proportion in the legislature as it has in the population.

One can calculate the average value of $R(y)$ for a group of voters by using the usual rules for calculating expected values. Thus, the average value of the representation function for all voters is 1.0:

$$E[R(y)] = \int_{-\infty}^{\infty} R(y) f(y)\, dy = 1.0. \qquad (6)$$

Other groups are defined relative to this group of everyone. For a group of voters, such as members of minority group B, characterized by a probability distribution over ideology of $f_B(y)$, we can also compute an average. We calculate the average value of the representation function among voters in group B as follows:

$$E [R (y_i) \mid \text{for all } i \in B] = \int_{-\infty}^{\infty} R (y) f_B (y) \, dy = 1.0. \qquad (7)$$

Understanding this average representation for various groups B provides insight into our model and therefore into this standard of racial fairness.

2.3.2 INTERPRETATION

In order to incorporate more of what we wanted in an idealized political system, the model here is more stylized than that in section 2.2 and requires specific distributional assumptions, for example. Important and reliable policy implications do emerge from this model. And, although we are confident of the direction of the effects and general character of these solutions we are about to describe, one would not want to set policy in any precise way on the basis of the specific numerical values calculated.

We portray the results from this model with two examples. In both examples, we study the average value of the representation function for a minority group, characterized in different ways.

Representation of Ideologically Extreme Minority Groups

In the first example, we study a minority group that is composed of the ideologically most extreme members of a political system. This roughly approximates the situation with blacks, who are considerably more liberal on average than others. This example models the worst situation from the perspective of members of minority group B in terms of the level of representation.

We can portray this situation by letting the ideology of black voters follow a normal distribution truncated from above at value $b < 0$:

$$f_B(y) = \begin{cases} \dfrac{1}{\Phi(b)} \, N (y \mid 0, 1) & \text{for } y < b \\ 0 & \text{otherwise} \end{cases} \qquad (8)$$

where $\Phi(\cdot)$ is the cumulative normal distribution function. We can then calculate the average representation function for this ideologically extreme group of minorities with the rule in equation 7:

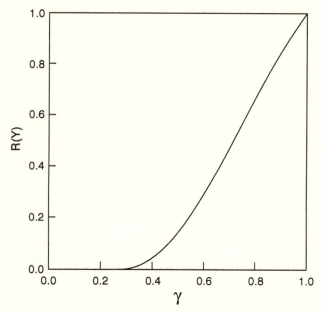

Figure 4.2. Average Representation of Ideologically Extreme Minorities

$$E[R(y_i) \mid \text{for all } i \in B] = \int_{-\infty}^{\infty} R(y) f_B(y) dy \qquad (9)$$

$$= \frac{\Phi(b/\gamma)}{\Phi(b)}$$

To interpret this result, consider the situation where $b = -1.0$, so that blacks comprise about $\Phi(-1) = 16$ percent of the electorate. (We use $b = -1$ for simplicity and because it corresponds roughly to the proportion of blacks nationwide and in some states. The interpretation is similar for other values of b.)

The relationship between the ideological homogeneity of districts as indexed by γ and the representation function $R(y)$ is portrayed in figure 4.2. At the extreme, when $\gamma = 1$ and districts group voters in an ideologically homogeneous way, blacks would receive a proportional share of legislative seats. This special case of the present model leads clearly to the result of the model in section 2.2.

However, in the situation where $\gamma < 1$ and districts are less than perfectly homogeneous, blacks will receive less than a proportional share of legislators. This is the first qualification to the result in section 2.2: *If an electoral system contains color-blind voters and party nominations, but race is not independent of ideology, an ideologically extreme minority group will receive fewer seats than the proportional representation standard would in-*

dicate. Note again that the degree of independence between race and ideology is a feature to be chosen as our theoretical standard, not as a judgment about the empirical world.

This result is unambiguous, and it would hold even if the normal distributions and other assumptions were generalized. The model suggests that ideologically extreme minority groups, such as blacks, should receive fewer seats than proportionality would indicate, but it does not indicate precisely how much fewer.

Representation of an Ideologically Diverse Minority Group

In this final example, we parametrize both the degree of ideological extremism and the diversity of a minority group. We do this by letting the ideology of black voters follow a normal distribution with mean $\mu < 0$ and variance $\sigma^2 < 1$. The average value of the representation function for this group is calculated again according to the rule in equation 7:

$$E[R(y_i) \mid \text{for all } i \in B] = \int_{-\infty}^{\infty} R(y) f_B(y)\, dy \qquad (10)$$
$$= \int_{-\infty}^{\infty} R(y)\, N(y \mid \mu, \sigma^2)\, dy$$
$$= \frac{1}{(\gamma^2 + \sigma^2 - \gamma^2\sigma^2)^{1/2}}\, e^{-\frac{\mu^2}{2}\frac{1-\gamma^2}{\gamma^2+\sigma^2-\gamma^2\sigma^2}}$$

Three substantive results can be ascertained from equation 10. First, as before, if $\gamma = 1$ and all districts are homogeneous, leading to the distribution of voter and legislator ideology to be identical, then the representation function equals 1.0 and minority groups are proportionally represented. This is true regardless of the values of the other parameters.

To illustrate the remaining two substantive results, we set $\gamma = 0.7$, which moderately favors centrist candidates. Figure 4.3 plots $R(y)$ for corresponding values of the average ideology μ and internal ideological diversity σ of blacks. The figure clearly shows that as μ increases toward zero (the median position of voters across the state), black representation under this system increases. The model here is most relevant on the left side of the graph, where the minority group is more ideologically extreme, and this shows minorities receiving less than proportional representation $(R(y) < 1)$. If a minority group is able to remain ideologically homogeneous and, at the same time, be fairly centrist, then under this ideal political system, it would actually be represented more than proportionally. This latter result is of interest, and does reflect what happens to cohesive groups of centrist voters, but it is not relevant to minority groups of the sort that are protected under the law, since they tend to be more ideologically extreme. Indeed, if they are not politically distinctive from the majority group, then, except for purposes of descriptive representation, one could argue that they receive adequate representation.

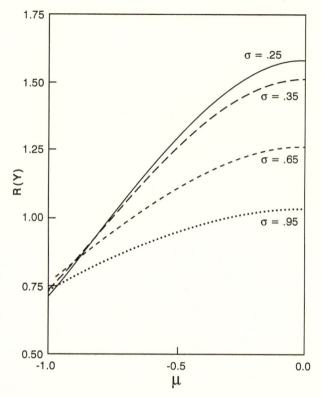

Figure 4.3. Average Representation of an Ideologically
Diverse Minority

In addition, for most fixed levels of average minority ideology, black
voters under this model increase their representation as they become internally less diverse ideologically. Thus, black voting power, and the resultant
level of representation, increases when blacks are more centrist on average
and more ideologically homogeneous as a group.

In this model, we have developed a standard under which voters and
party nominations are color-blind, but we have allowed blacks to differ
ideologically from other voters. The results clearly demonstrate that
proportional representation would be fair only under relatively limited circumstances. Under a more general standard, with no race-based voting or
nominations, ideological distinctiveness generally guarantees that racial
minorities will receive less than proportional representation. Of course,
even ideologically extreme minorities could receive proportional representation in the legislature if they happen to live in segregated areas and the
line-drawers choose to create homogeneous districts.

2.3.3 RELAXING MODEL ASSUMPTIONS

We briefly discuss two portions of this model that might be profitably generalized in future research. First, we assume that the variance of voters within each district is constant across the state (γ is constant). This could be generalized by allowing γ to vary systematically or via a probability distribution. It is unlikely to have substantial effects on our conclusions.

Second, we assume that legislators are elected from the center of the ideological spectrum of their districts. That is, a district with mean ideology θ_j will elect a legislator with the same ideology. This assumption is reasonable in one-party dominated districts (conditional on the electoral system); it should be generalized to produce a two-party model. The likely consequence is that our representation function would be somewhat higher, although not universally, for extreme ideological groupings.

3. Empirical Standards: Cross-Group Comparisons

A final way to define racial fairness in redistricting is by comparison with other groups in society that are fairly treated. We do not offer this standard as a general policy recommendation since it is not always practical to find reasonable comparison groups or to measure their representation. But it will be practical in some states and for some minority groups, particularly if a detailed sample survey can be conducted.

This definition of fairness is both absolute and relative. It is an absolute standard in that all similarly sized minority groups would get the same seat proportion for a given vote proportion. One could even restrict the comparison groups to those of similar size and ideological and partisan preferences. But it is also a relative standard since it is defined only in relation to other groups. This standard might be considered better than the purely relative standards discussed in section 2.1, from some perspectives, since a priori normative decisions are somewhat less a part of the judgment. After the comparison group is chosen, normative decisions are not necessary. Of course, in practice, one must choose a group with which to compare, and this can involve extremely important normative judgments.

This standard is more flexible than proportional representation, since situations in which all minority groups receive less than (or more than) proportionality could be defined as fair. It is also similar to the widely accepted partisan symmetry standard; both standards substitute cross-sectional factual comparisons with time-series counterfactual ones. The advantage of this comparative standard for racial fairness is that it does not require assessing the counterfactual situation where a minority group will quickly attain numerical majority status.

TABLE 4.5
Selected Comparison Groups in the United States, 1989

	Proportion of Population	Proportion of U.S. House Seats
Religion		
Catholic	0.28	0.27
Jewish	0.02	0.07
Methodist	0.04	0.14
Race		
Black	0.12	0.09
Gender		
Female	0.51	0.06

Source: Compiled from U.S. Statistical Abstracts.

Table 4.5 provides examples of selected comparison groups in the U.S. Congress as a whole. Here we can see that blacks (and women) are represented far less than proportionally, whereas religious groups are much closer to, or even represented more than, the proportional representation standard. We emphasize that any practical use of this standard would involve a more detailed study in the particular state in which it is applied, and particular care must go into choosing the comparison group. One would ideally find many groups of similar size to the one being evaluated. The groups in table 4.5 were chosen on the basis of available data, and, unfortunately, not much data are readily available. As a result, the comparison list is admittedly narrow. Although choosing the appropriate comparison groups is not difficult, finding data on both legislators and population groups turns out to be impossible in many cases. In practice, at least some of these comparison groups should have similar ideological and partisan preferences, or at least be similarly extreme. For example, if adequate survey data were available, one could compare blacks to the same proportion of the electorate from the most conservative end of the ideological spectrum.

To give slightly more specific flavor for the types of comparisons that could be conducted in individual states, we also provide racial and religious groupings among the population and the lower houses of the state legislatures of selected states (see table 4.6). Again, one would need detailed, careful work—such as complete analyses of state public-opinion polls—to apply this method within a particular state. But this table provides some interesting comparisons, some states giving roughly the same level of legislative-to-population representation to religious and racial groups. Others give considerably less representation to blacks, possibly indicating, according to this standard, that blacks should receive more representation.

TABLE 4.6
Selected Comparison Groups in Selected States, 1989 (Percentages)

	Black	Catholic	Baptist	Jewish
		Religion		
Massachusetts				
Population	5.0	50.0	—	4.6
Legislature	3.0	62.2	—	1.9
West Virginia				
Population	25.0	6.0	—	—
Legislature	2.0	9.9	—	—
Georgia				
Population	27.0	4.0	20.6	—
Legislature	11.0	1.0	44.4	—
Mississippi				
Population	36.0	25.0	24.6	—
Legislature	16.0	5.7	42.3	—
Tennessee				
Population	16.0	—	22.1	—
Legislature	10.0	—	36.4	—
Missouri				
Population	11.0	16.0	12.2	—
Legislature	7.0	22.1	18.4	—
Michigan				
Population	14.0	25.0	—	—
Legislature	11.0	29.1	—	—

Source: Analyses by the authors of the U.S. Census and individual state blue books.

4. Concluding Remarks

After substantial gains for minorities as a result of the 1991–1992 redistricting process, thirty-eight African Americans were elected to the U.S. House of Representatives. Blacks thus comprise about 8.7 percent of this legislature, as compared with roughly 12 percent of the U.S. population. Under the theoretical standard we develop in section 2.3, determining what constitutes a "fair" number of black members of Congress depends on how ideologically extreme black citizens are compared to nonblack citizens. If we make the reasonable assumption that blacks are about a standard deviation more ideologically extreme than whites, then (under our stylized assumptions) black citizens are now fairly represented in the U.S. House of Representatives, since they have only one fewer member of Congress than our standard indicates.[24] Of course, different numbers can be obtained based on different assumptions about the parameter values. A very important area of future research would be to estimate the distribution of the ideology of voters in the population (the results in table 4.1 being suggestive but imprecise).

Alternatively, if one is interested in judging fairness on the basis of a different hypothetical world in which blacks suffer no discrimination and have no unique cultural experiences (as in section 2.2), and as a result have no distinctive ideological preferences, a proportional representation standard is preferable. In this situation, a fair number of black members of the House of Representatives would be about fifty-two—an increase of fourteen members over the present thirty-eight.

Of course, neither these standards nor the comparative standard offered in section 3 can provide any automatic answer to the fairness of the American electoral system in the treatment of minority citizens. Our models are intended to clarify an important aspect of standards of racial redistricting, but in practice one will also need to look closely at the process. Outcome-oriented measures such as ours are essential in assessing the general situation with respect to the fulfillment of minority rights, but only a complete analysis, which includes such features as the degrees of discrimination and enfranchisement, differential campaign spending, racial cues taken and given during election campaigns, and many other factors, will produce a satisfactory conclusion in a real legislature.

Our primary purpose in writing this paper is to propose a directed research agenda for studies of racial fairness in legislative redistricting. We first discussed the goal of deriving an absolute standard of racial fairness, as opposed to the many relative standards that have been offered. We also offered the outlines of three possible absolute standards of racial fairness.

The academic community has made impressive contributions to the debate about the role of minorities in American electoral politics. However, public law has gone well beyond our empirical analyses and philosophical deliberations—exactly the opposite situation to political gerrymandering. It is time we caught up. The study of absolute standards of racial fairness in redistricting should be a high priority in future scholarly research.

Notes

1. As of this writing, the Supreme Court has not overturned any redistricting plans on the grounds of partisan gerrymandering.

2. The Voting Rights Act of 1965 was the first effective legislation in this area, although the previously enacted civil rights bills had some limited effects. Voting discrimination on the basis of "race or color" was prohibited, and the Justice Department was given a variety of mechanisms with which to force reluctant southern states to end discriminatory practices. The five-year extension of the act in 1970 included lowering of the voting age to eighteen in all elections (part of which were

later rejected by the courts) and reduction of the residency requirement to a maximum of thirty days in every state. In 1975, the Voting Rights Act was extended for seven years, and it was expanded to cover language and racial minorities, some outside the South, and to permanently ban literacy tests. The act was extended most recently in 1982 for twenty-five years. The most significant change was to add tests based on results for the existing intent tests in Section 2 vote dilution cases. See Grofman, Handley, and Niemi 1992 for a review of the jurisprudence in this area.

3. As Bruce Cain (1992, 262–63) writes, "The debate over voting rights is a modern and peculiarly American variant of a long-standing issue in political science—the relative merits of more or less proportional representational systems. The matter is rarely stated that way, especially by proponents of expanded voting rights legislation, because proportionality is something of a dirty word in the Anglo-American tradition. Americans prefer to use terms such as *fairness* and *nondilution* of minority votes without explicitly defining them, which causes significant confusion because electoral fairness could in fact mean something other than proportionality."

4. Of course, any question itself narrows the range of possible normative answers. For example, an attractive and quite defensible standard would be entirely process oriented, although this article is largely concerned with outcome oriented measures.

5. Shockley, 1991.

6. Pitkin 1967.

7. The courts have been divided on this issue; see Shockley 1991 and Soni 1990.

8. Of the sixteen new black members of the U.S. House of Representatives in 1992, thirteen came from largely black districts created during this redistricting process. The remaining three replaced black members of Congress from existing black districts.

9. Figure 4.1 was drawn by us using data from *Black Elected Officials: A National Register 1990.*

10. Key 1949.

11. Guinier 1991a and 1991b; Shockley 1991; Soni 1990.

12. Karnig and Welch 1982; Welch and Hibbing 1984; MacManus 1987; Darcy and Hadley 1988; Grofman and Handley 1989.

13. Latimer 1979; Davidson and Korbel 1981; Karning and Welch 1982; Grofman, Migalski, and Noviello 1986; Bullock and MacManus 1987; MacManus 1987; Teasley 1987; MacManus and Bullock 1988; Welch 1990; Zax 1990.

14. Bledsoe 1986.

15. Thernstrom 1987.

16. Exactly the opposite is true with respect to political gerrymandering; see Gelman and King 1994b.

17. See Grofman 1983; Niemi and Fett 1986; King and Browning 1987; King and Gelman 1991; Gelman and King 1994a. One of the few dissenting voices in the near consensus supporting partisan symmetry is Lowenstein and Steinberg 1985.

18. The Voting Rights Act says explicitly that "Nothing in this [Act] establishes a right to have members of a protected class elected in numbers equal to their proportion in the population." Yet, as many note, the courts have often used a departure

from proportional representation in the legislatures as evidence of minority voting dilution or disenfranchisement. See Cain 1992; Guinier 1992; Turner 1992; and Grofman and Davidson 1992. While the role of proportional representation in litigation cannot be ignored, we believe proportional representation will not be acceptable as a first principle in choosing an absolute theoretical standard of racial fairness.

19. See O'Loughlin 1979.

20. Similarly, the partisan symmetry standard may not apply to states uniformly dominated by one party. See Gelman and King 1994b.

21. Actually, uncontestedness is a severe problem in some southern states. For example, between just under one-half to just over two-thirds of seats in the Virginia House of Delegates have been uncontested in recent elections. It is also a growing problem across the states in the United States. See Gelman and King 1994b.

22. Recall that the usual "realism" criterion does not apply here, since we are intentionally trying to model an ideal standard for fairness that does not presently exist. If it did exist, we could do empirical estimations instead of theoretical analyses.

23. For the normal distribution, the mean voter is also the median voter. We are assuming that all party cues are subsumed within ideology.

24. That is, when $\mu = -1$ (standard deviations), the representation function is $R(y) = 0.75$ (see figure 4.3) which, when multiplied by 12 percent of the population (from table 4.5, which assumes that $\gamma = 0.7$), gives 9 percent of the legislature. This is just over 39 of the 435 members of the House of Representatives, which is one more than the current 38 black representatives.

5

Race, Representation, and Redistricting

DAVID IAN LUBLIN

SINCE THE REDISTRICTING round following the 1990 reapportionment, the policy of advancing African American and Latino representation through the creation of new majority-minority districts has come under increasingly intense attack from both the right and the left. Advocates of racial redistricting claim that few African Americans or Latinos would win election to the House of Representatives without the creation of majority-minority districts. They further view the election of black and Latino representatives from majority-minority districts as essential to the advancement of authentic black and Latino viewpoints during congressional deliberations.[1]

In contrast, conservative opponents lambaste racial redistricting as going beyond the original intent of the Voting Rights Act and perpetuating racial distinctions in both law and society. They further argue that blacks and Latinos can win election to the House of Representatives and promote their policy interests without what those on the right view as a form of political affirmative action. Indeed, conservatives contend that drawing new majority-minority districts ghettoizes blacks and Latinos into a few congressional districts. Minorities gain control over a few representatives at the cost of losing influence over a much larger number of members of Congress.[2]

Liberal critics view racial redistricting as largely ineffective at assuring minorities real influence over the political process. While the number of black and Latino representatives has increased, the proportion of minority members of Congress remains much lower than the proportion of minorities in the general or voting age population. More importantly, liberals contend that minority representatives are often tokens without real political influence. Just as winner-take-all systems of election regularly deny minorities election from majority Anglo constituencies, winner-take-all procedures within the House prevent minorities from gaining any real influence over the public policy.[3]

In this paper, I examine the effect of racial redistricting on the election of African American and Latino representatives and on African American influence over public policy. In particular, I focus on the trade-off between the election of greater numbers of black representatives and the advancement of African American policy interests. My previous work on this topic has been devoted to exploring the relationship between the racial composition of congressional districts and the ideology of individual representatives and Congress as a whole.[4] In this short paper, I discuss mainly the results and implications of this analysis.

The Election of Black and Latino Representatives

Black Representatives

African Americans rarely win election from districts that do not contain either a black majority or a combined black and Latino majority. In the history of the Republic, only six African Americans have ever won election from districts with clear Anglo majorities. All thirty-six of the black Democrats elected to the House in 1994 represent majority-minority constituencies. However, black Republicans Gary Franks of Connecticut and J. C. Watts of Oklahoma won election from districts with only a small proportion of African Americans.[5]

Some scholars have argued that African Americans can win election from majority Anglo districts in greater numbers.[6] Carol Swain highlights the success of some African Americans at winning election from heavily Anglo constituencies as evidence that blacks can win election outside black dominated constituencies.[7] African Americans have had particularly notable success at winning election to the mayoralty of several majority Anglo cities around the nation. Norm Rice currently serves as mayor of Seattle; Wellington Webb beat another African American in the runoff to become the first black mayor of Denver. Swain views the election of Doug Wilder as governor of Virginia and Carol Moseley-Braun as senator from Illinois as signals that the political process is increasingly open to blacks. Even when blacks lose elections from majority Anglo constituencies, they often garner many white votes. In his failed senatorial bid, former Charlotte mayor Harvey Gantt did as well as previous white challengers to North Carolina senator Jesse Helms.

Ironically, even these successes point to the difficulty that blacks face when trying to win election to the House from majority Anglo districts. Norm Rice lost a bid to represent Seattle in the House shortly before winning the mayoralty. Doug Wilder eked out a very narrow victory as governor, trailing his running mates substantially in votes. Since Wilder's victory in 1989, no African American has won a gubernatorial election, and no African American currently serves as governor. While the election of people like Rice and Wilder provides hope for the future, their victories attract attention precisely because of their exceptional nature. Empirical evidence indicates that the racial composition of the electorate overwhelms all other factors in determining the race of a district's representative.[8] The protection of majority black and majority-minority districts remains vital to the election of more than token numbers of blacks to Congress.

Nevertheless, Swain rightly points out that creating additional black majority districts will be very difficult.[9] During the round of redistricting following the 1990 reapportionment, mapmakers drew new majority-minority districts virtually everywhere possible. African Americans now represent all but one of the existing black majority districts. Future increases in black representation will have to come from outside black majority districts.

Moreover, proponents of racial redistricting often overestimate the percentage of African Americans required to make a district likely to elect a black member of Congress. Under the Voting Rights Act, the question of how high the percentage of blacks needs to be to assure black community control has important legal ramifications. In *Kirksey v. Board of Supervisors of Hinds County*, the district court ruled that the minority percentage of the population must be sufficient to provide members of the minority group a "realistic opportunity to elect officials of their choice." Some have argued for the creation of 65 percent black districts, rather than merely black majority districts, to take into account the higher levels of voting age population, registration, and turnout among whites as compared to those levels among blacks. While civil rights advocates strong endorse the so-called 65 percent rule, research indicates that the 65 percent threshold is higher than necessary to assure the election of a black representative. Fifty-five percent black districts have nearly as high a probability of sending an African American to Congress as 65 percent black districts.[10]

Latino Representatives

In 1994, seventeen Latinos won election to Congress. All of the Latino members of Congress won election from majority-minority districts and all but two represent Latino majority districts. Mexican Americans have traditionally dominated the Congressional Hispanic Caucus. Before the 1992 elections, only one Puerto Rican and one Cuban American sat in Congress. Today, three Puerto Ricans and three Cuban Americans join eleven Mexican Americans in the House. Republicans have had greater success among Latinos than among African Americans. Both of the Cuban American representatives from the Miami area caucus with the Republicans, as does Mexican American Henry Bonilla of southern Texas.

Like their African American colleagues, Latino members of Congress depend heavily upon majority-minority districts for reelection. However, Latinos fare worse in mixed black and Latino districts than do African American candidates. While adding Latinos to a district generally height-

ens the electoral chances of a black candidate, placing greater numbers of
African Americans in a district does not usually aid the electoral chances of
Latino candidates. African Americans invariably win mixed black and
Latino majority-minority districts unless Latinos substantially outnumber
blacks.[11]

However, empirical evidence also reveals that Latinos may find it easier
to gain election to the House in the future. The only other variable consistently related to the election of Latino representatives besides the percentage of Latinos in the population is the percentage of citizens in the
population. The presence of many noncitizens in the Latino population
undermines Latino candidates at the polls. Many districts with Latino population majorities lack Latino voter majorities. As greater numbers of Latinos gain citizenship, the percentage of Latinos required for a congressional
district to become likely to elect a Latino representative should drop. For
any given percentage of Latinos in the population, Latino candidates will
find it easier to win election than will African Americans running in districts with the same percentage of African Americans in the population.[12]

Latino candidates may find greater support among a largely Anglo electorate than do African American candidates. While Doug Wilder was the
first African American governor since Reconstruction, Latinos have won
gubernatorial races in both Florida and New Mexico. Despite these favorable future prospects, Latinos currently still require the protection of Latino
majority districts to assure the election of substantial numbers of Latinos to
the House. Low turnout and Anglo opposition combine to make election to
the House a difficult climb for most Latino candidates.

The Advancement of African American Policy Interests

The Conflict between Party and Race

Maximizing the number of black majority congressional districts clearly
makes the election of greater numbers of African Americans more likely.
However, this same redistricting strategy can actually undermine congressional support for the liberal policies favored by the black community.
The inherent conflict between maximizing the number of black majority
districts and the number of Democratic districts lies at the heart of the
problem.

Setting the impact of party aside for a moment, an increase in the percentage of blacks in a district always makes a representative more likely to
support legislation favored by African Americans. This liberalism of members of Congress rises linearly with the black percentage of the population,
except that there is a jump in liberalism once a district becomes around 40
percent black.[13] Raising the percentage of blacks in one district necessitates

lowering the percentage of blacks in another. Unless there is a net change in the number of districts above or below the 40 percent threshold, there will be no net change in the overall liberalism of a state's congressional delegation. The increase in the liberalism of the member from the district that has more blacks will be matched by a decline in the liberalism of the member or members from the districts that lost blacks, unless some of the districts cross the 40 percent threshold. An increase in the number of districts over 40 percent black would result in a rise in a delegation's overall liberalism, and thus would advance black policy interests.

The location of the threshold for an increase in liberalism at 40 percent black is noticeably lower than the 50 percent threshold required to make probable the election of a black representative. African Americans seemingly gain ideological control of a district before they can actually elect a member of their own group to the House. The voting behavior of the Anglo population accounts for this difference. The Anglo population is ideologically diverse enough for the black population in coalition with white liberals to elect a liberal member. Together, African Americans and white liberals can thwart the election of conservative members in 40 to 50 percent black districts. While Anglos do not generally lend enough support to black candidates for them to win in Anglo majority districts, enough Anglos are willing to support white liberal candidates to elect a liberal to the House.[14]

Once party is taken into account, the impact of creating additional black majority districts on a state delegation's overall support for black legislative goals becomes far cloudier. Black majority districts do not concentrate just blacks. Due to the exceedingly high level of support for the Democratic Party in the black community, black majority districts also concentrate Democratic voting strength. Inevitably, the concentration of Democrats within these districts raises the percentage of Republicans in the remaining districts. While black majority districts invariably become impregnable Democratic strongholds, Republican candidates in other districts may benefit from the depletion of black Democrats in their districts. If racial redistricting does result in the election of greater numbers of Republicans, support for black interests in the House could decline dramatically. Due to the ideological differences between the two parties, the election of one more Republican would more than negate the pro-black effect of drawing one new district greater than 40 percent black.[15]

The actual partisan impact of racial redistricting depends heavily upon the distribution of the population in the nonblack majority districts as well as upon the degree of concentration of African Americans within the new black majority district. Racial redistricting does not inherently benefit the Republicans. The vagaries of redistricting combined with partisan calculation often produces plans with districts that pack white Republicans within districts just as black majority districts concentrate blacks. As the following examination of the Alabama and North Carolina redistricting plans reveals, the actual constituency boundaries determine whether racial redistricting has any partisan effect.

The next two sections examine the impact of the very different types of redistricting plans enacted in Alabama and North Carolina on black descriptive and substantive representation. While minority groups win descriptive representation by electing members of their group to public office, they gain substantive representation by exerting influence over the policy process.[16] Descriptive representation can serve as a mechanism for advancing substantive representation. However, as the Alabama case shows, minority groups can gain descriptive representation at the same time as they lose substantive representation.

Case Study I: Alabama

Redistricting in Alabama worked exactly as the Republicans hoped. Since the Alabama lines are the product of a plan suggested by the Republicans and imposed by a federal court, this outcome is not altogether surprising. As figure 5.1 shows, the major changes occurred in the Sixth and Seventh Districts. The Seventh District shed most of its white suburban Republican territory around Birmingham to the Sixth District and picked up most of Birmingham's black Democratic precincts in exchange. The new Seventh District also took in new black precincts around the state capital of Montgomery that were formerly in the Second District. As a result, the Seventh District went from being 33 percent black before redistricting to 68 percent after redistricting. The black percentage of the population plummeted from 34 to 9 percent in the Sixth District and from 31 to 24 percent in the Second District. Incumbent Claude Harris, a white Democrat, decided to retire rather than seek reelection from either the new Sixth or Seventh districts. In 1992, Earl Hilliard won election from the Seventh District and became the first African American to represent Alabama in the House since the close of Reconstruction. White incumbent Democrat Ben Erdreich decided to fight for his seat. However, despite a strong effort, Erdreich was unable to overcome the strong Republican advantage in a Sixth District denuded of most of its African-American voters. Republican Terry Everett won a tight contest for the open Second District that he almost certainly would have lost if redistricting had not reduced the percentage of African Americans in his district.

The net result of these changes was to shift the partisan balance of the Alabama delegation and diminish black substantive representation. Thanks

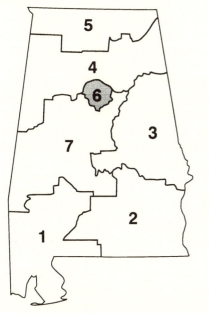 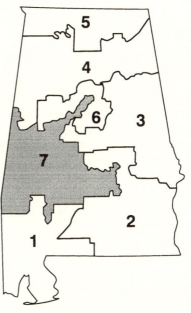

102nd Congress, elected 1990   103nd Congress, elected 1992

Name	% Black	Name	% Black
1 *Callahan (R)*	31%	1 *Callahan (R)*	28%
2 *Dickinson (R)*	31%	2 *Everett (R)*	24%
3 Browder (D)	28%	3 Browder (D)	26%
4 Bevill (D)	7%	4 Bevill (D)	7%
5 Cramer (D)	14%	5 Cramer (D)	15%
6 Erdreich (D)	34%	6 *Bachus (R)*	9%
7 Harris (D)	33%	7 **Hilliard (D)**	68%

Figure 5.1. Alabama Redistricting Plans

virtually entirely to favorable redistricting, Republicans won one new seat in 1992 and held on to one seat that they otherwise would have lost. Packing black voters into the Seventh District wasted Democratic voting strength and cost Democrats their hold on the Sixth District as well as an opportunity to win the open Second District. Instead of electing three moderate white Democrats, the Second, Sixth, and Seventh Districts now send one liberal black Democrat and two conservative white Republicans to Washington. Although a clear gain for black descriptive representation, this change on balance reduced black substantive representation. Prior to the 1992 elections, blacks had a good shot at gaining the vote of either of the two moderate Democrats representing the Sixth and Seventh Districts for pro-black legislation with any chance of passage. After redistricting, Alabama blacks can count on one sure vote on the floor of the House in the form of African American Earl Hilliard, but African Americans will find it exceedingly difficult to gain the vote of Sixth District Republican Spencer Bachus. Having few blacks in his district, Bachus has little reason to worry about black concerns. In effect, redistricting increased the size of the opposition to legislation supported by African Americans by one vote. The 1994 elections confirmed the new partisan balance of the Alabama congressional delegation. Despite the Republican tide, all incumbents won reelection in 1994.

Case Study II: North Carolina

After the 1990 Census, North Carolina found itself in the enviable position of having its congressional delegation increased from eleven to twelve. Although North Carolina had a Republican governor, Democrats entirely controlled the redistricting process because North Carolina governors lack the power to veto legislation. As figure 5.2 shows, prior to redistricting, North Carolina had no majority black districts and no blacks represented its people in the Congress. Intense competition marked North Carolina congressional elections throughout the 1980s. While the rest of the nation bemoaned the permanent Congress and the seemingly undefeatable incumbent, congressional seats regularly changed parties in many North Carolina districts.

North Carolina Democrats wanted to bolster their party's marginal incumbents during the reapportionment process. However, they faced the dilemma of protecting incumbent white Democrats while drafting new black majority districts to satisfy the Voting Rights Act. Partisan Democrats skillfully crafted a redistricting plan that met these twin goals. As a result, the 1992 North Carolina plan stands out as a truly creative work of art (see figure 5.2). County and town boundaries are regularly violated by districts that meander all over the map in shapes no salamander could hope to approximate. Even the contiguity standard was thrown to the winds. Districts one and three, and six and twelve bisect each other repeatedly and each district is at times contiguous only at points.

Two majority black districts arose out of the redistricting process. The First District, which elected African American Eva Clayton in 1992, was largely carved out of the seat of retiring white Democrat Walter Jones. Clayton was not only one of the first two African Americans elected to the House from North Carolina since Reconstruction, but the first woman ever elected to the House from North Carolina. Continuing this pattern of success, Clayton won election as president of the large House freshman class in 1992.

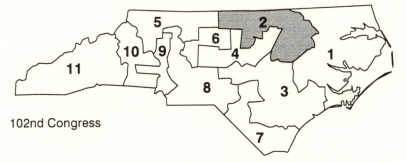

102nd Congress

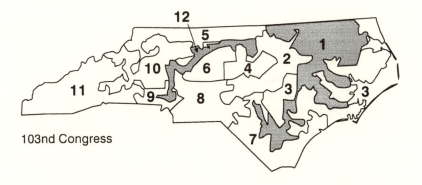

103nd Congress

102nd Congress, elected 1990		103nd Congress, elected 1992	
Name	% Black	Name	% Black
1 Jones (D)	35%	1 **Clayton (D)**	57%
2 Valentine (D)	40%	2 Valentine (D)	22%
3 Lancaster (D)	27%	3 Lancaster (D)	21%
4 Price (D)	20%	4 Price (D)	20%
5 Neal (D)	16%	5 Neal (D)	15%
6 *Coble (R)*	21%	6 *Coble (R)*	7%
7 Rose (D)	27%	7 Rose (D)	19%
8 Hefner (D)	20%	8 Hefner (D)	23%
9 *McMillan (R)*	23%	9 *McMillan (R)*	9%
10 *Ballenger (R)*	11%	10 *Ballenger (R)*	5%
11 *Taylor (R)*	5%	11 *Taylor (R)*	7%
		12 **Watt (D)**	57%

Figure 5.2. North Carolina Redistricting Plans

Democratic state legislators proved their ingenuity in the drafting of North Carolina's second black majority district. Using its Section 5 preclearance powers, the Department of Justice vetoed North Carolina's original redistricting plans on the grounds the plan diluted minority representation by not drawing a second majority nonwhite district. The department hinted that North Carolina could solve this problem by drawing a new majority black and Lumbee Indian district in southeastern North Carolina. Republicans loved this idea because it concentrated more Democratic voters and might have cost incumbent white Democrat Charlie Rose his seat. However, the Democrats solved this new problem by drawing a new majority black district in the central portion of the state. Following Interstate 85, the Twelfth District connects the black communities of Gastonia, Charlotte, Winston-Salem, Greensboro, and Durham. According to reports, anyone driving along the highway with both of their car doors wide open would kill most of the district's residents. The Department of Justice approved this plan, and the Twelfth District sent African American Melvin Watt to Congress in 1992.

Although North Carolina created two new majority black districts, white incumbents did not fare badly in the process. In avowedly anti-incumbent 1992, all the incumbents in the white majority districts sought reelection and all of them won. Packing Republicans into a few very safe Republican districts helped Democrats achieve their goals, so no Republican incumbent was endangered by the plan. While some white Democrats still held marginal seats, a couple saw their reelection prospects enhanced. The Democrats did not waste black votes by packing too many black voters into the new majority black districts. African Americans composed 57 percent of the population in both Clayton's and Watt's districts. When white majority districts had to lose black population, Democrats replaced the blacks with rural white Democrats rather than suburban white Republicans. In the 1992 elections, North Carolina Democrats improved their majority in state's congressional delegation from a margin of seven to four to that of eight to four.

However, the 1994 elections revealed that even clever gerrymanders cannot necessarily protect white moderate Democrats against losses due to racial redistricting over the long term. Despite the best efforts of the Democratic legislature to draw two new black districts without weakening their hold on the remaining seats, North Carolina Democrats lost four seats in the 1994 congressional elections. Racial redistricting accounts for at least two of these losses. If the Second and Third Districts had retained the same proportion of blacks as prior to redistricting, Democrats probably would have carried them. In both districts, the proportion of blacks excised during redistricting exceeds the Republican margin of victory. Additionally, if the legislature had focused its creativity in districting solely on protecting Democrats, it might have prevented incumbent Democrat David Price's narrow defeat in the Fourth District.

The election of two African American members of Congress in 1992 did not just represent major gains in black descriptive representation. These new liberal black representatives were also more responsive to the interests of the black community than past white representatives had been. Nevertheless, black North Carolinians paid a heavy price for these gains in terms of the overall level of substantive representation. African Americans now have two reliable votes on the floor of the House in the form of Eva Clayton and Mel Watt. However, blacks can similarly count upon the new highly conservative Republican representatives to regularly vote against the policy preferences of African Americans.

The Aggregate Effect of Racial Redistricting in 1992 and 1994

Nine states created new black majority districts between the 1990 and 1992 elections. Louisiana, Texas, and Virginia adopted Democratic gerrymanders similar to the North Carolina plan. In all of these states, legislators worked hard to protect incumbent white Democrats in the process of drawing a total of five additional black majority districts and two new Latino majority districts. Strategic Democratic mapmakers relied largely on packing as many Republican voters into as few districts as possible in their effort to prevent the Republicans from benefiting from racial redistricting. While they did not lose seats on balance, Republicans failed to gain new seats in 1992 from the concentration of black Democratic voters in black majority districts in these states. In 1994, Republicans won seven new seats in the Democratic gerrymander states, but only three of those gains, all in North Carolina, can be attributed to racial redistricting rather than to national trends favoring the Republicans.

Alabama, Florida, Georgia, Maryland, and South Carolina did not work to protect Democrats. In these non-Democratic states, blacks won an impressive eight new seats. However, Republicans also posted substantial gains. Republicans held only 36 percent of the House seats prior to the 1992 election. After the election, Republicans won nine additional seats and controlled 49 percent of the House delegation from non-Democratic gerrymander states with new black districts. Republicans and African Americans gained largely at the expense of white Democrats, who saw their share of seats plummet from 46 percent before redistricting to 25 percent after redistricting. Only three of the nine seats gained by Republicans in 1992 can be explained by to population growth in Republican suburbs or Democratic losses in marginal districts. Republicans gained six seats in 1992 and held on to one open seat almost entirely due to the creation new majority-minority districts.[17] Democrats lost an additional six seats in the non-Democratic gerrymander states in 1994, but racial redistricting accounts for no Democratic defeats in this heavily Republican year.

Overall, racial redistricting caused African Americans to make sizeable gains in descriptive representation at the cost of the loss of some substantive representation. The number of African American representatives rose by a total of thirteen. The election of new liberal black legislators raises the number of solid votes for legislation supported by African Americans. However, Republicans gained at least nine seats in 1992 and 1994 due to racial redistricting, out a total of twenty-two new seats won by Republicans in states with new black districts. The Alabama open seat held by Republicans, thanks to racial redistricting, brings the total number of seats won by Republicans due to the creation of new majority-minority districts to ten. Republican gains decrease the total number of potential votes on the House floor for legislation supported by African Americans. While moderate white Democrats often support liberal legislation favored by blacks, the newly elected Republicans are staunch conservatives. Due to both racial redistricting and regional trends favoring the Republicans, the white moderate Democratic representative is a vanishing breed in the southern states, where almost all of the new black districts are located. Prior to redistricting, white moderate Democrats held fifty-two (49 percent) of the seats in states that drew new black districts. Their numbers dropped to thirty-nine after the 1992 elections (34 percent) and to twenty-seven (23 percent) after the 1994 elections.

The Republicans won a majority of seats in the House in 1994 largely due to national tides favoring their party. Nevertheless, racial redistricting played an important secondary role in assuring Republicans control of the 104th Congress. The Republican majority would have been razor thin without the seats won by Republicans due to racial redistricting. If anything, the analysis that forms the basis for these conclusions underestimates both the short- and long-term effects of racial redistricting. The calculation of Republican gains excludes marginal Republican seats made safer thanks to racial redistricting. It also neglects to consider Democratic seats that state governments controlled by Democrats might have made safer during redistricting if they had not been compelled to maintain existing black districts. Racial redistricting not only helped Republicans win a majority of the House in 1994, it may also aid their efforts to retain control throughout the remainder of the decade.

The Outlook for the Future

Recent court decisions should exacerbate the negative impact of drawing new black majority districts on black substantive representation. The Supreme Court's decision in *Shaw v. Reno* threatens the redistricting plans of all of the states that drew Democratic gerrymanders and created new majority black districts. In order to create new black districts and protect white Democratic incumbents, these states invariably had to sacrifice the compactness requirement. The North Carolina plan disputed in *Shaw* exhibits exactly this type of trade-off. The Democrats protected white Democratic incumbents and created two new majority black districts by drawing districts that even the most charitable observer would have difficulty labeling contiguous, let alone compact. While the North Carolina plan spectacularly failed to protect white Democrats in 1994, similar gerrymanders in Louisiana, Texas, and Virginia successfully protected the seats of most white Democrats.

In *Shaw v. Reno*, the Supreme Court expressed strong disapproval of plans like the one in North Carolina, which ignore traditional districting requirements like compactness in the effort to draw new black districts. As Justice Sandra Day O'Connor wrote:

> We believe that reapportionment is one area in which appearances do matter. A reapportionment plan that includes in one district individuals who belong to the same race, but who are otherwise widely separated by geographical boundaries, and who have little in common but the color of their skin, bears an uncomfortable reference to political apartheid.[18]

While leaving to the lower courts to decide if the North Carolina plan violated the Constitution, the Court left little doubt as to its view when it ruled that the claim of racial gerrymandering in this case was justiciable under the Equal Protection Clause. At the same time, the Court specifically refused to relieve jurisdictions of the necessity of drawing new majority-minority districts, leaving that question open for future cases. Despite the radical departure in *Shaw* from past cases, the Department of Justice remains free to continue using its preclearance powers to compel states to draw new majority-minority districts.

Federal courts have been quick to apply the Supreme Court's reasoning in *Shaw*. Judges in Georgia, Louisiana, and Texas have vitiated congressional redistricting plans in these states on the grounds that they violate the Equal Protection Clause as racial gerrymanders. In *Hays v. Louisiana*, the U.S. Court of Appeals, Fifth Circuit, went even farther than the Supreme Court in *Shaw* toward undermining the basis of racial redistricting under the Voting Rights Act. In *Shaw*, the Supreme Court carefully left open the question as to whether North Carolina was required to create two majority-minority districts under the Voting Rights Act. However, the judges in *Hays* made a point of declaring that Louisiana could not be legally compelled under Sections 2 and 5 of the Voting Rights Act to create a second majority-minority district unless it was feasible to draw a geographically compact district. Reflecting the shift in tone from earlier voting rights cases, the court declared that states could not even voluntarily create new majority-minority districts unless the district was reasonably compact. Surprisingly, on remand from the Supreme Court as *Shaw v. Hunt*, the district

court in North Carolina upheld the contorted lines that inspired the Supreme Court's decision in *Shaw v. Reno*. At the time of this writing, the
decisions in the Georgia, Louisiana, North Carolina, and Texas cases are
all on appeal to the Supreme Court.

In drafting redistricting plans, legislators must now navigate carefully
between the Scylla of racial gerrymandering accusations and the Charybdis
of vote dilution claims. If the Supreme Court upholds *Hays*, the number of
black representatives will probably decline as states eliminate black majority districts with ungainly district lines. On the other hand, if the Supreme
Court vitiates *Hays* while reaffirming *Shaw*, the price of gaining additional
black members of Congress in terms of substantive representation will rise
substantially. In this legal context, drafting plans that protect white Democratic incumbents while creating new majority-minority districts becomes
far more difficult, if not impossible. Republicans may substantially benefit
from the fallout of the *Shaw* decision. As plans favorable to Democrats are
overturned and new ones that draw majority-minority districts without protecting Democratic incumbents are adopted, Republicans ought to win
many new House seats.

Needless to say, these changes will hardly benefit black substantive representation. By severely constraining the manner in which new majority-
minority districts may be drawn, the Supreme Court has taken away the one
tool that can effectively mitigate the negative impact of drawing new black
districts on black substantive representation. African Americans already
experienced an erosion in policy support in the House thanks largely to
redistricting. Thanks to *Shaw*, this erosion seems likely to continue
throughout the 1990s as plans favorable to African Americans fail to with-
stand legal challenges and are replaced by plans inimical to either black
descriptive or substantive representation.

Conclusion

Racial redistricting remains a key component of any strategy designed to
assure the election of more than token numbers of African Americans
and Latinos to the House of Representatives. Under the current electoral
system, eliminating majority-minority districts would probably drastically
reduce the number of blacks and Latinos elected to Congress. Due to the
inherent conflict between maximizing the number of black majority districts and the number of Democratic districts, drawing additional black
majority districts tends to make the Congress less likely to pass legislation
supported by most African Americans. The enactment of extremely creative Democratic gerrymanders can greatly reduce the negative impact of
racial redistricting on support for black policy interests within the Con-

gress. However, the Supreme Court's ruling in *Shaw v. Reno* that racial gerrymanders are justiciable under the Equal Protection Clause of the Constitution makes such plans extremely vulnerable to legal challenges. In the future, African Americans face the unpalatable alternatives of either accepting a reduction in the number of black majority districts or paying a steeper price for these districts through a loss of influence within the House.

Notes

1. McDonald 1992, 74–76; Parker 1990, 41–51.
2. O'Rourke 1992, 109; Swain 1993, 198–204; Thernstrom 1987, 3, 23, 74–75, 154, 167–68, 215–20, 226–27.
3. Guinier 1994a, 41–156.
4. Lublin 1994, 149–246.
5. Aside from Republicans Gary Franks and J. C. Watts, Democrats Ron Dellums, Katie Hall, Alan Wheat, and Andrew Young are the only African Americans who have ever represented Anglo majority districts. According to the 1990 Census, Franks's district is 4 percent black and Watts's district is 7 percent black.
6. O'Rourke 1992, 109; Swain 1993, 198–204; Thernstrom 1987, 215–20.
7. Swain 1993, 116–41, 207–9.
8. Grofman and Handley 1989, 439–40; Lublin 1994, 83–98.
9. Swain 1993, 200.
10. Grofman and Handley 1989, 439–40; Lublin 1994, 83–98.
11. Grofman and Handley 1989, 440–43; Lublin 1994, 98–108.
12. Lublin 1994, 104–8.
13. Ibid., 191–93; Walters 1994, 190–91.
14. Lublin 1994, 93–96, 193.
15. Ibid., 210–13.
16. Pitkin 1967; Swain 1993, 5.
17. Lublin 1994, 228–31.
18. *Shaw v. Reno*, 113 S. Ct. 2816 (1993), 2827.

Part II

RACE AND INSTITUTIONAL DEVELOPMENT

6

African Americans in U.S. Social Policy

THEDA SKOCPOL

LISTENING RECENTLY to a talk by two of my colleagues, I heard what might be called standard wisdom about the impact of relations between white and black Americans on the development of national social policies in the United States. America developed a welfare state very belatedly and incompletely, my colleagues argued, in large part because workers have always been divided by ethnicity and—especially—by race. Throughout U.S. history, it was further suggested, policies to help the poor have been particularly stigmatized, because "the poor" have been seen as likely to be people of color.

I found myself thinking: No, it is not quite as simple as that. Some U.S. social benefits developed "early" in international terms, and some have been quite generous.[1] Although African Americans have always been disproportionately among the most impoverished people in the United States, the stigma of policies targeted on the poor cannot be attributed mainly to the presence of the black minority. Until recent decades, blacks were overwhelmingly concentrated in the South, where there were few public social policies of any kind. Even so, antipoverty policies were very stigmatized in the North, where most of the poor were white.[2] Since the 1940s, and especially since the 1960s, stigmas of race and poverty have undoubtedly become mutually reinforcing for U.S. "welfare" policies. But it is hard to doubt that there would have been a deep and persistent stigmatization of policies targeted on the poor, even if African American slaves had never been brought to this nation, and even if black sharecroppers had not migrated in huge numbers to urban areas from the 1940s onward.

African Americans have *not* invariably been excluded from U.S. public social benefits, nor have they always been stigmatized when they did receive them. The overall dynamic since the Civil War has not been a linear evolution, moving from the exclusion or stigmatization of African Americans toward their (however partial) inclusion and honorable acceptance within mainstream U.S. politics and policies. There have been more ups and downs, more ironies and reversals in the history of African American relationships to U.S. social policies across major historical eras.

Provoked by my unease with the standard wisdom, this chapter is a preliminary effort to characterize and explain the changing places of African
Americans—as actors and as policy beneficiaries—within successive historical phases of U.S. social policy. For the sake of manageability, only
some types of policies are discussed here. I say little about education, housing, and health care; nor do I have much to say about socially relevant tax
credits. I focus primarily on public social expenditures. Although this exercise certainly does not provide a full picture, it may suggest something
about the complexly intertwined socioeconomic, political, and cultural
forces that have influenced the access—or lack of access—of African
Americans to pensions, social insurance, and welfare from the nineteenth
century to the present.

A Polity-Centered Perspective on
Major Policy Eras

Modern U.S. social policies did *not* start with the Social Security Act of
1935. Between the 1870s and the 1920s, U.S. federal and state governments established many policies aiming to protect, first, veteran Union soldiers and their dependents, and then mothers and their children.[3] As appendix table 6.A summarizes, I label the first two (often-overlooked) eras of
modern U.S. social policy the Civil War Era and the Maternalist Era. Two
more recent eras are better known: the New Deal Era and the contemporary
Era of "Welfare" Controversies.

To make sense of the four major phases of modern U.S. social provision
from the Civil War to the present, I use a "polity-centered" theoretical
framework.[4] This perspective begins with the historical development of
U.S. governmental institutions, political parties, and electoral rules. It ana-
lyzes the impact of such arrangements on the policy initiatives of officials
and politicians. It also looks at the impact of such arrangements on the
identities, goals, and capacities of the various social groups that have become active, at one period or another, in political alliances contending over
the shape of U.S. public policies. Finally, my perspective highlights "policy feedbacks" over time: the influences that earlier social policies have
upon the institutional arrangements and social groups that shape later social policies.

An essay such as this is hardly the place to go into great detail about my
explanatory approach. Still, before moving to situate African Americans in
the four eras, let me briefly characterize each phase and show how I use my
polity-oriented approach to make sense of overall developments in that
period.

The Civil War Era

From the 1870s to the 1910s, there was an enormous expansion of disability, survivors', and de facto old-age benefits for veterans of the Union armies of the Civil War.[5] By 1910, about 28 percent of all elderly American men, and nearly one-third of elderly men in the North, were receiving from the U.S. federal government pensions that were remarkably generous by the international standards of the day; many widows and other dependents of deceased veterans were also pensioners; and extra aid was often available to Civil War veterans and survivors from state and local governments. Union soldiers and their dependents, it was argued, had "saved the Nation," and should in return be cared for by the government to prevent the possibility of their falling into dependence on private charity or public poor relief.

The expansion of benefits for Union veterans of the Civil War was rooted in competition between patronage-oriented political parties within a nineteenth-century U.S. state that lacked centralized civil service bureaucracies, yet encouraged party politicians to use distributive policies to assemble cross-class and cross-regional electoral support from a highly mobilized and competitive male electorate. Between the mid-1870s and the mid-1890s, the Republican Party in particular learned to combine tariffs and pension expenditures. Tariffs, minutely adjusted in Congress to fit particular industries and local groups, appealed to many businessmen and workers, and raised plentiful revenues for the federal government. In turn, the revenues could be spent on pensions for beneficiaries scattered across all classes, and the application process could be manipulated in ways that helped the Republicans to appeal to electorally competitive states just before crucial elections.[6] Along with party politicians, thousands of veterans' clubs federated into the Grand Army of the Republic became key supporters of pension generosity from the mid-1880s onward, keeping congressmen across many northern legislative districts keenly interested in such social expenditures from the federal fisc.

The Maternalist Era

During the early 1900s, various policies aiming to help women workers and mothers and children proliferated. The federal government established the female-run Children's Bureau in 1912, and expanded its mission in 1921 through the enactment of the Sheppard-Towner program, partially to fund state and local health care education to help American mothers and babies. Meanwhile, dozens of states enacted protective labor laws for women workers, arguing that their capacity for motherhood had to be protected. And forty-four states also enabled local jurisdications to provide "mothers' pensions" to impoverished caretakers of fatherless children.

Around 1900, the nineteenth-century U.S. "state of courts and parties" was undergoing major structural transformations that opened opportunities for maternalist reformers.[7] The Democrats and Republicans became less electorally competitive in most parts of the nation, and elite and middle-class groups were calling for reforms that would weaken patronage-oriented parties. Until 1920 (or a few years before in some states), American women lacked the right to vote—yet they were hardly "outside" of politics.[8] Elite and middle-class women formed voluntary organizations to engage in charitable, cultural, and civic activities. By the turn of the century, nation-spanning federations of women's voluntary associations had formed, paralleling the three-tier structure of U.S. local-state-federal government. Women's federations allied themselves with higher-educated female professional reformers, arguing that the moral and domestic values of married homemakers and mothers should be projected into public affairs. Organized women urged governments to enact new social policies to help families, communities, and—above all—mothers and children. During a period when U.S. political parties were weakened, and when male officials and trade unions could not readily take the lead in enacting social policies for workingmen, U.S. women's voluntary federations were uniquely well positioned to shape public debates across many local legislative districts.[9]

After American women were admitted to the formal electorate by the Nineteenth Amendment of 1920, the civic engagement of many women's groups (ironically) weakened. For this and a variety of other reasons, the expansion of maternalist social policies came to a halt by the later 1920s, and indeed was partially reversed. Then came the Great Depression, bringing with it social and political upheavals that ushered in the next great era of U.S. social policy innovation.

The New Deal Era

This watershed period featured various federal programs to help the (temporarily) unemployed, along with the Social Security Act of 1935, which included national Old Age Insurance (OAI), federally required and state-run Unemployment Insurance (UI), and federal subsidies for optional, state-controlled Old Age Assistance (OAA) and Aid to Dependent Children (ADC, which was a continuation of the earlier mothers' pensions). In the public discourse of the 1930s and 1940s, the most "deserving" recipients of social benefits were said to be normally employed men who were temporarily forced out of work by the Depression, and the elderly. By the

early 1950s, it was clear that social insurance for retired elderly wage earners and their dependents had emerged as the centerpiece of such generous
and comprehensive public social provision as there would be in post–
World War II America.[10] The only other truly generous and comprehensive
part of postwar national social provision was the GI Bill of 1944, which
featured employment assistance and educational and housing loans for military veterans.

A number of structural changes set the stage for these policy innovations. The federal government—and within it the executive—came to the
fore in the emergency of massive economic depression. Economic crisis
spurred the unionization of industrial workers as well as protests by organizations of farmers, the unemployed, and—perhaps most important—old
people. Among the elderly, there emerged a widespread federation of local
Townsend Clubs demanding generous pensions for the elderly.[11] Economic
crisis also spurred electoral realignment, shifting votes from Republicans
to Democrats—and transforming the Democrats from a warring camp of
southern "dry" Protestants versus northern "wet" Catholics into a nationwide conglomerate of local and state political machines all hungry for new
flows of economic resources.

What the Depression, the New Deal, and even World War II did *not* do,
however, was to remove contradictory local and state interests from
"national" U.S. policymaking. Even at their strongest, President Franklin
Roosevelt and the assorted New Deal reformist professionals who flocked
into executive agencies during the 1930s all had to compromise with congressional coalitions rooted in state and local interests.[12] Above all, they
had to respect southern Democrats' determination to protect their region's
sharecropping agriculture and low-wage industries from actually (or potentially) unsettling "intrusions" by northern unions or federal bureaucrats.
Southerners were happy to have resources from the federal government but
did not want either centralized controls or benefits that might undermine
existing southern labor and race relations. And if the truth be told, congressional representatives of other localities and states in the nation felt pretty
much the same protective way about whatever the major labor and social
relations of their areas might be. There was a broad congressional consensus throughout the New Deal and the 1940s to preserve a great deal of
federal variety in economic and social policy.[13]

From this perspective, the shape and limits of the major social and economic programs of the New Deal era are not surprising. Federally run employment programs did not survive the mass unemployment of the 1930s
because efforts to institutionalize executive-run "full employment planning" and "social Keynesianism" ran afoul of congressionally represented
southern, business, and farm interests. The Social Security Act included
only one truly national program—Old Age Insurance—enacted in an area

where no states had previously established programs. Unemployment Insurance, meanwhile, was made federal rather than national, not only because represenatives of the South wanted their states to be able to establish terms of coverage, benefits, and taxation, but also because representatives of Wisconsin and New York wanted their "liberal" states to be able to preserve the terms of the unemployment insurance programs they had already established, prior to the Social Security Act. Public assistance programs for the elderly and dependent children were given federal subsidies under Social Security but otherwise left largely in the hands of the states.

During World War II, New Deal reformers tied to the National Resources Planning Board talked about permanently "nationalizing" and expanding both public assistance and unemployment insurance. But their proposals got nowhere at all, and Congress disbanded the National Resources Planning Board soon after they were made. Only Old Age Insurance tended to expand coverage and become more comprehensive after 1935. Widows and orphans of wage-earning "contributors" were added to OAI in 1939, transforming it into Old Age and Survivors' Insurance. During the 1950s, benefits for disabled wage earners were added to what was now known simply as Social Security, and coverage was extended to more occupations. The American "welfare state" that emerged from the New Deal and World War II was hardly comprehensive by the international standards of the day, yet it did eventually become relatively complete and generous for retired, disabled, or deceased regular wage earners and their dependents.

The Era of "Welfare" Controversies

Policy legacies and institutional features inherited from the New Deal era shaped and limited the ways that were available to reformers during the 1960s and 1970s. As Margaret Weir has explained, liberals, unionists, and Civil Rights activists were not in a good position to create public full-employment programs that might have jointly benefited the black poor along with white and black unionized workers.[14] Instead, institutional and intellectual legacies from the New Deal and the 1940s encouraged a split in economic policy between "commercial Keynesian" macroeconomic strategies, on the one hand, and relatively weak federal efforts to reeducate the poor to make them "employable," on the other. These latter efforts never really succeeded. As the War on Poverty gave way to the Great Society and the Nixon reforms, the emphasis shifted from job training and community development programs toward helping the poor through new or expanded categorical social benefits such as Aid to Families with Dependent Children (AFDC), Food Stamps, and Medicaid. These helped welfare mothers and their children, above all, and more needy single-parent families than ever before were added to the welfare rolls. During this same period, too, the Social Security Administration took advantage of the heightened concern with "antipoverty policy" to put through long-laid plans for Medicare, nationalized Supplemental Security Income, and indexed Social Security benefits, all of which helped to pull most of the American elderly out of dire poverty for the first time in history.

But that was not the end of the story. By the later 1970s, and particularly during the 1980s, political backlashes set in against the social policy innovations and extensions of the 1960s and early 1970s. Leaving aside important exceptions and nuances, one can say that expanded public provision for the elderly (poor and nonpoor alike) remained popular with broad, bipartisan swatches of American voters and politicians, while public "welfare" assistance to the working-aged poor became an increasingly contentious issue among politicians and intellectuals, and within the electorate as a whole.

Certainly, the rhetoric of "welfare reform" among politicians and intellectuals of vitually all political persuasions has changed markedly from the 1960s to the 1980s and early 1990s. Where once welfare reform meant finding ways to enroll more needy families and make benefits and services more adequate, it now almost always connotes finding ways to get people off welfare, or out of the ranks of the unemployed whose children may end up on welfare, and into paid jobs. Welfare reform now also means finding ways to force unmarried fathers to contribute to the support of mothers and children on AFDC. The issues back in the 1960s were similar—mothers and children on public assistance; poor men not fully in the labor force—but the ways they are defined has changed, in the wake of the conservative, Republican, and white backlashes against more generous public social provision for the poor.

African Americans in U.S. Social Provision

Against the backdrop of the general sketch of the historical development of modern U.S. social policies that I have just offered, what can be said specifically about the places—past, present, and future—of African Americans? There are two major propositions I hope to make plausible. Let me state them in general terms, and then say more about African Americans during each policy era.

The first proposition is this: While the regional and labor-force situation of African Americans has undoutedly determined a great deal about their place in U.S. politics and social policy, taking into account the changing position of blacks in U.S. federal democracy also does much to help us make sense of their exclusion or inclusion in social policies of different sorts. Both labor-force situation and political rights must, in short, be specified for each era—and the latter cannot simply be reduced to the former. We must pay careful attention to factors that have sometimes given African Americans (or some of them) more, or less, political leverage than one might expect for groups in their socioeconomic situation.

Secondly, as we look at the changing political position of African Americans, we must begin—but certainly not end—with questions about their formal political rights and ability to engage in self-conscious political mobilization. Historical evidence suggests that African Americans, including the poorest, have gained access to honorable public social benefits not only through their own efforts as voters, or protestors, or organized advocates. To be sure, they have gained access in those ways. But African Americans have also, at times, obtained honorable social benefits by virtue of being included in broad, cross-racial political coalitions, where they themselves were not the politically decisive force. And African Americans have also done well when they were included in politically and culturally defined categories of "honorable" beneficiaries—beneficiaries of public social provision thought to have "earned" support from the nation.

My polity-centered theoretical approach to the analysis of national systems of social provision leads me to notice instances when bureaucrats, professional reformers, or elected politicians take the lead in devising policies about—rather than at the behest of—social groups. My perspective refuses to take it all for granted that any social group—whether defined by class, or race, or gender—necessarily benefits most from governmental actions that it has consciously demanded; groups may be hurt by getting what they thought they wanted, and they may benefit from (as well as be hurt by) measures devised "over their heads" or for purposes that seem tangential to their needs. Finally, my perspective also highlights the political construction over time of movements and coalitions that may demand particular sorts of social policies, or else fight for their expansion or contraction. In democracies, I hypothesize, social policies expand over time when they are supported by cross-class majority coalitions. For blacks in America, who are inescapably a minority, this means that they may well gain the most when they can be symbolically included in a broad "honorable" category of beneficiaries *and* simultaneously included in a majority political coalition devoted to supporting the relevant policy over time.

African Americans and Civil War Benefits

The plausibility of both of my major points is well borne out by the place of African American Union veterans and survivors in the very generous and honorable system of federal Civil War pensions that was the keystone of the first era of modern U.S. social provision, from the 1870s to the early 1900s. Culturally and attitudinally, this was certainly an unabashedly racist—indeed, white supremacist—era in American history. African Americans were almost invariably at the bottom of socioeconomic hierarchies: they owned little land or capital, and were overwhelmingly agricultural tenants and laborers in the South, while a tiny minority consisted of (more or less skilled) wage earners in the North. Here was a time, moreover, when "poor relief" was certainly demeaning, and when many categories of whites, as well as most blacks, were *not* eligible to participate in the pension largesse of the federal government.

Yet the approximately 180,000 African American men who had served in the Union military during the Civil War, or their survivors, were formally eligible for the same order of pension benefits as the whites who had fought for the Union. A historian studying Union veterans and survivors in New Bedford, Massachusetts, has concluded that racial differences made little difference in their fate in the federal system; native-born whites, Irish Americans, and African Americans seem to have had similar experiences in applying for benefits, and all benefited greatly.[15] Even illiterate liberated southern slaves who served in the Union military became eligible for honorable and (relatively) generous Civil War pensions. Remarkably, there is some evidence that officials in the U.S. Pension Bureau of the late-nineteenth century made special efforts, at least for a time, to help former slave veterans or widows establish their eligibility in an application system that routinely more easily rewarded those who were literate and led settled lives.[16]

Was the eligibility for pensions and other Civil War benefits of certain African Americans due to their own political rights and efforts? Obviously yes—at least to the "effort" part of this question. Not until late in the Civil War did African Americans win the right to participate fully (as privates and lower officers, but not as higher officers) in the Union military effort. As soon as they were allowed to serve, African American men volunteered in impressive numbers, and often served with amazing valor under horrendous conditions.[17] Valorous service is surely what won African Americans enough grudging respect among Union veterans in general to make it politically feasible for them to be given benefits on formally equal terms. Of course, African Americans also formally gained the right to vote as an immediate result of the Civil War and Reconstruction; they became, even for a time in the South, formally defined as full citizens (see the discussion by Richard Valelly, chap. 8 in this volume).

But the interesting thing is that African American eligibility for Civil War benefits persisted over many decades, even as black voting rights and other progressive legacies of the Civil War petered out. African American eligility for pensions certainly outlasted voting rights for southern blacks. This signals that more was politically at work than formal political rights or continuing black participation as citizens. The Civil War was an indelible experience for a certain generation of northern politicans and voters,

138THEDA SKOCPOL

operating in a competitive patronage democracy that encouraged the formation of broad, cross-class electoral coalitions fueled, in part, by pension
generosity. The Grand Army of the Republic always included local clubs
of black veterans; predominately white locals in some states, such as Massachusetts, included individual African Americans. By the organizational
and political standards of the day, such inclusions were remarkable. Northern politicians, voters, and veterans' groups alike—talking to a believing
northern citizenry—constructed an honorable category of recipients of
public largesse: the "Saviors of the Union," who had "earned" the enduring
gratitude of a grateful nation. Here was a category that, despite white racism, continued to include African American Union veterans and survivors,
even former slave sharecroppers among them, to the end of their days.

African Americans and Maternalist Social Policies

Most maternalist social policies were state-level enactments that spread
rapidly during the 1910s across about forty states—yet were often not enacted at all (or else were enacted only during the 1920s and early 1930s) by
southern states, where the vast majority of African Americans lived during
the early 1900s. What is more, particular localities or occupations with
many blacks were often omitted, even when given states had such measures
on the books as hour limits for women workers or statutes to allow mothers' pensions to be paid by local authorities. In contrast to the nationally
run Union veterans' pensions of the Civil War era, most state-level maternalist regulations and benefits of the Progressive Era followed a pattern that
would persist in the United States throughout much of the twentieth century: a great deal of local and cross-occupational variety was built either
into the enactments themselves or into their practical application (i.e.,
whether particular local areas chose to establish programs). De facto, this
allowed the vast majority of African Americans to be left out of eligibility—even for benefits or protections to which they might seem to be have
been nominally entitled. Of course, it is also true that similarly situated
poor whites in the same occupations and localities were also excluded.
Thus, women workers in southern states worked long hours regardless of
race; and widowed mothers, black or white, in most southern states were
unlikely to be able to apply for mothers' pensions.

In "most northern and western states, the proportion of black families
receiving mothers' pensions was roughly equal to the proportion of blacks
in the total population"—a proportion which was, of course, very tiny.[18]
Historians and social scientists have, so far, developed only local case studies and anecdotal information about the implementation of mothers' pensions in the 1910s and 1920s. From that spotty information, some scholars

have made overly strong claims that blacks were excluded from mothers' pension programs primarily because white social workers tended to assume that African American widows were "unfit mothers." No doubt this sort of thing did happen; systematic cross-local studies of the implementation of northern mothers' pensions would probably show underrepresentation of needy black applicants (perhaps along with applicants from certain Eastern European ethnicities). Still, the most important reason why many needy widows, black or white, were excluded was the severe underfunding of mothers' pension programs, even in localities that established them in the first place. This underfunding reflected the general unwillingness of U.S. citizens to vote public monies to help "the poor."

Significantly, the one maternalist program that did the best job of including—and even reaching out for—poor rural women of all races was the only nationally designed and run effort of the early 1900s: the Sheppard-Towner program of federal matching funds for maternal and infant health education, which was planned and implemented by the U.S. Children's Bureau. When she was working out the legislative proposal for Sheppard-Towner during the 1910s, the first chief of the Children's Bureau, Julia Lathrop, made two deliberate decisions that had great importance for rural and nonwhite mothers. First, Lathrop decided to emphasize outreach to rural areas, not just to supplement the federal subsidy of already established urban maternal health programs. Lathrop knew that the need was greatest in rural areas, especially in the South and West. Moreover, she was thinking about what it would take to get her legislation through Congress, and she deliberately modeled her agency's programs on those of the U.S. Department of Agriculture, which she knew had established excellent relationships with local groups and legislators across the entire nation, not just in the urban-industrial districts. Secondly, Lathrop deliberately chose to explain in the enabling legislation for Sheppard-Towner that "this act is not a charity." She believed that Sheppard-Towner programs, like the public schools, should be open to all Americans, not just the poor. Otherwise, she felt, "the services would degenerate into poor relief."[19] Lathrop intended to carry out the cultural theme of the maternalist era: that motherhood was honorable service to the nation, that all children were resources for the nation.

After Sheppard-Towner state and local programs began to function with federal matching funds, the choices Julia Lathrop had made back in the planning stage had real-world consequences. According to public health historian Richard Meckel, the extension of these programs was "particularly noteworthy in southern and western states." The southern states that fully utilized Sheppard-Towner matching funds included ones such as Alabama and Georgia that had not enacted mothers' pensions or protective labor laws. Meckel also points out that at least some of this [Sheppard-Towner] work was reaching non-whites, who had been virtually ignored up to this time. Minnesota and Nebraska targeted their Native American populations for special attention. New Mexico, Arizona, and Texas employed Spanish-speaking nurses to give lecture-demonstrations and make home visits within the Hispanic community. And the South, although keeping its programs segregated, for the first time made an effort to extend public health services to blacks.[20]

How are we to explain the patterns of exclusion and inclusion of African Americans in the maternalist social policies of the early 1900s? One thing is certain: it would be difficult to attribute much to formal voting rights. True, southern blacks were disenfranchised in this period, and this correlates with their exclusion from state-level maternalist policies. Yet until 1920 or just before, most American women of all classes and races lacked the right to vote, and that did not prevent the enactment of many social policies aiming to help or protect mothers and children. Nationwide federations of local women's voluntary groups were the key actors in pressuring dozens of states legislatures to act during the 1910s. These federations were also crucial to the enactment of Sheppard-Towner in 1921, just after American women gained the right to vote (including black women in the North, but not in the South).

Were African American women part of the women's voluntary alliances that successfully agitated for maternalist social policies?—a very tiny and marginal part, at best. To be sure, middle-class African American women did form voluntary charitable, cultural, and mothers' clubs, just as white women did. But African American local women's clubs could not join the General Federation of Women's Clubs or the National Congress of Mothers. Unlike the Grand Army of the Republic during the Civil War era, these women's federations had southern state and local affiliates, and despite the desire of many northern white women to include black clubs, the national organizations chose to exclude them when faced with threats by southern white women to secede if blacks remained. African American women thus had separate groups, both locally and extralocally, which did at times cooperate in friendly ways with white women's clubs.[21] The evidence we have so far suggests that African American women concentrated on private charity and support for black education in this period, and were little involved in legislative campaigns.[22] Most African Americans were in the South, where they were excluded from political and civil rights, so the concentration on voluntary civic and service activities made sense.

Such inclusion of blacks as there was in the maternalist era—especially in northern mothers' pensions and in Sheppard-Towner programs, South and North—must be attributed to the moral inclusiveness of the mother-centered policy rhetoric of this period. Although the women who campaigned for and implemented maternalist social policies were overwhelmingly privileged and white, they spoke unabashedly of the "honor" of all mothers, and they meant to reach out fully to include mothers and children quite different from themselves on class, racial, and even behavioral lines. Mrs. G. Harris Robertson, the married lady from the Tennessee Congress of Mothers who kicked off the nationwide campaign for mothers' pensions in 1911, even went so far as to advocate in her speech that "our provision include the deserted wife, and the mother who has never been a wife," on the grounds that we must "honor the *mother* wherever found—if she has given a citizen to the nation, then the nation owes something to her."[23]

Equally pertinent, the nonpartisan political strategies followed by women's voluntary federations and by the leaders of the Children's Bureau depended on casting a wide net across many local communities and states. These strategies were necessary to shape public and legislative opinion in a huge, federally organized polity, during a period when political parties were weakened and strong civil service bureaucracies were absent. The breadth of women's strategies and the inclusiveness of their rhetoric of honoring motherhood made it possible to extend some social benefits and services to African American mothers and children—even in a period when racism was rampant and the electoral involvements of blacks were minimal. The focus on mothers also made it somewhat easier to include blacks than it might otherwise have been during an epoch when African Americans were rarely the sorts of wage-earning industrial workers who were at the core of early European social provision. This final point is an important one, for I am arguing that maternal policies were more racially inclusive than class-oriented ones might have been during the early-twentieth century.

African Americans and New Deal Social Policies

The Great Depression, the New Deal, and World War II brought a momentous increase in the role of the federal government in economic and social life. From this fact alone, one might suppose that African Americans would have been more fully included than ever before in public social provision. In terms of the absolute numbers of blacks helped by federal programs—and particularly by the emergency relief and employment-relief programs of the 1930s—this was certainly true. Black Americans suffered terribly during the Depression, for they were concentrated in the rural South, where agriculture was in dire crisis, and in domestic service, laborer, and less-skilled industrial positions in northern cities, where massive unemployment struck and persisted. African Americans were deeply appreciative for help from New Deal emergency relief and works programs.[24] Participation in emergency New Deal programs literally saved many black families from starvation during the depths of the Depression. Historian Nancy Weiss argues that gratitude for this was enough to inspire many blacks in the North to switch their voting allegiance away from the "party of Lincoln" to the "party of Roosevelt" from 1936 onward.[25]

Still, we must make a clear distinction between what the New Deal did for blacks through emergency programs and what it did for them in more permanently established social and economic policies. New Deal price supports for agriculture, for example, did not have to be shared between owners and tenants in the South; they also promoted the mechanization of cotton cropping, which pushed masses of African American laborers and sharecroppers off the land from the 1930s onward.[26] New Deal administrative supports for the unionization of wage workers were not extended to agricultural laborers, thus excluding southern blacks. And agricultural workers were left out of New Deal wage and hours regulations as well.

For the purview of this essay, the most important thing to notice is what happened to African Americans under the various social insurance and public assistance programs established by the Social Security Act of 1935. The Social Security Act is often celebrated as the launching of America's "modern welfare state"; the Old Age Insurance (OAI) program in particular is seen as the beginning of something approximating universalism in modern U.S. social provision. One might suppose that the promises of inclusion of blacks in honorable, "earned" social benefits—promises hinted at in the federal Civil War pension program of old—were taken up again, and carried through more fully, in the federal Social Security Act. But actually the various programs launched in 1935 more closely resembled a federalization (and, in OAI, a nationalization) of the de facto racial patterns that occurred in the cross-state enactments of the early 1900s. As the National Association for the Advancement of Colored People argued at the time, "from a Negro's point of view it look[ed] like a sieve with the holes just big enough for the majority of Negroes to fall through."[27]

The social insurance programs of Social Security—those for the retired elderly and the unemployed—excluded most African Americans by leaving out of "national" coverage the domestic service and agricultural occupations in which two-thirds of black workers were employed (when employed) in the 1930s. Relatively few African Americans were industrial workers or corporate white collar employees at the time the social insurance programs were launched—although many more blacks did join the ranks of industry during and after World War II, thus gaining elibility for social insurance coverage.

In chapter 7 of this volume, Robert Lieberman shows that blacks eventually benefited from fair treatment in the nationally administered programs established by the 1935 Social Security Act. During the 1950s, domestic service and agricultural occupations were added to Social Security; thus many blacks became newly elibible, if they were regularly employed. But, of course, such service and agricultural employees had already (compared to most other workers) lost many years of building eligibility for generous retirement pensions. Covered workers in Social Security have always "earned" retirement pensions pegged to numbers of years of regular covered employment, and pegged also to wage and salary levels. Thus African Americans have received less even from this relatively universal part of U.S. social provision than have whites.

From the start in 1935, African Americans were nominally eligible for the public assistance programs newly federally subsidized under Social Security (even when their predominant occupations were excluded from OAI and UI). But nominally was not really, because the congressional committees considering the proposals of the Committee on Economic Security stripped from the public assistance provisions of the Social Security Act of any language that would have allowed federal administrators to supervise the decisions of state and local officials about such vital matters as eligibility for old age pensions or mothers' pensions, or decisions about the adequacy of the benefits offered to those accepted onto the rolls. After 1935, therefore, local and state adminstrators were free to discriminate in the most blatant ways against impoverished African American old people and mothers. And they did exactly that, especially in the southern states and cotton-belt districts, where most blacks lived and worked.

Southern authorities feared that even small public assistance grants to nonworkers would cause entire black families to stay out of the cotton fields. They prevented this by excluding blacks altogether or by suspending assistance payments during harvest. Even when grants were given, moreover, "although discrimination was illegal, southern states were allowed to pay blacks lower grants than whites by using different criteria for determining need, and by paying Confederate veterans and their dependents the maximum grant."[28] In broad historical perspective, it is amazing that southern states were able to use federal subsidies after 1934 to enrich assistance to Conferedate veterans and survivors, the very persons who had been excluded altogether from the federal Civil War pensions of the nineteenth century!

A final important consequence for African Americans of the social policy developments of the New Deal era lay in the realm of political symbolism. From 1935 into the 1950s, federal Social Security administrators undertook many administrative and ideological efforts to distinguish between "earned" Social Security benefits versus "unearned welfare handouts" from public assistance programs.[29] Their motives were not racial, but some of the consequences were. Those eligible for public assistance to the elderly or dependent children were much more likely to be black than those covered by retirement or survivors' insurance through Social Security. Thus blacks and "welfare" became associated in U.S. discourse about social provision from the 1950s onward, much more than they had been prior to the 1930s.

Having summarized the various implications of New Deal social policies for African Americans, I want to address *why* these developments occurred with the specified racial consequences. Scholars often argue that the New Deal excluded marginalized blacks simply because they were mostly in the South, working in agriculture, and not able to vote. These reasons are certainly the basis for any explanation—yet, in historical perspective, they are clearly not the complete explanation. These regional, labor-force, and political aspects of the African American situation were just as true, indeed more true, prior to the 1930s. Yet if we leave aside the issue of absolute numbers of persons reached by various social programs (particularly the emergency relief programs of the 1930s), in many ways African Americans were as much excluded and marginalized—and, perhaps, over time, more symbolically stigmatized—by the major social policies of the New Deal era as they were by the major policies of the Civil War and Maternalist eras.

The political reasons for this are not hard to specify. The enhanced federal interventions of the New Deal era were enacted and implemented by a presidents and reformers who had to work out repeated compromises between an expanded but poorly coordinated executive branch of the federal government and a Congress that gave plenty of scope to state and local interests. New Deal social policies were also shaped by a newly hegemonic Democratic Party. African Americans were just a tiny part of the New Deal electoral coalition—because only northern blacks could vote, and they joined Democratic ranks only from 1936 onward. Worse, from the African American point of view, the New Deal Democratic Party was an internally contradictory compromise between northern liberals and southern Democrats. The southern Democrats had a strong stake in repressive labor control of blacks and in their exclusion from democratic political rights. The southern Democrats were vital to Roosevelt's presidential electoral coalition, and they controlled key committees in Congress that could prevent enactment of any economic or social legislation that might upset or modify southern economic and racial relations.

All of these facts are, of course, well known. It is simply worth underlining in the context of this essay that the African American political problem during the New Deal was not only one of electoral weakness. Their additional problem was that the New Deal coalition in power—quite in contrast to the hegemonic Republican coalitions in power after the Civil War— would be strongly threatened if African Americans were fully included as beneficiaries in nationwide social programs. That is why the enhanced federal powers of the New Deal period—particularly in more "permanent" programs—*did not* straightforwardly recapitulate and extend the inclusionary trends for blacks started back in the Civil War era. Instead, African Americans found themselves facing a Social Security Act that was of little benefit to African Americans, as the NAACP had reminded members of Congress at the time. Eventually, once Social Security expanded to categories of wage earners originally left out in 1935, many blacks benefited from the administrative fairness of the most national and inclusive social programs launched by the New Deal. But down to the present day, many impoverished African Americans suffer from the local discretion and stigmatization of the poor that was built into the New Deal's welfare programs for nonelderly families who did not enjoy access to regular private employment.[30]

African Americans and Social Policies since the Sixties

African Americans have, in several ways, moved to the fore in the politics of U.S. social policy since the 1960s. They have become major political actors in their own right, as African Americans have gained rights to vote everywhere and as blacks have been elected to local, state, and national offices in considerable numbers. What is more, blacks of all socioeconomic strata have been included in U.S. social policies, rather than left out altogether, as most were previously. Yet this inclusion, occurring during a period of new black political rights and mobilization, has also brought ironic consequences, especially for those African American single mothers who find themselves at the vortex of intense—and apparently endless—controversies over "welfare reform."

The Civil Rights revolution of the 1950s to the mid-1960s brought southern blacks into the electorate for the first time since the post–Civil War interlude of African American suffrage. This change, along with massive postwar migrations of blacks into northern cities, transformed black voters into a major factor in the urban and the presidential electoral coalitions of the Democratic Party. At the same time, both the Civil Rights movement and its northern spin-offs aroused black groups and white liberal sympathizers to demand reworkings and extensions of U.S. public policies to include the black poor, whether rural or urban.

Many of the policy innovations of the sixties and seventies certainly occurred quite apart from any efforts of the Democrats to appease newly mobilized blacks. For the War on Poverty, reformist professionals took advantage of the coming to power of the Democrats in the early sixties to launch new federal programs to reach "the poor" and "pockets of the unemployed" who were obviously left out of U.S. social provision even in an era of economic prosperity.[31] Taking advantage of antipoverty ferment, the Social Security Administration put through long-gestated plans for Medicare and Medicaid in 1965. And during the presidency of Republican Richard Nixon, policy advocates in Washington, D.C., were still using the rhetoric of "fighting poverty" to put through innovations such as the indexing of Social Security, extension of eligibility for Food Stamps, and the nationalization of minimum support for the elderly.

But efforts to help "the poor" soon became understood by many reformers and citizens as efforts targeted on underprivileged blacks. The Democratic Party and Democratic President Lyndon Johnson sought ways to incorporate new black voters, and they wanted to propitiate black protest movements that, after the Civil Rights movement moved north, increasingly highlighted issues of racial economic disadvantage. Starting with Watts in 1965, racial riots in cities across the nation spurred state and local authories in many places to conciliate blacks—at times, by expanding access to AFDC and establishing social services for the urban poor to be run by African American pubic employees.[32]

Between the mid-1960s and the mid-1970s there occurred what antipoverty historian James Patterson has called an "explosion" in social welfare. The sheer numbers enrolled in Aid to Families with Dependent Children grew from 4.3 million in 1965 to 6.1 million in 1969 to 10.8 million in 1974.[33] Public expenditures also grew enormously. To be sure—and this is worth underlining—the bulk of expanded social expenditures in this period went for non-means-tested programs, including Social Security and Medicare for the elderly and Unemployment Insurance for previously regularly employed covered workers. "But [means-tested] public aid also rose during these years, accounting for 1.3 percent of the GNP in 1950, 1.9 percent in 1968, and 2.8 percent in 1974. Public assistance payments per recipient increased both in constant dollars and in comparison to average wage rates."[34] In-kind means-tested aid to the poor, such as Medicaid, Food Stamps, and public housing, accounted for even bigger public social spending increases than did increases in cash welfare.

African Americans were helped considerably by the innovations and expansions in U.S. social provision during the 1960s and 1970s. Regularly employed middle- and working-class African Americans benefited, of course, from improvements in social insurance. And we need to keep in mind that a certain amount of black upward occupational mobility in this period was due to the expansion of public social service jobs.[35] Also, many blacks were among the elderly Americans whose economic lot was improved more than any other group in society by the operations of Supplemental Security Income, Medicare and Medicaid, and improvements in Social Security for low-wage retired workers and their dependents. African American elderly people are still three times more likely to be poor than white elderly people, but since the 1970s the elderly no longer predominate in the ranks of the American poor.[36]

Instead, single mothers with children crowd the ranks of the poor. While not pulled out of neediness, impoverished single mothers of all races were significantly helped by the massive expansions of means-tested cash and in-kind transfers that occurred mostly between the mid-1960s and the mid-1970s. The positive effects were especially important for blacks, among whom poverty has become substantially "feminized." According to Reynolds Farley, in "1959 two-thirds of the impoverished blacks were members of husband-wife families and about one-fourth were in families headed by women. By 1980 the situation had reversed: about 60 percent lived in families headed by women and one-fourth lived in husband-wife families."[37] In general, single-mother-headed families are more prevalent among African Americans (and Hispanics) than among whites, and the nonwhite single mothers are more likely to be enrolled in AFDC than are white single mothers.[38]

But if African Americans were greatly helped by the 1960s to 1970s expansion of U.S. social policies that provided them more access, more benefits, and more public-sector employment, then it is also true that blacks were put in an increasingly awkward situation when political backlashes undermined popular and official support for the expanded American welfare state. From 1964 onward, conservative and Republican politicians began to take advantage of racial tensions within the late–New Deal Democratic electoral coalition.[39] As African American voters became more numerous, and realigned into the Democratic camp, and as protest movements demanded more economic leverage and social benefits for blacks, white southern voters and many white ethnic working-class voters grew restive about liberal Democratic attempts to use the regulatory and spending powers of the federal government to help the poor and/or blacks. The institutional limits that Margaret Weir has pointed to were crucial, because they cut off possibilities for creating a truly universal full-employment welfare state—devoted to providing broad benefits to all working families, rather than just expanded programs for the poor.[40] Liberal Democrats, in effect, asked their most beleaguered working-class supporters to bear heightened costs to pay for benefits for "the poor" (such as Medicaid) that sometimes were unavailable to their own families. The working-class Democrats were mostly white, while the poor getting improved benefits were disproportionately black and Hispanic.

The liberal Democratic and moderate Republican social policy expansions of the 1960s and early 1970s were not anywhere near enough to overcome black poverty and un- or underemployment. But occurring in a context of slow economic growth, high inflation, and tax bracket "creep," they were enough to arouse resentment among white working-class people, many of whose votes helped to bring Ronald Reagan and the conservative Republicans to national power in 1980. The Reagan administration accepted the continued growth of generous "social security" for the elderly, while it cut some "welfare" programs and slowed the growth of others (in effect, bringing about real economic cuts). States cut or slowed the growth of welfare, too. Moreover, the symbolic changes were as important as the material ones, and perhaps portended worse material effects for blacks in the future—for Reagan and his supporters engaged in public rhetoric that functioned to delegitimate a strong governmental role in social welfare and to make "welfare handouts" seem downright dishonorable. African Americans could not help but see Reaganism as threatening, for both middle-class and poor blacks had gained a strong stake in public social expenditures and services in the aftermath of the Great Society and the Nixon reforms.

Single mothers on Aid to Families with Dependent Children were, by the late 1980s, in an increasingly tenuous position. The consensus about "helping the poor" that had seemed to be there two decades before had changed into an increasingly obvious agreement between conservatives and neoliberals that future reforms should aim to "reduce welfare dependency." Larger shifts in public opinion than those associated with the "Reagan revolution" may well lie behind this consensus. One factor surely must be middle-class uneasiness (mostly white uneasiness) about the changing characteristics of AFDC recipients: "In 1973, the largest single welfare category used to be women who were separated or divorced; now it consists of mothers who have never married," most of whom are blacks.[41] Whether or not AFDC actually encourages out-of-wedlock childbearing, the structure of this social program tends to make this phenomenon more visible and its racial associations more apparent than would be the case if, for example, the United States had developed the sorts of universal "family allowances" that emerged in many other industrial capitalist democracies between the 1930s and the 1950s.

Another factor affecting changing attitudes toward AFDC may be the rise of modern feminist consciousness, which emphasizes equality between men and women, and the need to create "equal opportunities" for women to do paid work. The ideal mix of roles for middle-class women has changed sharply in America, and this tends to affect what public opinion wants to see happen in "welfare." Back when mothers' pensions were originally established in the 1910s, the women's movements of the day stressed that female domesticity and motherhood were an honorable kind of work. Federations of married middle-class ladies argued that public policy for poor mothers should enable them to avoid low-wage drudgery in order stay home and raise their children. That was seen as "service" to the community and the nation. But now, poor mothers on Aid to Families with Dependent

Children (the policy granddaughter of mothers' pensions) are criticized for being the "nonworking poor."[42] While it is true that modern feminists are rarely the ones who voice this criticism, nevertheless general changes in public opinion about middle-class women's roles probably make it easier for conservatives to advocate forcing AFDC recipients into "workfare"— with barely any attention to what will happen to their responsibilities as mothers if they are forced to work at all-day, all-week, all-year minimum-wage jobs. Current critics of welfare dependency often speak as if single mothers should be expected to function as traditional fathers and traditional mothers at the same time, combining full-time breadwinning with full-time parental responsibility. Yet only 27 percent of all married women who work do so in full-time positions.[43]

It is hard to avoid the conclusion that for AFDC mothers there is a special stigma in operation, stemming both from the nonwhiteness of about half the beneficiaries and from the relative dishonor that attaches to policies targeted on the poor. As Andrew Hacker points out,

> As it happens, one group of single mothers has been exempted from rules requiring employment. These are widows with school-age children, whose husbands had held steady jobs, and contributed every payday to their Social Security account. Women in this position do not have to apply for welfare, nor are they expected to become self-supporting. Since they cannot be held responsible for the demise of their husbands, the Social Security law entitles them to full "survivor's" benefits. The presumption is that these stipends are not handouts, but were earned by dint of their husband's work. Currently, some 300,000 widows who have children are supported under this statute, and they can receive as much as $24,000 a year, more than four times the average AFDC award. If they choose to work, as many do, they still receive separate payments to assist their children. In short, they bear no stigma, nor do they have to apologize for living on public funds. Nor is this very surprising, since those receiving these Social Security benefits are overwhelmingly white.[44]

In short, the "worthy widows," who were the original beneficiaries of mothers' pensions, still exist as an honorable group within U.S. social provision; they were incorporated into Social Security in 1939. That they still do exist as an honorable category, despite the rise of new feminist ideals for women, is testimony to the power that New Deal ideals about "earned benefits" still have within contemporary American policy discourse. The problems that African Americans face in U.S. social provision today— problems ranging from the absence of employment programs to the inadequacies and stigma of welfare—are still, in many ways, traceable to the institutional limits of New Deal state building, and to the exclusion of most blacks from core Social Security programs created for (only certain kinds of) wage earners and their dependents.

The Future of American Social Policies

In 1992, a new Democratic president of the United States took office, the first in over a decade, and one who clearly hoped to overcome the racial tensions about domestic policy that helped undermine his Democratic predecessors in presidential politics since the mid-1960s. In his campaign for the presidency, Bill Clinton promised to "put people first," but he had very little to say about poverty or programs to help African Americans. He also vowed to get rid of welfare "as we know it," and promised not to raise middle-class taxes.[45] How should African Americans, particularly the less privileged, including single mothers on welfare, regard the Clinton presidency and the "race-neutral" policy preferences of the Democratic Party in the 1990s?[46] From a historical perspective, there are two possible readings of what may happen to blacks and social policy under this new Democratic leadership.

The pessimistic reading would look back to the nonracial, economistic liberalism of the New Deal.[47] From this point of view, Democrats obsessed with winning and holding white votes in the national electorate are quite willing to push black interests to the side, especially any black interests than seem contradictory to what key constituencies of whites are demanding. Of course, things are different electorally in the 1990s than they were in the 1930s. African American voters are a vital minority within Democratic Party presidential coalitions, and the South is no longer a white racial oligarchy. But a pessimist about moderate Democrats who downplay talk of race and pro-black progams might still predict that they will favor white taxpayers over black welfare clients, and that they will emphasize social and economic reforms that help business and the middle class, if necessary, at the expense of the poor.

Yet there is also another, more optimistic reading of what President Clinton, Hillary Rodham Clinton, and various other progressive social reformers are trying to do. Perhaps an effort is under way to build a new broad coalition—cross-class and cross-racial—in support of public sector initiatives to help all children and families in America. Perhaps efforts are under way to change the categories of public discourse about social provision, away from the New Deal's opposition of "Social Security" versus "welfare," and toward new ideals of "leaving no child behind" and helping all Americans who "play by the rules," combining work and responsible parenting in one way or another. Relevant programs favored by today's progressives include measures as wage supplements for low-wage workers; improved job training and retraining for all American workers; child support for all single custodial parents; access to health care for all American families; and assistance to working families in obtaining child care.

Were programs such as these to be put into effect, less-privileged African Americans would undoubtedly benefit enormously.[48] Low-wage male workers would have an easier time helping to sustain a family. And single mothers would surely be happy to say good-bye to "welfare as we know it," trading it in for part-time work with reasonable wages and access to health care, along with honorable and predictable child support payments (ideally similar to the survivor's insurance of Social Security).[49] Perhaps most important, single mothers—African Americans and all others—would escape relegation to a dishonorable category of persons receiving "unearned benefits," for all single mothers would combine paid work and public support. And the public support they received, like the mothers' pensions of old, would acknowledge the value to the community and nation of the work they do as parents.

I acknowledge that the optimistic reading I have just sketched about the possibilities of progressive politics today is unlikely to be realized immediately. The victories by conservative Republicans in the 1994 congressional elections have shifted debates over welfare reform sharply to the right. President Clinton can articulate moderate, racially inclusive ideals, but he cannot enact them. In any event, this hopeful reading is the formula for a *possible* eventual improvement in the relationship of African Americans to U.S. social provision that follows from the historical analysis I have presented in this essay. A look back over the sweep of the history of modern U.S. social policies reveals that African Americans have always done best—gotten the most material help for the least stigma—when they have been part of broad, victorious political coalitions, and when they have been included in the most honorable categories of social beneficiaries in any given era. Let us hope that the day will come when all African Americans—and indeed all Americans—will be so included.

TABLE 6.A
African Americans during Major Eras of U.S. Social Policy

Factors Influencing Social Policy	*Civil War Era, 1865–1900*	*Maternalist Era, 1900–1920s*
Major innovations or expansions	Federal and state Civil War benefits for Union Soldiers and survivors	Maternalist regulations, benefits, services (state and federal)
Political actors	Party politicians Male voters Veterans' federations	Professional reformers Married women's federations
Institutional context	Patronage democracy Electoral competition Republican hegemony	Bipartisan public opinion Emulation across states Court acceptance of some laws
Honorable beneficiaries	"Saviors of the Union"	Mothers and their children
African American Situation		
Labor force and regional position	Former slaves, becoming sharecroppers; most in South, except some free northern blacks	Sharecroppers in South; slightly increasing flow of migrants to unskilled labor in northern cities
Political rights	Gained right to fight for the Union late in the Civil War; gained voting rights, then lost them	Forcibly excluded from voting and civil rights in the South
Included in honorable beneficiaries?	Yes: black Union veterans and survivors No: most southern former slaves (except for brief efforts of Freedmen's Bureau)	Northern blacks were marginally included; Southern blacks were virtually all excluded

TABLE 6.A (*cont.*)

Factors Influencing Social Policy	New Deal Era, 1930s–1950s	Era of "Welfare" Controversies 1960s–1990s?
Major innovations or expansions	Social Security Act (insurance for nonagricultural employees; terms of public assistance left to states)	War on Poverty; Food Stamps, Social Security/SSI improvements, Medicare and Medicaid AFDC expansions
Political actors	FDR and Democratic Party New Deal reformers Various protest movements, especially Townsend	Civil Rights and Black Power groups Social Security Administration and federations of the elderly Professional policy advocates
Institutional context	Electoral realignment toward and within Democratic Party Congressional compromises with stronger Executive	Liberal hegemony (brief) in 1960s Proliferation of advocacy groups and "issue networks" Conservative backlash among whites benefits Republicans
Honorable beneficiaries	Retired wage earners and their dependents Unwillingly unemployed (during 1930s only)	Elderly (all of them) "The poor" very briefly honorable; then backlash sets in against "nonworkers" and "welfare mothers"
African American Situation		
Labor force and regional position	Most remain sharecroppers or service workers; some in unskilled industrial jobs Exodus from rural South, 1940s–50s	Massive exodus from rural South and sharecropping, to urban areas, including northern cities; two-thirds remain working class or poor
Political rights	Southern blacks cannot vote or safely organize; Northern blacks, from 1936, begin voting Democratic	African Americans gain voting rights in all parts of the nation; black officials are elected in South and North
Included in honorable beneficiaries?	Most at first excluded from social insurance (farm and service jobs not covered); most excluded from public assistance in South.	Less privileged blacks are caught in controversies over welfare and other measures to help the poor

Notes

1. Amenta and Skocpol 1989.
2. Katz 1986, pt. 1.
3. Skocpol 1992.
4. Ibid., introduction.
5. Ibid., pt. 1 offers full documentation on Civil War pensions.
6. McMurry 1922; Sanders 1980.
7. Skowronek 1982.
8. Baker 1984.
9. For full details, see Skocpol 1992, pt. 3.
10. Amenta and Skocpol 1988.
11. Amenta and Zylan 1991.
12. Patterson 1967.
13. Skocpol and Amenta 1985; Weir and Skocpol 1985; and Amenta and Skocpol 1988.
14. Weir 1992.
15. Mulderink 1988.
16. See Skocpol 1992, 596 n. 131. For new research on these issues, see Donald R. Shaffer, "The Quest for Security: Black Union Veterans in the U.S. Civil War Pension System," paper presented at the Organization of American Historians, Washington, D.C., March 31, 1995.
17. Cornish 1956.
18. Howard 1992, 201.
19. Covotsos 1976, 123. For more on Lathrop, see Skocpol 1992, chap. 9.
20. Meckel 1990, 212.
21. Higginbotham 1993.
22. Gordon 1991.
23. Robertson 1912.
24. Sitkoff 1978, chap. 3.
25. Weiss 1983.
26. McAdam 1982, 73–81.
27. Quoted in Weiss 1983, 166.
28. Quadagno 1988a, 246. Eventually the southern states became willing to give somewhat more generous federally subsidized pensions to needy blacks—but only from the 1950s onward, when mechanization of cotton cropping had reduced their need for black labor, and after migrations of young blacks to the North had left "too many" dependent elderly people in the South.
29. Cates 1983.
30. W. Wilson 1987.
31. Patterson 1981, chap. 7.
32. Brown and Erie 1981.
33. Patterson 1981, 171.
34. Ibid., 164.
35. Brown and Erie 1981; Hout 1984.

36. Farley 1984, 161.
37. Ibid.
38. Hacker 1992, 86.
39. Carmines and Stimson 1989; Edsall and Edsall 1991b.
40. Weir 1992.
41. Hacker 1992, 86.
42. Mead 1992.
43. Hacker 1992, 90.
44. Ibid., 91–92.
45. Clinton and Gore 1992.
46. W. Wilson 1990.
47. Kirby 1980.
48. Skocpol 1991.
49. Garfinkel 1992.

7

Race and the Organization of Welfare Policy

ROBERT C. LIEBERMAN

MOST ACCOUNTS of racial classification in American politics ascribe the problems of racial division and stratification either to individual and collective attitudes or to underlying social and economic factors. The politics of race, in these accounts, appears as a horrible deviation from America's true liberal and pluralist path. But the persistence of racial classification as a force in American political life suggests that rather than a grim mistake, racial politics is built into the structure of American politics more profoundly than we would like to admit. In his eloquent essay "Many Thousands Gone," James Baldwin maintains that American identity is to its very core steeped in race. "Our dehumanization of the Negro," he writes, "is indivisible from our dehumanization of ourselves; the loss of our own identity is the price we pay for our annulment of his."[1] So in politics as well. We cannot overcome the boundaries that racial classification has imposed on our political institutions because without those boundaries, our politics would be something else altogether.

Among the strands of American political development most mired in racial conflict is the growth of the welfare state. The American welfare system is barely a system at all. It is a fragmented array of programs that serve different groups of people, with funding and administration at a variety of levels of government. The face that this welfare state, such as it is, presents to African Americans is dramatically different from the far friendlier one it shows to white Americans.[2] And yet many of the most important elements of the American welfare state trace their roots to a common origin, the Social Security Act of 1935, which had a unified goal of alleviating poverty caused by factors beyond individual control, such as age, unemployment, or widowhood. How and why did these policies diverge so widely from the same source to create today's racially segmented system of social policy? To answer this question requires a consideration of race as a fundamental problem of institutional development, rather than simply one of interpersonal or intergroup relations. Racial classification in civic life is not only a construction of institutions and policy; it plays a role in constructing them as well.[3]

This essay considers the impact of race as a structural factor in the development of American social policy and its administration by considering two of these policies: Old Age Insurance and Aid to Dependent Children (with some consideration of Old Age Assistance, which was at its inception structurally similar to Aid to Dependent Children). The comparison between these two policies will examine the proposition that the racial structure of American society and politics has impeded the growth of a unified administrative state. The examination focuses on the effects of the racial balance among potential beneficiaries of the programs on the policy choices on 1935 and looks at the arguments offered by actors in the debate on the Social Security Act to defend their preferences. By manipulating the terms of the legislation, the Congress created both a strong national old-age insurance system that systematically excluded most African Americans and, at the same time, a weak and decentralized system of public assistance that, while open to black recipients, invited discrimination.

The comparison does not suggest, however, that these outcomes came about simply because policy makers had racist intentions, although some of them probably did. Rather, it suggests that the structure of racial classification that underlay American, and particularly southern, politics in the 1930s provided social groups and political actors with incentives to make particular choices in designing new social policy institutions, institutions that have since had profound consequences for both social welfare and racial politics. This structural approach to the politics of race differs from most approaches to racial classification in American politics, which take race as a characteristic of individuals and groups and ask how this characteristic affects the experience of African Americans in the American political system. The structural approach asks neither how African Americans behave in politics nor how politics affects African Americans particularly, but how the existence of racial classification in American society has shaped the development of American institutions, policy, and political behavior.[4]

Race and Institutional Development

The New Deal was a pivotal moment in the evolution of the American national state, an era that has been a perplexing problem for students of American political development. In his pioneering work, Stephen Skowronek demonstrated the important limitations imposed on the United States by its relatively "stateless" past, dominated not by nationalizing central institutions but by the decentralizing influences of courts and parties.[5] Subsequent work has focused on the development of the relatively stunted American welfare state in the wake of the transformation that Skowronek describes. Much of this work has emphasized the failure of American development to emulate European development, particularly the absence of socialism in the United States and the consequent absence of political pressure for state-oriented solutions to the economic ills of industrial capitalism. But these approaches, like Skowronek's, reveal more about what the American state did not become than what it has become.

Theda Skocpol offers an essential corrective to this outlook in her work on the American welfare state.[6] Like Skowronek, she emphasizes the characteristics of American politics—notably the system of patronage-based mass political parties and the pattern of voluntary organizations—that account for particular features of the state. She rightly criticizes earlier work on the American welfare state for assuming, implicitly or explicitly, that "the modern welfare state" is a universal category, "inherently progressive, growing in recognizable stages in all industrializing and urbanizing nations," and she rejects the rather facile premise that if only the United States had had a proper working-class party, it would have developed a European-style, comprehensive welfare state. Skocpol's most fundamental insight is her insistence that explanations of institutional development focus on what *is* there, rather than what is not, and Skocpol rightly makes much of the structure of the American state, the party system, the legacies of past policies, and gender lines in politics and society to account for the peculiar development of the American welfare state.

But surely no feature of American political history is more present, or more distinctive, than the presence on this continent, almost since the beginning of European settlement, of two races, juxtaposed with each other in hierarchical legal, political, economic, and social relations to varying degrees. Certainly no factor has been more prominent in American politics while receiving less systematic attention from students of American political development than has race. Since the Civil War emancipated over three million slaves, racial conflict has always been a central problem of American politics as whites have attempted to impose, and blacks have attempted to overcome, segregation, discrimination, and economic dependence, and yet there is little account of how this obsessive struggle has shaped our politics and our institutions.

Moreover, Skocpol's approach, while compelling, leaves open the question of administrative structure. The decision to enact a particular policy does not necessarily entail a particular decision about how to organize the administration of that policy. The structure of administrative institutions determines who benefits from a policy decision, whether it is fairly or capriciously applied, and whether politics or professionalism matters more in carrying it out. In the case of social policy, so fraught with consequences for economic and social status, the structure of administrative institutions can take on tremendous importance for racial classification. Moreover, policy decisions and their institutional consequences play a crucial role in determining the political logic of a policy's future development. In fact, the question of administration was an important theme in the debates on the Social Security Act, perhaps as important as the content of the policies that it enacted.

The focus on the administrative structure of policies as well as on their content arises from James Q. Wilson's assertion that "organization matters."[7] If race contributed to the structure of social policy, then as the racial pattern of policy beneficiaries varies, we should observe differences across policies in their organization and operation. This connection between race and administration is, I suggest, more consequential than the more straightforward racial differentiation that can occur in legislative policy making. While statutes can be altered and policies amended, administrative institutions, once established, are harder to change. These institutions establish patterns of procedure, behavior, and expectations that can have an important impact on subsequent developments.[8]

Race influenced two critically important structural dimensions of the Social Security Act in particular: the level of governmental control and the extent of coverage under the policies. The framers of the Social Security Act hoped to establish a comprehensive and coordinated program of economic security under the close direction of the federal government. While they built on a foundation of state welfare programs, they anticipated that centralized direction would "be an instrument for improving standards in backward States" and for improving the reach and adequacy of public assistance.[9] But in promoting strong centralized controls over the administration of welfare, they ran up against resilient structures of localism. The New Deal had already demonstrated that federal direction could overcome some racial bias in the administration of emergency relief, so southerners had an interest in maintaining tight local control over any new social policy initiatives. To the extent that African Americans had any political power in the 1930s, it was in the cities of the North that were an essential part of Franklin Roosevelt's electoral coalition; the southern congressional barons did not answer to them. These factors suggest that the level of administration was an important racial battleground in the development of welfare policy.

On the inclusion dimension, the central issue was the status of agricultural and domestic workers. The administration's proposed Social Security bill excluded from Old Age Insurance and Unemployment Compensation coverage only government employees and railroad workers, almost all of whom were already covered by public pension plans. These categories totaled slightly over four million workers. To these exclusions Congress added another seven million workers, five million of whom worked in agriculture or domestic service. Not only were these the largest categories of

excluded workers, but they received the most attention and were acknowl-
edged at the time to be the most consequential for the Social Security program.[10] They also included an enormous share of the African Americans in
the labor force. Thus debate over these groups was perforce debate over the
racial structure of the welfare system.

Along both dimensions, policies were designed to undermine the New
Deal's universalistic aims in a racially biased way. Moreover, the two dimensions were linked by racial considerations. To pass a centralized, nationally administered old-age insurance program, the Roosevelt administration had to accept the exclusion of agricultural and domestic employees
from the program, with notably imbalanced racial consequences. At the
same time, Congress eased proposed federal controls over state administration of the public assistance programs on which poor African Americans
would be forced to rely. The racial structure of American society and politics rendered the enactment of racially inclusive, nationally administered
social policies impossible in the 1930s. Many factors clearly contributed to
the divergence of institutional structure between these two antipoverty policies created under the same legislative umbrella, among them constitutional objections; class, labor market, and administrative considerations;
and the legacies of past policies. But there is strong evidence that race
played more than an incidental role in structuring the American welfare
state at one of its critical founding moments.

An enterprise of this kind raises important questions of evidence and
inference in assessing the extent to which race was a decisive or even influential factor in these decisions. In this century, race has often been subtext
rather than text, and racial motivations, even when real, have frequently
gone unexpressed. Even the most assiduous historical research is not likely
to uncover explicit acknowledgment that the desire to maintain racial supremacy was a motivating factor behind behavior. But the argument is not
that individuals self-consciously acted from racist motives, although they
may have done so. It is, rather, that the structural position of racial groups
in society affects the motivations and behavior of political actors and that
political actions may arise as a consequence, whether intended or unintended, of the racial structure of society.[11]

To establish the effect of race on the design of the Social Security Act,
I rely principally on two kinds of evidence. The first is numerical data,
mostly from the census, about the extent to which the bill, in its initial and
final forms, included or excluded blacks from the population of potential
beneficiaries of the different programs. These data identify, with reasonable accuracy, the racial imbalances that resulted from the Social Security
Act and document that at the very least the outcome of the debate is consistent with a race-based interpretation. The comparison between the
Roosevelt administration's proposal and the law that Congress enacted

will allow an assessment of the racial consequences of congressional action in the two policies. Contrasting the two policies will allow an examination of the reasons that politics produced such widely varying administrative forms.

The second source of evidence is the historical record of the debates, both public and private, over the essential issues, and it is this evidence that points more directly to a link between racial concerns and administration. The documentary record can tell us several things. First, it reveals who was concerned about the relevant issues. By and large, it was members of Congress from the South and border states, where racial concerns were central to politics and the political economy, who raised questions and voiced concerns about these matters, even though the data show that the racial effects were by no means limited to the South. Second, this material reveals what kind of arguments actors made in support of their positions. Arguments based on local prerogative, often couched in the language of states' rights and sovereignty and ranging from skepticism to contempt in their attitudes toward the federal government, surfaced regularly, and coming from the mouths of southerners, such arguments must constitute strong circumstantial evidence that racial concerns were prominent, if not preeminent. Third, the testimony and opinions of black political leaders reveals what African Americans (or at least African American elites) considered to be in their interest. Their testimony corroborates an important assumption, namely that African Americans would have been better served by more inclusive, nationally administered policies. Finally, the record also reveals the alternatives that were rejected in favor of the outcomes that were chosen, offering a basis for comparing actual with possible outcomes.

Historians, political scientists, and sociologists have often noted racial disparities that resulted from the Social Security Act.[12] Several, especially Jill Quadagno, have stressed the racial structure of the South's distinctive political economy to account for the racial divisions in the Social Security Act.[13] Southern society combined labor-repressive agriculture with racial disenfranchisement and segregation to subdue African Americans both economically and politically. The hegemony of the Democratic Party in the South—built on these twin pillars of planter dominance and racial disenfranchisement—and the institutional structure of Congress combined to give white southerners both a strong interest in directing new social benefits away from African Americans and power beyond their numbers in the federal government, power they used to protect their racial and economic dominance of southern society. But the racially shaped welfare policies of the New Deal did more than simply exclude African Americans from benefits; they created institutions that carried the racial legacy of their origins, with profound consequences for both African Americans and the shape of the American welfare state.

Roosevelt and the Origins of Social Security

President Roosevelt raised the issue of federal-state relations in a special message to Congress in June 1934, in which he sketched the rough outlines of an economic security policy.[14]

> I believe there should be a maximum of cooperation between States and the Federal Government. . . . Above all, I am convinced that States should meet at least a large portion of the cost of management, leaving to the Federal Government the responsibility of investing, maintaining, and safeguarding the funds constituting the necessary insurance resources.[15]

Although he left it to the Committee on Economic Security (CES), appointed three weeks later, to fill in these rather vague outlines, his preference for federal-state cooperation guided the committee's deliberations and helped shape the resulting legislation.

Roosevelt had good reasons to suggest that a purely federal program would be unacceptable. Perhaps most important, Congress would never pass legislation creating such a program. The Congress was largely dominated by southerners, some more conservative than others, but generally united in their skepticism of excessive federal domination of domestic policy to the exclusion of state and local governments. V. O. Key demonstrates that while the image of southern solidarity against the nation during the New Deal is somewhat exaggerated, Southern members did coalesce reliably on issues of perceived federal intervention, especially those touching on race relations.[16] Roosevelt could ill afford to alienate powerful southern committee chairmen, and he perceived the South not only as an essential piece of his electoral coalition but also as his adopted home because of his deep emotional ties to Warm Springs, Georgia.[17]

But congressional politics aside, there were other reasons for the president to propose a cooperative federal-state economic security program. The federal government of the 1930s was poorly equipped to administer public assistance to individual citizens on anything like the scale he contemplated. Grants-in-aid to the states, on the other hand, were by then commonplace, existing in areas such as highway construction, vocational education, and public health.[18] The Supreme Court, too, loomed as an apparent obstacle to the extension of federal policy. Although the Court had on occasion upheld state regulatory power, the challenge to the federal enactments of the First New Deal was mounting. The constitutionality of the act's expansion of federal responsibility was an important concern of the framers of the Social Security Act, and there was tremendous uncertainty about the path the Court would take, uncertainty that would explode into despair before the act's passage with the overturning of the NRA the following spring.[19] Finally, the notion that states should tailor social policy to local conditions was congenial to the Brandeisian ethic of decentralization and policy experimentation that would overtake the doctrine of national planning in the transition from the First to the Second New Deal.[20]

For these reasons, and perhaps for others, Roosevelt proposed a cooperative federal-state security program. But his message to Congress and his charge to the Committee on Economic Security set forth only this broad directive along with the principle, only marginally more specific, that the states should participate in administration while the federal government should handle the money. The sticky work of translating these statements into concrete policy he left to the CES and the Congress, and the proper balance between state and federal responsibility—the power that the federal government would exert over state policy and practices—became an important and contentious issue in the deliberations of the next fourteen months.

The boundaries of inclusion and exclusion in the various provisions of the act were not so public or cataclysmic an issue, but their consequences were at least as great. The two largest categories of workers ultimately excluded from old-age insurance were agricultural workers and domestic service workers (household servants). While there were barely any black farmers in the North, farm labor of some sort was the most common occupation for blacks in the South; just over half of the southern black labor force in 1930 worked in agriculture.[21] The exclusion of domestic workers, however, affected blacks throughout the country. Despite a decline after World War I in the demand for black domestic labor, domestic service was still the second most common occupation for black Americans, and the most common outside the South.[22] The decision to exclude these workers from the employment-related provisions of the act had important effects on the evolving shape of federal social policy and its administrative institutions.

There was precedent for such selective coverage in social insurance programs. Nonindustrial workers had been excluded from the workmen's compensation laws that most states adopted in the 1910s and 1920s. But it was specifically industrial conditions that gave rise to these laws, which were intended both to prevent industrial accidents and compensate their victims for wages lost as a result.[23] More than half of the other countries with compulsory, contributory old-age insurance systems covered farm workers and domestics.[24] Roosevelt did not conceive of Social Security as a protection against industrial dangers but against the "hazards and vicissitudes of life," dangers that were not restricted to industrial workers. "There is no reason," he told Frances Perkins, why everybody in the United States should not be covered. I see no reason why every child, from the day he is born, shouldn't be a member of the social security system. . . . And there is no reason why just the industrial workers should get the benefit of this. Everybody ought to be in on it—the farmer and his wife and his family.[25]

The president maintained this position, although he did not press the issue, even after the legislation had passed and undergone its first major amendment. Later in the 1930s and during World War II, he called for the inclusion of uncovered workers in the old-age insurance system.[26] Roosevelt's conception of a social security program was clearly a program that would address the economic security of all Americans, regardless of race or occupation.

Administration and Exclusion in the Development of the Social Security Act

In the wake of his message to Congress, President Roosevelt created the Committee on Economic Security in late June 1934. With the secretary of labor as its chairman, the committee consisted as well of the secretaries of agriculture and the treasury, the attorney general, and the federal emergency relief administrator. In its deliberations, which stretched through the summer and fall and on into the winter of 1934–35, the Committee on Economic Security considered the extent of coverage that was desirable. The members and staff of the committee accepted the president's stated preference for universal coverage, and the question became one of feasibility—how difficult would it be to administer a program of economic security that included not just industrial workers but farmers, servants, the self-employed, and other categories that might pose particular problems?

The committee's staff, which tended to be more attuned to potential administrative problems than were its cabinet-level members, was divided on the possibility of including agricultural and domestic workers in the Social Security programs. While many agreed with the president's goal of universal coverage, some influential staff members were pessimistic about the feasibility of adopting a European tax-collection system that would have facilitated the administration of unemployment insurance to farmers and servants. Others worried that including farm and other seasonal workers might force their employers to pay taxes for employees who would never be eligible to collect benefits because they did not work enough weeks out of the year.[27]

In its initial draft of a report and proposed legislation, the staff recom-

mended the exclusion of agricultural and domestic workers, but the committee itself, led by Frances Perkins and Federal Emergency Relief administrator Harry Hopkins, supported full inclusion.[28] "We are opposed," the
committee stated in its final report, "to exclusions of any specified industries from the Federal act." And later, "we recommend that the contributory
annuity system include, on a compulsory basis, *all* manual workers and
nonmanual workers earning less than $250 per month." The committee
also addressed directly the particular problems of groups at the margin of
the economy.

> Agricultural workers, domestic servants, home workers, and the many self-em-
> ployed people constitute large groups in the population who have generally re-
> ceived little attention. In these groups are many who are at the very bottom of the
> economic scale. We believe that more attention will have to be given to these
> groups than they have received heretofore. We cannot be satisfied that we have a
> reasonably complete program for economic security unless some degree of pro-
> tection is given these groups now generally neglected.[29]

The committee's report reflected the president's desire for universal coverage. It paid particular attention to the needs of these politically powerless,
economically marginal workers and thus, at least indirectly, to the plight of
African Americans.

The extent of federal control over the economic security system received
more attention in the committee's deliberations. In general, the committee's aim was to ensure adequate benefits nationwide, promote maximum
uniformity from state to state, and encourage professional and competent
administration of the various programs that might be established, and it
tried to square these aims with the president's preference for federal-state
cooperation. As a rule, these goals called for more rather than less federal
control of Social Security programs, but on this issue the committee took
more serious account of the political problems that might ensue. The principal barrier to an entirely federal system that the committee members fore-
saw was constitutional. Social policy advocates had severe doubts about
how far the Supreme Court would be willing to go in allowing federal
innovation, and this was an important consideration in the committee's
decisions. A second barrier to a federal system was politics. Perkins re-
marked that where "state jealousies and aspirations were involved," Congress would be unlikely to accept a system of social insurance that gave the
federal government too much power.[30] The economic security bill it prepared struck an artful balance between the administration's concerns with
adequacy, comprehensiveness, and administrative competence and the anticipated concerns of Congress and the courts. Still, the scheme was a risky
proposition both constitutionally and politically.

On old-age insurance, the CES's staff was unanimous in advising the committee against a state-by-state program because of the tremendous difficulty involved in tracking millions of individual workers and their tax payments over their entire careers in a highly mobile population. The committee preferred to propose a strictly national program it thought constitutional by relying on the scope of the federal government's power to tax and spend.[31] For the various public assistance programs—programs for the aged, the blind, and dependent children, which many states had already established—the committee proposed grants-in-aid to the states. This part of the committee's recommendation was developed, according to Arthur J. Altmeyer, chairman of the CES Technical Board and later of the Social Security Board, "without the necessity for extended consideration," but not without a staff study on the mechanisms available for federal control of state expenditures under grant-in-aid programs, including the power to withhold federal contributions for noncompliance.[32] The committee's provisions for federal control of public assistance programs would be among the most contentious issues in the congressional debate on the bill.

Congress, the South, and Social Security

The legislation the Committee on Economic Security proposed along with its final report in January 1935 was structurally much the same as the bill that the president would sign seven months later—national old-age insurance, cooperative federal-state unemployment insurance under a tax offset plan, and grants-in-aid to support state public assistance programs. There is little evidence to suggest that race played a direct role in the committee's considerations. But the Congress altered the legislation in several significant ways that suggest that race was a critical part of the political logic behind the mixed administrative design of the Social Security Act. The congressional amendments, in particular the exclusion of agricultural and domestic workers from certain programs and the loosening of federal control over public assistance, did not amount merely to tinkering around the edges. Rather, they fundamentally structured the Social Security programs to conform with, or at least not to conflict with, the basic fact of black economic dependence, particularly in the South.

The Social Security bill was introduced in the House by David Lewis of Maryland and Robert L. Doughton of North Carolina, chairman of the Ways and Means Committee, and in the Senate by Robert Wagner of New York. The House Ways and Means and Senate Finance Committees held hearings on the bill in January and February, compiling over two thousand pages of testimony. The House passed the legislation in April, the Senate in June, and the conference committee completed its work of reconciliation and compromise in August. On August 14, 1935, President Roosevelt signed the Social Security Act into law.

An important factor, perhaps the most important factor, in considering the impact of race on the shape of the legislation is the position of southerners in Congress. The pivotal structural position of the South in the Congress is, of course, a commonplace in the American political universe of the New Deal era.[33] Because of the South's one-party politics, southern congressional delegations were overwhelmingly Democratic, and individual southern Democrats, once elected, were nearly assured of reelection.[34] Because of the strict seniority system by which members of Congress were promoted to positions of power, southern Democrats tended to rise disproportionately to these positions, most notably as committee chairs, who were more powerful than ever in the 1930s due to the norms of committee autonomy and reciprocity that had developed in Congress over the preceding quarter century.[35] And regardless of their general political outlook, southerners tended to coalesce in opposition to racial liberalism and encroaching federal power.[36] As Roosevelt well understood, southern cooperation was essential to the success of the administration's legislative agenda, and southern votes were essential to the coalition that had nominated and elected him.

Specifically, southerners played pivotal roles in the passage of the Social Security Act. Southern Democrats held a commanding position on the Senate Finance Committee. Chairman Pat Harrison of Mississippi was a key administration leader in the Senate. Out of fifteen Democrats, six were from the Deep South and three more were from border states. On a committee of twenty-one members, this group held formidable power. Chairman Doughton of the Ways and Means Committee had somewhat weaker ties with the administration, but he too took an active role in promoting the legislation.[37] Only four of the eighteen Democrats (on a twenty-five member committee) were southerners, and another four were from border states.

But southerners were not, as they are often portrayed, monolithically conservative during the New Deal. It is true that many southern Democrats were among the most vehement critics of the New Deal, but all southerners were not conservative, nor were all conservative members of Congress from the South.[38] But the South was of two minds in its relationship with the New Deal. While always wary of expanding federal power, especially in areas like social policy that might undermine the South's racially stratified socioeconomic structure, the South desperately needed the New Deal's largesse. The Depression had worsened conditions in the already poor South, and the southern states had neither the programs nor the fiscal capacity to respond.[39] Hence southern members of Congress took a decidedly ambiguous stance toward the administration's Social Security proposal; they needed to capture as much as they could of the new federal spending for relief and social insurance while at the same time resisting the threat of racial interference and federal domination. Southerners and northerners alike recognized the New Deal's potential to undermine the traditional pattern of southern race relations.

The hearings of the Ways and Means and Finance Committees covered a variety of issues, from competing social insurance proposals such as the Townsend revolving old-age pension plan and the Lundeen proposal for federal unemployment relief, to the equity of the various taxes contemplated by the bill and the economic effect of building up large reserves in the old-age insurance account in the federal treasury. But the two issues under consideration here—occupational exclusions and federal control— took center stage, both because they led to the most far-reaching amendments to the administration's proposal and because they were raised almost exclusively by southerners.

The public record of the debate in the committees and on the floors of the chambers is, of course, imperfect and incomplete evidence of the intentions of the principal actors, especially because the key decisions were made and the bill rewritten in executive sessions of the committees, for which no official records exist. But a combination of factors indicates that race was at least one prominent factor that lay behind the arguments and decisions made by members of Congress. First, the issues that concerned the southern members of Congress were the issues that most directly affected the racial balance of the Social Security Act's operation. A careful examination of quantitative evidence will show that the changes that the southerners sought and won were far from racially neutral. Second, the kind of arguments offered by southerners, while not directly racial, indicate that race played a large role in shaping their positions. They relied primarily on arguments about state sovereignty and the limited powers of the federal government. These were claims of dubious constitutional and theoretical merit, increasingly associated since the Civil War with segregation to the exclusion of all other meaning. Southerners invoked states' rights arguments selectively and inconsistently during the 1930s, betraying their deep ambivalence about the New Deal and ultimately rendering states' rights merely a stand-in for white supremacy. Finally, although there was little vocal support for inclusion and federal control during the hearings or the floor debate, what support there was came from black groups such as the National Association for the Advancement of Colored People and the National Urban League, and inclusion of agricultural and domestic workers in Social Security programs became an important item on the political agenda of these groups in subsequent years.[40]

Old-Age Insurance

The question of the inclusion or exclusion of agricultural and domestic workers was argued most strenuously in the debate on compulsory, contributory old-age insurance. The CES's decision that these workers should be covered came under immediate and persistent questioning in the hearings, and the Ways and Means and Finance Committees' decisions to eliminate them from coverage came under attack as well. The terms of the debate are instructive because the arguments on the merits of the issue were generally a stalemate, with one important exception. The argument over the racial impact of excluding these workers went unanswered because it was unanswerable.

The most prominent argument against inclusion was based on administrative feasibility. It would be too difficult, critics argued, to devise a system to collect payroll taxes from workers who worked not for large industrial or commercial firms but, generally, for private individuals or small farmers. This argument was raised most tellingly by supporters of the legislation, particularly by Secretary of the Treasury Henry Morgenthau. Morgenthau told the Ways and Means Committee, apparently on the advice of the Bureau of Internal Revenue, that the Treasury Department already faced an "extremely formidable" task in devising a system to collect payroll taxes for Social Security. If agricultural, domestic, and casual workers were included, he said, "the task may well prove insuperable—certainly at the outset."[41] Morgenthau's testimony was something of a bombshell to his colleagues on the Committee on Economic Security, who had unanimously taken the opposite position on precisely this question.[42]

While advocating exclusion for administrative reasons, Morgenthau made it quite clear that he supported inclusion on philosophical grounds. "I want to point out here," he told the committee, "that personally I hope these three groups can be included." When Doughton and Vinson responded approvingly to Morgenthau's testimony, Representative John W. McCormack of Massachusetts answered that to exclude farmers and servants for administrative reasons would be to take "an attitude of defeatism." Recognizing that an affirmative act of Congress adding them to the program in the future would be difficult to achieve, if not impossible, McCormack suggested that they be included at the outset, but with a time lag of several years before coverage began, giving the Treasury Department ample time to devise a method of collection and reporting. To this proposal Morgenthau responded simply, "I would say that that would be ideal."[43]

While some advocates of inclusion recognized that the coverage of agricultural and domestic workers presented a potential administrative burden, others made a strong case for a tax collection system that could potentially overcome it. J. Douglas Brown, a Princeton economist who served as a staff consultant to the CES on old-age security, gave detailed testimony to the Ways and Means Committee on the stamp-book system for collecting payroll taxes, which was then in use in several European social insurance systems.[44] Under the stamp system, each employee would be issued a blank booklet into which employers would paste stamps purchased from the post office or some other government agency indicating the amount of payroll tax paid. Brown even included in his a testimony an example of a stamp book from the British system of contributory health insurance, which illustrated how a stamp system might work. Edwin E. Witte, the executive director of the CES, also referred to the stamp system as the most efficacious way of collecting taxes from groups such as domestic servants, and he suggested that there need not be a single system for the collection of taxes but that different systems might be used for different kinds of workers. The original administration bill, while it left administrative discretion in the hands of the Treasury Department, explicitly provided for a stamp-book system, a stipulation that the Ways and Means Committee dropped.[45] These points, along with the suggestion of deferred inclusion that Morgenthau supported, offered the Congress an array of options to make inclusion of agricultural and domestic workers feasible.

The committee members who brought up the issue were invariably southerners. Both chairmen were relatively quiet during the hearings, preferring to let other members take the lead in questioning witnesses. But both Harrison and Doughton dropped their usual silence to pursue the question of the inclusion of agricultural and domestic workers. Harrison, in fact, uttered barely a word beyond procedural formalities for more than a week after the Finance Committee began its hearings until he engaged Witte in a line of questioning searching for some evidence that there was opposition among the "experts" to the inclusion of farm workers.[46] Doughton similarly awoke from his general public silence to probe on this issue, and other southern members also expressed interest. Ironically, one of the most vehement objections to exclusion came from an opponent of the bill. Republican Representative Daniel A. Reed of New York, arguing that the whole contributory system was unconstitutional, castigated the Ways and Means Committee for discriminating (his word) against farm workers and domestics.[47]

One witness who testified before both committees explicitly argued against exclusion on the grounds that it would deny benefits to African Americans. This was Charles H. Houston of the NAACP. Houston argued that because of the concentration of black workers in agricultural and domestic jobs, the system of contributory old-age insurance was itself inadequate. Providing old-age payments as a *substitute* to earnings rather than as a *supplement* to earnings, he contended, would not adequately protect blacks in these low-paid and often irregular occupations. Furthermore, he pointed out, sharecroppers and tenants were excluded even from the administration's bill because they would be considered self-employed or independent contractors, not employees, an interpretation offered elsewhere by Witte. The NAACP's preference was for a single national old-age security plan covering all workers.[48]

Houston's claim that the old-age provisions of the bill advantaged white workers was undoubtedly true, but how true was it? To what extent would the exclusion of farm workers and servants have a disparate racial impact on the population that would benefit from old-age insurance? How would this impact be geographically distributed? After all, the entire South was heavily agricultural, and exclusion would eliminate many whites from coverage as well.[49] An examination of census occupational data from 1930 shows that the exclusion of farm workers and servants contemplated by the bill did, in fact, have a racially imbalanced effect, and that this effect was not only national but was larger outside the South.

Census data are a rather blunt instrument for examining these occupational categories. First of all, the census is done only every ten years, so it offers only a snapshot of a single moment in a fast-changing labor force. This problem is especially acute for the 1930s, when the Great Depression caused greater than normal economic dislocation. The timing of the Social Security debate could not be worse for a comparison of its provisions with census data, since it is equidistant from the 1930 and 1940 censuses. Second, the occupational categories reported in the census do not correspond precisely with the categories in the law, making the enumeration of potentially included or excluded workers difficult. However, no other source provides such a comprehensive picture of the national labor force during the 1930s. I have used 1930 census data here because its information would have been available to the actors in 1935, or at least it represents a demographic and political reality that they could have (and, in many cases, would have) perceived and understood. The categories of agricultural workers counted in 1930 map easily onto the relevant Social Security categories. To approximate the number of domestic workers, I have used the 1930 census category "servants," which comes closest to approximating the sense that the act intends. If anything, this usage slightly undercounts the number of domestic workers actually excluded, since it does not capture household employees classified under other categories such as "launderers" or "cooks." Were it possible to include these workers in the data, I do not believe the findings would differ significantly.[50]

Table 7.1 shows the percentage of the work force in agricultural and domestic service by state, both for the total labor force and for blacks. These data include all workers occupied in agriculture—owners, tenants and sharecroppers, managers and foremen, wage laborers, and unpaid fam-

TABLE 7.1

Gainful Workers in Agricultural and Domestic Employment, All Workers and Black Workers, 1930 (Percentages)

State	All	Black	Difference	State	All	Black	Difference
United States	25.5	51.3	25.8	Vermont	31.3	38.9	7.6
				Maine	20.5	27.8	7.3
South	47.5	61.6	14.1	Ohio	15.5	22.1	6.6
North	17.6	25.6	8.0	Nevada	24.4	30.8	6.4
Border	30.4	36.8	6.4	Illinois	14.8	21.0	6.2
				Washington	19.1	24.3	5.2
New Jersey	7.9	32.5	24.6	Tennessee	44.0	48.5	4.5
Rhode Island	6.5	28.8	22.3	Oregon	23.4	27.4	4.0
Delaware	22.9	45.0	22.1				
Massachusetts	7.2	28.2	21.0	Arizona	26.9	29.0	2.1
Maryland	18.4	38.9	20.5	Michigan	16.2	18.2	2.0
Connecticut	9.3	28.9	19.6	Missouri	29.1	30.6	1.5
New York	9.8	29.1	19.3	Colorado	29.8	31.3	1.5
District of Columbia	10.6	29.7	19.1	Indiana	22.9	21.6	–1.3
California	17.4	35.6	18.2	Kentucky	42.8	39.5	–3.3
Oklahoma	40.0	57.6	17.6	Utah	26.9	22.5	–4.4
				New Mexico	44.8	38.2	–6.6
South Carolina	55.0	71.2	16.2	West Virginia	23.9	17.1	–6.8
Louisiana	42.2	58.3	16.1	Kansas	35.9	25.6	–8.3
Texas	42.1	58.0	15.9				
Pennsylvania	10.7	25.5	14.8	Wisconsin	28.8	15.8	–13.0
New Hampshire	15.1	28.6	13.5	Wyoming	36.2	22.3	–13.9
Florida	29.1	42.3	13.2	Minnesota	34.5	19.9	–14.6
North Carolina	48.3	61.2	12.9	Montana	39.6	24.7	–14.9
Arkansas	60.6	73.1	12.5	Nebraska	42.0	26.3	–15.7
Virginia	36.1	46.5	11.4	Iowa	39.3	23.5	–15.8
Mississippi	69.6	80.3	10.7	South Dakota	55.5	38.3	–17.2
				Idaho	42.7	24.7	–18.0
Georgia	48.6	58.8	10.2	North Dakota	59.4	24.7	–34.7
Alabama	52.6	61.6	9.0				

Source: U.S. Bureau of the Census 1931, vol. 4, tables 6, 11.

ily workers—as well as servants. The first two columns are simply the percentage of the total labor force and of the black labor force in these occupations. The third column is the difference between these two percentages, indicating the extent to which blacks were over- or underrepresented in these occupations compared with the entire population.

The first striking point is that while these categories include one-fourth of all workers, they include fully half of the black work force. Not surprisingly, the disparity is greatest in the South, where the black percentage is 14 percentage points higher than the total percentage, but in the aggregate the positive difference appears in the rest of the country as well. The 25-percentage-point difference for the entire country, an apparent anomaly since it is higher than the difference for any state or region, results from the concentration of blacks, and especially of black agricultural workers, in the South.[51] The nationwide percentage of black farm workers is heavily weighted toward the South, while the overall percentage is weighted toward the North, where there were both fewer blacks and more industry.

But it is not in the southern states that the greatest disparities are found. In the state rankings, the South is clustered in the second and third quintiles, with differences ranging from 16 down to 4.5 percentage points. The states in which blacks are most overrepresented in excluded occupations are not southern, but mostly industrial northeastern and border states with relatively few farmers, black or white. In these states, as in the other nonsouthern states, servants account for most of the black percentages. Other major industrial states such as Pennsylvania, Ohio, Illinois, and Michigan also show positive differences, indicating overrepresentation of blacks. In fifteen states, the percentage of blacks in these occupations is lower than the percentage for the whole labor force. These are mostly midwestern farm states and mountain states that had very small black populations. Only two—Kentucky and West Virginia—had populations more than 5 percent black, and most were under 1 percent. The striking conclusion from these data is that the disproportionate presence of blacks in excluded occupations was nearly a nationwide phenomenon and, while heavy in the South, was heaviest in the Northeast.

These figures present a partial picture of those excluded from the old-age insurance coverage under the Social Security Act. The self-employed were excluded by definition from the legislation, since there is no employer-employee relationship. Employees of governments and nonprofit organizations were also excluded, the former because many already had pension plans, the latter because it was felt the tax would be burdensome. It is likely that in these categories most workers were white and that a tally of these groups would show that blacks were not disproportionately excluded from old-age insurance. But the data in table 7.1 do not precisely identify those workers who were the subject of the fight over agricultural and domestic workers. As Houston and Witte pointed out, neither farm owners nor tenants were considered employees for the purposes of the Social Security Act, and were thus excluded from coverage as self-employed persons or independent contractors. Many farm workers were classified as unpaid family workers—the spouses and children of farmers—who received no wages and therefore would not participate in the system. The workers that the exclusion controversy affected were those who received wages for their work on farms, wage laborers, and managers or foremen.

Table 7.2 replicates table 7.1 for this restricted class of workers, those whom the congressional amendment actually removed from the coverage they would have received under the administration bill. The new results are basically similar with some important differences. The most important difference is that there is only one negative number in the table. In only one state, North Dakota, were blacks underrepresented in farm labor and domestic service compared to the whole population. In every other state, blacks were more likely to be found in these occupations than was the population at large. This pattern indicates strongly that the exclusion of these workers from the old-age insurance provisions of Social Security had a racially imbalanced impact throughout the country.

Second, the South no longer appears distinctive. Removing tenants and sharecroppers from the data removes many southern farmers, both black and white. As a result, the overall racial disparity in the South declines somewhat from 14 to 11 percentage points, and the uniformity of the southern states disappears. Whereas in table 7.1 the South was bunched together, here the southern states are arrayed up and down the list. Deep South states such as Mississippi and Alabama, in which tenant farming was especially common, fall to near the bottom of the chart, while others stay in essentially the same position. Ironically, the states in which racial politics was most prominent, and whose congressmen in fact played the greatest role in excluding these workers, are among the states where the racial disparity that results from the exclusion appears the smallest. And yet even over relatively small numbers of workers, these senators and representatives spent political capital to amend the bill, suggesting that administrative and labor-market concerns were not at the center of their motivations. There were, however, still far more blacks in the South than in the North, and to most northerners the politics of race was still a rather distant concern.

On the contrary, the exclusion of agricultural and domestic workers affected the northern states considerably more. For both the northern and border states, the disparity between black and overall percentages is greater than for the South, and the top ten states remain unchanged, merely shuffled. And finally the national percentages reflect the persistence of the basic trend. While the amendment excluded only one in ten workers overall, it removed one in four black workers from the benefits of old-age insurance.

TABLE 7.2
Gainful Workers in Farm Labor or Domestic Service, All Workers and Black Workers, 1930 (Percentages)

State	All	Black	Difference	State	All	Black	Difference
United States	9.8	25.0	15.2	Washington	8.8	22.4	13.6
				North Carolina	12.8	26.0	13.2
Border	10.3	28.9	18.6	Illinois	7.4	20.4	13.0
North	8.5	25.0	16.5	Nebraska	12.6	25.5	12.9
South	13.7	24.5	10.8	Tennessee	12.0	24.8	12.8
				Texas	13.2	25.7	12.5
Delaware	12.3	38.8	26.5	Indiana	8.3	20.7	12.4
New Jersey	6.2	32.0	25.8	Georgia	15.9	28.3	12.4
Rhode Island	5.4	28.6	23.2				
Maryland	11.7	34.5	22.8	Kansas	9.8	21.8	12.0
California	12.1	34.5	22.4	New Mexico	19.4	31.2	11.8
New York	6.9	29.0	22.1	Utah	10.2	21.6	11.4
Massachusetts	5.9	27.7	21.8	South Carolina	17.1	28.3	11.2
Connecticut	6.9	28.6	21.7	Michigan	6.8	17.6	10.8
Oklahoma	11.1	30.6	19.5	Arizona	16.6	27.0	10.4
District of Columbia	10.5	29.7	19.2	Louisiana	14.9	25.2	10.3
				Iowa	13.0	21.6	8.6
Pennsylvania	6.3	25.3	19.0	West Virginia	8.5	15.8	7.3
New Hampshire	8.5	27.4	18.9	Alabama	12.5	20.9	8.4
Kentucky	10.9	29.1	18.2				
Colorado	13.2	29.9	16.7	Minnesota	11.9	19.1	7.2
Florida	17.6	34.1	16.5	Montana	15.0	21.3	6.3
Vermont	15.1	31.6	16.5	Arkansas	12.2	17.7	5.5
Oregon	10.1	26.6	16.5	Wisconsin	10.2	14.1	3.9
Missouri	9.5	24.6	15.1	Mississippi	10.4	14.1	3.7
Maine	9.5	24.3	14.8	Idaho	15.3	19.0	3.7
Virginia	14.9	29.6	14.7	South Dakota	16.1	18.8	2.7
				Wyoming	16.6	19.0	2.4
Ohio	7.1	21.2	14.1	North Dakota	20.0	17.8	−2.2
Nevada	15.4	29.3	13.9				

Source: U.S. Bureau of the Census 1931, vol. 4, tables 4, 6, 11.

Note: South = 11 Confederate states; Border = District of Columbia, Kentucky, Maryland, Missouri, Oklahoma, West Virginia; North = all other states.

While the champions of exclusion were from a region whose politics was infused with race, the result of exclusion was a nationwide racial disparity.

In contrast to the question of inclusion, the issue of the national administrative structure of the old-age insurance program received very little attention during the hearings or the floor debate. The reasons for exclusively federal administration, Witte explained to the Finance Committee, were the long-term nature of the program and the tremendous mobility of the American work force, and once the bill had been amended so that a majority of African American workers would be ineligible to receive this benefit directly from the federal government, Congress accepted this logic without question.[52] In the end, only after the program's coverage had been defined by the exclusion amendment was the national administration of old-age insurance possible. Ironically, despite its exclusionary origins, old-age insurance smoothly incorporated African Americans both through fair administration and legislative expansion, and has grown into a nearly universal, color-blind program.

Aid to Dependent Children

A second major feature of the Social Security Act was public assistance—grants-in-aid to the states for purposes including Old Age Assistance (OAA) and Aid to Dependent Children (ADC). While the former was more prominent in the public assistance debate in Congress—it was the immediate political response to the demands of the Townsend movement—the provisions for the two grant programs were substantially the same. Over the subsequent decades, as old-age insurance matured and grew, OAA declined in significance; ADC, on the other hand, has become the most prominent, controversial, and racially divisive of the public assistance programs. Under each program, the federal government would grant funds to each state to defray part of the cost of its relief program, provided that the state program met certain minimum standards. The major difference between the two was that for OAA the federal government was to pay one-half of the state's cost up to a certain amount per recipient, while for ADC the federal share was one-third. But the administrative arrangements, which southern congressmen fought to change, were the same for both.

The exclusion of certain categories of workers was not an issue in the public assistance debate as it was for old-age and unemployment insurance. In fact, several witnesses carefully reminded congressmen that farmers, while ineligible for the contributory old-age program, could receive noncontributory pensions if they found themselves in need in their old age.[53] The principle behind these public assistance programs was the relief of the "deserving poor," those who, due to life circumstances beyond their con-

TABLE 7.3
Wage Earners with Annual Incomes Less Than $1,000 and $600, by Color, for United States and Regions, 1939 (Percentages)

	< $1,000			< $600		
	White	*Nonwhite*	*Difference*	*White*	*Nonwhite*	*Difference*
United States	54.5	89.2	34.8	33.8	72.6	38.8
New England	54.6	78.3	23.7	30.4	49.3	18.9
Mid-Atlantic	50.7	78.6	27.9	30.7	53.8	23.1
East North Central	50.0	75.1	25.1	30.7	50.0	19.3
West North Central	61.5	85.0	23.5	41.9	65.0	23.1
South Atlantic	59.8	92.5	32.7	35.8	78.8	43.0
East South Central	66.8	94.5	27.7	44.1	81.7	36.9
West South Central	64.1	95.4	27.7	44.8	83.2	38.4
Mountain	56.8	81.7	24.9	37.5	60.4	22.9
Pacific	48.3	80.7	32.4	29.8	50.2	20.4

Source: U.S. Bureau of the Census, *Sixteenth Census of the United States: 1940, Population, Wage or Salary Income in 1939* (Washington, D.C.: Government Printing Office, 1943), pp. 75–86, table 5.

trol such as old age or widowhood, could not support themselves. Furthermore, since these programs were to be funded out of general revenues and since benefits did not depend on an individual's contributions or work history, they did not pose administrative problems such as tax collection and payroll reporting. But it was precisely because of these structural features of public assistance policy, as well as the racial composition of ADC's target population, that southerners demanded stronger local control over the program.

Because eligibility for ADC was in principle universal and blacks were not systematically excluded, as they were from other benefits, blacks throughout the country were more likely than whites to be among its beneficiaries. Blacks were substantially more likely to be poor than whites, for a variety of reasons. Not only were black workers more likely to be unemployed, but their earnings were likely to be insufficient to bring them above the level of poverty, as table 7.3 shows.

It is impossible to estimate with any precision the number of families, black or white, who would have been eligible for ADC in 1935. First, the federal act did not specify such eligibility requirements as residence and citizenship. Second, sufficiently detailed data that describe the income of black and white single-parent families do not exist for the period. But we can infer, from a variety of aggregate data, that blacks were more likely to be eligible to receive ADC benefits than were whites. Table 7.3 presents the racial disparity in wage income by region in 1939. These data include all wage or salary workers, including those with no wage income and excluding those on emergency work. They include workers with nonwage income as well as those for whom wages were the only income. A drawback of these data is that farmers and tenants did not receive wages and are not included in these data, so that the table does not capture farm poverty. The data are also for individuals, and so do not give a picture of family poverty, the criterion for ADC eligibility. But the table does suggest the large difference between the earnings of black and white workers. Because ADC benefits were not generally available to workers, even unemployed workers, these figures do not say anything directly about ADC eligibility, but they do provide a vivid picture of the racial gap in economic levels.

The table reports the percentage of wage workers in 1939 earning below two different wage levels: $600 and $1,000 per year. The higher figure approximates the poverty threshold for a family of four in the mid-1930s. A 1935 Works Progress Administration study of the cost of living in fifty-nine cities reported that the average minimum annual income required to maintain a family of four was $1,261, a level that was "completely beyond the means of the general Negro population, particularly in the South." The study also found that an emergency budget, consisting of the merest subsistence, was possible at an average annual income of $903.[54] As a comparison, the average federal poverty threshold for a family of four in 1990, converted to 1939 dollars, was about $1,420.[55] The lower figure considered in table 7.3 approximates the annual level of support contemplated by the Social Security Act for a medium-sized family. The act provided for federal reimbursement for monthly payments of up to $18 for the first child and $12 for each subsequent child, although states were free to pay higher benefits at their own expense. Payments at these levels would translate to annual benefits of $504 for a family of three children and $648 for four children. Table 7.3 thus provides a glimpse at the extreme poverty of black wage earners.

Table 7.3 shows that blacks earned less than whites throughout the country. While one-half of all wage workers earned less than $1,000, nine of ten nonwhite workers fell short of this threshold. One-third of white workers were below $600, compared to nearly three-fourths of nonwhites. In every region, the racial differential appears at both levels, and the disparity is greater in the South than elsewhere, despite higher overall levels of poverty in the South. These figures suggest that black poverty was prevalent throughout the country, and that any government program to combat poverty would find more blacks than whites among its clients.

Another aspect of ADC eligibility was the presence of only a single parent. ADC was a federal extension of state mothers' pension laws, which provided support for impoverished single mothers who could not otherwise care for their children at home.[56] Blacks in the 1930s were not only more likely to be poor, but black families were also more likely to be headed by a single parent. In 1930, 30 percent of all black families in the United States were single-parent families, and two-thirds of these were headed by women. By comparison, only 20 percent of native white families had a single parent, about three-fifths female-headed. Single black mothers also tended to have more children than did single white mothers.[57] Each link in the chain, from the incidence of poverty to family structure and size, indicates that blacks were considerably overrepresented among potential beneficiaries of ADC.

Because blacks stood out as potential recipients of public assistance programs, particularly ADC, the question of administrative control became perhaps the most contentious issue of the congressional debate, and it certainly raised the ire of Southerners more than any other issue did. The controversy focused on the nature of the requirements that the bill established for state plans. There were both general and specific objections. Specifically, members opposed the requirement that old-age and ADC payments be sufficient to provide "a reasonable subsistence compatible with decency and health," and to the requirement that state administrative operations, including the hiring of personnel, be acceptable to the federal government. More generally, they charged that the administration bill gave unelected federal officials arbitrary and unrestricted power to withhold funds from states that did not measure up to their standards of professionalism and liberality. Wilbur J. Cohen, Witte's assistant at the CES, later called the deletion of these standards, especially the "decency and health" mandate, "the bill's most significant long-range loss."[58] This significance was not lost on members who viewed these provisions as an unprecedented and dangerous intrusion into states' rights. The invocation of states' rights regarding public assistance requirements contrasts sharply with the striking absence of such arguments in the debate on old-age insurance, surely a much greater assumption of federal power. A consistent constitutional objection to centralization ought to have appeared there as well. But a national program that systematically excluded black workers provoked no such "principled" objection, suggesting that race rather than the Constitution motivated this argument.

The most vociferous critic of the bill on this count was Senator Harry F. Byrd of Virginia. On the third day of hearings, Byrd launched into a tirade against Witte, claiming that the bill gave the federal government "dictatorial power . . . over what the State is permitted to do. . . . The administrator in Washington is to be the sole judge as to whether or not a State receives any of this appropriation from the Federal Government." A few moments later, Byrd turned up the rhetorical heat, invoking the classic phrases of states' rights:

SENATOR BYRD. Do I understand, Doctor, that this Administrator has supreme power to deny a sovereign state of this Union any benefits of this pension system at all unless that State complies with the regulations that he makes and thinks are proper?

MR. WITTE. That is putting it in little stronger terms than I would.

SENATOR BYRD. Is that not the truth under this legislation if it is enacted as it is now?

MR. WITTE. Perhaps, theoretically, so.[59]

Witte's rather weak and disingenuous response was that while the Social Security Board technically could suspend payments to a state for noncompliance, the idea was that the board would simply review the state *law* establishing the program. Moreover, he pointed out, these provisions were no different from standards in other federal grant-in-aid laws, which had only rarely resulted in an outright suspension of payments to a state.[60] Moreover, as one student of welfare policy has noted, "unlike the situation in highway policy . . . public assistance introduces problems of race, of sex, of religion, and of family relationships. It is hard to think of four areas most American politicians would rather avoid."[61]

Byrd was the loudest but not the only congressional critic of the federal control provisions of the bill. Harrison expressed concern about this question several times over the course of the hearings, but so did Hugo Black of Alabama, a New Deal supporter and one of the most perceptive members of the Finance Committee, who referred to the bill as "federal coercion." The provisions for federal control also provoked opposition from Republicans Allen T. Treadway of Massachusetts, the ranking member of the Ways and Means Committee, and Senator Daniel O. Hastings of Delaware, who eventually supported the bill despite "the great damages which such action . . . will bring to the principles on which our Government was founded"— namely, state sovereignty.[62]

The race question lurked just beneath the surface of this debate, precipitated as it was largely by southerners. When Representative Howard W. Smith of Virginia—who was to become famous when, as chairman of the House Rules Committee, he obstructed the passage of Civil Rights legislation—appeared before the Ways and Means Committee to oppose excessive federal controls, the race issue broke through. Smith proposed adding to the bill "a provision that would allow the States to differentiate between persons" in paying benefits. He went on to note that of Virginia's 116,000 people over 65, "practically 25 percent are of one class that will probably qualify 100 percent." Thomas A. Jenkins of Ohio asked Smith what he meant, provoking an exchange that is worth quoting in full:

MR. SMITH. Of course, in the South we have a great many colored people, and they are largely of the laboring class.

MR. JENKINS. This is what I thought the gentleman had in mind. I should like
to ask the gentleman, and also any member of this committee, whether in this law
it is contemplated that there be any loophole by which any State could discriminate against any class of people?

MR. SMITH. No sir; I do not think so, and you will not find in my remarks any
suggestion to that effect. It just so happens that that race is in our State very much
of the laboring class and farm laboring class. But you will find no suggestion in
my remarks of any suggested amendment that would be unconstitutional, if I may
use that expression.[63]

This exchange demonstrates that Smith, and probably other southern congressmen, clearly saw and understood the racial implications of the legislation, and it exposes for a moment the reason behind their concern with state
control. Smith's invocation of the "constitutionality" of the South's concerns taps into a discourse of racial exclusion that has its roots in the voting
restrictions of the Jim Crow period.[64] Moreover, his denial that he is interested in restricting black access to benefits rings as false as Captain Re-
nault's expression of shock at discovering gambling at Rick's Café just as
he pockets his winnings.

On the other side, the NAACP supported nationalizing public assistance,
and opposed the bill precisely because the standards, which Byrd and others so strenuously opposed, were too weak to prevent discriminatory
administration at the state level. "From the point of view of the Negro,"
Houston told the Finance Committee, "it would be much easier to get fair
enforcement of a Federal law than to get a really effective old-age assistance law passed by southern legislatures."[65] Representative Arthur W.
Mitchell of Illinois, the first black Democrat ever to serve in Congress,
made his maiden speech to the House on the bill, criticizing state administration of public assistance and calling for greater federal financing and
control.[66] The view that blacks were better served by federal than by state
administration of government assistance was common among black leaders in the 1930s, and there is some evidence to suggest that this was so.[67]

Nevertheless, the Ways and Means Committee, in executive session, relaxed the federal control provisions substantially. The committee eliminated the "decency and health" clause, giving states much more leeway in
setting benefit levels; removed personnel matters from the administrative
requirements; relaxed the minimum eligibility standards; and provided for
a hearing before the federal government could cut off a state's funding.
Witte, who attended many of the committee's executive sessions, had little
doubt that these amendments resulted from southern fears of federal interference. "The Southern members," he wrote, "did not want to give authority to anyone in Washington to deny aid to any state because it discriminated against Negroes in the administration" of public assistance.[68]

The southern assault on the federal control potential of the bill continued in the floor debate, even after the Ways and Means amendments. One member, Representative E. E. Cox of Georgia, gave the classic Jeffersonian argument in defense of states' rights. Lamenting the decline of the Democratic Party's adherence to decentralized and limited government, he predicted the rise of a third party "to lead the people of this country who adhere to the belief that the Federal Government is a government of delegated powers, and is sovereign only to the extent of supreme and exclusive exercise of those powers."[69] This was perhaps the most overwrought attack on the bill, but it was not atypical. Even Harrison, whose legislative prowess helped shepherd the bill through the Senate, was almost apologetic in explaining to his colleagues that the public assistance titles of the bill contained "an absolute minimum of Federal participation," which provided a striking contrast with Wagner's defense of the bill's "fundamental requirements."[70]

These rhetorical attacks on the bill, however, masked deep ambiguity among southerners about the federal role in Social Security and once again revealed the inconsistency in their invocation of states' rights. While they attacked excessive federal control, many supported a series of amendments to provide federal funds for public assistance to poor states that could not afford the matching funds required by the grant-in-aid programs. In support of one such amendment, Representative William M. Colmer of Mississippi raised the specter of "a new imaginary line . . . like a veritable Mason and Dixon's line that would divide this great country of ours into two sections," rich and poor. The imagery of his remarks left little doubt about where he thought that line would be drawn. All of these amendments were either withdrawn or defeated by voice vote, but of ten members who spoke in favor, five were from the South and three from border states. It took John McCormack to point out to these members the logical, not to mention political, inconsistencies of their position—in favor of entirely federal funding of public assistance but opposed to federal control.[71]

The decentralization of ADC, which had its roots in the racial structure of American politics, had clear and predictable racial effects—African Americans were less likely to get ADC and got it in smaller amounts than whites, despite greater need. The direct evidence for racial disparities in the administration of ADC is sketchy and anecdotal. But a quantitative analysis of ADC administration at the county level shows clear patterns of discrimination.[72] Because data breaking down ADC recipients by race are not available for the decades following the New Deal, an ecological analysis of county-level data is the only way to observe racial patterns systematically. Using regression analysis, this study examines differences in ADC administration between 1940 and 1960 in counties with high and low concentrations of black population, controlling for other factors that might affect the availability of ADC coverage, such as wealth and urban-rural and regional differences.

The results show that there were significant systematic differences between black and white access to ADC benefits. Southern counties with high black populations provided no more benefits than other areas, despite objectively greater need. In the North, by contrast, more heavily black counties had higher levels of ADC coverage, even controlling for urban-rural differences that might be suspected to lie behind such a result. Since there is no reason to believe that the stigma attached to being on welfare was greater in the South than in the North, these results suggest that rules regulating access to ADC were applied differently to blacks, especially in the South. In addition to restricted access to ADC benefits, recipients in heavily black areas nationwide received lower benefits. Finally, the analysis shows that in cities, where most African Americans outside the South lived, the most important factor affecting the treatment of black ADC recipients was the presence of traditional, patronage-based party organizations. In machine cities, African Americans did considerably better under ADC than in nonorganization cities, suggesting that traditional party organizations used ADC's decentralized institutional structure to seize control of public welfare and treat it as a political benefit. The decentralized structure of ADC thus promoted racial discrimination in administration, which inhibited the program's development and produced a legacy of retrenchment and intensified racial division that is today more virulent than ever.

Conclusions

Racial classification has had a profound effect on the development of the American welfare state. The legacy of racial division lies deep within the structure of American social policy institutions, dating back to one of the defining moments of public welfare in America. The politics of race and the politics of welfare are linked not simply because demographics bring African Americans into more frequent contact with the makers and administrators of social policy, but because the institutions of social policy were sculpted out of stone already hewn by racial division. The story of race and Social Security suggests that in order to understand the meaning of race in American politics, we must explore not only the current state of race relations but also the deeper connection between race and American political development. Racial conflict, whether subtle or overt, structures American political life. It shapes and reshapes our politics in ways that we often nei-

ther anticipate nor intend. It can confound even the best of intentions, cor-
rupting apparently "neutral" institutions and policies. The better we understand how these processes have worked over history and still operate today,
the better equipped we will be to confront the dilemmas of racial classification that haunt us still.

Notes

1. Baldwin 1984, 25. See also Smith 1993; Lieberman 1993.
2. M. Brown 1988.
3. Lieberman 1995.
4. Lieberman 1993. On the reciprocal relations between politics and institutions,
particularly administrative organizations, see Moe 1989; and March and Olsen
1989.
5. Skowronek 1982.
6. Skocpol, with many collaborators, has produced voluminous work on this
subject, culminating in Skocpol 1992; quotation from 39.
7. J. Wilson 1989.
8. March and Olsen 1989.
9. U.S. Social Security Board 1937, 247–48.
10. Ibid., 213.
11. Lieberman 1993.
12. Sterner 1943, 214–23; Myrdal 1944, 357–58; Weiss 1983, 166–67; Katz
1986, 244–45; Orloff 1988; Finegold 1988.
13. Quadagno 1988b; Bensel 1984, 147–74; Alston and Ferrie 1985a, 1985b.
14. The narrative and analysis that follow rely heavily, of course, on the indis-
pensable work on Social Security, Derthick 1979.
15. Roosevelt 1938, 291–92.
16. Key 1949. For a more nuanced view, see Katznelson, Geiger, and Kryder
1993.
17. Roosevelt cited southern leadership in Congress when he told Walter White,
secretary of the NAACP, that he could not support antilynching legislation in 1934.
"I did not choose the tools with which I must work," he told White. "Had I been
permitted to choose them I would have selected quite different ones. But I've got to
get legislation passed by Congress to save America. The Southerners by reason of
the seniority rule are chairmen or occupy strategic positions on most of the Senate
and House committees. If I come out for the anti-lynching bill now, they will block
every bill I ask Congress to pass to keep America from collapsing. I just can't take
that risk." White 1948, 169–70; Weiss 1983, 105–6. See also Brinkley 1984, 98–99.
On Roosevelt's relationship with the South see Freidel 1965.
18. Key 1937.
19. Schlesinger 1960, 252–55, 275–80; Perkins 1946, 286.
20. See Schlesinger 1960, esp. 385–408.
21. Compiled from U.S. Bureau of the Census 1931, vol. 4, tables 6, 11.

22. Greene and Woodson 1930, 224–46; M. Anderson 1936, 66–67.

23. Lubove 1986, 45–65.

24. U.S. Social Security Board 1937, 183.

25. Roosevelt 1938, 291; Perkins 1946, 282–83. In her memoir, Perkins expresses skepticism about the both the feasibility and the wisdom of universal coverage, but this contradicts accounts of her behavior in the Committee on Economic Security and is probably retrospective validation of a position adopted out of necessity. When her book was written, agricultural workers were still excluded from Social Security programs.

26. Altmeyer 1966.

27. Merrill G. Murray, "The Case for Payroll Recording as Against the Stamp System," October 16, 1934, Box 20, National Archives; Bryce Stewart, "Unemployment Insurance," p. 3, box 21, National Archives.

28. Witte 1962, 131, 152.

29. U.S. Committee on Economic Security 1985, 38–49. Emphasis added. See also Witte 1962, 32.

30. Altmeyer 1966, 14–15; Perkins 1946, 291–92.

31. Altmeyer 1966, 25–26; Witte 1962, 146–47. The committee here undoubtedly took as a cue Justice Harlan Fiske Stone's remark to Perkins, in response to her fears about the constitutionality of the economic security program, that the taxing power of the federal government "is sufficient for everything you want and need." Perkins 1946, 286.

32. Altmeyer 1966, 16; Jane Perry Clark, "Analysis of Types of Federal-State Relationships in Relation to a Program of Economic Security," box 17, National Archives.

33. See Key 1949; Potter 1972.

34. In the Seventy-Fourth Congress, which passed the Social Security Act, all 22 senators and 100 of 102 representatives from the South (the eleven former Confederate states) were Democrats. The two exceptions were representatives from eastern Tennessee, a traditional Republican stronghold since the Civil War. Data compiled from U.S. Congress 1935.

35. On the seniority system see Price 1977; Polsby 1968; Matthews 1960, 164–65. On the committee system and the New Deal see Bensel 1984, 155–74, 317–67. In the Seventy-Fourth Congress, 9 of the 20 most senior senators and 38 of the 86 most senior representatives were southerners. The speaker of the House and both majority leaders were southerners. Southerners chaired 12 of 33 committees in the Senate and 21 of 47 in the House. These included the tax, appropriations, military and naval affairs, agriculture, and banking committees of both houses as well as the House judiciary and commerce committees. Compiled from U.S. Congress 1935.

36. Key 1949.

37. In fact, administration strategists, who had considered seeking the creation of a special committee to consider the economic security program, were somewhat surprised when Doughton expressed interest in sponsoring the bill. Witte 1962, 79–80; Perkins 1946, 296.

38. See Patterson 1967.

39. Patterson 1969; U.S. Social Security Board 1937, 156–67, 233–46; Skocpol et al. 1993.

40. Hamilton and Hamilton 1992.

41. House Committee on Ways and Means 1935, 902.

42. Witte 1962, 152–53; Perkins 1946, 297–98.

43. House Committee on Ways and Means 1935, 902, 911.

44. J. Brown 1972, 19–20; McKinley and Frase 1970, 313–14.

45. House Committee on Ways and Means 1935, 112, 244–47.

46. House Committee on Ways and Means 1935, 219–20.

47. *Congressional Record* 1935, 5991.

48. House Committee on Ways and Means 1935, 796–97; Senate Committee on Finance 1935, 199, 640–44.

49. In 1930, 42.7 percent of the southern labor force worked in agriculture. U.S. Bureau of the Census 1931, U.S. Summary, table 5, p. 18; state volumes, table 4. Unlike voting restrictions in southern states, this provision offered no loopholes such as grandfather clauses or literacy tests to limit its impact on whites. Alston and Ferrie 1985a, 98.

50. Ewan Clague, a Social Security Board statistician, used 1930 census data for a similar analysis in 1937. "Were data available for 1937," he argued, "it is likely that the proportions would vary somewhat but not enough to alter the picture in any appreciable degree." He estimated that there were approximately 2.1 million workers in domestic service in 1937. My estimate totals 2.0 million. Ewan Clague, "The Problem of Extending Old Age-Insurance to Cover Classes Now Excluded," presentation to the Advisory Council on Social Security, November 5, 1937, box 9, National Archives.

51. In 1930, nearly 71 percent of American blacks, but nearly 94 percent of black agricultural workers, lived in the South.

52. Senate Committee on Finance 1935, 199.

53. Senate Committee on Finance 1935, 66, 509.

54. Sterner 1943, 83–88.

55. U.S. Bureau of the Census 1991.

56. See Skocpol 1992.

57. Sterner 1943, 48–58, 280–81. As Herbert Gutman and others have pointed out, poverty and family structure may not be entirely independent of each other (1976, 462–63).

58. Cohen 1985, 9.

59. Senate Committee on Finance 1935, 70–71.

60. Clark, "Analysis of Types of Federal-State Relationships." Grant-in-aid programs already in place in 1935 employed a wide variety of mechanisms for federal direction of state activity, some more overtly coercive than others. Key 1937.

61. Steiner 1966, 4.

62. Senate Committee on Finance 1935, 12, 122, 220–22, 338–39, 344, 78–79; House Committee on Ways and Means 1935, 125–26; *Congressional Record* 1935, 9419.

63. House Committee on Ways and Means 1935, 974–77.

64. Smith 1993, 561.

65. House Committee on Ways and Means 1935, 641–43. See also Weiss 1983, 166–67.

66. *Congressional Record* 1935, 5692–93.

67. See Weiss 1983; Bunche 1973, 106; Wolters 1970.

68. Witte 1962, 144–45. Witte's personal assistant, Wilbur Cohen, was present at all the executive sessions of both congressional committees.

69. *Congressional Record* 1935, 5780.

70. Ibid., 9268, 9285.

71. Ibid., 5796, 5976–83.

72. The following analysis is summarized from Lieberman 1994.

8

National Parties and Racial Disenfranchisement

RICHARD M. VALELLY

ABOUT A CENTURY ago, conservative southern white politicians began to institute a system of electoral rules—literacy and good understanding tests, the poll tax and the like—intended to destroy their political opposition. When they finished around 1910, they had in effect killed off African American voting in this country, since the great majority of African Americans lived in the South. Lacking robust political representation, black Americans became vulnerable not just to Jim Crow but also to a gradual strengthening of de facto color lines in the nation as a whole. Color lines grew brighter in national and public settings (e.g., the District of Columbia, the federal civil service, the dining rooms of the Congress), in national institutions (e.g., the armed forces), and in national policies (e.g., social security and federal work relief in the 1930s)—all influenced by Congress and by southern Democrats. Such public segregation in turn tacitly legitimated efforts by northern party machines with white ethnic clienteles to establish color lines in public employment, schooling, and housing. The stage was thus set for the ghettos that greeted black migrants from the South for decades to come. By the 1930s and 1940s color lines were so much a feature of national life that Gunnar Myrdal aptly characterized their existence as an "American dilemma."[1] This chapter on disenfranchisement tells a tale worth telling, therefore, not only because disenfranchisement was an extraordinary process, a shocking reversal of Reconstruction's democratic gains that ushered in Jim Crow, but also because it clarifies the political origins of racial hierarchy in America today.

My approach to disenfranchisement focuses on *national party conflict* and its impact on the region. Such factors as poverty among black southerners, the restoration of the cotton kingdom and its quasi-feudal relationships, and continuing white racism, in both North and South, all abetted disenfranchisement.[2] But Reconstruction's democratic gains had depended critically on the decisions of national Republican leaders. So too the eventual destruction of these gains in the 1890s, some two decades after the end of Reconstruction, also depended on the decisions of national Republican leaders.

This chapter thus joins a growing literature that corrects two widely held

misconceptions: that disenfranchisement dates from the collapse of Reconstruction and that the politics of racial equality dropped from the national
agenda after the Compromise of 1877. The prospects of African American
suffrage dimmed, to be sure, with Reconstruction's collapse—but voting
continued, often at high levels, well into the 1880s. Black elected officials
served in southern state legislatures and in Congress to the end of the nineteenth century. In the 1890s a militant biracial movement gained control of
North Carolina's government. Parts of the South, even the Deep South,
remained highly contested terrain long after 1877.[3]

Below I consider how national party dynamics affected (1) African
American politicians and white allies, both southern Republicans and
third-party independents (consider them "inclusionists"), and (2) regional
conservative and race-baiting white Democrats (consider them "exclusionists"). Although the best literature on post-Reconstruction politics adequately covers regional and state-level party dynamics, rather less is known
about the *interaction* between region and nation. The distinctive contribution of this article is to show that the eventual certainty of disenfranchisement depended on far-reaching change in the structure of national party
competition.[4]

Party Dynamics, Systemwide Competition, and Democracy

Party competition is rightly regarded as a condition of democracy. It gives
rival parties incentives to monitor each other for abuses of rights of political association and speech. Rallies, appeals to the public, and open meetings are crucial for the business of conducting campaigns and winning office. Party competition also can give parties incentives to work to include
new social groups, either competitively or even singly, as the case of southern Republicanism during Reconstruction shows.

But these desirable consequences of party competition depend critically
on whether parties compete and mobilize throughout an entire system. The
political prospects of African Americans often have been linked to major
party commitment to systemwide conflict. This was particularly true in the
nineteenth century, given the demographic concentration of African Americans in the South.

During the Reconstruction, the Republican Party made a commitment to
contest elections in the South, leading to the establishment of a national
electoral regulatory system. That system survived the fall of the Reconstruction. The Republican Party still needed the South, as we will see, so
persisting in its commitment to contest southern elections, often enough to
add considerably to the political uncertainties of the region. The party not
only sought to enforce the electoral regulatory system; it also advertised its

persistence in party platforms, carried on congressional campaigning, and insisted on mounting investigations of electoral fraud and intimidation.

To be sure, the Supreme Court weakened much of the electoral regulatory system. Yet the Court also greatly strengthened the Federal Elections Act of 1871, governing congressional elections. This helped to set the stage for a fierce congressional battle between 1889 and 1891 over the wide-ranging Federal Elections Bill (commonly known as the Force Bill or the Lodge Bill). A briefer battle between 1893 and 1894 also followed. Congressional Democrats, empowered by the first unified Democratic government since the antebellum Buchanan administration, then undertook a largely successful repeal of all the Reconstruction-era federal elections statutes. Still, from 1894 to 1896 there was sharp rearguard sniping from congressional Republicans as they sought investigations of election fraud and unseated southern Democrats in the House.

To put the story another way, from the Reconstruction to the 1890s Democratic-Republican contestation in and over the South was marked by (1) fundamental disagreement over the boundaries of the suffrage, due to a Republican commitment to contest elections in the South, and therefore by (2) intense but opposed preferences within the two parties over electoral institutions. Let me briefly consider both features of this contestation before sketching the conditions of a shift in the terms of Democratic-Republican conflict in the region.

Fundamental Disagreement over Boundaries of the Suffrage

While the post-Reconstruction party system had a variety of formal democratic features, in a key respect it was unusual: one party, the Democratic Party, preferred to demobilize a significant portion of the Republican Party's electoral base. The term *compromise* in a sense is misleading when applied to the Compromise of 1877. America's two competing party leaderships did not compromise in 1877 their disagreement over the boundaries of the suffrage because the Republicans had already invested so many resources in the South. Here the concepts of *commitment to contest* and *sunk costs* are helpful.

U.S. parties have no natural stake in generating processes of mobilization and contestation across the entire system—they must be motivated to do so. Such features of the American system as the electoral college provide strong incentives for a selective approach to mobilization that achieves unified government, in contrast with, for instance, a parliamentary system of proportional representation, where pressures for systemwide mobilization to gain control of government are greater. Thus an American party leadership does not always mount a contest in jurisdictions where historically their party has had no strong presence. But if it does, the result can be a dramatic increase in the system's scope of contestation, as happened during the Reconstruction.[5]

Once made, furthermore, a commitment to contest is abandoned only (*a*) when the commitment clearly becomes politically very costly and (*b*) when alternatives to it open up. Parties, like firms, do not easily write off the very large sunk costs of making a commitment to contest. The rate of return (in terms of winning national offices) to developing other commitments to contest must be manifestly higher than the rate of return to existing commitments. Unless the rate of return to existing commitments drops rapidly, new commitments will not rapidly take over at the margin. Political actors who must evaluate alternative rates of return are always uncertain in their evaluation. They also often have some level of ideological attachment to existing commitments to contest and their anticipated rates of return.[6]

The problem, then, with the conventional wisdom about the Compromise of 1877—holding that Republicans abruptly abandoned their African American constituencies—is that it asks one to ignore these kinds of considerations. Implicitly it holds that the huge sunk costs of the Republican commitment to contest southern elections, undertaken during Reconstruction, were summarily written off. Echoing the wisdom that the Compromise of 1877 was so grand and sweeping that it lasted until the 1960s, two analysts recently stated that the "ending of Reconstruction marked the end of race as a national political issue" for many decades. But in fact the national salience of race reemerged fairly soon after the Compromise was struck—as suggested (we see below in table 8.1) by a technique that these same analysts devised. In other words, sunk costs were not summarily written off.[7]

Let me turn to another general feature of the post-Reconstruction situation. If the parties disagreed over the boundaries of the suffrage and if the *same* region mattered to both of them, then one would expect that they also had strong preferences about the rules of the electoral game. One might expect that they cared deeply whether *national* or *local* electoral rules applied in the South. If the rules were national, then Republicans had a better chance of shaping electoral outcomes; if they were local, then Democrats had the advantage. In fact, the two parties did have intense and opposed preferences about electoral institutions.

Intense and Opposed Preferences about Electoral Institutions

In the post-Reconstruction period, both parties renewed their previous Reconstruction-era struggle over electoral rules and institutions. Both remained cohesive with regard to electoral regulatory policy. The Republicans preferred national rules developed during the Reconstruction; the Democrats opposed such rules, preferring regional or local rules.[8]

There were, of course, debates within the Republican Party about its southern policy after 1877, and they seem to have had effects on platform writing as shifts in the figures reported in table 8.1 below will suggest. But even amid the worst outbreak of factionalism over southern policy that occurred after the Reconstruction (during the 1890–91 battle for the Federal Elections Bill), most of the Republican Party was united behind national electoral regulation.

In making an effort to regulate national elections, Republicans were hampered by decisions the Supreme Court had made during Reconstruction and, of course, by southern Democrats. But in one particular area of electoral regulation, congressional electoral regulation, the basis for an expansion of national regulation became possible through successful Justice Department litigation and cases won by Republicans in lower federal courts. The most important decision came when the Supreme Court announced in March 1884 in *ex parte Yarbrough* that a national statutory effort to regulate congressional elections was permitted under article 1, section 4. The Court stated what it had declined to declare during Reconstruction, despite opportunities to do so: that the Fifteenth Amendment conferred a *national* and nationally enforceable right to vote on African Americans. In other words, the rate of return on the southern commitment to contest did not clearly seem to drop monotonically after 1877. Indeed, after *Yarbrough* key Republicans could well conclude that any drop in the rate of return could be reversed sharply with appropriate statutory effort.

The time to act on this opportunity occurred during the Harrison administration in connection with the Federal Elections Bill of 1890–91. The politics of the bill is sometimes treated as a charade that no one really took seriously. The problem with this view is that not only Republicans but also southerners took the bill very seriously. The Democratic Party made electoral institutional reform its leading issue in the 1892 presidential election, as we will see.

Given (1) disagreement over the boundaries of the suffrage and similar regional commitments and (2) sharply diverging preferences over electoral institutions, Republican-Democratic conflict over the future of southern politics was, in fact, surprisingly deep and intractable. What the Compromise of 1877 settled, in other words, was the presidential election of 1876 and whether or not federal troops would be used to police elections. Further conflict was not ruled out. This was good news for the democratic inclusion of African Americans. For their own reasons, the leaders of a major institution, the Republican Party, continued to invest resources in resisting black demobilization from the political system. The result was a continuing and high level of systemic conflict.

One condition, of course, for resolution of this conflict was abandonment by Democrats of their bid to demobilize African Americans from politics. But there was a consensus between both the northern and southern wings of the post–Civil War Democratic Party that African American suffrage posed a threat to the Democratic Party's chances of ever reexercising control of national institutions.[9]

Thus resolution at the national level of the conflict over the control of electoral institutions and ultimately over African American suffrage required (1) that somehow the anticipated rate of return to Republicans' historic commitment to contest southern elections drop appreciably, unmistakably, and quickly, and (2) that somehow the rate of return to newly developed commitments to contest, or to preexisting nonsouthern commitments to contest, rise. Either new voters, new jurisdictions, or both new voters and new jurisdictions had to be brought into the political system to offset losses to the party threatened with demobilization—that is, the Republican Party. In other words, *full* Republican abandonment of its Southern commitment to contest—one that would clearly alter the political opportunities facing African Americans, their allies, and their opponents—depended on a manifest change in Republican opportunities in the national electoral market.

Yet where would this shift in market opportunities come from? There was a pro-Republican realignment at the electoral level in the 1890s in the North and the Midwest—but was it sufficient to motivate Republican abandonment of the South? How was it possible for the Republican abandonment actually to occur? This conundrum gets to the relationship between geography and party competition.

Geography, Realignment, and a Western Commitment

The geographic boundaries of most modern political systems are fixed or change very slowly, seeming to preclude the addition of new jurisdictions to compensate any party threatened by demobilization of a constituency. But the United States in the late-nineteenth century was unusual in the extent to which geography could rapidly affect the relative positions of the parties in the electoral market.[10] The system had a large "reserve" of unorganized territory that had been acquired through conquest of a militarily weak Native American population. This territorial expansion had an intricate link to black disenfranchisement and thus to the making of modern America. Republican organization of western territories during the Harrison administration—accelerating a process that Republicans had engineered for decades—immediately preceded Republican mobilization of new voters and conversion of existing voters in the older, existing jurisdictions of the Northeast and Midwest, amid the heat and turmoil over monetary and trade policy that marked the realigning sequence of the 1890s.

Together these phenomena—acquisition of new voters through acquisition of new territories (i.e., a Western commitment to contest) and acquisition of new voters through mobilization and change in voter preferences (i.e., realignment)—helped to set the stage for a Republican withdrawal from southern affairs in the closing years of the nineteenth century. A southern policy was thus no longer needed. The South became unnecessary to the Republican Party as a vote-getting, office-seeking political organization. Also, the costs of continuing to compete in the southern electoral market increased due to sharp Democratic resistance to the Federal Elections Bill, further outlined below.

This final Republican withdrawal from southern politics in turn critically affected the political capacities of regional actors and made black disenfranchisement quite unstoppable. Here I borrow the concept of *political opportunity structure* from the social movement literature. The simple ideas here are: (1) repeated signals from the political environment are either promising or forbidding and political actors respond accordingly; and (2) whether national political parties sustain a regional strategy of mobilization is a crucial signal to regional actors engaged in struggle with each other that will affect their calculations and behavior.

Of course, between the weak and the strong there are differences in how quickly they can respond to shifts in the political environment. But even the seemingly weak are inserted within networks that are often easily overlooked by observers. Reconstruction necessarily left a legacy of democratic institutions—black churches, schools, and newspapers and autonomous black settlements and neighborhoods—and it left a large class of trained and skillful black politicians. The resulting networks permitted political communication, debate, and contact among potential leaders, activists, and followers. The political capacities of actors in these "networks of the weak"—African Americans and their white allies in the region—were critically influenced by how national party politics created a regional political opportunity structure. When that structure changed, both exclusionists and inclusionists appear to have understood the character of the change and to have reacted accordingly.[11]

Let me turn from this overview of the argument to its elaboration. This elaboration proceeds by my first sketching in the Republican Party's Reconstruction-era commitment to contest southern elections. Then I very briefly consider selected aspects of the Republican Party's post-Reconstruction commitment to contest southern elections. Third, I treat the logics of the Republican abandonment of the South that occurred during the McKinley administration. Fourth, I consider the regional impact of this abandonment. I conclude with both a summary of and a brief reflection on the implications of my account.

A Commitment to Contest, 1867–1877

The Confederate States of America's military defeat in 1865 settled the issue of whether two nations would exist where one had existed before. But that settlement simultaneously opened up basic questions about the future both of political representation in the restored Union and of the role of parties in representation. By 1867 the Republican Party partly resolved these questions by sponsoring far-reaching change in three areas: (1) national constitutional law (the Thirteenth, Fourteenth, and Fifteenth Amendments) and the statutory law of national constitutional implementation (the military Reconstruction acts); (2) the policy orientations, tax codes, and institutions of the former Confederate states via the recasting of their constitutions under the aegis of military Reconstruction; and (3) the structure of the party system, as Republican organizations were rapidly built in the former Confederate states.

These were tightly linked domains. The changes in national constitutional law were also changes in the rules of representation and in the electoral rules. They permitted the establishment of new civilian governments in the former rebel states based on radically different constitutions that embodied new social commitments. The establishment of these governments in turn permitted the rapid creation of a new concentration of party elites—black politicians; indigenous white politicians active before the war in southern electoral politics who committed themselves to new forms of social and political representation (known today as the scalawags); and, finally, northern white politicians and men on the make who came South, carrying a mix of ambition, career self-interest, and new, egalitarian social commitments (known today as carpetbaggers). A large array of offices was made available to this new political elite by national-level constitutional change, and the resulting, state-level elections and constitution making. In turn, the provision of offices to a new political elite aided the crash construction of a southern wing for a political party that had never had any presence in southern jurisdictions—the Republican Party.[12]

Development of a Protective, Regulatory Apparatus

Southern Democratic backlash to the Republican Party's sweeping commitment to contest electoral politics throughout the South came, to a considerable degree, in the form of widespread, clandestine, paramilitary violence directed against the new Republican leadership in the South and against freedmen institutions—newspapers, schools, churches, political clubs. In response, Republican Congresses reinforced the Fifteenth Amendment, which stated that the "right of citizens of the United States to vote" could not be abridged or denied "on account of race, color, or previous condition of servitude." The Enforcement Act of May 1870 protected national, state, and local electoral processes from discriminatory administration, and implemented this goal through criminalizing both private and public obstruction of the right to vote related to racial conflict and through placing administration of the act within the federal courts and the Justice Department. It authorized the president to use military force "to aid in the execution of judicial process" and, further, permitted federal judges, marshals, and attorneys to form posses in aid of judicial process. The Ku Klux Klan Act of April 1871 was a wide-ranging statute that authorized "action at law" for a victim deprived of rights by a person acting "under color of any law," held that private conspiracies to interfere with the exercise of a citizen's rights were a "high crime" subject to certain specific and harsh penalties, and permitted military suppression of "insurrection, domestic violence, unlawful combinations, or conspiracies" crippling state governments in the maintenance of their law-and-order responsibilities.[13]

Through the Department of Justice (established in 1870), the Republican Party regularly deployed special (if temporary) Justice Department lawyers and U.S. attorneys, and other personnel (U.S. marshals, federal troops, special election commissioners) on behalf of its southern constituencies. A special fee system for the marshals and attorneys (the more violations tried and the more often process served, the greater one's income) tied together their pecuniary interests, their political loyalties, and the enforcement of a new, radically more inclusive system of representation. Besides the frequent military interventions and deployment of federal troops initiated by the president or on his authority, the Department of Justice launched a total of 3,635 criminal cases between 1870 and 1877 in the South.[14]

In addition, Republicans attached their southern policy to a program of northern "urban reconstruction" via the Federal Elections Act (1871), sometimes known as the Second Force Act. The Federal Elections Act created a quite different electoral regulatory system than the Enforcement Act and its followup, the Ku Klux Klan Act, had. Those statues were largely Fifteenth Amendment enforcement statutes, although the Ku Klux Klan Act also permitted criminal enforcement of the Fourteenth Amendment (at least until the Supreme Court halted this use of the act.) They depended on the Department of Justice and the president for their effective administration, and were clearly aimed at the South. The 1871 Federal Elections Act, in contrast, had a different and northern origin and established a different, largely northern system. Still, it was later amended so that in principle it applied to all rural districts as well, thus creating the rudiments of a fully national system. It would become the basis for the Federal Elections Bill of 1890–91, mentioned above.[15]

Limits of the Reconstruction Commitment

By 1877, though, Republican efforts to invest heavily in building a series of new state-level parties in the former Confederate South seemed a failure—with seemingly obvious implications for the recent increase in the system's scope of contestation. In addition, the Supreme Court had weakened the Fifteenth Amendment electoral regulatory system. In this connection, a key Fifteenth Amendment case is relevant—*United States v. Reese* (1876), involving denial of ballots to African Americans by Kentucky officials. *Reese* damaged the federal criminal enforcement machinery by holding two provisions of the Enforcement Act of 1870 unconstitutional. At a time when black voting rights and southern Republican Parties were facing challenge all through the South, the decision's political impact was deeply discouraging to federal attorneys. Another 1876 decision handed down with *Reese*—*United States v. Cruikshank*, a Fourteenth Amendment case on appeal from Louisiana involving a gruesome massacre of over one hundred African Americans—also suggested hostility among the Supreme Court's justices to national involvement in southern affairs. In *Cruikshank* the Court held that criminal justice in Fourteenth Amendment matters was a state, not a national, prerogative. If Louisiana failed to punish a massacre, the Court suggested there was not much scope for federal action.[16]

To sum up: The Reconstruction developed into a relatively thorough effort to recast the party system of the South. A national regulatory apparatus reinforced this effort. But by the end of Reconstruction this apparatus faced a severe judicial challenge. Yet, we will see, the Republican Party persisted after the Reconstruction in its commitment to systemwide competition. Let me turn to briefly sketching the persistence of a commitment to contest.

Renewed Involvement: Indicators and Incentives

Republican involvement, and an effort at electoral regulation in the South, hardly died after the Reconstruction. Several indicators show that fairly soon after 1877 there was a significant revival of the Reconstruction-era involvement. Consider the first of these in table 8.1. It displays scores for the parties on salience to them of their struggle over enforcement of equal

TABLE 8.1
Priority Index of Equal Suffrage for Major Party Platforms, 1868–1892

	1868	1872	1876	1880	1884	1888	1892
Republicans	0.93	1.0	0.89	0.14	0.04	0.85	0.76
Democrats	0.37	0.93	1.0	0.72	0.45	0.00	0.96

Source: Porter and Johnson 1966.

TABLE 8.2
House Races Contested in the Former Confederacy, 1878–1892 (Average Percentages)

	1878	1880	1882	1884	1886	1888	1890	1892
All	85%	94%	94%	91%	67%	92%	81%	93%
Reps.	48%	76%	61%	91%	52%	86%	66%	54%

Source: Congressional Quarterly's Guide to U.S. Elections 1985, 2d ed.
Note: States are Alabama, Arkansas, Florida, Georgia, Louisiana, Mississippi, North Carolina, South Carolina, Tennessee, Texas, and Virginia.

suffrage in the South and (after 1870) of the Fifteenth Amendment. The crucial assumption here is that the earlier an issue appears in a platform, the more important it probably is. Importance of the equal suffrage issue is measured by 1.0 minus the ratio of the number of the paragraph containing the first explicit reference to black suffrage rights and the total number of paragraphs. The higher the number, the greater the importance, and vice versa; the maximum value is 1.0, the lowest 0. By this measure Republican involvement initially dropped, but then grew substantially.[17]

A second indicator of a continuing involvement is participation in congressional races. Consider the rows in table 8.2. The first is the regional average of *all* House races contested in general elections; the second is the regional average of all House races contested in general elections by candidates willing to label themselves as Republicans or willing to run fusion candidacies that retained a Republican label. Clearly there were ups and downs, but overall one sees a strong performance—a party persisting in candidate recruitment and campaigning.

Yet another indicator is the number of congressional investigations of southern election fraud and violence. Table 8.3 shows, first, the number of congressional investigations of southern elections fraud and violence in two periods, Reconstruction and the period after Reconstruction up to and through the Fifty-fourth Congress. These investigations led to published reports, and they differ from contested elections cases. The table shows, second, the number of investigations sponsored by the two parties during the two periods.[18] Overall, three times as many investigations occurred in the Senate, where Republicans continuously organized the chamber from

TABLE 8.3
Congressional Investigations of Southern Election Fraud and Violence,
during and after Reconstruction

	40th–44th Congresses	45th–54th Congresses
House investigations		
Republican	5	0
Democrat	2	2
Senate investigations		
Republican	14	7
Democrat	0	0

Sources: Congressional Information Service, 1985; Goldman 1976.

TABLE 8.4
Contested Elections Politics, House of Representatives, 45th–54th Congresses

Congress	Total Cases	Southern Cases	Disposition
45th (1877–79) (D)	5	2 (40%)	100% D
46th (1879–81) (D)	2	2 (100%)	50% R/50% D
47th (1881–83) (R)	8	6 (75%)	75% R/25% D
48th (1883–85) (D)	7	3 (43%)	100% D
49th (1885–87) (D)	0	0 (0%)	N.A.
50th (1887–89) (D)	0	0 (0%)	N.A.
51st (1889–91) (R)	9	6 (67%)	89% R/11% I
52nd (1891–93) (D)	1	0 (0%)	100% D
53rd (1893–95) (D)	3	0 (0%)	100% D
54th (1895–97) (R)	11	6 (54%)	82% R/18% I

Source: Martis et al. 1989.

Reconstruction to the rise of McKinley, except during the Fifty-third Congress. While Senate Republicans were clearly much busier during the Reconstruction, they stayed vigorously investigative during the post-Reconstruction decades.

Consider, as well, table 8.4, presenting data on contested elections politics in the House during the Congresses between the end of Reconstruction and the election of McKinley. The rows list the Congresses, their dates, and, in parentheses, the designation of which party organized the House of Representatives in that Congress. The columns list from left to right (1) the total number of contested elections cases that actually affected who was seated; (2) the number of such cases from the South and a parenthetical listing of the percentage of the total composed by the southern cases, and; (3) the disposition of all of the cases. The cells for disposition of the cases list the percentage of cases won by either party for that Congress—hence, a percentage figure in front of either D, R, or I (Democrat, Republican, or

Independent, such as a Greenbacker, Readjuster or Populist). Not all of the cases involve Republican-Democratic conflict—for instance, two of the three southern cases for the Forty-eighth Congress involved Virginia independents allied with the Republicans.

Table 8.4 indicates several things. First, Republican control of the House produced more contested elections politics (26 cases) than Democratic control (18 cases), even though Republicans controlled only 3 out of the 10 Houses organized between 1877 and 1895. Second, such politics, whether Democrats or Republicans controlled the House, was primarily southern contested elections politics. Indeed, if one considers a fact not in the table, that southern seats made up, on average, slightly fewer than 20 percent of the seats in the House during this period, then a scan of the parenthetical percentage figures in the middle column shows that not only was contested elections politics largely southern, it was also disproportionately southern. Fourth, the party controlling the House tended to rule in its favor. In this connection it is worth noting another fact not in the table: In several cases of Republicans ruling against Democrats, they ruled for opponents that were not Republicans—two Populists, one from Alabama and one from North Carolina, won their cases before the Fifty-fourth Congress. In other words, Republicans were not picky about building up congressional opposition to Democrats so long as they built up opposition.[19]

In addition to these tabular data, consider as well evidence concerning the enforcement of electoral law. During the Arthur administration (1881–85), the Department of Justice mounted an aggressive Fifteenth Amendment enforcement effort. The Arthur administration's criminal enforcement effort did not match the level reached during the Reconstruction. Of the nearly 5,000 criminal indictments brought in the South between 1870 and 1894 under statutes implementing the Fourteenth and Fifteenth Amendments, over 1,260, or only about 26 percent, occurred after Reconstruction, almost all between 1878 and 1884. Still, despite the *Reese* and *Cruikshank* decisions of 1876, Fifteenth Amendment enforcement was evidently possible during the Arthur administration under surviving sections of the 1870 Enforcement Act.

There are certain interesting patterns in the enforcement data. About 60 percent of the Reconstruction effort occurred between 1872 and 1875 in two states alone, South Carolina and Mississippi. These had black-majority populations and were likely to experience high rates of criminal action by whites against blacks seeking to vote. In contrast, the post-Reconstruction effort focused less on protecting rights and more on building political opposition. Although indictments were brought in all former Confederate states, five states saw a *higher* number of indictments than during the Reconstruction: Arkansas, Florida, Texas, Louisiana, and Virginia. These

TABLE 8.5

Republican Electoral Performance in Its Historic Base, before and
after Reconstruction (Percentages)

	1860–72/4 (% won)	1876–92/4 (% won)
Electoral vote		
Northeast	89	69
Midwest	98	79
House seats		
Northeast	73	60
Midwest	70	52
Senate seats		
Northeast	92	84
Midwest	84	61

Source: Stewart 1991.

were states with relatively weak Democratic establishments or with anti-
Democratic insurgencies.[20]

Clearly the Republicans *had* a southern policy—but what were the incentives for a southern policy? As suggested by table 8.5, the Republican
Party faced a much more competitive context. In its historic regional bases,
the Northeast and Midwest, the Republican Party lost ground, even though
its absolute strength was still quite high. National percentages (not listed in
the table) show also a much more evenly matched competitive situation
between the parties. The Republican Party's average percentage of House
seats dropped from 61 percent during the 1860–74 period to 46 percent
during the period from 1876 to 1894. Its average percentage of Senate seats
went from 71 percent to 51 percent. Its average electoral (different from
popular) vote went from 75 percent to 49 percent. In this more knife-edged
context, the 11 percent of the former Confederacy's House seats held by
Republicans during the 1876–94 period and the 10 percent of Senate seats
might provide a margin for unified government. Or, to put it in another
way, national Republicans had incentives to regenerate, through further
investment in Southern politics, a positive rate of return to their Reconstruction-era sunk costs.[21]

For example, during the Garfield-Arthur administration, an alliance
with the Virginia Readjusters proved crucial in assuring Republican
unified government for the first time since 1872. The Readjuster movement, which captured the Virginia legislature in 1879, was a militant,
biracial party committed not only to a free ballot and a fair count but
also to strengthening public education and making taxes less regressive.
The Republicans needed an alliance with the Readjusters badly and were
willing to pay a high price for it. A Virginia Readjuster senator, William

Mahone, a Confederate war hero turned railroad magnate and ultimately a political reformer who built a biracial coalition, helped the Republicans to organize an evenly divided Senate during the Forty-seventh Congress (1881–83) and thus to give the vice-president a tie-breaking vote. In return, Mahone received the chairmanship of the Senate Committee on Agriculture during that Congress and membership on three other Senate committees.[22]

Readjuster success in Virginia hinted at the possibility of challenge, in other states, to Democratic control of the governorships, a position crucial to a fair certification of victorious, non-Democratic congressional candidates. They often lost close contests when Democratic governors would certify Democratic candidates as the winners. Yet the populations of about 33 percent of the ex-Confederacy's seventy-three congressional districts in 1881 were majority black. An "anti-Redeemer" (i.e., non-Democratic) governor in another key state or two might generate stronger Republican and black representation in the House. The rate of return on the southern commitment could thus be increased at the margin.[23]

There were serious judicial threats to a southern policy: the *Civil Rights Cases* of 1883, in which the Court overturned the Civil Rights Act of 1875, and *United States v. Harris*, curbing Fourteenth Amendment federal action to punish private violence by whites against blacks.[24] But the Arthur administration's legal enforcement effort scored a major and often overlooked victory in Georgia. There a leader in the Republican-Independent alliance was a U.S. attorney. He ran for Congress in 1882 and won criminal convictions in 1883 in federal district court against key members of a night-riding, Klan-style organization, the Pop and Go Club, that sought to punish black supporters of the Republican-Independent alliance. He also won on appeal to the Supreme Court in *ex parte Yarbrough* (1884). *Yarbrough* was critically important because it opened up rich new possibilities for national electoral regulation in the South. In *Yarbrough* the Court unanimously announced a constitutionally valid connection between the Fifteenth Amendment and Congress's Article 1 power to regulate its own elections. It held that the Fifteenth Amendment created a national and congressionally enforceable right to vote for blacks; suffrage came from the United States as well as from any given state in which a black citizen resided. Second, it held that Congress "must have the power to protect the elections on which its existence depends from violence and corruption." In effect, what Congress could not do through the Enforcement Act of 1870 or the Ku Klux Klan Act of 1871, it could do through Article 1 *for congressional elections*. The decision thus fused the Fifteenth Amendment to the electoral regulatory system put into place under the Federal Elections Act of 1871.[25]

The potential impact of *Yarbrough* was enormous. But not until the administration of Benjamin Harrison, when Republicans briefly again enjoyed unified government, could the effort to act on these implications begin. That effort took the shape of the Federal Elections Bill of 1890–91, which built on the Federal Elections Act. Often treated as a half-hearted echo of Reconstruction, the bill is more accurately read as an effort to seize the opportunities provided by *Yarbrough*. The bill did fail in the Senate—in a moment of high drama in which a small Republican faction torpedoed what the rest of the Republican Party clearly desired.

To sum up: The Republicans had a post-Reconstruction southern policy. Some of it ran aground on the reefs of judicial action. Also, a key initiative was killed in the Senate by a minority faction within the party. But this post-Reconstruction policy was vigorous—strong enough to call forth an even more vigorous Democratic backlash. Let me turn to the Democratic response to a southern policy.

Democratic Backlash

During the Harrison administration, southern Democrats in Florida and Tennessee enacted legislation to restrict the suffrage. In Mississippi they rewrote the state constitution for that purpose. These states thus joined South Carolina and Georgia, which already had suffrage-restrictive legislation on the books. But the Democratic presidential platform for 1892 went further. It made the Elections Bill and, by implication, the very idea of a federal electoral-regulatory system its first objects of attack. Both in its printed material for public circulation (booklets and posters) and in the themes chosen by Democratic speakers touring the country, the Democratic campaign made electoral regulation the party's most important—its first and paramount—issue. This is a little-known fact about the 1892 campaign, but another look at table 8.1 helps to confirm it.[26]

When Cleveland won his second presidency, the Democratic party found itself—for the first time since the Buchanan administration of 1857–61—enjoying unified control of the national government. It used this control to act on its 1892 platform and campaign. In 1893 and 1894 congressional Democrats repealed twenty-eight of the sections in the United States Statutes under the title of "Elective Franchise," and ten of the sections, and a part of an eleventh, under the title of "Crimes."[27]

Meanwhile, regional change in electoral law continued. In 1895 South Carolina's disenfranchising constitutional convention instituted a poll tax (which in poor, rural, credit-starved areas had a devastating impact) as well as literacy and good understanding tests. Alabama and Virginia put per-

sonal registration and the Australian ballot on the books. Personal registration increased the costs of voting, requiring a potential voter to take time
away from the field or factory, and placed enormous discretion in the
hands of local registrars. As for the Australian ballot, it undercut local Republican or third-party formations, since they no longer were the intermediaries between the voter and the ballot box that provided ballots. It was
subtly disenfranchising in another way because such a ballot placed a premium on literacy.[28]

Republican and Populist Resistance to
Democratic Backlash

Republicans sought to resist these trends. Although space precludes an account of the Republican-Populist alliance in the South, it is worth noting
that northern Republicans arranged fusions with southern Populists in
1894. Senator George Hoar (R-Mass.), the Senate manager of the Federal
Elections Bill in 1890–91, raised money for Reuben Kolb, an Alabama
Populist. Senator William Chandler (R-N.H.)—the architect of the Arthur
administration's southern strategy—called for and got a Senate investigation of the Alabama elections in a Senate newly returned to Republican
control. In North Carolina, white fusionists gained control of the legislature, undoing suffrage-restrictive legislation in the 1895 session and encouraging black organization. George White, the last black southern
congressman until 1973, was elected as a Republican from North Carolina
to the first of two terms in 1896. Two fusionist senators, Marion Butler
and Jeter Pritchard, went to the U.S. Senate in 1895 and 1897, respectively.

   Two other indications of Republican resistance are contested elections
politics and the 1896 platform. The Republican-controlled House during
the Fifty-fourth Congress was active in unseating southern Democrats, getting rid of as many as it had during the Fifty-first Congress, when it took up
the Federal Elections Bill. Second, the 1896 Republican platform condemned lynching and disenfranchisement.[29]

   In short, as late as 1896 the Republican party's southern policy was,
despite setbacks, alive and well. Let me turn now to the McKinley administration, during which the historic southern policy of the Republican Party
collapsed. In the standard narrative of a steady Republican retreat from the
South from 1872 on, the post-1896 developments within the Republican
Party are the last act in the betrayal of southern African Americans. But it
is more of a puzzle than that—and it is explicable from within this chapter's party-centered approach.

The Logic of Disinvestment

Within a few years of McKinley's election it was clear that the Republican Party had abandoned a historic southern policy. There was silence about race riots and lynchings. Republicans literally did nothing in the Fifty-fifth Congress about disenfranchisement. In the Fifty-sixth Congress Republicans failed to assist fusionist politicians in North Carolina.[30] In time it became clear that the first McKinley administration was a watershed. From 1901 to 1929 Congressional Republicans and African American leaders periodically sought to place disenfranchisement on the national legislative agenda. Also, Republican presidential platforms raised the issue in 1900, 1904, and 1908 (although not thereafter). The priority index of equal suffrage, introduced in table 8.1, above, yields scores for these years of 0.58, 0.32, and 0.59. But the political counterpoint to these legislative efforts and platform stances comprised death in committee, overwhelming procedural votes against further pursuit of the issue, and led to efforts by prominent Republicans to change delegate representation at Republican national conventions so as to destroy the remaining influence of the South's Black-and-Tan Republican politicians within presidential nominating politics. Republican leaders actually voiced dismay (in Theodore Roosevelt's words) over "the folly . . . of reconstruction based on universal Negro suffrage."[31]

What explains this shift? During the Harrison administration, a brief two-year period of Republican unified government was the occasion for a major electoral regulatory effort, the Force Bill, that probably would have succeeded had one vote on a procedural motion in the Senate gone differently. Also, during the second Cleveland administration, Republicans resisted the Democratic counterattack, allying themselves with Alabama and North Carolina Populists. As late as the 1896 presidential nominating convention black Republican delegates from the South played a key role in convention politics.

Republicans might well have found it easy, furthermore, to return to their historic role. In 1904, for instance, the Republican presidential platform noted that the party "entered upon its present period of complete supremacy in 1897." But despite "complete supremacy" nothing really happened—why?[32]

A key part of the answer surely has to do with new tariff, monetary, and foreign policy issues. But much of the answer *also* has to do with the change that occurred between 1893 and 1897 in the costs and benefits of a historic policy. Given scarce organizational resources and a historic context that provides incentives for selective mobilization, American party leaderships have always faced choices about whether they will contest all

206 RICHARD M. VALELLY

jurisdictions in the system. They are strategic about rates of return on commitments to contest. By the late 1890s it was clear that the rate of return on the southern commitment had dropped. Also, the national electoral cycle's outcomes had begun to provide clear information of increased electoral success in other regions. That is, the rate of return on other commitments had simultaneously increased. The net result was rapid disinvestment from the South.

Democratic Resistance

Bear in mind that the Democratic Party simultaneously combined national *and* regional change in the rules of the electoral game and that there were threats of widespread resistance to a vigorous national policy, such as mob and paramilitary violence in 1889 and 1890 in northern Florida, which had led to the assassination of a deputy U.S. marshal and the resignation of the U.S. marshal for northern Florida.[33]

More fundamentally, perhaps, the new state-level rules restricted the electorate to a pool of white conservative Democrats that Republicans could never mobilize. The disenfranchising conventions and the southern legislatures had devised rules that shrank the legal registrant pool. Under *Yarbrough* only national regulation of national elections was protected; states could pretty much do what they wanted. But what point was there to national regulation of national elections if the registrant pool was minuscule, white, and strongly Democratic? Only a massive new commitment— a true "second Reconstruction"—could cope with this problem.

The South's New Superfluousness

The potentially exorbitant costs of a renewed southern policy also have to be laid against the South's superfluousness to the incipient Republican restoration, a restoration that looked by 1904 to be a "period of complete supremacy." Here the key facts are the basic differences between the 1877–97 phase in U.S. party politics and the phase after 1897 in (1) the Republican Party's capacity to achieve unified government and (2) the marginal contribution of southern Republicanism to that capacity.

During the former phase, the Republican party struggled to achieve unified government, and succeeded both times only for brief two-year periods—1881–83 and 1889–91—that ended abruptly after midterm, off-year elections. Yet in both two-year periods Republican involvement in the South played important roles. In the 1881–83 episode, alliance with the Readjusters permitted the Republicans to organize the Senate during the

TABLE 8.6
Shifts in Regional Bases of National Politics, 1876–1892/4 and 1896–1908/10 (Percentages)

	Presidential Electoral Vote		House		Senate	
	1876–1892/4	1896–1908/10	1876–1892/4	1896–1908/10	1876–1892/4	1896–1908/10
Confederacy	26	25	19	13	28	24
Northeast	29	26	31	29	23	20
Midwest	21	19	26	27	13	12
Border	11	10	11	12	13	12
West	13	19	13	19	25	33

Source: Stewart 1991.

Forty-seventh Congress by giving the vice-president tie-breaking power. Without the Republican-Readjuster alliance, there would have been no unified government.[34] In the 1889–91 episode, a contingent of fifteen Southern Republicans contributed to the 179–152 advantage that the Republicans had in the Fifty-first Congress, at a time when the policy agenda of the party was long and when the pent-up demand for new legislative initiatives was unusually strong. Without them, the margin to legislate decreased considerably.[35]

After 1897, in sharp contrast, the Republican Party was continually able to create unified government—and without any southern presence. For the elections between and including 1896 and 1908, the mean of the Republican percentage of the presidential electoral vote (distinct from the presidential popular vote) was 65.7 percent. The mean of its percentage of the House seats between the Fifteenth Congress (1897–99) and the Sixtieth Congress (1907–9) was 56.9 percent, and for the Senate the comparable figure was 60.7 percent.

The party's strength in its historic base, the Northeast and Midwest, returned after McKinley's election in 1896, in the wake of the intense Republican mobilization during that campaign. Further, the party's strength increased in two other areas, the border states and the western states. Consider also table 8.6. The rows are for regions and the columns are for pairs of percentages by national institution. The first number in the pair is the percentage corresponding to the period 1876–92/4; the second number in the pair is the percentage corresponding to the period 1896–1908/10. The percentages are for the proportion of individuals from that region elected to the House or the Senate for the period, or the percentage of electoral votes for the region for the period. For instance, the cell for the Confederacy and the House shows two things: (1) between 1876 and 1894, 19 percent of all of the individuals elected to the House were from the ex-

Confederate states and (2) between 1896 and 1910 13 percent of all the individuals elected to the House were from the ex-Confederate states. The same principles apply to all of the other cells in the table.[36]

Political and organizational incentives for the pursuit of a southern policy, of the kind that existed between the Compromise of 1877 and the election of McKinley, disappeared after 1896. The Republican Party's strength returned in its historic base—in part the result of mobilization around tariff and monetary policy issues in the high-stakes 1896 election. Also, Republican strength grew in the border states, and it was high in the western states. These changes coincided with important shifts in the regional bases of national politics that added to the South's new irrelevance to the Republican Party.

The former Confederacy grew less important, relative to other regions. Other regions also grew less important, but their decline in importance was not as great as the Confederacy's. Thus Republicans grew stronger in regions that were only slightly less important than they once had been. At the same time Republican strength remained considerable in the region that became the winner in the regional shift—the western states.

That the western states proved to be an important component of the new Republican period of "complete supremacy" was a planned outcome. The same degree of political insecurity after the Compromise of 1877 that motivated a Republican southern policy *also* motivated a Republican *western policy*. At the outset of the Harrison administration, six new states, the largest number ever to be admitted in any presidency and five of them safely Republican, were admitted to the Union. This relative flood of new states resulted from careful Republican maneuver in Congress to sustain partisan advantage. Ironically, the party's western policy, based on the kinds of motivations that also had gone into a southern policy, ultimately contributed to the Republican Party's disinvestment from the South: the western policy helped to make the South superfluous to Republican Party interests.[37]

Here we see the influence of geography on party competition. In most modern political systems the boundaries of the system are fixed. New jurisdictions cannot be added. But the nineteenth-century U.S. party system had a "reserve" of unorganized territory, acquired through military conquest of Native Americans and colonized by small numbers of voters and practicing politicians with links to the party system in the older jurisdictions. This reserve provided one of the conditions for the resolution of the Democratic-Republican struggle that first erupted in 1867 over the boundaries of the suffrage in America. It meant that if the Republicans developed a western policy they could, in effect, be "compensated" for the demobilization of a historic constituency and for the destruction of electoral regulatory institutions they had built up and tenaciously defended for decades.

The rate of return on an investment in the West could replace at a higher level the current rate of return on investment in the South.

Let me sum up before turning to the regional impact of the Republican Party's disinvestment from the South. By the middle of the first McKinley administration, when McKinley toured the South praising the Confederate war dead, it had become clear that the consummation of the Compromise of 1877 was finally at hand. New issues, such as foreign policy, figured in the GOP disinvestment. But their influence on the GOP also interacted strongly with an abrupt change in the costs and benefits of the party's historic southern policy. The costs of a southern policy were now very high indeed, and the benefits were nil. Both a resurgence of strength in historic Republican areas and new strength in the West made the South superfluous to Republican capacity to achieve unified government.

By the end of the Cleveland administration, the Democratic Party had gone very far toward altering the rules of electoral politics, making a return to the status quo ante prohibitively costly for the Republican Party. And by the end of the 1896 presidential campaign, it had become clear for Republicans that there were likely to be rich alternatives to a southern policy. It would take a few more electoral cycles for this structural change in national party dynamics to become completely clear—thus, debate about the emerging "southern system" continued within the party, leaving its mark on presidential platforms until 1908. But the change in national party dynamics appears to have been clear enough during the McKinley administration to motivate the kind of sharp change in the Republican Party's symbolic stance toward the South represented by McKinley's southern tour.

Let me turn now to consideration of the South's regional political opportunity structure. Political signals from the national political environment were a key feature of the political opportunity structure of the South. Such signals, and change in them, had a large impact on the political capacities of the South's political actors.

The Impact of Disinvestment

What impact did the Republican Party's final disinvestment have on the South? Since the Reconstruction, the region's inclusionists—to recall a term introduced earlier—had been an active force in the South's politics. These included (1) African American politicians and activists and (2) their white allies, both local Republicans and leaders of white-led economic insurgencies, for example, the Readjuster movement, the Arkansas Agricultural Wheel, and the North Carolina Populists, all of which explicitly called for a "free ballot and fair count" and broad-based educational and tax policies favored by African Americans. Their opponents, whom I have called exclusionists, sometimes adopted paternalistic stances toward African Americans and sometimes were openly white supremacist. Republican disinvestment—the inaction toward the South that became clear by 1898—strongly affected these actors' political capacities.

Republican inaction was not, of course, the only influence on the political capacities of the South's protagonists. But it is an influence whose role has not yet been fully appreciated. Because the Compromise of 1877 is seen as so pivotal, there is a tendency to cast subsequent processes leading to disenfranchisement in largely regional terms. In doing so, the critical interaction between national and regional dynamics can easily be overlooked.

The process of final disinvestment that began sometime about 1897–98 necessarily decreased the political capacities of inclusionists. It accomplished this both by shutting off resources and by ensuring that there would be no favorable political opportunities, thus extinguishing political hope. Correlatively, therefore, disinvestment also augmented the political capacities of exclusionists. Southern Democratic parties had of course already grown stronger—but now there was less expectation of a national challenge.

The sharpness of the shift in the region's structure of political opportunities can be appreciated by reviewing the impact that Republican persistence in a southern policy had in the decade and a half or so between the Arthur administration's southern strategy and McKinley's 1898 tour of the South. Consider, first, the impact of continuing to contest congressional elections.

The continued presence of Republicans, or candidates willing to be public about fusion with Republicans, meant that money would be sent south, after consultation between local and national Republicans. It also meant that state-level Republican parties had to be staffed in order for ballots to be provided to voters. Until the 1890s and the advent of the Australian ballot in American politics, parties printed and provided ballots to voters, if sometimes under state regulation. For them to provide ballots on election day there had to be at least a skeletal party infrastructure. With such an infrastructure came county- and statewide conventions. These often were sites of struggle between white officeholders and black politicians vying for shares of federal patronage—but they could also be forums for participation, debate, platform drafting, and reaffirmation of principle. They played key roles in the development of a regional cadre of black politicians.

Here the federal patronage and the system of U.S. attorneys and U.S. marshals, who were often empowered to hire temporary assistants, proved crucial in providing a political infrastructure. In many states, both a party staff and at least a smattering of "mobilizers" and "contacters" worked the electorate. Supporting these party workers were networks of regional and local institutions, such as African American churches (among other associations), that were used for communication of political directives.[38]

Second, consider the impact of federal criminal prosecutions. There were about 1,260 federal criminal cases bunched into the 1877–84 and the 1889–93 periods of Republican control of the presidency, with most in the former period. Some of these—how many is very hard to say, of course—created some hope of justice, and some created financial burdens for the defendants or otherwise gave pause to them. [39]

Consider, third, the impact of congressional investigations. The publicity of such investigations created hope of further federal intervention. An investigation was sometimes seen as a party-building technique by politicians in the region. In order for these investigations to proceed, networks of local activists had to be contacted and witnesses had to be brought to Washington or to where the investigation was sitting.[40]

Finally, consider the impact of commitment to national legislative reform. The national party repeatedly called for "free ballots and fair counts" in the South. State-level southern parties echoed this commitment in their own platforms. Thus, when the party achieved unified government in 1889, something like the Federal Elections Bill was widely expected and there were regional reactions. In Mississippi, for instance, the bill's introduction led African American leaders to hold a state convention in Jackson, a move characterized by a standard history as a "shock" to the white establishment. The convention communicated a request to Democratic leaders for fusion candidacies, per the policy of black leaders of working with Democrats "until it was possible to vote once more as Republicans." When Democrats refused, perhaps not unexpectedly, the convention entered the first statewide Republican ticket since 1875. Eventually, violent attacks on campaign rallies forced the withdrawal of the entire ticket. The episode nonetheless says much about the quickness with which African American leaders could and did organize in response to major political opportunities in their national and regional environment.[41]

In sum, there was a continuous provision of encouragement and resources involved in Republican persistence in a southern policy. This national-regional interaction played at least a modest role in sustaining the often high levels of African American voting discovered by Kousser and, as well, by Rusk and Stucker, both for the Deep and peripheral South states. Rosenstone and Hansen have shown that electoral participation depends much more than had previously been thought on political mobilization, and less on attitudes and individual-level political resources. Thus the level of hope and the local, albeit fragile, Republican institutions that were encouraged by national inputs partly explain the persistence of African American local, state legislative, and congressional political careers well into the 1890s.[42]

National-regional interaction also helped to stimulate biracial coalitions under the banner of third-party economic insurgencies. Fusion candidacies in states where the Republican Party was reasonably strong lowered the threshold of political entry for such insurgencies. While black politicians often had mixed feelings about these insurgencies, a look at the preponderance of evidence in a recent treatment of Chester Arthur's southern strategy suggests that black support for fusion was strong, if primarily tactical in nature. Furthermore, in two cases, the Readjusters (1879–89) and the North Carolina Populist-Republicans (1896–99), such insurgencies permitted the rapid mobilization of very strong, county-level and municipal black politics. Only savage race riots instigated by conservative Democrats sufficed to crush these mobilizations.[43]

Thus the almost complete cessation after 1897 of national inputs into southern politics was, in itself, an important intervention into regional politics. A seemingly remarkable feature of disenfranchisement in its later stages was the lack of overt black protest in the region. While many factors produced apparent quiescence, one of these was surely the rational judgment that protest would not spark national assistance and that it would provoke exceptional violence.

By the same token, the Republican failure to return to a southern policy affected exclusionist capacities. It combined with the cumulative effects of violence, intimidation, and pre-1897 state-level rules changes to create a context within which disenfranchisers considered themselves freer to complete the process of disenfranchisement. There may be more than just a correlation in the fact that much of the activity of disenfranchisement occurred *after* the rise of McKinley Republicanism. North Carolina instituted sweeping change in 1899 and 1900. Alabama's disenfranchising convention of 1901 established a poll tax, literacy and property tests, and a grandfather clause for registration prior to 1902. Virginia's disenfranchising convention of 1902 established a poll tax, a literacy test, a property test, and an understanding test. Texas established a poll tax in 1902. Georgia established a literacy test, a property test, and an understanding test in 1908. Final Republican disinvestment from the South may well have shut off, as it were, a yellow light in the region that signaled "proceed with caution" and may have turned on a green light.[44]

GOP disinvestment from the South toward the close of the century helped to make disenfranchisement an unstoppable process. It deprived inclusionists of resources and hope. It encouraged exclusionists to recast entirely the basic electoral foundations of political democracy in the South—and, in the process, to shift the 90 percent of America's black citizens living in the South well to the margins of the political nation's boundaries. The introduction of the Australian ballot (placing a premium on voter literacy), seemingly nominal poll taxes (which captured a surprisingly large percentage of the total annual disposable income of debt-burdened sharecroppers, tenants, and freehold farmers), literacy tests, good understanding clauses, grandfather clauses, and white primaries all combined to erect impassable barriers between African Americans (and many whites) and the electoral system. When complete by about 1908, the "southern system" was much more efficient in establishing racial exclusion than earlier, relatively scattershot mechanisms of intimidation, fraud, violence, and vote dilution. And its efficiency set the stage for a new phase in America's long and epic struggle over black voting rights. Considering that phase is beyond my scope, however—so I will turn now to brief summary of my party-centered analysis of disenfranchisement.

Party Dynamics, Disenfranchisement, and
American Democracy

After the Reconstruction, party competition strongly influenced the political prospects of African Americans. Given the demographic concentration of African Americans in the South, their role in electoral politics depended on the persistence of at least one of the major parties in forcing systemwide conflict and mobilization. Such persistence was there. National party dynamics from 1877 to the mid-1890s helped to sustain some of the inclusiveness achieved by the Reconstruction. Such dynamics preserved some of the "refounding" of the American system represented by the Reconstruction.

But party dynamics were also tightly connected to regional calculations. When the incentives to the more inclusionist Republican Party to engage in systemwide mobilization and competition finally and irreversibly changed, the "new Constitution" instituted after the Civil War then truly lost much of its life. Republican disinvestment from the South did much to permit the establishment of the "southern system."

Disenfranchisement had a regional *location*. But it left many imprints on the system as a whole, influencing the future of American life. All southern black—and many southern white—voters lost direct electoral influence over state legislatures, county commissions, and city and town councils. Segregationists completed the construction of an elaborate system of color lines and codified it in law. Without any political representation for the great majority of black Americans, African Americans were also vulnerable to a gradual strengthening of de facto color lines in the nation as a whole. To paraphrase C. Vann Woodward, the Southern Way became the American Way in race relations.[45] Disenfranchisement thus contributed to the deepening and magnification of racial stratification in America. It has, in fact, taken decades of African American struggle in building national groups, planning litigation, and mounting broad movements of protest to help in creating the closely related processes—still underway, with many steps backward and forward—of both restoring life to the "new Constitution" instituted after the Civil War and of dismantling racial hierarchy in America.

Notes

1. Katznelson, Geiger, and Kryder 1993; Myrdal 1944.

2. Cf. Rueschemeyer, Stephens, and Stephens 1992, 122–32; and McAdam 1982, 66–67, focusing on social and economic factors.

3. Wang 1993; Ayers 1992; Kousser 1992; Rusk and Stucker 1978; and Kousser 1974 exemplify the new understanding. Examples of misconceptions about the Compromise of 1877 are Swain 1993, 21; and Carmines and Stimson 1989, 29.

4. Terms *inclusionist* and *exclusionist* from Valelly 1993.

5. This understanding of the relationship between mobilization and institutional context derived from Powell 1986, esp. p. 21.

6. On "sunk costs," see Stinchcombe 1968, 120–25. "Commitment to contest" is my term.

7. DeSantis 1982, discusses the scholarly controversy over the longevity of the Compromise. Carmines and Stimson 1989, 29.

8. See Kousser 1974 for basic theory of parties having preferences over electoral institutions. See Stewart and Weingast 1992, 225, 270, and 225 n. 11, for a succinct, clear statement. On party unity and its electoral systemic origins, see Kousser, 1992. On internal politics, see Wang 1993, chap. 6.

9. Kousser 1992 is quite important for understanding this consensus.

10. For an important work that makes this clear, see Martis and Elmes 1993.

11. A basic discussion of "political opportunity structure" is in McAdam 1982. For an overlooked discussion of an important case, enslaved African Americans and their responses to shifts in their political opportunity structure, see Du Bois [1935] 1992, chaps. 1–7. See also Foner 1988, chap. 3.

12. Cf. Valelly 1993 and cites therein.

13. Ibid., 39–40.

14. On the fee system, see Goldman 1976, 279, 283, 302; for the enforcement effort, entire vol.; enforcement statistics for 1870–77 are at 70 n. 31.

15. 16. On the 1871 Federal Elections Act, see Burke 1968; and Wang 1993, chap. 2 and app. 3, reproducing the statute.

16. See Benedict 1978; Nieman 1991, 92–99; Kousser 1992, 160–64; Magrath 1963, chap. 7.

17. Adaptation of the Racial Priority Index of Party Platforms, Carmines and Stimson 1989, 56–57. For coding equal suffrage priority, I counted all paragraphs that explicitly referred to a "free ballot," a "free ballot and a fair count," the Fifteenth Amendment, the merits of federal vs. state control of elections, and equal adult male suffrage. First paragraph of platform coded as a *preamble* and

not a paragraph if it ended with a colon, notwithstanding any substantive statement in the preamble.

18. Why would Democrats sponsor investigations? For equally partisan purposes is the answer. Thus, in connection with the 1876 contested presidential election, the House of Representatives, organized by the Democratic party, sponsored a total of four investigations.

19. For more on the politics of contested elections, see Allen and Allen 1981, 176–78.

20. See Burke 1968, 146–54; and Goldman 1976, 311–12.

21. Data from Stewart 1991, 208, 210, 212, 217, tables 9.3–9.6.

22. Readjusters sought "readjustment" of the state debt downward via partial transfer to West Virginia and the upping of revenues through corporate taxation. Both moves would redress looting of the school fund for debt retirement and reduce the tax system's regressivity. Cf. Ayers 1992, 46–47; Doenecke 1981, 50–53; Degler 1982, 270–315. See also Martis et al. 1989, 45. See U.S. Congress 1989, 1414, for Mahone's committee appointments.

23. Percentage of districts majority black estimated from Parsons, Beach, and Dubin 1986, 146–223.

24. For concise discussion of these cases, see Wang 1993, 398–405; Kousser 1992, 160–62; McCurdy 1986; and Wiecek 1988, 96–101.

25. See Burke 1968, 153–66 for doctrinal background to *Yarbrough* and for impact. McCurdy 1986 succinctly describes the cases. Regarding *Yarbrough* itself, see Goldman 1976, 192–204. Cf. also Wang 1993, 391–408.

26. Knoles 1942, 8–12, 91–92, 136, 138–39, 144–45, 161–62, 168–170, 171–72, 173–74, 177–78, 193–94, 208–9, 213–16 (esp. summary remarks at 216 and discussion in n. 66), 220–21, 224–25.

27. Schwartz 1970, 806.

28. Kousser 1974, 239.

29. DeSantis 1959, chap. 6; Sherman 1973, 2, 8–9, 16. While the Priority Index of Equal Suffrage is not especially high (0.30), it is still higher than it is for 1880 or 1884, the two years bracketing the Arthur administration's southern strategy.

30. Sherman 1973 chap. 1.

31. Ibid., 72, 77, 95–97, 169, 170–71, 221–23. See also Allen, Clausen, and Clubb 1971.

32. Johnson and Porter 1966, 137.

33. Goldman 1976, 250–68.

34. Further, the Republican capacity to hang onto the Senate in the Forty-eighth Congress, thus preventing Democratic dominance of the Congress as a whole in the second half of the Arthur administration, depended critically on the 1882 election of a second Readjuster senator from Virginia, creating a Republican-Readjuster coalition of forty, against thirty-six Democrats. On the relative importance of this, see Stewart and Weingast 1992, 259–69.

35. On pent-up policy demand, see Socolofsky and Spetter 1987, 47.

36. Stewart 1991, 208, 210, 212, 217. Cf. also Stanley and Niemi 1992, 139; and Martis and Elmes 1993, 70–84.

37. See Stewart and Weingast 1992, 236–42, 258.

38. The evidence is fragmentary, and sometimes offered from within the "Republican betrayal" framework, but suggestive enough. See Anderson 1981, esp. 159–61, 340–42; Bacote 1955, 65–67; Uzee 1950.

39. Again, the evidence in secondary sources is not extensive, but see Cooper 1968, 32, 70–71, 84–85, 94–106; Anderson, 1981, 91, 112, 340–42.

40. Congressional Information Service 1985, 515–16, 525, 528–29, listing witnesses for major post-Reconstruction investigations. In 1894 in South Carolina's Second District, which was not the historic "black" Seventh District, Republicans organized poll watching in order to trigger a House contested election investigation that deprived Democrats of the seat. See Tindall 1949, 212–34, at 231. Also, see Uzee 1950, 48–49.

41. Wharton 1965, 203–9.

42. Kousser 1974; Rusk and Stucker 1978; Rosenstone and Hansen 1993, chaps. 5–7.

43. Degler 1982, 292–300 (on the Danbury, Va., riot and its role in the collapse of the Readjuster movement) and 359–66 (on the role of the Wilmington, N.C., riot in the collapse of the Populist-Republican fusion movement of North Carolina).

44. Kousser 1974, chaps. 6–7, and p. 239.

45. Woodward 1974, 67–118 and 115.

9

The Politics of Racial Isolation in Europe and America

MARGARET WEIR

THE ONCE-HOMOGENOUS nations of Europe are now struggling with the social tensions of racial diversity. Clusters of disadvantaged minorities have emerged on the metropolitan landscape of many European nations as economic growth has slowed and unemployment has risen. In the face of racial conflict and ethnic disadvantage, the press and some politicians have warned that European nations are developing American-style ghettos, populated by ethnic minorities who are excluded from the mainstream of social and economic life.[1] Such concentrations raise thorny questions for liberal democracies because they suggest that racial difference creates disadvantages that pervade all spheres of economic and social life.

Yet even a cursory review of the evidence reveals substantial national differences on issues related to race and poverty. Nowhere do the levels of ethnic and racial segregation reach the virtually total separation of the races that exists in many American cities.[2] Likewise, the extreme violence and deep poverty that characterize the poor areas of American cities have no counterpart in Europe. Perhaps most striking, however, is the sheer extent of the physically separate and deteriorated areas of American cities. Any remotely similar set of problems emerging in European nations is surely on a much smaller scale.

Some observers have sought to reconcile this set of differences and similarities by arguing that European countries are on the same trajectory as the United States, only a decade or so behind.[3] An alternative approach contends that nations can and do challenge the forces leading to racially linked economic and social exclusion by adopting policies that promote inclusion and opportunity.

In this article, I argue that national differences are indeed significant but that the policy and political mechanisms that create concentrations of racially defined poverty have not been adequately understood. I contend that to assess the direction of change, we must examine the spatial dimension of politics and the division of policy responsibility between central and local governments. Without an understanding of these mechanisms, it becomes difficult to judge national trajectories. Drawing on these features of politics and policy, I show that recent changes have moved European nations closer to the American model of concentrated poverty but that underlying political differences will limit the process of "ghettoization" in Europe.

I develop this argument by comparing the emerging problems of poverty and race in Britain and France with those existing in the United States. France and Britain provide a useful comparison because both countries have significant populations of ethnic and racial minorities who are citizens and who are spatially concentrated in deteriorated areas. Moreover, both countries have experienced social disturbances centered in these areas of disadvantage. And, like the United States, France and Britain have had to cope with structural changes in the economy during the 1980s that have been especially severe for workers at the bottom of the labor market. However, France and Britain have different political systems and have been governed by quite distinct political coalitions over the past ten years. They thus offer some variation for understanding the way that politics interacts with the economic and demographic forces that produce racial disadvantage and concentrated poverty.

In the pages that follow I compare the emergence of concentrations of poverty and pay special attention to the racial dimensions of this issue in the United States, Britain, and France. I first examine theories explaining why racially identified concentrated poverty emerges, presenting my own argument about the importance of the spatial dimension of politics and policy. I then analyze the American model, noting a fundamental continuity in a "bias for localism" that created racially separated areas of poverty in cities since World War II. The third section examines the more centralized politics and policies adopted in postwar Britain and France, showing how they created spatial distinctions that were less isolating than those in the United States. The final section of the paper argues that changes in policy and politics in the 1980s pushed Britain and France in an American direction but it also shows how institutional and political differences will limit the process of ghettoization.

Explaining Exclusion

Analysts of poverty and race make two types of arguments: one highlights the entwined effects of economic and demographic change; the other stresses political responses to emerging problems. Neither explanation is sufficient to account for both national differences and direction of change. Economic and demographic arguments overstate similarities because they pay insufficient attention to politics. But political arguments must be able to specify the underlying mechanisms that shape how governments respond to new economic and demographic pressures in order to capture the likely direction of change.

Economic and Demographic Pressures

The emerging literature on "global cities" argues that the globalization of manufacturing and the rise of finance as a central function of advanced economies have created a new urban form.[4] As major cities such as New York and London have become international financial centers, they have elaborated a fundamentally new kind of local economy based on the provision of highly specialized services. The transformation of the local economic base brings with it significant changes in the labor market, creating a sharp bifurcation between a highly paid, specialized professional sector and a poorly paid, casual labor market of lower-level jobs. Thus, according to this literature, the new economic base of cities also transforms social structures, introducing a more polarized society with a declining middle class.

Because workers are increasingly able to cross national boundaries, the new social polarization has taken on a racial dimension, as immigrants fill the lower levels of the labor market. Such social divisions take on a spatial form, in part because native whites leave the city for the suburbs. These processes are so strong that they make the problem of the "inner city"—poor and deteriorated areas of minority concentration—a concern of all advanced economies.

Other analysts point to economic trends to explain the emergence of comparable centers of disadvantage in older manufacturing cities. Kasarda and Friedrichs, for example, contend that a similar phenomenon of concentrated disadvantage has appeared in older German and American cities, "with the West German experience lagging behind that of the U.S. by approximately 10 years."[5] As these cities changed from goods-processing to information-processing centers, they argue, "demographic–employment opportunity mismatch" appeared. A significant proportion of the blue-collar population lacked the skills to perform the white-collar jobs that now dominate the economy. Without the ladders of mobility once provided by industrial employment, these groups have become occupationally blocked. And, significantly, they are geographically stuck as well. Kasarda and Friedrichs argue that social policies providing subsistence exacerbate the problem because they discourage moves to more prosperous areas. "The outcome" they note, "is that increasing numbers of potentially productive minorities find themselves socially, economically, and spatially isolated in segregated areas of urban decline where they subsist, in the absence of job opportunities, on a combination of welfare programs and their own informal economies."[6]

These economically based perspectives draw our attention to the major shifts in the world economy that have affected Europe and the United

States. But the emphasis on similarities masks important cross-national differences that might make for very different national trajectories. First, there is little agreement on how international trends are affecting domestic labor markets. Sassen argues that they create a new casual labor market. In contrast, Kasarda and Friedrichs maintain that they create skilled jobs for which existing workers are unprepared. Second, these approaches do not sufficiently explore nationally specific factors—such as labor market institutions, social policies, and government action—that might intersect and alter the impact of these economic forces.

Moreover, these accounts pay insufficient attention to the effects of noneconomic factors. Why does the United States have by far the highest levels of racial segregation, and what does this difference mean for the trajectory? Does the greater number of poor minorities in American cities create a threshold effect that make their problems qualitatively worse and more difficult to attack? If these nations began feeling the effects of these international forces from different starting points in terms of social policy coverage, patterns of industrial relations, and the organization of public and private investment, why should they be pushed in the same direction? In other words, cannot initial differences affect the trajectory and ultimately the outcome?

To answer these questions, we need a better understanding of how politics intersects with economic trends. What prompts governments to try to influence these developments? What do they try to do, and what are they able to do?

Explaining National Differences

A second perspective on race and poverty emphasizes national differences. In this view, significant cross-national variation in the characteristics of concentrated disadvantage indicates qualitative differences, not simply time lags. Moreover, the diverse ways that governments respond to these problems are taken as evidence that national trajectories will differ.

This perspective has been advanced by Loic Wacquant in his telling comparison of the Parisian suburb La Courneuve and the South Side Chicago neighborhood of Woodlawn.[7] Wacquant dismisses facile arguments about the growth of American-style ghettos in the high-rise public housing on the outskirts of Paris. He shows that the Parisian areas are far more racially and socially integrated than those in the United States. For example, in one of the major housing estates commonly thought of as the center of La Courneuve's "ghetto," 75 percent of the residents are white French people and the majority of household heads are employed.[8] In contrast, Woodlawn is virtually all African American and has far higher levels of hardship, with nearly half of all households receiving public assistance.

Wacquant attributes these differences to the fundamentally distinct processes creating them. In the United States, the process is one of "hyperghettoization," in which both the market and the state have withdrawn from a racially defined urban core. In France, race is not the defining characteristic of the process; emerging economic divisions that fragment the working class are key. Central to these differences is the role of the state and, in particular, the welfare state. Wacquant points to the vigorous efforts of the French state to reverse the deterioration of the *banlieues* (suburbs) and to find ways to "reinsert" the poor into the mainstream of social life. In contrast, the American government sought to reduce its responsibility for the poor in the 1980s.

Wacquant provides an insightful comparison, attentive to the experiential similarities of these disadvantaged areas but stressing their distinctive structural underpinnings. Nonetheless, his account provokes questions about the origins, and hence the durability, of the distinct processes he has outlined. What is it about American society or American politics that makes race so central, and why is race less pivotal in France? Wacquant suggests that welfare states play a key role in organizing these processes, but he does not specify the features of the welfare state that are important. The British case makes such distinctions especially salient. Despite the adoption of a social policy path quite similar to that of the United States in the 1980s, Britain does not have the sharply racialized isolation and government/market-withdrawal characteristic of the United States. This raises the possibility that welfare state policies may not be the most important aspect of government activity, or at least that they act in concert with other policies.

These questions suggest that we need to know more about the dynamics of the political and policy processes that Wacquant identifies. Wacquant highlights the different responses of the American and French governments in the 1980s, but we have no means of knowing whether such actions are contingent on temporary political coalitions or whether they are more securely rooted. The measures that the French government has initiated to address concentrated disadvantage sound suspiciously like some of the programs created by the American government in the 1960s: the creation of a cabinet agency responsible for cities and a new program of special assistance for poor areas. Are these initiatives more likely to endure than the American policies, which were diluted within several years and virtually abandoned a decade later? To answer such questions we must understand how this set of issues fits into the existing organization of political coalitions and what opportunities and incentives these issues present for political actors.

In an illuminating account of national differences, Hilary Silver provides some clues as to how political dynamics affect different national patterns of exclusion.[9] As she notes, class segments may form diverse political alliances in different political systems; furthermore, national political institutions and changing welfare programs selectively mobilize some groups and not others. This emphasis on the interaction among political institutions, social policies, and political alliances provides a lever for considering political dynamics and national trajectories. I argue below that a particular feature of politics and policy—their spatial organization—is key in understanding such national differences.

The Political Underpinnings of National Differences

Two clusters of policy are particularly important in understanding national differences and trajectories. The first set of policies are those that help organize local space, uniting or dividing people of different income levels and races. Such policies include, most centrally, land use and housing policies. The second cluster of policies are those that intensify or mitigate spatial divisions. Most important are arrangements for financing the social policies that affect quality of life and future life opportunities, such as education and basic public services. Both sets of policies create incentives for the private and public actions that together create concentrations of disadvantage.

The possibilities for different spatial configurations are deeply affected by technological developments, such as the invention of the automobile and the computer, but governments also profoundly influence the way populations and economic activity organize spatially. Most central is the framework for making decisions about land use. What is the unit of government responsible for such decisions? What is the extent of public authority in this domain? Equally important is the way local units of government are created and what authority they have to control the activities that occur within their borders. Thus, rules about creating new jurisdictions and determining the power of local jurisdictions not only over land use, but also over budgets and taxes, are critical determinants of population and business location. Housing policies also create powerful incentives that shape locational choices. The size of the public- or "social"-housing sector and rules for siting and allocating such housing are of paramount importance, but financing arrangements for housing construction and purchase are also significant.

The second cluster of policies, including education and public services, may either reinforce or mute spatial differences. When benefits and services vary substantially across jurisdictional boundaries, they create incentives for movement. By contrast, benefits that are uniform or that vary little across jurisdictional boundaries will do little to reinforce spatial differences. Such differences are governed in the first instance by decisions about which level of government is responsible for financing these services or benefits. When localities bear substantial responsibility for funding these benefits, the size and economic base of localities will create differences across jurisdictions, as will local decisions about taxing and service levels.

These two clusters of policy shape how individuals and businesses respond to income and racial differences because they create exit options and an array of incentives and disincentives to act on preferences or fears. The extent of the exit options and the strength of the incentives are significant because processes of social and economic division can become self-reinforcing. Accordingly, they may also affect the possibilities for reversing emerging social and racial isolation.

Policies, of course, change. Thus, it is important to understand how these two sets of policies fit into politics if we are to assess how readily they can be altered and in what directions change is likely to emerge. Two features of politics are key: What power do central governments have to affect the division of local space by race and poverty? And what incentives do central government actors have to prevent or ignore the emergence of concentrations of racially identified poverty? As these questions indicate, relatively enduring political structures (such as constitutional design) as well as more situational factors (including political strategy) will underlie political responses.

Politics and Racial Isolation in the United States

Racial ghettos have long existed in American cities. In postwar America, African American migration from the rural South and the suburbanization of whites created a new division between cities, which housed blacks and other racial minorities, and suburbs, which became home to a broadly defined white "middle class." In the past decade, suburbs have become more racially and economically diverse, but nothing has challenged the fundamental forces isolating the black poor. In fact, policy changes in the 1980s combined with existing practices to drive even deeper wedges between cities and suburbs, making it increasingly difficult for cities to address the deepening poverty within their borders.

Institutionalized Localism and Racial Separation

The political feature that most distinguishes the United States in land use, housing, and other social policies is localism—the power of local governments to determine the activities that occur within their borders. Localism was the salient feature of American politics and policy prior to the New Deal, but it did not disappear with the nationalizing thrust of the 1930s. In fact, after World War II, the federal government helped re-create new forms of localism as it sponsored, but did not control, the suburbanization of the metropolitan landscape.

Local control over land use is one of the most important factors in creating the distinctively fragmented organization of American metropolitan areas.[10] Through zoning and other measures formally meant to ensure local health and safety, localities have acquired the power to determine what kinds of people can live and what kinds of business activities can be conducted within their borders. Although states exercise formal control over land-use, they have devolved considerable power to localities and regularly defer to local land-use decisions. Further exacerbating local political fragmentation is the relative ease with which new jurisdictions are formed in most states, compared with the difficulty of expanding older jurisdictions, via annexation or consolidation.[11]

Housing policy reinforced spatial differentiation of the population by income and race. Public housing, launched during the 1930s, remained a small program for the very poor, housing less than 3 percent of the population.[12] Building industry opposition and the right of localities to accept or reject public housing made public housing a residual sector concentrated in cities. Crucially, the local housing authorities that built public housing also ensured that it was racially segregated. This meant that public housing for African Americans was located in the already crowded and deteriorating ghettos of the inner city.[13]

The organization of social policy reinforces the impetus to form separate political jurisdictions differentiated by income and race. Most important in this regard is education. The tradition of financing education from local property taxes and the long-standing middle-class expectation of sending children to public schools has provided a central impetus for populations to separate in the United States. Although states have taken on a much greater role in educational finance in the past twenty years, the significant role of the local property tax continues to generate substantial inequalities across jurisdictions.

Thus, the organization of social policy, the power of localities to determine levels of services and taxation, and the ease of forming separate political jurisdictions provided powerful incentives for populations to separate out by income and by race. American metropolitan areas, particularly in the Northeast and Midwest, were carved into distinct jurisdictions defined by income and race. Significantly, these distinctions are marked by political boundaries. Because such boundaries function as symbols and clear information-transmitting devices, they reinforce and solidify processes of population sorting.[14]

The federal government has played a dual role in creating this pattern of spatial division. On the one hand, federal actions promoted suburbanization, fragmentation, and racial division for two decades after World War II; on the other hand, federal urban policy, launched in the 1950s and 1960s, compensated cities with specially targeted aid.

Washington's support for suburban life by building highways, promoting the use of the automobile, and subsidizing private home ownership is well known.[15] But the federal government also engaged in practices that encouraged racial exclusion. Most significant was federal sanction of discrimination in housing markets by promulgating rules that prevented racially changing neighborhoods from receiving Federal Housing Administration (FHA) mortgages. This practice effectively prevented blacks from joining the postwar exodus to the suburbs. Similarly, the federal government bowed to local opposition to subsidized housing that might promote integration; federal housing policies were predicated on local acceptance. As a consequence, subsidized housing was concentrated in cities; very little was located in the suburbs.[16]

Beginning in the 1950s, several federal programs helped mitigate the spatial inequalities that accompanied the suburban exodus. For the most part, these funds did not directly serve the urban poor, nor did they appreciably stem the flight to the suburbs, but they did provide a cushion that allowed for higher levels of public services such as libraries, police protection, and infrastructural maintenance that improve the quality of urban life.

The urban renewal program of the 1950s helped local governments underwrite major physical renewals of their central business districts. In the 1960s, the human costs of this approach led to other urban programs, such as Model Cities, that focused on rehabilitation and quality of life for the poor urban residents. The creation of the Department of Housing and Urban Development (HUD) in 1965 signaled the special place that urban aid would have at the federal level.[17] Even with the Democratic defeat in 1968, assistance for poorer localities continued as a legitimate federal government responsibility. No-strings-attached revenue sharing and Community Development Block Grants enacted under Richard Nixon and the Carter administration's Urban Development Action Grant (UDAG) employed different approaches but reflected a similar sensibility that localities, and especially cities, required special aid from the federal government.

During the 1980s, the federal government sharply reduced its compensatory role. The only programs totally eliminated during the decade were those that particularly benefited urban areas. For example, in 1981 Congress terminated the Comprehensive Employment and Training Act (CETA), which cities had used (unofficially) to bolster the ranks of their employees. General revenue sharing, which provided extra untargeted revenue for localities, ended in 1986. By the end of the Reagan administration, UDAGs had also been denied funding. Demetrios Caraley has estimated that grants for places were cut some 46 percent between 1980 and 1990.[18]

Cities fared only sightly better at the state level. Long dominated by rural interests, state governments instituted reforms during the 1960s and 1970s that equalized urban representation and modernized administration. By this time, however, suburban influence had grown so strong in many state legislatures that cities still operated at a disadvantage in state politics. Although some states compensated cities for the withdrawal of federal aid in the 1980s, others took only limited steps, and state actions frequently exacerbated the problems of cities. For example, urban efforts to raise local taxes were often rejected by unsympathetic state legislatures.[19] Moreover, states did little to guide the development that continued to spur the exodus from the cities nor did they do much to improve possibilities for regional cooperation. The recession of the late 1980s and early 1990s put a severe strain on many state budgets, revealing the limits of state financial aid.

The localistic bias of American land use, housing, and social policies thus created two sides to the face of metropolitan America: suburban sprawl and concentrated urban poverty. Over this time, the federal government not only failed to challenge the fundamental organization of policies that created these features of metropolitan America, it actively abetted them. The federal government did, however, directly compensate, then disengage from, cities. To understand these policy patterns, we must examine the politics of race and localism in national politics.

The Political Predicament of American Cities

Two aspects of politics shape national approaches to concentrations of race and poverty in the United States. The first, stemming from constitutional design, limits the federal government's purview over local land-use decisions. This means that federal efforts to change the organization of local space or to alter the distribution of people across space will be sharply challenged from below. The second aspect of politics affecting urban poverty is played out in the realm of party politics. Because the federal government has no formal responsibilities for cities, the various forms of compensatory aid described above were highly contingent on conjunctural forces that made cities, racial inequalities, and poverty national political concerns.

The constitutional limitations on federal action regarding local land use proved difficult to work around when reformers sought to promote planning in the late 1960s and 1970s. In contrast to France and Britain, where central governments have substantial planning capacities, constitutional authority over land use is lodged at the state level in the United States. The federal government has very limited legal authority to intervene in local land-use decisions, although it can greatly affect land use with a variety of tax and expenditure policies that create incentives for particular kinds of development.

By the late 1960s the negative consequences of the new metropolitan settlement pattern for the urban minority poor became evident to planners and advocates for the poor. In a variety of reports on urban problems, national commissions recommended state action to overcome local fragmentation. The cause of local land-use planning was taken up in the Senate and then embraced by the executive branch.[20] Proposed legislation initially aimed to encourage states to plan by offering financial incentives. But a wide range of locally based opposition, including urban officials, greatly diluted the legislation that emerged from the House of Representatives. The National Land Use Policy Bill that ultimately emerged in Congress exempted incorporated areas from its provisions, thus preserving the autonomy of local officials. However, even in this weakened form, the legislation did not pass. By the mid-1970s, the federal government had withdrawn from any comprehensive efforts to influence metropolitan organization.

Federal efforts to change the distribution of people across space by "opening up the suburbs" in the early 1970s were likewise short-lived. For a brief period, the federal government sought to build subsidized housing in the suburbs, using its power over the federal purse strings to force localities to accept public housing. Faced with violent opposition, federal officials quickly backed down.[21]

The obstacles to providing compensatory aid for cities were less forbidding. In fact, in the 1960s, providing benefits for cities was good politics for Democratic presidents. The urban vote—along with the "solid South"—had comprised the electoral core of the national Democratic Party since the New Deal. The strong organization of political parties in many cities, especially in the East and the Midwest, magnified the importance of cities and gave urban leaders special access to national policy makers. The dominance of urban interests within the Democratic Party as a whole was clear in Congress, where Democrats from suburban areas in the North voted heavily in favor of measures to aid the cities.[22]

In addition, the Civil Rights movement gave minority interests special political significance in the 1960s. The moral authority of the movement helped to create a national climate unusually sympathetic to black interests. Urban aid was a comparatively easy way for the federal government to address black concerns in the North. Although the urban programs of the 1960s grew controversial as they became associated in the public mind with riots and "black power," they never challenged the fundamental patterns of racial separation. Moreover, urban poverty policies fit neatly into the pattern of group politics that characterized much of American policy.

The power of cities and the sympathy generated by the Civil Rights movement were short-lived. Demographic shifts, changes in party organization, and the decline in the Civil Rights movement contributed to the political eclipse of cities and the decline in urban aid in the decades after the 1960s. In 1960, the nation's population was evenly divided among cities, suburbs, and rural areas. By 1990, both urban and rural populations had declined, leaving suburbs with nearly half of the nation's population. The urban population declined to 31 percent. And, as cities lost population, they became poorer and more minority in their racial composition.

The dynamics of partisan competition exacerbated the decline of urban political influence as Republicans showed that national elections could be won without urban support. The shift of population into suburban areas made it possible to win national elections without the urban vote. In 1968, suburbs cast 35.6 percent of the vote for president; by 1988 that figure had risen to 48.3 percent. By the 1992 election, suburbs comprised a majority of the electorate.[23]

The terms of partisan competition did not take long to register these changes. During the 1980s a sharp disjuncture between urban and suburban voters in the North and the Midwest attested to Republican success in mobilizing a distinctive suburban political identity. In contrast to the pattern prevailing during the 1960s and 1970s, when central cities and suburbs tended to vote in similar directions, by 1980 a marked split between the suburban and urban vote emerged. Central cities remained the only stronghold of the Democratic Party, while the majority of suburban areas voted Republican.[24]

These political shifts revealed how contingent the urban aid policies of the 1960s were. Even the return of a Democratic president in 1992 could not put cities back on the national agenda. When President Clinton tried to provide special assistance to cities as part of a 1993 stimulus package, Congress rejected the proposal as "pork."[25]

As the federal government sharply reduced its compensatory role, urban governments have had to shoulder the burdens of needy populations and a precarious economic base. They have responded above all by attracting private development, offering tax abatements and other special incentives for business, in the process heightening interjurisdictional competition.[26] Their many successes in attracting and maintaining investment during the 1980s highlighted the advantages of the comparatively high level of local autonomy enjoyed by American cities.

But, for the most part, these successes came at a cost to poor urban populations. Tax abatements drained future tax revenues, reducing the scope for local public action. Other strategies, such as the formation of special taxing districts within cities (with a variety of names such as Business Improvement Districts), further fragmented the public tax base. Some cities sought to capture part of the benefits of development for poorer residents by established "linkage" programs, which required developers to contribute to building low-income housing, but these programs remained small in light of the problems they aimed to alleviate.[27]

Changes in industrial structure and the location of industry have exacerbated the burden and political isolation of cities in the 1980s. The revolution in information technologies in the past decade combined with the lack of metropolitan-level planning to produce a substantial deconcentration of economic activity. As new businesses and commercial centers appeared in suburban "edge cities," the connections between city and suburb further attenuated.[28]

Federal disengagement, the failure to create new forms of regional cooperation, and the absence of policies to help the urban poor cross political boundaries has left cities politically and economically isolated. In each of these policy areas, racial considerations played a significant, if often unspoken, role. The easy identification of cities, racial minorities, and poverty in American politics allowed racial meanings to be understood without being said. Moreover, preexisting concentrations of poor minorities in cities meant that these policy decisions had racially targeted consequences. It also meant that the politics of race would affect the fate of any proposed solutions to cope with urban poverty.

Centralized Power and Metropolitan Development in Postwar Europe

In postwar Britain and France, the central governments exercised substantial control over urban development and population movements. Government housing policies had racial implications, but race was not the central organizing element in process of spatial sorting, as in the United States. The centrality of race in urban development and social-policy formation after World War II distinguishes the United States from Britain and France. Race could not be an organizing principle in social policy and urban development in these European countries because the numbers of racial minorities were so small. And when the numbers of minorities grew in the 1960s and 1970s, already existing social policies and established practices meant that whites could not so effectively act on their racial antipathies as they had in the United States. Moreover, because central governments shouldered more responsibility for funding social policies and public services, sharp local differences in taxes and services did not reinforce the spatial differences that did exist.

As a consequence, central government decisions about land use and housing shaped the distribution of people and economic activity in metropolitan areas much more than did individual evaluations of incentives to move and individual choices about exit. And because of the reduced incentives and possibilities for exit, spatial differences tended not to have the spiraling qualities evident in the United States. A closer look at how government actions after World War II helped to sort populations will highlight the very different way postwar Europe built its metropolitan areas and the distinct political factors that supported these policies.

Urban Council Housing and the British Working Class

In contrast to the United States, which sought to meet postwar housing needs by underwriting private home ownership, the British government took the lead in building housing. By the end of the 1970s, a third of British households lived in "council housing."[29] The very size of the British public housing sector made some level of income mixing inevitable.

Council housing also had more locational variation in Britain than in the United States. Intent on decentralizing the urban population, the government initially constructed public housing outside the central city. Most of this early postwar development took place in "new towns" and peripheral areas well beyond areas of existing settlement. The government also built large housing estates in peripheral areas to house overspill population from urban redevelopment. By the 1960s, however, the government redirected public housing back to the cities. Bowing to spatial constraints and architectural fashion, the dominant form of new construction was the high-rise project.

The important role of local authorities in constructing public housing created dynamics that produced something of an "inner-city problem" by the 1960s. But the political forces that generated such spatial divisions in Britain were somewhat different from those in the United States. As in the United States, middle-class homeowners, who dominated existing suburbs, resisted council housing.[30] But, in contrast to the United States, suburbs were not wholly successful in blocking council housing. On the other hand, urban Labour authorities had positive financial and political incentives to build substantial amounts of high-rise council housing within the cities. By the early 1980s, these dynamics created a pattern in which London's council housing was more concentrated in poorer inner London (43 percent), but sizable amounts also existed in Central London (roughly equivalent to the central business district) (29 percent) and outer London (23 percent).[31] The range of people housed in urban flats encompassed a wide swath of the British working class, not simply the poorest of the poor, as in the United States.

The spatial patterns produced by public housing generally followed the lines of private development: suburban areas were geared toward the middle class, who could afford the more expensive private homes built there. The working class and the poor remained in the city. The government used regional planning to guide metropolitan development, relying on greenbelts to contain the urban population and limit sprawl. Such planning objectives were reinforced by a rural upper class of property owners that staunchly opposed suburban development and was able to impose some limitations on suburbanization. These efforts at limiting suburban development were only partially successful. The London population, for example, had been leaving the city for suburban areas since the 1930s; postwar planning did not reverse this trend.[32] However, the combination of limited suburban development and the absence of government policy to subsidize suburbanization ensured that a significant part of the British working class did not find their postwar housing in the suburbs.

The sorting of populations that occurred after the war also had some negative consequences for racial mixing. Again, however, it did not create the sharp racial segregation characteristic of the United States. Initially, the point system used for allocating public housing (one element of which was length of tenure in the borough) worked against members of racial minorities, most of whom were recent immigrants.[33] Although this discrimination was substantially remedied by the passage of the Race Relations Act in 1968, minorities had missed the first wave of the more desirable council housing built outside the central city. In most major British metropolitan areas, therefore, minority populations concentrated in the inner city. This pattern was reinforced by the departure of the middle classes to private suburban homes and the upper working class to suburban council housing. Immigrants typically settled in urban areas that were losing population.

The extent of segregation within the cities was tempered by the existence of integrated public housing, which was never deliberately segregated, as in the United States. Because there were no preexisting racial ghettos, public housing was built and sited without racial considerations in mind. Much public housing was located in working-class districts, which were not racially defined. Moreover, the more restricted opportunities for the working class to move to owner-occupied housing in the suburbs (due to less favorable tax treatment of mortgages and more limited financing) limited the suburban exodus in Britain until the 1970s.[34]

The British government had a variety of tools to reduce the spatial inequalities that did appear. The central government's ability to redraw local political boundaries meant that local tax bases could be enlarged by the central government. The importance of the central government also made it far easier than in the United States to redistribute resources to reduce territorial inequalities. The majority of local expenditures were financed by the centrally provided rate support grant, an amount calculated in part on the basis of local need.[35] In addition, an "inner city" policy, modeled after that in the United States, offered special assistance to the poorest areas.

The strong role of the central government in financing education, social programs, and public services also arrested the impulse to individual exit that characterized the United States. The place of cities in the British political structure is diametrically opposed to that in the United States. In the highly centralized British political system, local authorities exist at the pleasure of the central government. They have had access to only one source of local revenue, the property tax, levied on property owners and businesses. Because they have so little autonomy and discretion in financing, sharp differences across localities and the dynamic of interlocal competition so central in the United States was less evident in Britain.

Politically, these measures benefited from the strength of the Labour Party, which took the lead in creating an expanded public sector after the war. But Conservatives also supported the financing arrangements and special expenditures that aimed to reduce or compensate for place-based inequalities. There was, likewise, cross-party agreement on using planning to guide metropolitan growth. Thus, when Thatcher came to power, Britain had a large working-class public-housing sector concentrated in cities (along with the isolated outer estates), a disproportionate minority presence in declining areas of cities, and limited suburban development.

Central Planning and Spatial Organization in France

In France, the process of population sorting after World War II was more centrally directed than in Britain, overseen by the central planning agency, the Commissariat Général du Plan.[36] After initially emphasizing industrial development, the Plan turned to housing. As in Britain, decades of depression and war had left a dilapidated and meager housing stock. The housing shortage was exacerbated by the belated urbanization of the French population, which occurred only after the war. The French government looked to the fastest and cheapest means possible to address housing problems: construction of massive housing projects developed on new sites outside the city. Deeply influenced by the architect Le Corbusier, who pioneered the *grands ensembles* (large high-rise housing blocks), French planners saw such high-rise housing as the epitome of functional modernism.[37]

HLM (Habitations à loyer modéré) housing, as the subsidized housing program was called, came to serve 14 percent of the French population, considerably less than the British but substantially more than the residual American program.[38] In addition, the state provided subsidies for nonprofit associations to build housing. Planners conceived the suburban housing estates as workers' lodgings, located near (and often subsidized by) the major industries in the Parisian suburbs. As in Britain, rules governing access to HLM housing initially worked against immigrant racial minorities. In fact, HLM housing tended to serve the middle- and lower-middle classes rather than the very poor, who concentrated in private rental housing in the slums of the cities. And, as in Britain, central government subsidies for education and public services reduced the emergence of sharp and spiraling spatial differences across local jurisdictions.

Thus, postwar France developed a spatial pattern of suburbanizing working-class housing, with cities increasingly reserved for the well-off and the poor, many of whom were immigrants. The central government played the key role in continuing population movements with its plans for urban redevelopment, which often displaced the poor from the cities.

The Americanization of Europe?

The recent pattern of population movement and government actions in Britain and France reveals some striking similarities that seem to support the argument that these nations are "ten years behind the United States." And, indeed, racially identified concentrated poverty has become a deeper problem in France and Britain in the past decade. I will argue, however, that in these European countries, distinct starting points and political brakes on the processes of socioeconomic and racial separation make the dynamics of ghettoization far less encompassing than in the United States.

Among the key policy shifts that have fostered new spatial differences in Britain and France are central government policies promoting home ownership and loosening planning restrictions. Together these shifts have encouraged a trend of private suburban homeownership among the middle class. Furthermore, high rise public housing has generated similar problems in all three nations. Difficult to maintain, many of the housing blocks quickly became dilapidated, undesirable places to live, propelling those who were able, to find housing elsewhere.[39] Finally, during the 1980s, changes in public finance in both Britain and France have created possibilities for more differences to emerge among places.

Despite these trends, important differences in the original design of housing policies and continuing distinctions in the political factors that shape population movements suggest limits on the process of "Americanization." The initial racially defined location of most public housing in the United States, along with the small size of the program, has given American public housing a racial identity and level of isolation that is unlikely to emerge in Britain or France. Moreover, in neither Britain nor France was suburbanization accompanied by the abandonment of cities as residential areas. The central governments continued to treat cities as a national resource to be developed. Finally, changes in public financing that handicap poor places have been limited by political factors—even within conservative governments—that have no counterpart in the United States.

Together, these different starting points and limits on policy change mean that "tipping" mechanisms so central to the process of ghettoization and isolation in the United States are less forceful and more spatially contained in Britain and France.[40] When they do occur, they are likely to be more confined (to a particular housing project, for example) and more readily addressed by government intervention.

The Government and the Market Reshape Britain

In the 1980s, Prime Minister Margaret Thatcher recast the relationship between central and local government in Britain. Her government changed many long-standing policies and introduced new frameworks for implementing local policy, replacing political authority with private action. In contrast to the United States, where the central government withdrew from cities, the British government used extensive intervention to redefine the modes of local activity. These actions have left cities with fewer resources and heavier social burdens. The changes in public finance, social housing, and land-use planning have moved Britain closer to the American model, but important differences continue to limit the process of urban isolation and deterioration.

Margaret Thatcher's new brand of Conservative politics put an end to the postwar party consensus about local development patterns. Anxious above all to reduce public expenditures, the new prime minister made local government a central target. This was a highly partisan battle since the local authorities most resistant to her initiatives were Labour-controlled councils that used their local base to mobilize political opposition and devise policies at odds with Thatcher's market vision.[41]

Thatcher introduced a variety of changes that reduced the equalizing role of the central government and left localities more on their own and less able to cope with the rising needs of their populations. New methods for calculating the central grant reduced its size and made it less redistributive across territory.[42] In addition, new measures allowed the central government to limit the rates that local authorities could levy, thus hampering authorities that sought to compensate for the central government cutbacks.

The Conservative government also undermined council housing. The 1980 Housing Act allowed council housing tenants of three years standing to purchase their units. The measure proved to be one of the most popular of the Thatcher administration. By 1990, one-fifth of the council housing stock had been sold to tenants. The effects on concentrated disadvantage have been mixed. The bulk of sales have occurred in suburban areas, where the most attractive detached units were located. Very little of the block housing located in the inner cities has been sold.[43] Since sales patterns followed existing lines of division, they did not increase racial or income segregation, but they did help to weaken public support for council housing. As the government reduced funds for council housing, it has become less attractive as a place to live. The result has been to increase the proportion of the poor in public housing and to create more racial isolation in deteriorating estates as whites leave.

After a decade of Thatcherism, British politics has been transformed in ways that will make it more difficult to assist disadvantaged areas than in the past. The extreme centralization of government and the abolition of metropolitan county governments that sought to address the problems of the urban poor have removed important arenas for political mobilization around these dilemmas. Social class continues to define the central political cleavage, accompanied by a sharp regional division, with a Conservative south and a Labour north. However, during the 1980s an increasingly suburbanized working class largely abandoned Labour in national elections.[44]

Margaret Thatcher introduced enormous changes in the powers and resources of local government, many of which have been detrimental to cities (and suburbs) with large concentrations of poor minority residents. However, existing structures of policy and politics limited Thatcher's reach and lessened the government's ability to impose losses on poor places. Because localities can raise revenue only from property taxes, not only poor Labour authorities but richer Conservative-governed local authorities also opposed drastic reductions in the central grant. Unlike American middle-class localities that can make up for withdrawn central funds by raising a variety of local taxes or fees, all local authorities in Britain are still heavily reliant on central government support.

This dynamic was responsible for the repeal of Thatcher's proposed "poll tax," opposition to which was a central factor in her resignation. The poll tax, proposed in 1986, would have replaced the local property tax by an equal tax levied on each voter, with the amount to be decided by the local authority. It replaced the local business rate with a uniform rate to be collected by the central government. A far more regressive tax on individuals, the new tax aroused enough opposition in Conservative constituencies to provoke a party revolt against Thatcher. Under Prime Minister John Major, the poll tax has been replaced by a council tax, which combines a personal and a property element.[45]

In addition to these brakes on policies that increase the burdens on poor places, the strong role of the central government has made it harder for the British government simply to ignore the problems of the inner city, as has the federal government in the United States. Throughout the 1980s, the government launched new policies to promote urban economic development, including Enterprise Zones and Urban Development Corporations. Although the government has sought to redirect urban policies toward economic redevelopment and at the same time pay little attention to the poor, the very existence of such programs has created pressure to address urban poverty. The task is one of diverting a resource flow rather than trying to revive federal or create state-level responsibility, as American urban advocates must do.[46]

The more centralized nature of British politics and land-use planning have also facilitated the emergence of a national opposition to unchecked suburban development that has no counterpart in the United States. When the government relaxed local planning controls in the 1980s, new suburban commercial development exacerbated suburban sprawl and began to undermine city shopping areas. The current movement to reimpose stricter planning guidelines includes Conservative members of Parliament anxious to limit the destruction of the countryside as well as urban representatives concerned about the impact on cities.[47]

In sum, the Thatcher government increased concentrated disadvantage by undermining council housing, reducing territorial redistribution in public finance, and loosening metropolitan planning restrictions. Yet two factors keep Britain from replicating the American experience. The continued importance of public housing in cities and the integrated status of that housing has slowed down the tendencies to extreme racial and income segregation. Moreover, the power of the central government has limited the differentiation between cities and suburbs and consequently avoided the more extreme degree of urban isolation and abandonment characteristic of the United States.

Decentralization and the French War on Poverty

In France, increased owner occupation in the 1970s, combined with important changes in central-local government responsibilities during the 1980s, has created more spatial differentiation by income and race. The most obvious problems occurred in the deteriorating *grands ensembles*, or large public housing projects on the outskirts of cities. But changes in public finance and in land-use and economic development policies also created dynamics that increased spatial differences. In contrast to the United States and Britain, the French government responded with a variety of policies aimed at economic *and* social revitalization of poor places. The politics supporting these policies reveal important features of French politics that differ from the United States and Britain. However, whether these remedial policies will significantly alter the underlying forces creating concentrations of racially identified poverty remains open to question.

During the 1980s, the French Socialists introduced sweeping changes in central-local relations. The decentralization laws of 1982 are likely to have significant repercussions for the treatment of concentrations of poverty. With political aims and a constituency far different from those of Reagan and Thatcher, the Socialists sponsored changes that exacerbated the problems of poor localities. Decentralization began to introduce into France some of the interjurisdictional competition that has characterized the United States, and, as in the United States, it has left poor localities with fewer resources. As the effects of the changes became apparent, however, the government has enacted a series of measures designed to spread poor people among different localities and to compensate those areas economically hurt by decentralization.

Decentralization was introduced with the official aim of producing more local democracy by decreasing the power of the central government and enhancing local public powers.[48] Like American local government, French local government is fragmented into a large number of small units, the most of any European nation. Although the central government has the formal authority to reduce the number of units, in practice the penetration of central power by local authorities (by the *cumul des mandats*, which allows local officeholders to hold multiple offices simultaneously) has blocked territorial rationalization. Central power was exercised over this fragmented political terrain by the departmental prefect, whose approval was needed for most local actions.

The 1982 decentralization has given localities much more autonomy in urban planning and in allocating expenditures by implementing a system of block grants and devolving some social responsibilities and taxing requirements to lower levels of government. Not surprisingly, given the diverse sizes and resources of the communes, decentralization has introduced new territorial inequalities. Some localities have been able to use their new autonomy to attract investment and enrich the local tax base; others have had to levy higher taxes.[49] These differences have been exacerbated by an overall decline in public spending as France, like other western nations, has sought to reduce public expenditures. In addition, the strong central hand that allocated economic activities and populations among different regions and within metropolitan areas has been replaced by the myriad development decisions of local governments. The considerable power that the central government enjoyed in the siting of social housing after the war has also been considerably curtailed. Local power to reject such housing, or to resist accepting undesirable tenants, has grown considerably. In practice, this means that the least powerful and least well-off localities end up with more social housing.

By the late 1980s, fearful of generating new inequalities, the Socialists passed a series of laws that aimed to compensate poor places. One new law transfers resources from rich localities to poorer localities. Another obliges localities to pay a penalty if they refuse to accept a certain percentage of social housing. A third law seeks to remedy the housing problems of the extremely poor by helping them to pay back rent.[50] Reflecting worries about the fate of cities, in 1990 they created for the first time in the history of France a Minister for Cities. Finally, in 1988 the central government enacted a new minimum income financed by the central government for those not covered by existing social assistance. The new Revenue Minimum d'Insertion (RMI) seeks, as its name implies, to "insert" the poor into French society by providing financial resources in exchange for which recipients seek work or training.[51]

The government has also introduced new programs to revitalize public housing. Large public housing buildings have posed a special problem in France as in Britain. By the 1970s, HLM housing had been opened to immigrant racial minorities, and the proportion of immigrants in HLM housing quickly grew, reaching 30 percent in some estates.[52] At the same time, national programs to promote home ownership prompted the exodus of many middle-class families from HLM housing. This cycle of exit by better-off native French citizens and entry by minority immigrants increased the concentrations of the poor in these settings. In the 1980s, the problem was greatly exacerbated by the economic decline in the industries around which much of this housing was constructed. High unemployment, deeper poverty, and social isolation created a spiral of decline.

The French government has sought to stem this development with a variety of social programs reminiscent of the American War on Poverty of the 1960s. Most important have been programs overseen by the Commission Nationale de Développement Social des Quartiers (DSQ, Commission for the Social Development of Neighborhoods).[53] The programs bring housing authorities and local and regional government together with national government to sponsor programs of social and physical renewal for the designated areas, most of which are *grands ensembles*. The commitment to provide special aid to distressed areas was renewed by the conservative government of Edouard Balladur, which came to power in 1993.[54]

Many of the inequalities that the French government has sought to combat are closely linked to its fears of developing American-style ghettos.

Unlike in the United States and Britain, deep concerns about "national solidarity" cross party lines in France. The republican tradition of citizenship and French nationality is sufficiently compelling that neither governments of the right or the left want to be accused of allowing pockets of difference and exclusion to grow. And, in contrast to the United States, such issues are a legitimate national responsibility.

Thus, French governments of the left (and now the right) have sought to combine the benefits of decentralization—greater local democracy, freeing of local economic initiative, and the reduction of central government responsibility for administering austerity—with a commitment to equalizing the territorial distribution of economic resources. But questions can be raised about the political durability of these new policies as well as their efficacy. By most accounts, the growth in the number of elected officials has not promoted local democracy; it has merely increased the power of local notables.[55] Moreover, the emergence of local competition introduces a dynamic into French politics familiar to Americans: representatives of localities with different resource bases may interpret not only the local interest but also the national interest quite differently.

Nor is there evidence that remedial programs are working. Reviews of programs to aid distressed areas have found that such programs have had only a limited impact in promoting "inclusion" or significantly improving life conditions for the residents.[56] The political durability of the French "War on Poverty" can also be questioned. Although these programs emerge from a political impulse quite different (and more enduring) from the urban power and racial interests that underlay the American War on Poverty, the French quest for national solidarity is two-sided. The current anxiety about immigrants in France and the desire to promote their integration has a darker side represented by the racist National Front of Jean-Marie Le Pen. Although Le Pen's appeal has been waning, resentment against "immigrants" (many of whom are now second generation) who appear unassimilable is still strong. Political shifts could give more expression to this repressive response to racial diversity in France.

Conclusion

The United States, Britain, and France have all experienced wrenching economic changes in the past decade, creating new forms of poverty and calling into question existing social and economic policies. Racial diversity has added a volatile element to the uncharted social and economic terrain that governments now face. Yet governments play a key role in determining the social consequences of these changes. This article has highlighted the nexus among policy, politics, and the organization of space as the key to understanding diverse national trajectories. Public policies help to sort groups spatially by race and income; the political links between central and local governments determine the way such spatial divisions feed back into politics. Governments must accordingly pay attention to the way a range of policy arrangements not only create such spatial divisions, but also set off a self-propelling spiral isolating the poor, particularly racial minorities.

The American strategy of federal withdrawal from cities and social policy decentralization in the 1980s reinforced existing arrangements that have isolated the black poor. In the context of sharp economic change and diminishing wages for those at the bottom of the economic ladder, the results of isolation and policy withdrawal have been catastrophic. In France and Britain, changes in policies and political structures have created new possibilities for an American-style cycle of racial separation and poverty. Although different starting points and political processes are likely to limit spiraling and avert isolation as deep or as extensive as in the United States, the emergence of such sharp divisions remains deeply troubling for liberal democracies.

Notes

1. See the news articles cited in Silver 1993, pp. 347–48.

2. Ceri Peach notes that Indices of Segregation in the European context tend to be significantly lower than those for blacks in the United States. Only at a very localized level are rates of segregation (with Indexes of Segregation above 70) comparable to those of American blacks found. The Indexes of Segregation are more typically in the 30–60 range. And, as he notes, "the high indices that are found in Britain, seem to be more voluntary than imposed." See Peach 1987, 47.

3. See for example, Kasarda and Friedrichs 1986, 221; and the comments in Laquain 1992, 23.

4. For a recent comprehensive analysis of the development of global cities, see Sassen 1991.

5. See Kasarda and Friedrichs 1986, 221.

6. Ibid., 223.

7. See Wacquant, 1995.

8. Ibid.

9. Silver 1993.

10. Mills 1987, 562–63; Danielson 1976, chap. 2.

11. See Briffault 1990.

12. There were some exceptions, where state governments supplemented the federal program. The most outstanding case is New York, where public housing accommodates a sizable working- and middle-class population.

13. For an illuminating case study, see Hirsch 1983.

14. This argument is developed in Weiher 1991.

15. See Jackson 1985, chaps. 11–12.

16. Danielson 1976; on the FHA see K. Jackson 1985, 203–18.

17. See Gelfand 1975, chaps. 7, 10.

18. See Caraley 1992.

19. On state-city political tensions over finances and social policies see Specter 1991, 1; and Kolbert 1991, E6.

20. On commissions see, for example, the U.S. National Commission on Urban Problems 1968, 323–45; on the National Land Use Policy Bill, see Plotkin 1987, chaps. 5–6.

21. Danielson 1976, chap. 8.

22. See Caraley 1976, 19–45.

23. See the figures reported in Edsall and Edsall 1991b, 229; Schneider 1992, 33–44; Reinhold 1992, 1.

24. On the older pattern of suburban-urban voting, see Zikmund, 1968, 239–58; and Wood 1960; 272–73. On the splits in urban-suburban voting in the 1980s see Morin 1988, A29–30. Clinton captured a plurality of the suburban vote, with 44 percent; Bush received 36 percent, and Perot 20 percent. See Schmalz 1992.

25. On the defeat of the stimulus bill and urban spending, see Peirce 1993.

26. See for example, Mollenkopf 1992, chap. 8.

27. On linkage in Boston, see Dreier and Ehrlich 1991, 354–75.

28. See Stanback 1991. On "edge cities" see Garreau 1991.

29. Willmott and Murie 1988, 8.

30. See the discussion in Young and Kramer 1978.

31. Savitch 1988, 191.

32. See Buck and Fainstein 1992, 45–50, 56–61.

33. See Rex 1988, chap. 6.

34. Willmott and Murie 1988, 19

35. See Jackson, Meadows, and Taylor 1982, 23–43. The determination of local need was not immune to political influence; see Pickvance 1991, 60.

36. See Phillips 1987.

37. Ibid.

38. On HLM housing, see Willmott and Murie 1988.

39. See the critique in Jacobs 1961; see also T. Schuman 1985.

40. On "tipping" see Schelling 1978, 137–66.

41. See Parkinson 1985; for the conflict between Margaret Thatcher and the Greater London Council, see Forrester, Lansley, and Pauley 1985.

42. King 1993, 200–202.

43. See Willmott and Murie 1988, 35–36, 46; Silver 1991, 167–68.

44. See the analyses of the 1992 election in Peter Millar "How Essex Man Showed Major the Path Back," *Sunday Times*, April 12, 1992; Colin Rallings and Michael Thrasher, "Essex Man Stays Loyal and the Older Women (*sic*) Is Won Over," *Sunday Times*, April 12, 1992.

45. See the discussion in King 1993, 196–200.

46. On British urban policy in the 1980s, see Lawless 1991; and the Centre for Local Development Strategies 1992.

47. W. Schmidt 1994, E16; Jacobson 1994, 1194–95.

48. On decentralization see V. Schmidt 1990.

49. For an analysis of the effects of decentralization at the commune level, see Preteceille 1991, 134–40; for an analysis at the department level see Bernier 1991.

50. See Grémion 1991 and Faberon 1991.

51. On the RMI, see Autes 1992.

52. See Willmott and Murie 1988, 51.

53. On DSQs see Castellan, Marpsat, and Goldberger 1992.

54. "Doté de 5 milliard de francs le 'Plan d'Urgence pour la Ville' renforce l'intervention de l'etat dans les quartiers en crise," *Le Monde*, July 30, 1993, 8–9.

55. See Mény 1992.

56. Bernard 1993.

Part III ————————————————————

RACE POLITICS

10

Racial Group Competition in Urban Elections

DAVID IAN LUBLIN AND KATHERINE TATE

AMERICANS TODAY more commonly vote in presidential or state elections than in local elections. During the late-nineteenth and early-twentieth centuries, however, electorally based political activism was more vigorously pursued at the local level. Not only were fewer state and national officials popularly elected as they are today, but American political parties during this period were more involved in mass participation at the local level of politics than nationally. Urban politics during this era was especially vigorous and rich. The entry and early suffrage of nearly twenty-three million immigrants to America at the turn of the century led to the emergence of political machines. Machines recruited, socialized, educated, and mobilized the scores of immigrants entering the cities at the turn of the century through patronage.[1] They capitalized on the new religious and ethnic lines of conflict within the cities.[2] Mayoral elections, in particular, became the focus for intense struggles between the competing ethnic and religious interests within cities.

America's urban centers hold a less vital place in American politics today.[3] Big-city mayors no longer have the national clout and authority they once possessed. Nor are urban voters as assiduously courted every four years by presidential contenders, who, instead, lavish much of their campaign activities on middle-class voters, many of whom fled the cities for the suburbs during the turbulent sixties and seventies. Political reform, the decline of American parties, new federalism, and federal policy toward the cities have diminished the vigor of urban politics. Local government has become "remote."[4] Unsurprisingly, urban voter participation has declined steadily since the 1930s as a consequence.[5] In this chapter, however, we argue that the rise of blacks as a new political force within urban centers has meaningfully altered the lines of conflict within the cities, revitalizing their politics. Utilizing data gathered for twenty-six major American cities from 1969 to 1991,[6] we show that mayoral elections involving black candidates are more competitive, resulting in rising levels of voter activity. In spite of the limited scope of city governments today, racial competition over control of city hall persists for a number of complex and complicated reasons.

The Racialization of Urban Politics

The Progressive Era launched an assault on parties. Progressive reforms did not, by themselves, rid cities of their political machines; established machines promptly adapted to the reform system.[7] Rather, the political reforms ultimately undercut the mobilization function of parties, transforming urban politics in the process. First, the introduction of the Australian ballot made voter recruitment through material inducements a less reliable method of winning elections. No longer able to enlarge the electorate through graft, machine bosses turned toward job patronage as their primary strategy of staying in power. The narrow electoral universe of municipal employees and their individual networks of families, friends, and neighbors kept the machines in power.[8] Second, the decline of American parties ended most of the two-party competition that existed in urban centers. Partisan or nonpartisan, most big cities today are firmly under Democratic control, and only rarely has the GOP or any independent party mounted an effective challenge against its leadership. It is the absence of party competition that has diminished voter participation.[9] Moreover, nonpartisan elections, a method favored by reformers for reducing the influence of party on the local vote, tend to generate lower rates of participation than do partisan elections.[10] Finally, city elections were staggered from national and state elections so that local, not national, politics would be the focus of such elections.[11] Freed from the vagaries of national politics, however, citizen interest in local politics declined, and fewer citizens turned out to vote.[12]

Even as the urban-based political machines reinforced the ethnic and racial tensions that arose as immigrants and southern blacks poured into the cities to compete for jobs and housing, they reduced such conflict. Machine organizations helped to curb outbreaks of ethnic and racial violence by rewarding ethnics and blacks with political office. Political office came to be viewed as the "dangling rope" of socioeconomic advancement for lower-status groups within the cities.[13] Although early analysts of the machine have emphasized the "rainbow" configuration of machines, postrevisionist political historians of this era, however, have shown that in spite of their long years of service and loyalty to the machine, blacks' share in the city's patronage system was meager. They received proportionately far fewer of the city jobs than favored white ethnic groups.[14] Moreover, blacks were always the most junior members within the machine's organizational hierarchy. Even the political clout of black submachine bosses like the legendary "Big Bill" Dawson of Chicago has recently been called into question. William Grimshaw contends that black machine politicians, such as Dawson, were firmly under the control of the Irish-led Chicago machine.[15] Likewise, the crop of young black leaders who rose to power through the infusion of antipoverty and Community Action Program funds into the cities from the federal government during the late 1960s and 1970s were either handpicked by calculating, entrenched white mayors or quickly co-opted.[16]

Black participation in machine politics served to limit and delay racial conflict that would engulf cities after Watts in 1965 and Martin Luther King's assassination in 1968. Even during the years of intense racial conflict and urban rioting, black Chicagoans remained relatively compliant under the Daley machine. Black politician Richard Newhouse, who had challenged Richard Daley, Sr., in the 1975 Democratic primary in Chicago, took only 8 percent of the votes cast, receiving little support from the black wards of the city, especially those on the West Side known as the "plantation wards."[17] Black Chicagoans, in fact, would not mount a serious challenge against the machine until almost a full decade after Daley's death in 1976.

Even as machine rule suppressed racial conflict, that conflict, once unleashed, hastened the death of machine organizations. Whites, fearing the rising crime rates and deteriorating public schools they attributed to the influx of blacks and other lower-income groups, fled to the suburbs. The urban riots only escalated such flights. The mass departure of many whites made the aging machine establishments more dependent on the black vote. As the proportion of blacks within the central cities spread, their demands for political empowerment intensified. Newly politicized and increasingly critical of their limited rewards under machine rule, blacks finally broke with the machines. In cities such as Philadelphia,[18] Chicago,[19] Baltimore, and Newark, black independents were elected.[20] This pattern was repeated, even in such cities as Detroit that lacked a history of machine activity.[21] Race relations in many Democrat-controlled cities had reached a critical point where the Democratic Party could no longer manage the ensuing white voter backlash against the emerging crop of black candidates.

The Civil Rights struggle brought race to the center stage of national American politics.[22] Eventually, race also became a dominant and contentious political issue in many American cities. Roused by the rhetoric of the Black Power movement, blacks began to mobilize.[23] Community Action funds from the federal government aided the mobilization process.[24] As table 10.1 shows, even though voter participation in cities of one million or more since 1966 in presidential and congressional elections has steadily declined, the racial gap in participation has narrowed during this period. The lower rates of black participation in 1988 and 1990 reversed this trend somewhat, but on the whole, the period from 1965 to 1991 represented one of heightened voter activity among urban blacks, whose rates of participation began to approximate those for urban whites. By contrast, the racial difference in turnout between blacks and whites living outside of the central

TABLE 10.1

Reported Voters in Presidential and Congressional Elections in Central Cities and Outside Central Cities, by Race, 1964–1990 (Percentages)

	1964	1966	1968	1970	1972	1974	1976	1978	1980	1982	1984	1986	1988	1990
Central Cities														
Whites	—	58.3	67.4	57.0	64.7	45.9	59.1	46.5	56.7	48.2	—	45.9	56.2	43.9
Blacks	—	47.7	61.4	48.6	56.4	37.0	52.5	41.4	54.0	48.5	—	44.4	53.6	39.1
Racial Gap	—	10.6	6.0	8.4	8.3	8.9	6.6	5.1	2.7	-0.3	—	1.5	2.6	4.8
Outside Central Cities														
Whites	—	60.5	72.7	58.1	68.8	48.2	63.6	49.9	62.5	51.0	—	46.2	60.5	47.3
Blacks	—	45.9	67.2	54.2	60.3	33.6	52.6	36.7	50.7	40.1	—	40.1	49.3	36.7
Racial Gap	—	14.6	5.5	3.9	8.5	14.6	11.0	13.2	11.8	10.9	—	6.1	11.2	10.6

Source: U.S. Bureau of the Census *Current Population Reports*, P-20 Series.

Note: Data reported for 1966 to 1986 include those cities of 1 million or more until 1986.

TABLE 10.2

Size of the Black Community, 1920 and 1960–1990 (Percentage)

	1920	1960	1970	1980	1990
Majority-black cities in 1990					
Gary, Ind.	9.6	38.8	52.8	70.8	80.6
Detroit, Mich.	4.2	28.9	43.7	63.1	75.7
Atlanta, Ga.	31.3	38.3	51.3	66.6	67.1
Washington, D.C.	25.3	53.9	71.1	70.3	65.8
Birmingham, Ala.	39.3	39.6	42.0	55.6	63.3
New Orleans, La.	26.2	37.2	45.0	55.3	61.9
Baltimore, Md.	14.8	34.7	46.4	54.8	59.2
Newark, N.J.	4.2	34.1	54.2	58.6	58.5
Memphis, Tenn.	37.7	37.0	38.9	47.6	54.8
30–49.9% black in 1990					
Cleveland Ohio	4.4	28.6	38.3	43.8	46.6
Oakland Calif.	5.7	22.8	34.5	46.9	43.9
Chicago, Ill.	4.2	22.9	32.7	39.8	39.1
Hartford, Conn.	3.2	15.3	27.9	33.9	38.9
New Haven, Conn.	2.9	14.5	26.3	31.9	36.1
Charlotte, N.C.	n.a.	27.9	30.3	31.0	31.8
20–29.9% black in 1990					
Kansas City, Mo.	9.5	17.5	22.1	27.4	29.6
New York, N.Y.	2.9	14.0	21.1	25.2	28.7
Houston, Tex.	24.6	22.9	25.7	27.6	28.1
Raleigh, N.C.	n.a.	23.4	22.7	27.4	27.6
Miami, Fla.	n.a.	22.4	22.7	25.1	27.4
Boston, Mass.	2.3	9.1	16.3	22.4	25.6
10–19.9% black in 1990					
Berkeley, Calif.	3.3	19.6	23.5	20.1	18.8
Los Angeles, Calif.	5.2	13.5	17.9	17.0	14.0
Denver, Colo.	2.7	6.1	9.1	12.0	12.8
San Francisco, Calif.	3.3	10.0	13.4	12.7	10.9
Seattle, Wash.	4.0	4.8	7.1	9.5	10.1

Source: Statistical Abstract of the United States, 1924, 1972, 1982–83, 1992 (Washington, D.C., U.S. Government Printing Office).

cities has remained relatively constant, and, except in the 1968, 1972, and 1986 elections, this gap has persisted at over 10 percentage points.

The mobilization of urban blacks during this period was undoubtedly tied to their large increases in population. As their numbers grew, blacks' political aspirations and feelings of efficacy expanded. Prior to 1970, none of the twenty-six cities selected in this study was majority black (see table 10.2). However, among these cities—seventeen of the fifty largest cities in the country—several (Gary, Atlanta, Washington, D.C., and Newark) had become majority black by 1970. Black urban populations continued to grow through the 1970s, and by the 1980s, blacks emerged as population majorities in Baltimore, Birmingham, Detroit, and New Orleans. Even in cities where blacks would remain minorities, their proportion expanded throughout the 1960s, 1970s, and 1980s. Only a few of the cities examined here (notably those located in California: Berke~~~ ~~~ ~~~les, Oakland, and San Francisco) experienced black ~~~ ~~~ ~~~ ~~~ ~~~e 1980s. As black voting power expan~~~ ~~~ ~~~ ~~~ ~~~ingly began to contest for e~~~ ~~~ ~~~ ~~~ ~~~ities, black mayoral of~~~ ~~~ ~~~ ~~~ ~~~f the elections held b~~~ ~~~ ~~~ ~~~ ~~~ held between 1989 ~~~ ~~~ ~~~ ~~~mayoral elections for ~~~ ~~~ ~~~ ~~~cks participated for ti~~~ ~~~ ~~~ ~~~ Baltimore, Denver,

The Impact of ~~~
Electoral Co~~~

The behavioral an~~~ ~~~ ~~~politics has generally been ~~~ ~~~ ~~~ttention because a number o~~~ ~~~ ~~~assumed that its effects would ~~~ ~~~...lation of groups. Echoing Dahl, Peter ~~~ ~~~ ~~~gued that racial conflict would diminish as blacks gai~~~ ~~~ve offices and as whites came to accept "black rule" in black-majority cities.[26] A few political scientists have notably disputed such claims, arguing that race remains a salient feature of city politics.[27] However, race still did not elicit much attention, because studies of voting behavior have tended not to focus on the political context even though it has been shown to have powerful and independent effects on electoral mobilization.[28] Most of the studies of voting behavior have focused instead on how the social characteristics of voters and electoral arrangements, such as voter residency requirements, affect turnout.

Elections that blacks won to become a city's first black mayor were usually dramatic, highly publicized affairs. In most instances, the turnout of the city's registered voters was markedly higher than average rates of participation for such elections. These elections were usually quite competitive; in many instances, black mayors were elected by narrow margins. The questions addressed here, therefore, are the following: First, what impact does the candidacy of a black have on the level of competition and voter turnout in mayoral elections? Second, has the impact of black office seeking lessened over time, as pluralists have long prophesied?

To estimate the independent effect of black office seeking on turnout and competition in mayoral elections, an ordinary least squares regression model was developed with voter turnout and competitiveness as the dependent variables. Turnout for all general, runoff primary, and primary mayoral elections was measured by the proportion of registered voters who cast ballots for mayor. Margin of victory served as our measure of competition. Races with a small margin of victory were deemed more competitive than races with a large margin of victory. To estimate the effect of race on competition and voter turnout in mayoral elections, we classified elections on the basis of black candidate participation; to further isolate the effects of candidate's racial group membership and other candidate characteristics, we also took into account the type of candidate involved and other racial characteristics of the election.[29] We have five measures of black office-seeking: (1) black candidate or candidates running generally, (2) black incumbent seeking reelection, (3) first-time black candidacy, (4) multiple black candidacies, and (5) no white candidate. Not all black candidates running for mayor were counted as "black candidates." In order to screen out fringe and truly minor candidates, we include only those black candidates who had previously held elective office or who managed to obtain more than 5 percent of the vote in the election. In addition, a "first-time black office seeker" represents the first time a black appeared in a particular election category (i.e., the first black to enter a runoff election is also a first-time black office seeker). In Chicago Democratic primaries, for example, the first-time black office seeker was not Harold Washington, who became the city's first black mayor in 1983, but Richard Newhouse, who challenged Richard Daley, Sr., in 1975. All of our black office-seeking measures are dummy variables. (However, Washington was the first black office seeker for Chicago general elections.)

Even though blacks still comprise a very small share of all elected officials, especially among higher offices, blacks now regularly pursue elected office. In the 315 general, runoff primary, and primary elections examined here, over half were elections in which black candidates participated. On average, 55 percent of the mayoral contests had black candidates running in them, while 21 percent of these elections were those where a black incumbent mayor was seeking re-election. Thirteen percent of the elections in our study were those having a first-time black office seeker. Finally, we distinguished between elections involving more than one black candidate and those having no white candidates present. Over the twenty-two-year period covered, only 14 percent of the elections had more than one black candidate participating, while 8 percent of the elections had no white candidates.

Different types of elections can affect different levels of competition and turnout. As part of reform, most big cities have nonpartisan primary elections followed by a runoff among the top two candidates if no candidate wins a majority—for example, Atlanta, Birmingham, Los Angeles, Memphis, Newark, and Oakland. Other cities, such as Cleveland, Detroit, Kansas City, and Seattle, have nonpartisan primary elections followed by nonpartisan general elections. Turnout in nonpartisan elections tends to be higher and more competitive in runoff or general elections where there are only two rival candidates than in primary elections where a large number of candidates can compete. But other cities, principally those "unreformed" cities located in the Northeast or Midwest, still hold partisan primary elections. Baltimore, Charlotte, Chicago, Gary, Hartford, New Haven, New York, and Washington, D.C., for example, all hold partisan primaries followed by a partisan general election.[30] Because many big-city governments are Democrat-controlled, the Democratic Party primary election is often more competitive than the general election. In fact, only Charlotte, Cleveland, and New York elected Republican mayors during the twenty-two-year period covered.[31] Not much is known about differences between mayoral primaries and general elections, but presidential primaries generally have lower turnout levels than do general elections.[32] An additional election-type variable was also created for partisan general elections. While nonpartisan elections and partisan primaries require voters to learn something about a candidate before they cast ballots, party cues enable voters to make a voting decision based on party. Turnout in partisan general elections is expected to be higher than turnout for all other elections because they impose fewer informational costs on the voter.

Party activity, especially in machine-controlled urban governments, has traditionally been viewed as positively related to voter participation. However, postrevisionist analysts of machine politics assert that machines depressed voter activity.[33] Our measure of party organizational strength is based on David Mayhew's "traditional party organizations" scale. In a comprehensive state-by-state analysis of party activity, Mayhew rated party strength in each state on a scale from 0 to 5. Because party organizations can vary widely within states, we assigned a different value to the city's level of party activity when there was a discrepancy between state and city levels of party activity.[34]

For the twenty-six cities during the period under study examined in this paper, average turnout in the mayoral general election or runoff primary was 50 percent, while the average turnout in mayoral primaries was 44 percent. Research has shown that competitive, close races generate high turnouts.[35] When a race is competitive, one would expect voters to express more interest in the campaign. Furthermore, if voters are Downsian rational actors, then they should be more likely to show up at the polls when their vote has a greater (but still infinitesimally small) chance of swaying the election.[36] Margin of victory is expected to be negatively related to turnout.

In addition, the lower levels of participation observed for elections involving black incumbents may not necessarily be any lower than for elections involving political incumbents generally. Therefore, the variable of open-seat versus incumbent races was added as a possible correlate of turnout and margin of victory.

Other control variables include those related to the city's political structure and its demographic characteristics. Demographic variables include the racial and ethnic composition of the city, its socioeconomic profile, and its region. The impact of the racial composition of a city's population on voter turnout should be considered both from an aggregate-level and an individual-level perspective. Verba and Nie[37] and Shingles[38] found that blacks tended to participate at higher levels than whites from similar socioeconomic backgrounds. Verba and Nie suggest that group consciousness among blacks explains this racial disparity in participation. Studies utilizing more up-to-date data bases having larger numbers of black respondents, however, have found that blacks no longer have participation rates higher than whites.[39] Race may play a different role in the aggregate population than among individuals. Once the percentage of blacks in the population rises to levels that virtually assure that an African American will occupy the mayor's office, turnout may be lower than for cities where blacks constitute a voting minority or are in a competitive situation with whites and other ethnic groups.

Wolfinger and Rosenstone found that Hispanics vote at a lower rate than do whites.[40] While there are differences in turnout among Hispanics based on their national origins, members of all Hispanic ethnic groups tend to vote at a lower rate than whites. Language and citizenship are often barriers to voting for many Hispanics. Accordingly, turnout should be negatively related to the Hispanic proportion of the population. Studies of voting behavior have also found that income, education, and age are related to turnout[41] Therefore, per capita income, the average level of educational attainment, and median age were added as control variables. These demographic variables might also affect the competitiveness of mayoral races. Finally, the year of election was added as a predictor variable to see if there are time trends not accounted for by the more substantive variables in the model.

Table 10.3 displays the results of the analysis. The presence of a black candidate clearly has a strong effect on aggregate turnout for all types of elections. According to the OLS results, if there is a black candidate in the race, voter turnout should increase by 4 percent. These results suggest that higher numbers of voters are mobilized to vote when a black candidate seeks election to the mayor's office. Black incumbent candidates, in contrast, generally depress voter participation by nearly 4 percent. The remaining black office-seeking measures did not have separate, independent ef-

TABLE 10.3

Voter Turnout and Margin of Victory in Mayoral Elections (Ordinary Least Squares Regressions)

	Turnout of Registered Voters		Margin of Victory	
	B coefficient	Standard error	Coefficient	Standard error
Intercept	57.69**	(11.25)	9.57	21.57
Black office-seeking measures				
Black candidate(s)	4.23**	(1.67)	−7.10*	(3.51)
Black incumbent	−3.71*	(1.98)	−5.36	(4.12)
First black office seeker	0.36	(1.97)	−1.17	(4.22)
Multiple black candidates	−0.02	(2.35)	−13.48**	(4.96)
No white candidate	−2.04	(2.84)	12.95*	(6.02)
Political variables				
Margin of victory	−31.39**	(2.70)		
Open-seat race	−1.72	(1.33)	−9.96**	(2.77)
State party strength	0.98	(0.72)	−2.76**	(1.15)
General election	8.82**	(1.45)	−7.53**	(3.09)
Partisan election	1.98	(2.51)	1.10	(4.15)
Partisan general election	−1.83	(2.33)	22.52**	(4.82)
Demographic variables				
Black population	15.98*	(7.48)	49.99**	(12.59)
Hispanic populaton	−23.45**	(7.26)	19.83	(12.87)
High school graduates	−29.19**	(9.05)	−0.14	(16.49)
Median age	0.22	(0.31)	0.18	(0.58)
Year	−0.23	(0.13)	0.38	(0.26)
Region and city controls				
South	—	—	−8.34**	(3.34)
West	13.86**	(2.69)	—	—
Midwest	−10.97**	(2.21)	—	—
Baltimore	−14.73**	(3.60)	22.97**	(6.59)
Chicago	16.64**	(3.33)	—	—
Charlotte	−14.27**	(3.45)	—	—
Gary	10.62**	(4.09)	—	—
Hartford	−8.45**	(3.01)	—	—
New Orleans	10.41**	(3.39)	—	—
Oakland	−12.54**	(3.75)	—	—
Raleigh	−5.10*	(3.38)	22.42**	(6.60)
Seattle	−13.05**	(3.63)	11.91*	(7.09)
Total number of elections	315		315	
R-squared	0.66		0.34	
Corrected R-squared	0.63		0.29	
Standard error of regression	9.18		19.75	
Mean of dependent measures	46.72		24.28	

Source: Data compiled by authors.

Note: Includes all mayoral elections held from 1969 to 1991 for the 26 cities. *$p < .05$. **$p < .01$. One-tailed test.

fects on turnout. Turnout for first-time black office seekers was not significantly higher than turnout in elections involving black candidates generally and in all other elections types. Browning, Marshall, and Tabb's
notion that turnouts peak the first time African Americans attempt to gain
control of the mayor's office was not supported by this analysis.[42]

Turnout in general elections is about 9 percent higher than for primary
elections, while turnout in partisan elections is no higher than it is for nonpartisan races. The results also validate for mayoral races what has been
shown for presidential and gubernatorial elections—namely, the more
competitive the race, the more people are drawn to the polls. While the
margin of victory is strongly related to participation rates in mayoral elections, open-seat races do not generate substantially higher turnouts than
those races in which incumbents seek reelection. Our measure of party
organizational strength was unrelated to turnout. We found no support for
traditional view that machine activity boosts turnout. But nor was there any
support for revisionist scholars who argue that political machines actually
depress voter turnout.[43]

The size of the black population was positively related to turnout, while
increases in the size of the Hispanic community decreased turnout. However, this analysis is based on aggregate data; one cannot conclude that
overall turnout is higher in cities having large numbers of blacks because
blacks are more likely to vote than other groups. Similarly, one cannot say
that turnout is lower in those cities having substantial Hispanic populations
because Hispanics are less likely to vote. Surprisingly, education was negatively related to turnout. Since education is the best predictor of whether an
individual decides to vote, this finding was completely unexpected. It is
likely that education is negatively related to turnout because we include
only major U.S. cities. Education does not vary nearly as much across cities
as across individuals. The relation of race to education might also explain
this unexpected finding. The size of the black community in these cities is
positively related to turnout in mayoral elections. Yet, blacks are usually
one of the least educated groups in these cities. African Americans may
vote at higher rates than whites, so education across the cities may truly be
negatively related to turnout. Age was unrelated to turnout in mayoral elections. Finally, western cities have turnout rates generally 14 percent above
those cities located in the North and South, while cities located in the Midwest have significantly lower turnout rates. A number of the cities, such as
Gary, Oakland, and Seattle, had participation rates that could not be fully
accounted for by the variables included in the model.

Mayoral candidates tend to win by comfortable margins, with the average margin of victory for the 315 elections examined here being 24 percent.
However, black candidacies also affect the competitiveness of the race.
When blacks compete for the mayoralty, the margin of victory tends to be
lower by about 7 percent. Similarly, when more than one black runs, the

race is more competitive than other races. However, when whites are absent and all the mayoral candidates are black, the race is far less competitive than other races; the margin of victory increases by about 13 percent. Political factors also relate to electoral outcomes. Open-seat races and general elections are more competitive than elections where incumbents mayors are seeking reelection or primary races. In contrast, partisan general elections are far less competitive than other types of mayoral elections. As explained earlier, in Democratic-led cities, partisan general elections are generally coronations and are not competitive. Surprisingly, however, states that have strong party organizations have slightly more competitive city elections. It is possible that state party organizations develop stronger operations in more competitive political environments.[44] Cities that have large black populations, such as Detroit, the District of Columbia, and Gary, have far less competitive mayoral elections than cities with smaller black populations. It is possible that black population size dampens competition because black mayoral candidates are able to win and remain in office for longer periods of time in majority-black cities. In addition, mayoral elections in southern cities tend to be more competitive than elections held outside of the South. Finally, Baltimore, Raleigh, and Seattle are all cities where mayoral candidates usually win by large margins.

While turnout has possibly dropped from 1969 to 1991 for the twenty-six cities examined here (the coefficient for year of election approaches statistical significance), elections did not become more competitive during this period. To determine if the effect of black office seeking on turnout and electoral competition has diminished over time, an interaction term between black office seeking and year was added to each regression model. The results of this analysis are not shown here since these interaction terms turned out to be statistically insignificant. Thus, except for cities in which black mayors are seeking reelection and those cities where whites were absent in the race, race continues to affect the campaigns and behavior of voters in urban elections. In general, black office seeking boosts turnout and heightens the competitiveness of urban elections, and this effect has persisted for more than two decades.

Conclusion: The Continuing Political Significance of Race

Race can strongly affect urban voting behavior. Efforts by blacks over the past two and a half decades to win the mayoralty are linked to electoral competition and higher rates of voter turnout in urban elections. Contrary to pluralist expectations, such race effects are not diminishing over time. Racial group competition in the urban political arena persists, even in those cities that have elected black mayors. In Los Angeles, the much heralded biracial coalition that made Tom Bradley his city's longest-serving mayor has collapsed.[45] Los Angeles voters in 1993 elected a white Republican as the city's chief executive, with votes split largely along racial lines.

There are two competing explanations for the continuing impact of race in American politics. One perspective is that the while old-fashioned racist attitudes are no longer publicly acceptable, the deeply negative ingrained attitudes that whites hold against blacks can lead them to mobilize and block blacks' efforts to win the mayoralty.[46] Since most researchers have found that Americans have become more racially tolerant over time,[47] an alternative view provides a more compelling explanation: that contemporary racial conflict is best understood as a realistic power struggle between blacks and whites,[48] and that this struggle animates the pattern of behavior and electoral politics revealed in our analysis. Blacks have traditionally viewed the elections of blacks as an important symbol of their progress, while whites may view the same election as a sign of their displacement and increased powerlessness. This symbolism can activate group loyalties in the political arena that would otherwise be absent. Moreover, since elected offices are strictly limited in number, black office-seeking can intensify conflict between the two racial groups. Relative status is a zero-sum good such that a rise in the status of blacks predicts a corresponding decline in the relative status of whites.[49] Elections involving blacks competing against whites also give rise to substantive as well as symbolic concerns. Long believing that their lack of adequate representation in the past worked against them, blacks consider the election of a black to be in their direct material interest. Whites, in contrast, believe that the loss of a white candidate to a black could result in the loss of previously enjoyed material benefits.

The group conflict framework garners additional support put into historical perspective as well. Susan Olzak's study of the period of massive immigration, industrialization, economic turbulence, and labor strife found that group conflict erupted when marginalized groups began to challenge the status quo.[50] In particular, the flood of European immigrants and African Americans caused group inequalities and racially ordered systems to break down as these groups competed for jobs, housing, educational opportunities, and social position. Such competition provoked unprecedented rates of riots, lynchings, violent strikes, and the like. Olzak also discovered that more than Asian and white European immigrants, African Americans were very often the targets of violence during this period.

The competition for political power among social groups can be no less intense when groups compete for jobs and status. However, channeled as such into democratic institutions, such conflict is less severe. In democratic states, electoral outcomes do not generally provoke riots or violence. Notably, Olzak argues that racial violence is less an enduring feature of Ameri-

can society than it is episodic and erratic. Even as race remains a central
feature of American society, the violence that erupted at the turn of the
century eventually abated. Will the competition between blacks and whites
lessen as blacks increasingly win executive posts within American cities?
The findings presented here are mixed. Black control of the city may ultimately reduce conflict because it is associated with lower levels of electoral
competition. Black political control, however, is achieved in fact only
when blacks have become mayors of the city and are seeking reelection, or
when all of the mayoral candidates are black. In most cities where blacks
are a numerical minority, black office seeking continues to heighten voter
activity. Perhaps the recent entry of Latino Americans and Asian Americans into urban electorates will blur the black-white dimensions of urban
political conflict as witnessed today. For now, the urban political environment is one where race remains politically potent.

Appendix 10.A: List of Cities by Region

Twenty-six cities that have a population of 100,000 or more were selected.
The cities are listed below by region. Of these twenty-six cities, seventeen
are among the fifty largest cities in the United States. These cities are indicated by an asterisk (*). The year each city elected its first black mayor is
also shown in parentheses.

Midwest (5)	Chicago*	(1983)
	Cleveland*	(1967)
	Detroit*	(1973)
	Gary	(1967)
	Kansas City*	(1991)
Northeast (7)	Baltimore*	(1987)
	Boston	(none)
	Hartford	(1981)
	New Haven	(1989)
	New York*	(1989)
	Newark*	(1970)
	Washington*	(1974)
South (7)	Atlanta*	(1973)
	Birmingham	(1979)
	Charlotte*	(1983)
	Memphis*	(1991)
	Miami	(none)
	New Orleans	(1977)
	Raleigh	(1969)
West (7)	Berkeley	(1971)
	Denver*	(1991)

Houston	(none)
Los Angeles*	(1973)
Oakland*	(1977)
San Francisco	(none)
Seattle*	(1989)

Appendix 10.B: Data Sources

While the Joint Center for Political Studies has conducted an annual count of the total number of black elected officials in the United States since 1977, there is no data bank that monitors the incidents and frequency of black candidates. Newspaper accounts of political campaigns as well as press endorsements were used to determine the number of races involving black office seekers. All of the seventeen major cities and many of the smaller cities selected have at least one daily newspaper. The remaining cities fall within the territory covered by at least one metropolitan newspaper. Election results and registration data were gathered from the appropriate city, county, and state offices. Except for New York, turnout data are from official sources. For New York, a combination of official sources and *New York Times* reports were used to calculate turnout.

Information regarding the form of government and election rules was based on newspaper accounts and city government offices. Demographic data regarding the city's racial composition and its socioeconomic profile were gathered from the results of the decennial U.S. Census and the Current Population Reports published by the Census Bureau. David Mayhew's typology of traditional party organizations (TPO) was used to code the level of machine activity in each city. In *Placing Parties in American Politics* (1986), Mayhew assigned each state a TPO score ranging from 0 to 5 based on the amount of organization activity. Modifying Mayhew's scores to account for variation in the level of machine activity within a state does not alter the results of the data analysis.

Notes

This research was funded by a grant from the National Science Foundation (#SBR-93-07924). The authors thank Sarah Laurence, Tamara Lyn, and Ray Joseph, Jr. for their research assistance.
1. Wolfinger 1965.
2. Piven and Cloward 1988; Cornwell 1964.
3. Cisneros 1993; Peterson 1985.
4. Berry, Portnoy, and Thomson 1993.
5. Karnig and Walter 1993.

6. These cities are a subset of incorporated cities that have populations greater than 100,000, and they are listed in appendix A. These twenty-six cities were selected to ensure regional diversity. To minimize sample selection bias, cities were selected that vary considerably as to the point in time when black mayoral candidates first appeared and the frequency of their bids. Details concerning how we gathered and coded other information are presented in appendix B. Since the cities were not selected randomly, the univariate statistics for the black office-seeking measures presented here may not be representative of all major U.S. cities. However, the set of relationships uncovered in this analysis should be generalizable for all major U.S. cities.

7. Erie 1988.

8. Ibid.

9. Kleppner 1981.

10. Alford and Lee 1968; Karnig and Walter 1983.

11. Welch and Bledsoe 1988.

12. Banfield and Wilson 1967.

13. Dahl 1961.

14. Katznelson 1976; Nelson and Meranto 1977; Erie 1988; Grimshaw 1992.

15. Grimshaw 1992.

16. Greenstone and Peterson 1973.

17. Grimshaw 1992.

18. Keiser 1990.

19. Kleppner 1985; Preston 1987; Grimshaw 1992.

20. Preston 1990.

21. Rich 1989.

22. Carmines and Stimson 1989.

23. A. Smith 1981.

24. Greenstone and Peterson 1973; Browning, Marshall, and Tabb 1984.

25. Dahl 1961.

26. Eisinger 1980.

27. Pinderhughes 1987; A. Reed 1988.

28. Kleppner 1981; Patterson and Caldeira 1983; Cox and Munger 1989; Tate 1991.

29. We rely on newspaper coverage of the city's newspaper to determine the race of mayoral candidates for each election. In some cases, we contacted local city officials to ascertain the race of candidates whose mayoral campaigns generated little media coverage. Since 1969 is the starting point of our study, we are unable to say with certainty that the candidate we label "first-time black office seeker" is, in fact, the city's first viable black mayoral candidate.

30. In New York, if no candidate wins at least 40 percent of the primary vote, a runoff primary election is held between the two top candidates. New York instituted primary runoffs after the divisive 1969 Democratic mayoral primary. Charlotte established partisan elections in 1973. Before that, Charlotte's election system was similar to Detroit's. Apparently, Charlotte also has a primary runoff provision like that of New York. However, since 1969, no mayoral nominee of either major party has failed to win majority support.

31. Los Angeles and New York, however, recently elected Republican mayors.

32. Ranney 1972.
33. Erie 1988.
34. The unmodified version of Mayhew's (1986) traditional party organization scale, nevertheless, still yielded the same results as our modified version.
35. Cox and Munger 1989.
36. Downs 1957.
37. Verba and Nie 1972.
38. Shingles 1981.
39. Wolfinger and Rosenstone 1980; Bobo and Gilliam 1990.
40. Wolfinger and Rosenstone 1980.
41. Ibid.; Verba and Nie 1972.
42. Browning, Marshall, and Tabb 1979.
43. Erie 1988.
44. Since most big-city governments are Democrat-controlled, the strength of the Democratic Party will be included as a correlate in these models in future analyses.
45. Sonenshein 1993.
46. Kinder and Sears 1981; Sears and Kinder 1985.
47. Schuman, Steeh, and Bobo 1985.
48. Glaser 1994; Huckfeldt and Kohfeld 1989; Bobo 1983.
49. Fossett and Kiecolt 1989.
50. Olzak 1990.

11

The Color of Urban Campaigns

DAVID HAYWOOD METZ AND KATHERINE TATE

My God, I sometimes wish we were all blue.
*(W. Otis Higgs Jr., candidate for mayor
of Memphis, 1983)*

OVER TIME, as more black politicians come face-to-face with whites in mayoral elections, it is inevitable that race will have a powerful influence on city politics. Race was especially salient in the first black-white mayoral confrontations that took place during the late 1960s and early 1970s. According to Thomas Pettigrew, "the fact that a leading candidate for mayor is a Negro becomes a dominant feature for both white and black voters, overwhelming in importance political party identification in Cleveland and Gary and scandals in incumbent administrations in Los Angeles and Newark."[1] Although crossover voting by voters of both races occurs in every election, most voters continue to cast their ballots along racial lines in elections involving black candidates.[2] A 1987 Gallup poll found that 54 percent of whites believed whites voted on the basis of race rather than of qualifications in black-white mayoral races, with 39 percent believing the same of black voters.[3]

Candidates have developed political strategies to exploit or compensate for the persistent tendency of Americans to vote along racial lines in black-white contests. Previous research, however, has ignored the strategic use of race by candidates in American elections. Beyond a handful of case studies that have identified racial campaigns and racial conflict as factors impeding black electoral success, few political scientists have attempted to formally define a racial campaign tactic or identify racialized campaigns. Instead, race-coded politics is treated in the profession like pornography—political scientists recognize it only when they "see it."[4] In this article, we assess to what degree black and white mayoral candidates use racial strategies in black-white contests, and what demographic and political factors, such as the size of the black and minority population and political incumbency, are associated with the racial strategies of black and white candidates in such elections. The central question addressed here is whether or not mayoral candidates emphasize or ignore race in order to maximize their political strength.

Our measure of a candidate's racial strategy is based on the major newspaper's coverage of the campaign for each city. The data analyzed in this study were a subset of mayoral elections (primary, runoff, and general) held in sixteen major American cities from 1969 to 1991 in which the two major candidates were black and white. There were seventy-five such contests. The sixteen cities, chosen for regional diversity, are Atlanta, Baltimore, Birmingham, Boston, Charlotte, Chicago, Cleveland, Denver, Detroit, Hartford, Kansas City, Los Angeles, Memphis, New York, Seattle, and Washington, D.C.

Race as a Campaign Strategy in Black-White Contests

As strategic politicians,[5] candidates can choose to make racial appeals in order to maximize their political strength. Offered as testimony in *Gingles v. Edmisten*, Paul Luebke's definition of a racial appeal is when "one candidate calls attention to the race of his opponent or his opponent's supporters, or if media covering campaigns disproportionately calls attention to the race of one candidate, or that of the candidate's supporters."[6] Another social scientist writes that since overt appeals to racist sentiments cannot be as effectively practiced by southern politicians who hope to win, today's racial slogans are often presented in "coded, sanitized language."[7] *Law and order* and *quota* are examples of terms that have strong racial connotations. Obviously, Luebke's definition of a racial appeal is easier to measure than a coded racial appeal, but an attempt to identify campaign issues that have implicit racial messages was made in this study. In our analysis, elections become racialized when one or both of the two major candidates make explicit appeals to members of their own racial group; when the major candidates limit their campaign appearances to members of their racial group; and when the candidates raise issues that are explicitly or implicitly racial.

For white candidates running against a black, race can be used as a wedge issue to divide voters racially. Given the sizable overlap between race, political ideology, and party membership, this use of race as a wedge issue generally advantages Republicans and conservative Democrats running in nonpartisan races. By arousing white racial fears, a white candidate can effectively siphon off votes from his or her black rival. Chicago's 1983 mayoral election is perhaps the most noted example of candidates making race a central issue in their campaigns. Becoming the first black to win the Democratic primary in a solidly Democratic city, Harold Washington was virtually assured of victory in the general election that followed. While his white Republican rival, Bernard Epton, a virtual unknown, began his campaign using conventional tactics to build name recognition and a positive image, he quickly shifted to attacking Washington's character, telling the press that others were unwilling to criticize Washington's past record because of their "fears of being called racist." Epton also called himself a victim of "reverse racism." But it was Epton's negative television ad that many felt carried a racially coded message; it ended with the line, "Epton for Mayor . . . Before It's Too Late!"[8]

While examples of how white candidates use race against their black opponents abound, black candidates can also emphasize race in order to augment their chances of winning. Since blacks, given their demographic profile as a group, often vote at lower rates than whites, race is generally used by black candidates as a means of galvanizing and mobilizing the black voters in the city. Chicago's 1983 mayoral race is, again, instructive. Paul Kleppner writes that although Washington's original strategy was to campaign in the entire city, he was forced to modify it when it became clear that he would not attract much white and Latino support. In order to motivate more blacks to register and go to the polls, Washington increasingly began to present himself as a symbol of black pride and progress. At one campaign rally, Washington told his predominantly black audience to enthusiastic applause, "We have given the white candidates our vote for years and years and years. Now it's our turn . . . it's our turn . . . it's our turn."[9] As William Nelson and Philip Meranto point out, black numeric strength must be augmented by strong leadership, a sense of group cohesion, and widespread political consciousness in the black community.[10] Black candidates who run highly racial campaigns emphasize their role as representatives of the African American community. They strive to mobilize as many black voters as possible, paying little attention to the voters of other races.

If emphasizing one's race, the race of one's rival, and issues that evoke racial interests and anxieties are tactical means for augmenting a candidate's chances of winning—unlike door-to-door canvassing and kissing babies—they do not always produce positive results. In fact, it would appear that, more often than not, racial campaigning can undermine a candidate's chances of victory. Since race baiting is considered to be politically unacceptable nowadays, candidates who manipulate race can encounter a barrage of voter disapproval. For white politicians, race baiting almost always takes the form of negative campaigning. It is more commonplace for white candidates to attack their black rivals on racial grounds than to emphasize their racial pride as whites. Negative, racially charged campaigning serves the purpose of elevating white fears about the black candidate's leadership abilities. A 1987 survey found that although 50 to 60 percent of whites felt that black and white candidates are no different in their personal leadership abilities, 34 to 35 percent still felt that white candidates are generally more intelligent, stronger leaders, and more knowledgeable than black candidates.[11] Thus, the negative campaigning will focus on the black candidate's character, or on his or her fairness and evenhandedness. However, while a negative, race-oriented strategy can mobilize racially conservative whites, as arch-conservative U.S. Senator Jesse Helms's anti–affirmative action commercial had in his 1990 reelection campaign,[12] particularly in communities where serious racial divisions already exist, it can also cause more liberal whites to reject those white politicians caught fanning the flames of highly racial, or in the extreme, racist politics. In Chicago, for example, once the media began to publicize the racist activities of Epton supporters, including the distribution of racist campaign literature, buttons, and T-shirts bearing slogans such as "Vote Right, Vote white," Epton became less appealing to liberal whites who did not want to be associated with such groups. Not only was Epton forced to condemn the racist activities taking place in his campaign, he began blaming the media for injecting race into the campaign in the first place. In the end, not only did the open racism in Epton's campaign drive some liberal whites away, it also motivated more blacks to register and vote. Washington won one-third of the white liberal vote in the city, and the black turnout was estimated to be 5.8 percentage points higher than the rate for whites.[13]

Washington, too, however, also found it necessary to moderate the racial tone of his campaign. Having adopted "It's Our Turn" as his chief campaign slogan, Washington also told black Chicagoans during the primary: "Every group, when it reaches a certain population percentage, automatically takes over. . . . They don't apologize, . . . they just move in and take over."[14] This statement greatly worried whites, raising the level of anxiety and misgivings they had about a black becoming mayor of the city. With Epton solidifying the votes of whites, who represented about 48 percent of the city, Washington needed to make a more universal appeal to pick up enough white support to win the election. Although, according to Kleppner, Washington failed to do this sufficiently, he still won, but by a narrow margin of just 4 percent.

Mobilizing the black community through the employment of strong racial rhetoric can backfire, therefore, causing the alienation and mobilization of the white community. In cities that are majority black, this trade-off may not matter. However, blacks are voting minorities in most American cities. Thus, analysts often have advised black candidates running in predominantly white jurisdictions to use deracialized strategies to build cross-racial coalitions in order to win the support of all voters. A deracialized strategy, according to McCormick and Jones, is one that avoids "explicit reference to race-specific issues, while at the same time emphasizing those issues that are perceived as racially transcendent."[15] It requires that candidates avoid issues that may prove racially divisive, such as affirmative action, and focus instead on issues like economic growth and jobs. Candidates who run deracialized campaigns devote almost all of their energy to discussion of these issues, and spend almost no time making rhetorical appeals to voters. As a strategist for former Philadelphia mayor Wilson Goode notes, issues may "legitimate" black candidates in the eyes of white voters.[16]

A deracialized approach has its shortcomings. Spending less time campaigning for black votes to court white support or downplaying the concerns that black voters may have, however, can lead to a low black turnout. Because black candidates often lack a secure base among white voters, they can lose without concentrated black support. Indeed, past black-white contests suggest that black candidates require anywhere from 85 to 95 percent of the black vote as well as a high black turnout rate to win office. Among the reasons why Andrew Young lost his runoff primary bid in 1990 to become Georgia's first black governor was the low turnout among black voters. In particular, Young's efforts to deemphasize race issues in order to pacify those whites concerned about his civil rights record reduced black enthusiasm for his campaign. Despite Young's extensive campaign for white votes, several surveys showed that about one-third of the white vote was beyond Young's reach.[17] Yet, a vigorous campaign for black votes can cause whites to reject the black candidate in favor of the white opponent. As a way out of this racial dilemma confronting black political aspirants, political scientist Jesse Borges argues that the optimal strategy for black candidates is a "dual campaign" approach, one where a highly racial style is employed in the black community and a deracialized style is adopted in white areas.[18] To some degree, black candidates have attempted such an approach through intensive personal campaigning in the black community and the employment of inclusive, biracial campaign rhetoric. In general, the type of racial strategy a black candidate employs should depend on the size of the black community. Whether the candidate is running for an open seat or for one where a white incumbent mayor is seeking reelection may also affect the racial cast of the black candidate's strategy.

Other than emphasizing the idiosyncratic and personal beliefs of certain white candidates, political scientists have failed to explore and identify the set of factors that may influence the racial style of white candidates. Whites who wage highly racial campaigns are generally thought to be politically conservative. However, this is not always the case. For example, white incumbent mayor Sam Massell had a won office with the strong backing of black voters in Atlanta, and was considered to be liberal. Challenged by black vice-mayor Maynard Jackson in 1973, however, Massell called Jackson a "racist," and declared that Jackson's goal was a "black takeover of the city." Whether the black opponent is an incumbent mayor or not may affect a white candidate's strategy. Lastly, as in the case for blacks, the size of the black community in the city may strongly affect the racial style of white mayoral aspirants.

Finally, elections can become racialized for reasons more complicated than calling attention to the race of one of the candidates. While many assume that the candidates, the parties, and the media can control and limit the level of race in a given campaign, racial issues can dominate a campaign regardless of what the candidates and their political organizations say or do. Race can unavoidably become the issue in an atmosphere of aggravated and newly inflamed racial tensions. For example, prior to his election as New York City's first black mayor in 1989, David Dinkins's political style could hardly have been characterized as racially threatening. Yet, enmeshed in the racialized climate brought about by the Tawana Brawley affair (now considered a hoax, in 1987 a black teenager claimed to have been kidnapped and raped by six white men), the murder of Yusef Hawkins (a black teenager) in the white section of Brooklyn, and the Central Park rape of a white woman by black and Latino teenagers, Dinkins could hardly avoid addressing racial issues.

Predicting the Racial Strategy of Black and White Candidates

Elections become racialized when the rhetoric of one or both major mayoral candidates consists of race-based appeals directed toward members of their own race. Secondly, campaigns become racialized when candidates limit their public appearances to members of their own group, ignoring, then, the other racial group in the city. Lastly, the degree to which a candidate incorporates race into his or her discussion of issues can elevate the salience of race. The types of issues that candidates raise can be overtly racial, such as the city's affirmative action policy, or covertly racial, as sometimes is the case in a white candidate's exclusive focus on the city's crime (read: black) problem.

In general, voters get most of their information about the campaign directly from the media or indirectly through their friends, coworkers, and family members. On the basis of newspaper coverage of the campaign, each of the two major candidates was assigned a numeric code to reflect the racial tone of his or her campaign (see appendix 11A for additional coding information).[19] Each candidate was assigned a 1 to 5 score for rhetoric and a 1 to 5 score for audience composition. Candidates' public statements were given the highest score of 5 when their campaign appeals were directed explicitly toward their own race and assigned the lowest score of 1 when their appeals were explicitly directed toward the other race. The mid-point of 3 is assigned to those candidates whose rhetoric was directed to all races equally. In terms of campaign appearances, candidates were assigned high scores if their audiences prominently consisted of their own racial group and low scores if they more consistently appeared in front of the other racial group. Lastly, up to four issues that each candidate emphasized most during the campaign were noted, and a score of 1 assigned to each if the issue was discussed in terms of race. The racialized issue content, there-fore, of each candidate ranged from 0 to 4. The three scores were combined into one additive index ranging from 2 to 14.[20]

Most candidates' racial strategies were moderate in tone, falling about midway between the two extremes. Black candidates challenging whites and white candidates challenging blacks earned fairly comparable scores near 7 (see tables 11.1 and 11.2).[21] While a handful of candidates directed their campaign appeals toward the other race exclusively, none restricted their appearances toward the other race exclusively. Those candidates cam-paigning for the votes of the "other" race were generally white.[22] In pre-dominantly white cities such as Seattle, several white candidates made ex-plicit statements for the need to broaden and expand job opportunities for blacks. But only rarely have candidates of either race directed the bulk of their energies toward winning the votes of "other" race. Instead, strategies have generally vacillated between focusing on both races equally or on concentrating on the votes from members of their own race.

If a racial campaign style is a vote-maximizing strategy, political factors, such as whether the candidate is running in a primary or general election, and demographic factors, such as the size of the black community, should be related to it. The type of opponent black or white candidates face should affect their strategies. Black candidates may adopt more racialized cam-paigns in their efforts to unseat a white incumbent mayor. The reverse is more plausible for whites challenging black incumbent mayors. After a black candidate has served for a few years and whites have seen that no catastrophes have transpired, racial strategies may be less effective. white candidates can less effectively exploit racial fears.

The percentage of blacks in the city should strongly affect the type of campaign candidates decide to run. In fact, out of the long list of factors, the size of the black population may be the most important consideration. When the black population is small, a highly racial strategy has little chance of succeeding for black candidates. However, as the size of the black community grows, so does the number of voters receptive to highly racial campaigning. Moreover, Mark A. Fossett and K. Jill Kiecolt have found that as the size of the black population increases, whites' perceptions of a threat from blacks also increases.[23] These white fears could undermine a candidate's ability to build a multiracial coalition, providing black candi-

TABLE 11.1
Racial Strategy Scores for Black Candidates in Black-White Contests (Percentages)

	Score							
	4	*5*	*6*	*7*	*8*	*9*	*10*	*11*
	1.4	25	30.6	12.5	9.7	6.9	4.2	9.7
(*N*)	(1)	(18)	(22)	(9)	(7)	(5)	(3)	(7)

Total *N* 72
Mean 6.90
S.D. 1.94

TABLE 11.2
Racial Strategy Scores for White Candidates in Black-White Contests
(Percentages)

	Score						
	5	*6*	*7*	*8*	*9*	*10*	*11*
	16.9	38	22.5	9.9	7	1.4	4.2
(*N*)	(12)	(27)	(16)	(7)	(5)	(1)	(3)

Total *N* 71
Mean 6.73
S.D. 1.48

dates even more incentive to run highly racial campaigns when the black population is large. Previous studies have found that the size of the black community determines black mayoral candidates' political success; it should have an equally profound impact on their choice of racial strategy.

The passage of time should influence a candidate's choice of racial strategy. Most researchers have found a steady, if somewhat uneven, decrease in racial prejudice in America over the last few decades.[24] Most observers have argued that deracialized strategies have become increasingly prevalent over time.[25] Black candidates also have a strategic incentive to implement highly racial strategies when a city's nonblack minority populations are large. The size of the Latino population should have a particularly strong influence on a candidate's choice of strategy. In most cities, Latinos constitute the largest minority group besides blacks, and their social, economic, and political status closely resembles that of African Americans.

If a racial campaign style that a candidate adopts is largely idiosyncratic, then few, if any, of these variables should be associated with it. Given the general difficulty black candidates have in winning white votes, black and white candidates might tailor their campaigns differently in similar political environments. Thus, the racial strategy scores for black and white

TABLE 11.3

Factors Predicting Black Candidates' Racial Strategy Score (Unstandardized Ordinary Least Squares Coefficients)

	B	SE
Intercept	2.82**	1.06
White incumbent (0–1)	1.42*	0.62
Democratic Party strength	−0.85	0.66
Partisan general election (0–1)	0.13	0.67
Margin of victory	1.44	1.51
Open-seat race (0–1)	1.59**	0.61
Black population	3.56*	1.59
Hispanic population	3.56	2.60
Midwest (0–1)	1.91**	0.55
Racial incident (0–1)	0.39	0.61
Year	0.05	0.04
Number of cases	70	
R-squared	.30	
Adjusted R-squared	.19	
Mean of dependent variable	6.93	

Note: Probability levels shown for one-tailed test. ** $p < .01.$ * $p < .05.$

candidates are analyzed separately. The results of the analysis are shown in tables 11.3 and 11.4.

In general, increases in the proportion of African Americans in the city heightened the racial tone of the black candidate's strategy.[26] Thus, in general, increasing the black population by 10 percent increased the black candidate's racial strategy score by one-third of one point. The size of the Latino population had no appreciable effect on black candidates' racial scores in black-white contests.

Black candidates tended to run more racially oriented campaigns against white incumbents than against white challengers. Running against a white mayor elevated the racial tone of the black candidate's campaign by nearly one and one-half points. Blacks may be more likely to emphasize race and racial issues in such elections in order to mobilize the black community and solidify its vote. Open-seat races had the effect of raising the black candidate's score by more than one and one-half points as well.

Whether or not political parties can minimize racial conflict has been the subject of some controversy. Machine organizations may have served to curb outbreaks of ethnic and racial violence by rewarding ethnics and blacks with political office. In this analysis, the strength of the Democratic Party's state organization had a decisive impact on the racial strategies of black candidates (see appendix 11A for details on this measure). Overall, strong state Democratic organizations reduce the likelihood that black

TABLE 11.4

Factors Predicting White Candidates' Racial Strategy Score (Unstandardized Ordinary Least Squares Coefficients)

	B	SE
Intercept	7.01**	0.90
Black incumbent (0–1)	−0.28	0.43
Democratic Party strength	−0.36	0.44
Partisan general election (0–1)	1.16**	0.48
Margin of victory	−2.47*	1.15
Open-seat race (0–1)	0.01	0.38
Black population	1.44	1.66
Hispanic population	0.06	1.87
West (0–1)	1.65**	0.68
Racial incident (0–1)	1.02**	0.42
Year of election	−0.07**	0.03
Number of cases	69	
R-squared	.39	
Adjusted R-squared	.28	
Mean of dependent variable	6.75	

Note: Probability levels shown for one-tailed test. ** $p < .01$. * $p < .05$

mayoral candidates will choose to run a highly race-oriented campaign. Strong party support that black candidates may obtain in states having strong Democratic organizations may reduce the need for black candidates to engage in high racial rhetoric and other racial tactics to mobilize blacks in the city, since they may already be mobilized. Moreover, strong party support may increase the likelihood of blacks winning higher levels of white acceptance and electoral support. Finally, black candidate strategies were more racial in the Midwest than in all other regions of the country.

In analyzing what factors are related to the racial strategies white candidates adopt when their principal rival is black, a strongly similar picture emerged. The racial tone adopted by white candidates was stronger in both partisan general elections and highly competitive races, suggesting that white candidates may use racial strategies as a means of holding off black advances. However, white candidates did not rely heavily on a racial strategy when their opponent was a black mayor seeking reelection. A race strategy may lose its strategic value in cities where whites have shown their willingness to elect black candidates or where the white votes' are marginal to the outcome. Moreover, the size of the black community, as depicted in any functional form, had no effect on the racial style of whites; nor, for that matter, did the size of the Latino community, or (not shown in table 11.3) the size of the white community. White candidates' strategies were not significantly more racial when the election was an open-seat race. Finally, the campaigns of white mayoral candidates running in western cities were more racial than those of white candidates running elsewhere in the country.

In contrast to the findings for black candidates, consistently related to the racial strategies of white candidates were the year of the election and whether there had been a recent racial incident in the city as reported by the press. White candidate strategies have become increasingly less racial over time, perhaps because it is increasingly less acceptable for white candidates to engage in racial politics. In contrast to black strategies, white racial approaches generally take the form of negative campaigning, which is more likely to elicit voter disapproval from all races, possibly making race strategies a riskier choice for white candidates. Moreover, given that the black urban population has grown considerably over the last fifty years, it may no longer be electorally possible for white candidates to court exclusively members of their own race. At the same time, when a racial incident had occurred in the city, such as a police beating of a black suspect, the campaigns that white candidates conducted were more likely to be racially oriented. A racial incident, however, increased the white candidate's racial strategy score by only one-half of one point. Thus far, the evidence suggests that the racial strategies adopted by black and white candidates in black-white contests tend to be based on a number of political and social factors and are more strategic than personal.

Conclusions

Any number of considerations could lead a candidate to emphasize race during the campaign. Candidates might be strategic actors who emphasize race only when doing so will have political benefits. Alternatively, candidates might choose to emphasize race for reasons that have nothing to do with political strategy, including their personal beliefs about racial issues, a genuine desire to establish good public policy regarding race, or a concern about the racial climate of the city. The analysis of the use of race by mayoral candidates in black-white contests reveals that the racial strategies that candidates adopt are based on certain considerations. When the black base of the population is small or when blacks form the large majority of the city, the campaigns that black candidates run tend to be less racial. Black candidates adopting a deracialized campaign style will spend equal time campaigning for both black and white votes and will take care to deemphasize racial issues in the campaign. The study confirms that generally, most black candidates opt for the politically advantageous strategy. In cities with small black populations, black candidates most often turn to deracialized strategies. In cities where blacks near a majority of the population, black candidates favor more highly racial strategies. In the latter case, blacks choose to pursue this more racial course in order to mobilize and consolidate the votes they expect to win from the black community, given that many believe majority support from whites to be out of reach. In elections where white mayors were running for reelection, the racial strategies black candidates employed were markedly more racial in tone.

As in the case of black candidates, whites' racial strategies were found to be systematically linked to a number of political and social factors. Their strategies tended to be more racial in the most competitive circumstances or in partisan general elections. White candidates' strategies were also markedly more racial when race relations had been impaired by a recent racial event or incident. Over time, the number of whites running highly racial campaigns has fallen. This may be because the proportion of black voters in cities has increased, and whites, like blacks, now recognize the importance of running deracialized campaigns. In black-white contests held in the West, the racial tone adopted by white candidates tended to be high. The finding that candidates manipulate the racial tone of their campaigns for political advantage in black-white contests has wide-ranging consequences for our understanding of urban politics.

Although the campaign strategies of white candidates are becoming somewhat less racialized, the findings presented here seem to contradict a growing body of literature which suggests that deracialized strategies are becoming increasingly prevalent.[27] Analysis of aggregate data revealed that the passage of time has no significant effect on the type of racial strategies that black mayoral candidates choose, and circumstantial evidence reinforces this finding. Coleman Young in Detroit, W. W. Herenton in Memphis, and Richard Arrington in Birmingham have all used highly racial strategies to win or retain mayoralties within the last five years.

It may be, however, the most of the highly racial campaigning that still occurs takes place in cities like Detroit and Birmingham, where blacks have occupied the mayor's office for years. Candidates like Young and Arrington, who have held office for over a decade and first came to power by using a highly racial strategy, may be unwilling or unable to modify their approach. Their past use of highly racial strategies may have alienated white voters, who will forever associate such candidates with black interests. If most of the highly racial campaigning that still occurs take place in majority-black cities with long-term incumbents, it may mask a trend toward deracialization taking place elsewhere.

Because we emphasize political and contextual factors, our theory differs substantially from earlier formulations purporting to explain the persistence of ethnic and racial politics only because Americans stubbornly cling to their racial and ethnic identities.[28] Because it becomes strategic for black and white politicians, under certain conditions, to engage in racial politics, racial group identities are strengthened in the process. And as long as it remains strategic, politicians will continue to cast issues as racial ones. Thus, race politics is how the game is played in the United States.

Appendix 11.A: Data Sources and Coding

To code the racial content of the campaign, the city's newspaper coverage of the final months of the election was reviewed. To facilitate coding consistency, a questionnaire was developed by the authors, on which each of the two major candidates' public statements, campaign appearances (as covered in the paper), and principal policy positions were recorded. In an earlier phase of the project, newspaper accounts of political campaigns were also used to determine the racial group membership of all of the mayoral candidates. Black candidates identified in the study are only those who have previously held elective office or those who managed to obtain more than 5 percent of vote in the election. In some instances, local government officials and newspaper reporters were contacted to ascertain the race of candidates whose race was not readily identifiable from newspaper sources. Election results and registration data were gathered from the appropriate city, county, and state offices. Except for New York, turnout data are from official sources. For New York, a combination of official sources and *New York Times* reports was used to calculate turnout. Information regarding the form of government and election rules was based on newspaper accounts and city government reports. Demographic data, such as the city's racial composition, were gathered from the results of the decennial U.S. Census and Current Population Reports published by the Census Bureau.

Dependent Measure

Racial strategy: Additive index of the candidate's racial rhetoric score, audience composition score, and racialized issue score.

Independent Measures

Black population: Percentage of the voting-age black population of the city, according to the 1970, 1980, and 1990 censuses.

Hispanic population: Percentage of the city's Hispanic population eighteen years of age and older, according to the 1970, 1980, and 1990 censuses.

Open-seat race: Coded as 1 when an incumbent mayor was not running for reelection, and 0 otherwise.

Black incumbent: Coded as 1 when a black incumbent mayor was seeking reelection, and 0 otherwise.

White incumbent: Coded as 1 when a white incumbent mayor was seeking reelection, and 0 otherwise.

Democratic Party strength: This is Cotter, Gibson, Bibby, and Huckshorn's state party organizational strength measure for the Democratic Party.[29] Organizational strength at the state level is measured by the researchers along such dimensions as the level of services state parties offer to their candidates and the resources in office facilities, staff, and budgets that the state party organizations have.

Partisan general election: Coded as 1 when the election was a partisan and general election, and 0 otherwise.

Margin of victory: The total percentage of the votes for the victor minus those for his or her major opponent.

Year of election: Beginning with 1969, coded from 1 to 26 for year of the election.

West: Coded as 1 for cities in the West; 0 otherwise.

Midwest: Coded as 1 for cities in the Midwest; 0 otherwise.

Racial incident: Coded as 1 when the newspaper reported a racial incident; 0 otherwise. An event classified as a racial incident included racial violence, discrimination, or confrontation that occurred during the election cycle.

Notes

This research is part of Katherine Tate's larger study of race politics and power in American cities and was supported by the National Science Foundation (#SBR-93-07924). This chapter is also partially based on David H. Metz's senior thesis submitted to Harvard College, June 1993, which earned the Government Department's highest honors (a summa). The authors thank Greg Strizek, Jeff Beatty, and Chris Martin for their research assistance.
   1. Pettigrew 1972.
   2. Karnig and Welch 1980; Bullock 1984; Kleppner 1985; Keiser 1990.
   3. 1987 Gallup/Joint Center for Political Studies poll cited in Linda F. Williams 1989.
   4. Grofman 1992b, 206.
   5. See Jacobson and Kernell 1983.
   6. Quoted in Grofman 1993, 206–7.

7. Quoted in Grofman, Magalski, and Noviello 1985, 215.

8. Kleppner 1985, 210.

9. Ibid., 154.

10. Nelson and Meranto 1977, 26.

11. Williams 1989.

12. McCorkle 1991. Helms had aired a television commercial that showed a black getting a job through affirmative action even through the white applicant was apparently "better qualified" than the black and "needed the job the most." McCorkle's (1991) research found that the commercial had not so much reduced white support for Helms's black opponent as converted those undecided white voters in the electorate to his side.

13. Kleppner 1985, 212–14, 149.

14. Ibid., 155.

15. McCormick and Jones 1993, 76.

16. Ransom 1987, 24.

17. Davis and Willingham 1993, 162.

18. Borges 1993.

19. Admittedly, this approach has its own shortcomings. Certain newspapers might give biased accounts in their coverage of the campaign, yet only one newspaper was used to code for the racial content of the campaigns. The bias could extend to how the newspaper reports the campaign activities of the black candidates; some newspapers may not give coverage to all racial aspects of a given campaign. They may not report, for example, that in order to draw attention to his black opponent's race, a white candidate printed the picture of his black opponent in the campaign literature that was distributed. If anything, the content analysis might result in *lower* estimates of the racial strategies employed by the major candidates and of the racial character of the campaign. Our approach, therefore, is fairly conservative. An alternative to newspaper content analysis might include interviews with local election officers and officials to record their assessments of how racialized these campaigns were. However, this technique would inject its own sources of bias and would be more costly than content analysis. Nor could this approach be as easily replicated as content analysis.

20. The inter-item correlations between the rhetoric, audience composition, and issue content for the first major candidate are 0.34 for rhetoric and audience, 0.41 for rhetoric and issue content, 0.29 for audience and issue content. For the second major candidate, they are 0.51 for rhetoric and audience, 0.26 for rhetoric and issue content, and 0.21 for audience and issue content.

21. Because cities were not selected randomly, the univariate statistics presented here are not necessarily representative of all major U.S. cities. However, the set of relations uncovered in this analysis should be generalizable for all major U.S. cities.

22. Asian Americans have made serious bids in mayoral contests in Seattle and, most recently, Los Angeles, as well as in other cities. Recognizing that a black-white framework does not adequately capture the politics of major American cities today, we made efforts in this study to record the ethnicity and race of other groups, specifically Latinos and Asian Americans. An analysis of these groups and their impact on racial politics in American cities will be included at a later stage of the project.

23. Fossett and Kiecolt 1989.

24. Schuman, Steeh, and Bobo 1985.

25. McCormick and Jones 1993; R. Smith 1990.

26. A number of different forms (linear, curvilinear, and logarithm) of the black population's effect on the racial strategy scores of black candidates were modeled. The one shown in tables 11.3 and 11.4 achieved the best model fit (i.e., highest R squared and t statistic).

27. McCormick and Jones 1993; R. Smith 1990.

28. Wolfinger 1974, chap. 3; Wolfinger 1965, 896–908; Parenti 1967, 717–26.

29. Cotter, Gibson, Bibby, and Huckshorn 1984.

12

Religious Institutions and African American Political Mobilization

FREDRICK C. HARRIS

RELIGIOUS INSTITUTIONS have provided critical organizational resources for protest mobilization both during the postwar Civil Rights movement and an earlier era. The black church has often served as the "organizational hub of black life," providing the structure and resources that fostered collective protest against a system of white domination in the South and elsewhere.[1] Those resources promoted mobilization through clerical leadership and through formal and informal networks of communication.

This chapter surveys the early history of black religious institutions in electoral politics, and argues that during Reconstruction, as now, black churches served as a source of information, organizational skills, and political stimuli. It then illustrates how black religious institutions operated under different opportunity structures for participation during the Jim Crow period. The analysis then turns to the present and indicates, through participant observation primarily in Chicago churches, how politicians' explicit courtship of black churchgoers brings these churchgoers information and political stimuli as well as providing politicians with an easily mobilizable constituency. The analysis then takes up the controversy over the appropriateness of church-based political activism, concluding that most black churchgoers approve of church-based activism so long as it does not include ministers' explicit endorsement of particular candidates. Survey research demonstrating a greater boost from religious activity to black political activism than to the participation of whites suggests that when congregants approve of church-based political activism, they then have a fairly clear idea of their political interests.

African American Religious Institutions in Historical Context

Understanding the emergence of the Civil Rights movement and subsequent church-based electoral activity requires understanding the history of black religious institutions. As Adolph Reed puts it, "Any rigorous analysis of the link between politics and the black church must delineate the developmental context—and the trajectory of actions and choices dictated by this context—through which the twentieth-century black church evolved."[2]

The following analysis will not assert, as many do, that religious institutions performed as independent actors in mass mobilization or that black clerics acted as "organic leaders" in African American communities. Rather, it will show that black churches as institutions interacted with other sources of mobilization. The churches' communication networks, their capacity to stimulate social interaction, provide material resources, and give individuals the opportunity to learn organizing skills, and, perhaps most importantly, their sustainability over time and physical space made them the only black institutions consistently promoting the collective resistance of African Americans through several historical periods, shifting political alliances and interests, and vastly differing opportunity structures for activism.

Other more elite-centered analyses center on the political action of black religious leadership.[3] Yet an exclusive focus on the political behavior of clerics presents a skewed view of religion and black political activism. Black clerics have championed, but have also undermined, mobilization efforts for racial integration, unionization, civil rights activism, and black electoral empowerment.[4] Recognizing the ambiguous role of clerical leadership in African American political mobilization, this analysis will emphasize the effects on that mobilization of religious institutions, particularly horizontally organized religious institutions.

Religious Institutions and African American Political Development

Robert Putnam's work on Italy demonstrates that institutions are shaped by historical circumstances that help determine if they will act as resources for political engagement. Specifically, Putnam argues that the nature of communication networks within social organizations affects the "social capital" needed for collective action. Putnam theorizes that "Some . . . networks are primarily 'horizontal,' bring[ing] together agents of equivalent status and power. Others are primarily 'vertical,' linking unequal agents in asymmetric relations of hierarchy and dependence."[5] In Italy, the horizontal linkages are associated with broader civic competence and governmental performance. In the United States, African Americans have historically gained greater social capital for civic engagement through horizontally structured Protestant denominations than through vertically structured Roman Catholic institutions.[6]

After Emancipation, for example, when opportunities opened for the political engagement of newly freed black men, religious institutions provided the organizational infrastructure for mass political mobilization. In the Reconstruction period, newly freed religious blacks organized autonomous Baptist denominations and joined the northern-based African Methodist Episcopal Church, which fiercely competed against the independent Baptist churches for the religious loyalties of newly freed slaves.[7]

Both the exclusionary practices of the white Protestant denominations in the South, especially regarding clerical leadership, and the newly freed slaves' own desire for self-determination led the former slaves to found and affiliate mostly with black-led denominational groups, represented almost exclusively by the Baptists and Methodists.[8] These institutions were, and still remain, the largest organizations of blacks in the United States. Although northern black churches and religious leadership were an integral part of the Abolitionist movement and the Underground Railroad before the Civil War, in the South there were few, if any, purely indigenous political organizations for freed slaves during Reconstruction politics.

Thus in Reconstruction, southern churches provided meeting space for political gatherings, and church leadership and laity were elected to state political conventions and to state and local elected offices. Black clerics were particularly prominent in Reconstruction politics. Historian Eric Foner estimates that "over 100 Black ministers, from every denomination from AME to Primitive Baptist, [were] elected to legislative seats during Reconstruction." Ministers used their churches as a political base and "among the lay majority of black politicians, many built a political base in the church." The initial phases of black mobilization during Reconstruction were fostered by religious institutions and organizations, which were strongest in the urban South. "Political mobilization . . . proceeded apace in Southern cities, where the flourishing network of churches and fraternal societies provided a springboard for [political] organization."[9]

With the end of Reconstruction, religious institutions as well as secular ones "accommodated" to white domination in the South. As a result of the repeal of civil rights laws that had legally protected black citizenship rights, black electoral mobilization came to a halt, leaving severe sanctions against organized opposition. In the presidential election of 1876, the Republican Party, once the party of the freed men and women, sabotaged black political development by promising to withdraw federal troops from the South in exchange for Republican control of the presidency.[10] Thus, the growing consensus of both major political parties to allow the erosion of black citizenship rights during the last decades of the nineteenth century prevented the inclusion of African Americans in the American political party system. Within the Republican Party, "lily-white" factions cropped up throughout the South, and the demobilized black Republican groups were relegated to separate "black and tan" factions that competed with southern white Republicans on the national level for party patronage.[11]

Although occupational differentiation in the North produced secular leaders and organizations, and political party machines attempted to incorporate black migrants along with European immigrants, in the South white southerners promoted their political interests through the Democratic Party, which in many southern states restricted participation to whites only. For African Americans in the South, participation in the American polity was confined to an ineffectual Republican Party.[12]

These events and policies intensified the development of racially separate political spheres, forcing African Americans to develop their own organizational resources for political mobilization. The growing exclusion of African Americans from the vote and from party activity left a void filled mostly by black religious institutions.

Diminishing Opportunity Structures and Rigid Sanctions

As a result of intensified legal barriers and physical and economic sanctions to black political mobilization in the South, religious institutions became, in E. Franklin Frazier's words, a "nation within a nation." Frazier argued that black interests in politics were increasingly confined to the internal politics of religious institutions and organizations as a result of the exclusion of African Americans from the American polity. He took a negative view of the internal politics of southern black churches, observing that after Reconstruction "as the result of the elimination of Negroes from the political life of the American community, the Negro church became the arena of their political activities" where "the struggle for power and the thirst for power could be satisfied." [13] Frazier's analysis did not recognize the way those churches also developed their congregants' organizing and civic skills.

Mays and Nicholson's extensive work on the black church during the Jim Crow epoch details how the elaborate church structures of the mainstream black denominations nurtured the civic and organizing skills of African Americans during a period of dim prospects for mass mobilization against white supremacy. Writing in the early 1930s, the authors observed:

> The Negro's political life is still largely found in the Negro church. . . . The great importance attached to the political manoeuvering at [religious conventions] can be explained in part by the fact that the Negro is largely cut off from the body politic. The local churches, associations, conventions and conferences become the Negro's Democratic and Republican conventions, his Legislature and his Senate and House of Representatives.[14]

The political skills that Mays and Nicholson observed during this period were not exclusively confined to the internal politics of religious organizations. As Evelyn Higginbotham's pathbreaking work on the history of black Baptist women indicates, the institutional resources of black churches enabled black women to challenge racial and gender domination during the Jim Crow epoch of white domination. Higginbotham argues that African American religious institutions functioned for both black women and men as a "public sphere" in which "values and issues were aired, debated and disseminated throughout the larger black community." Higginbotham also points out that the reform-oriented women's club movement among African Americans drew their early leadership and membership from black women's religious groups. "The club movement among black women owed its very existence to the groundwork of organizational skill and leadership training gained through women's church societies" because the "missionary societies had early on brought together women with little knowledge of each other and created bonds of sisterly cooperation at the city and state levels."[15]

By facilitating the development of politically relevant organizing skills, indigenous leadership, and the dissemination of information through church-affiliated networks and religious publications, black religious institutions thus directly influenced the political mobilization of women in the secular realm during a period of diminishing opportunities and rigid sanctions against participation in the South. These networks were particularly relevant to the political development of black women who—now as well as then—represent the bulk of churchgoers among African Americans, although clerical and denominational leadership has been, and still continues to be, male dominated.

Contrasting Churches and Black Electoral Mobilization in the North and South

Mass migration of African Americans to northern cities during the interwar period and after World War II opened opportunities for black political engagement. Church-based resources were forged for electoral and protest mobilization in cooperation with political parties and groups and civil rights organizations like the NAACP and the Urban League. As political scientist Harold Gosnell noted of Chicago during the interwar period,

> It is not uncommon on a Sunday morning during a primary or [general] election campaign to see a number of white candidates on the platform ready to present their claims for support at the polls as soon as the regular service is over and before the congregation is disbanded. . . . The church is an institution which plays an important role in [blacks'] social life and they look to it for advice on political matters.

Church visits by these political candidates undoubtedly informed parishioners about elections and encouraged them to vote. Gosnell also notes that many black ministers took part in the patron-client relations that characterized party machine politics. The machine gave ministers fees, loans, or gifts to allow candidates to speak to their congregation. "Sometimes Negro ministers [sought] campaign funds outright in return for the delivery of a block of votes." However, as Gosnell observed, "not every colored minister permits candidates to address his congregation and there have been occasions when the Negro clergymen as a group protested against political interference."[16]

In the research compiled for Gunnar Myrdal's *American Dilemma*, political scientist Ralph Bunche's mammoth and largely overlooked study of black mobilization during the interwar period provides insight into how different structures for participation among African Americans in the North and in the South affected overt activism. Bunche contrasted the quietude of southern black churches to the ties between urban machines and black clerics in northern cities during midcentury.[17] In Atlanta, Bunche wrote, the lack of social, economic, and political progress among blacks was largely "the fault of the ministers, who direct the social thinking of so a large part of the population." In Memphis, black ministers "avoided social questions" altogether. In Bunche's words, "They have preached thunder and lightning, fire and brimstone, and Moses out of the bulrushes, but about the economic and political exploitation of local blacks they have remained silent."[18]

By contrast, in the same period black churches in northern cities were engaged in electoral mobilization, although its nature and intensity varied from city to city and often depended on the strategy of political parties. In St. Louis, for instance, blacks held the balance of voter power between Republicans and Democrats. Both political parties consequently targeted churches to mobilize the black electorate. Bunche contended that electoral engagement by black churches was motivated by the self-interest of black clerics: "Generally the Negro preacher's interest in procuring the vote for his congregation varies in direct proportion to his own pecuniary interests." He added that the Democratic Party in the city exploited the "smaller churches of the store-front variety" and that the Republican machine in that city "had been running the Negro preachers, along with everything else in the town, and had on occasion paid fifty or sixty dollars for their help." In New York City, Bunche reported, "Harlem became 'political-minded' when these Southern Negroes migrated. . . . In fact, if a 'political machine' is defined as a 'deliverable vote,' the church is the only effective, disciplined machine that Negroes have developed."[19]

Ruby Johnson contrasts the community involvement of black Protestant churches in the North and South during the postwar period. Johnson noted that black ministers in South Carolina were "hesitant" to engage in "practical action" efforts to improve black communities, mainly, she implied, because of white sanctions for such involvement:

> Fear of the threat of application of sanctions to the disadvantage of the [Negro] person or group which seeks to institute change restrains action. This consideration is important with reference to a comparison of church programs of southern and northern [black] clerical leaders.[20]

In South Carolina, Johnson discovered churches working cooperatively in self-help efforts to produce community social services, but also reported some organized political opposition within black churches. For several years, she wrote, black clerics had been involved in the NAACP "by holding executive positions, making individual contributions, urging their congregations to contribute to this organization, and by carrying the organization directly into the church in spite of opposition from many members." Moreover, "ministerial action was conspicuously tremendous" during 1947 and 1948, when "preachers were active in actually executing the increase of teachers' salaries, in educating Negroes for citizenship by conducting classes and speeches, and in urging them to qualify to vote."[21]

In contrast to the limited church-based activism of African Americans in South Carolina, in Boston thriving religious institutions engaged in a variety of electoral and interest group politics. Johnson reported of the black churches in Boston during the midfifties:

> Most of the [Negro] pastors of Boston churches manifest some form of political action. . . . Most ministers impress upon audiences the importance of voting, making wise use of the ballot, and taking advantage of the opportunity to vote. Some present information on candidates for office and discuss various platforms in relation to the community. Some tell their congregation whom to support, while others do not. Some clergymen permit candidates for office to speak in their churches. . . . Some clergymen seek to be elected to public office.[22]

Political Parties, Churches, and Black Political Development

Church-based political activism in the urban North during the interwar and postwar periods demonstrates how opportunity structures for participation affected black mobilization. Martin Kilson has observed several stages of black electoral engagement during the inter-war period, none of which contributed significantly to the long-term political development of African Americans. Much of this early period of black electoral politics was characterized by patron-client relationships between urban machines and black leaders that operated with "a small group of blacks who fashioned personalized links with influential whites, becoming clients of the whites for a variety of sociopolitical purposes." As Kilson argues, northern political machines undermined black political development through the party system because of their exclusionary practices regarding African Americans. Unlike European immigrants, who, with a few exceptions, were effectively incorporated into machine politics, African Americans were treated as a guaranteed bloc of votes rather than as partners within the party machine apparatus. Kilson explains that "in the years 1900–1940 the goal of white-dominated city machines toward Negroes was to neutralize and thus minimize the political clout of the Negro urban community and not infrequently even to distort that community's social and political modernization." He argues that this strategy on the part of white party organizers "emanated largely from the racist perspective of the American social system."[23]

Black realignment during the New Deal, the Democratic Party's support of civil rights issues on the national level in the sixties, party reform initiatives in the sixties and early seventies, and the election of thousands of black elected officials within the Democratic Party during the seventies and eighties have gradually incorporated African Americans into the Democratic Party apparatus. These events have occurred along with the declining mobilization capacity of political parties and the advent of personality-and media-centered politics.

As indigenous institutions that have survived Reconstruction, Jim Crow, the Great Migration, urbanization, the Depression, machine politics, partisan realignments, and a host of other social and political movements throughout the late-nineteenth and much of the twentieth century, black churches continue to operate as an organizational resource for black mobilization. These churches gave many political actors their only experience with public speaking, planning meetings, managing finances, and making group democratic decisions—all skills necessary for collective action.

The rest of this chapter will examine how religious institutions today teach organizing skills, disseminate information about politics, produce political stimuli that increase political participation, and directly promote activism. It will also investigate the concerns of African Americans about church involvement in political activities.

Political Resources for Congregants

Learning Organizing Skills

The elaborate organizational structures of predominantly black denominations, as well as majority black congregations affiliated with majority white religious groups, give blacks the opportunity to learn organizing and civic skills through their participation in church work. In his study of the political behavior of black ministers in the early 1970s, Charles Hamilton recognized the role of African American religious institutions in developing organizing skills. "Many blacks," he noted, "learned about organizations, acquired political skills and developed an ability to work with and lead people through the institution of the church."[24] Mays and Nicholson had observed the same pattern during the 1930s, and E. Franklin Frazier had commented on it during the 1950s.

The recent work of Sidney Verba and his colleagues confirms the phenomenon in the post–Civil Rights era. Verba and his colleagues report from their extensive survey of volunteerism in the United States that many individuals learn civic skills through their religious institutions. The researchers asked respondents if they had written a letter, gone to a meeting where they took part in a decision, planned or chaired a meeting, or given a presentation or a speech. They report that although over two-thirds of individuals in the United States have learned civic and organizing skills at their place of employment and about two-fifths practice such skills through nonpolitical organizations, nearly one-third of respondents reported practicing such skills at their place of worship.[25]

They also found considerable variation by racial/ethnic groups and by religious orientation. Members of Protestant congregations report practicing political skills at their churches more than do members of Catholic parishes. For African Americans, religious institutions are a particularly important place to develop politically relevant skills. Nearly 40 percent of African Americans practice organizing skills at their place of worship, compared to only 20 percent of Latinos and 28 percent of Anglo-whites. Similarly, African Americans (38 percent) are slightly more likely than Anglo-whites (35 percent) and substantially more likely than Latinos to hear political messages at their place of worship. Verba and his colleagues conclude that "for several reasons, African-Americans derive more participatory benefit from their churches." This benefit derives from African Americans being more likely than Anglo-whites and Latinos to be a member of a church, to be affiliated with Protestant rather than Catholic churches, and to be exposed to politically relevant stimuli at their place of worship. Since Protestant churches are more congregationally-organized than Catholic churches, allowing churchgoers more participation in lay activities, and since the overwhelming majority of African Americans are Protestant, their learning civic skills within church settings may help offset the socioeconomic disadvantage of the group.[26]

These politically relevant organizational skills combine with political stimuli to increase the likelihood that a churchgoer will become politically activated. Sermons, church announcements, church bulletins, candidate visits to churches, church-sponsored forums, and clerical endorsements of candidates all make parishioners more aware of politics, stimulate political action, and, in some cases, facilitate political activities through church-based networks. The nature of information and appeals for political action varies but usually involves voter registration, support for political candidates and positions, details regarding government programs and assistance, and community organizing efforts.

Disseminating Information

The dissemination of information on political matters can occur within several church-based venues, offering congregants facts about political and social issues and giving them the opportunity to hear several points of view regarding candidates and issues. For instance, at the Second Baptist Church of Evanston, Illinois, a Sunday bulletin encouraged members to attend a rally for a candidate running for county office for the 1990 primary election.[27] The candidate, a "guest speaker" for the church's Black History Month program that Sunday, told congregants during his talk about the countywide office for which he was running, described his opponents, and gave his reasons for running for that office. A photographed, biographical and professional resume of the candidate were stuffed inside the bulletins, and alongside the regular announcements was what could be interpreted as an endorsement of the candidate:

> JUDGE R. EUGENE PINCHAM will be our Guest Speaker today, at both worship services. At 3:00 P.M. this afternoon . . . there will be a "RALLY" for those in support of the candidacy of JUDGE R. EUGENE PINCHAM, FOR THE PRESIDENT OF THE COOK COUNTY BOARD. Do join us! JUDGE PINCHAM, the man who will run the County Government to serve ALL THE PEOPLE!

Sermons also disseminate political information to congregants. Ministers can support their preferred candidate during regular worship services primarily by taking a position against that candidate's opponent. When Reverend Charles Adams of Detroit's mostly middle-class Hartford Memorial Baptist Church criticized the record of 1992 Republican presidential candidate George Bush during a sermon the Sunday before the Tuesday general election, he made known his preference for Democratic presidential nominee Bill Clinton without ever mentioning the candidate's name.[28] Telling the congregation "When you wake up Tuesday morning, say your prayers, but then let your prayers get in your hands and in your feet" and "go [to the polls] and vote," Reverend Adams assailed Bush's record as president and the Republican Party's Christian conservative supporters:

> Some of us are trying to make this election a referendum on God . . . as if God belongs to Bush and his party and his ideology. Well, I don't believe that's true.

He slammed the Democrats for leaving God out of their platform. They were just being honest. I don't like it when folk lie and put God's name in their political aspirations just to win an election.

While questioning the incumbent's belief in Christianity, Reverend Adams criticized the Bush administration's involvement with the Iran-Contra scandal, the incumbent's opposition to pending civil rights legislation, and his nomination of Clarence Thomas, a conservative black Republican, to the Supreme Court. As Reverend Adams trumpeted:

Bush doesn't even know God. If Bush knew God, he wouldn't have lied about Iran-Contra. If Bush knew God, he wouldn't have failed to sign the Civil Rights Bill in 1990. If Bush knew God, he wouldn't have put a handkerchief head on the Supreme Court. If Bush knew God, he wouldn't destroy and oppress the people of this United States.

Candidates themselves disseminate information to congregants through their visits to worship services. Many speak from the pulpit to present their stands on issues and sometimes use the opportunity to criticize their opponents. During a campaign stop the Sunday before the 1994 Democratic gubernatorial primary election in Illinois, candidate Roland Burris told congregants at the Corinthian Temple Church of God in Christ on Chicago's West Side what ballot numbers to punch for him and his running mate. After he had been introduced by a member of the church who told the congregation and the live radio broadcast audience that "we need an effective Christian leader on our side in government. . . . Roland Burris is that leader," Burris made these remarks from the pulpit:

We're talking about two punch numbers, two punch numbers. Number three and number six. So once you punch three, just double it and you'll give us your vote. You'll get double your money because we are going to create jobs in the state so that we can put people back to work.

The candidate then became more partisan in his remarks, specifically questioning his leading opponents' prospects for winning against the Republican incumbent:

I'm the only one who can make a change in Springfield and go out and stand toe-to-toe with [the Republican incumbent]. . . . And if the head of the Democratic ticket is a tax-and-spend Democrat who's soft on crime, the Republicans will not only win the governorship, they may even win the state House of Representatives.

Other church-based venues for disseminating political information are not as partisan. Church-sponsored political forums, for instance, allow several candidates to present their points of view and permit congregants to question candidates and public officials about their policy positions. In the strongly contested 1983 mayoral race in Chicago, several religious groups sponsored candidate forums. For example, the West Side Ministers' Coalition and West Side Baptist Ministers' Conference sponsored a forum "for scrutiny of candidates in the Mayoral race," in which candidates were sent fourteen questions "posed by various Ministers and their Parishioners" that would be covered during the event.[29] The questions addressed issues as diverse as affirmative action, neighborhood redevelopment, funding for education, election fraud, and support for lower utility rates.[30]

Facilitating Political Action

While religious institutions operate as a means for congregants to make judgments about political issues and candidates, church-based venues can also facilitate political participation by directly appealing to congregants. These appeals, made in church bulletins, by clerics, or by political entrepreneurs themselves, foster direct involvement in both electoral politics and community organizing efforts in African American communities. The Sunday bulletin of Chicago's Progressive Community Church, for instance, included this announcement about voter registration for the upcoming 1990 November general election:

VOTER REGISTRATION
IMMEDIATELY FOLLOWING OUR MORNING WORSHIP SERVICE IN THE LOWER LEVEL OF THE CHURCH, THERE WILL BE VOTER REGISTRARS SET-UP. . . . TUESDAY, OCTOBER 9TH IS OUR LAST CHANCE TO REGISTER AFTER TO-DAY. . . . DO IT TODAY—DON'T WAIT!

After the Scripture reading and the recognition of visitors, the minister emphasized the voter registration and encouraged members who were not registered to do so because, as he told the congregation, voting is their "civic duty as good Christians."[31]

Recruiting workers for political campaigns not only helps politicians, as we will see in the next section; it also helps to facilitate congregants' own actions. In the 1994 Illinois Democratic primary race for governor, Reverend J. L. Miller of Mount Vernon Baptist Church on Chicago's West Side endorsed gubernatorial candidate Roland Burris and asked congregants to assist with the church's effort in getting out the vote and passing out flyers in support of the candidate.[32] Criticizing polls that showed the candidate's support slipping and media predictions of a low voter turnout, the minister solicited the congregation for support:

Now I need you to use your car, telephone, and your fingers to push doorbells. Tomorrow—those of you [who are] not working, we're walking. . . . The flyers are out, the [copying] machine is still working, we will be running off some additional flyers. We're going to make certain that everybody knows the polling place if it's been changed. We're going to make certain that everybody knows the direction and route to take on Tuesday morning. We're going to make it happen in this political process.

Churches may also facilitate participation by asking congregants to contribute financially to political campaigns. Evidence from the campaign records of Harold Washington's 1983 mayoral campaign suggests that African American religious institutions are a significant indigenous source of money for black candidates. Even before Jesse Jackson's 1984 presidential campaign, which raised a considerable amount of money from church-based sources,[33] similar fund-raising took place during Washington's campaign.

For example, the middle-class congregation of Park Manor Christian Church requested Washington to appear at a church-sponsored rally at the end of a Sunday service, "at which time we are asking members to make a financial contribution to help support the campaign."[34] One member of a congregation requested the appearance of the candidate at a Sunday evening rally, where "the Pastor and members of Mount Pleasant Missionary Baptist Church are interested in our continued efforts to raise funds for you as a Mayoral candidate."[35] Church-based contributions during Washington's campaign ranged from $3,400 from South Park Baptist Church to $150 from Allen Temple C.M.E. Church.[36]

Resources for Political Entrepreneurs

In addition to serving as sources of information and facilitating political action among churchgoers, churches may also serve as resources for political entrepreneurs, who often nurture ties with black clerics to solicit black support for their political goals. For instance, Democratic congressional candidate Bobby Rush, who in the previous campaigns for alderman received the endorsement of several clergy in his Chicago ward,[37] solicited the support of ministers in his congressional district for the party's efforts in the 1990 general election. With a letter written on campaign stationary, the candidate invited clerics in his district to attend a "breakfast" with Ron Brown, then chairman of the National Democratic Party:

Dear Reverend ——
As you are well aware, the November . . . General Election provides all of us with the opportunity to utilize our votes to help bring about much-needed changes in state and federal government. Chairman Brown will be in Chicago to present the Democratic Party's plans for the future. Your participation in this pivotal gathering is indeed vital.[38]

Some political entrepreneurs cultivate ties with black clerics well ahead of an election. One candidate who lost in the 1992 Democratic primary for U.S. Senate in Illinois attempted to extend his relationships with ministers after his defeat in the primary. These contacts may have provided him with a wider church network when he successfully ran as the Democratic Party's nominee for state attorney general a year and a half later. Writing about six months after his defeat in the Senate race and looking ahead to future political aspirations, Al Hofeld wrote this letter seeking clerical support:

> You may remember me, I was the candidate for the United States Senate in the most recent Democratic primary campaign. I am now doing everything within my power to see that Carol Moseley Braun is elected as our next United States Senator. . . . Since the primary, I have been out in the community and seen for myself some of the hardships that exist. . . . I would like to come out and meet with you or Fellowship as a parishioner at your Church sometime in the near future.[39]

Recognizing the organizing skills of churchgoers, some political candidates recruit workers for their campaigns through church networks. One candidate in New York City, for instance, advertised jobs for her reelection campaign through the church bulletin of Harlem's Abyssinian Baptist Church:

> Manhattan Boro President Ruth Messinger is seeking a number of organizers to join her grassroots reelection campaign. The ability to work with a wide range of people, personal organization and commitment to progressive politics are among the qualities they are looking for, and a sense of humor wouldn't hurt. Specific requirements are listed with each job description.[40]

Some political entrepreneurs contribute money to churches or religious organizations directly from their political campaign funds. (Others are known to give cash contributions to ministers under the table.)[41] For instance, Chicago mayor Richard Daley contributed from the itemized expenditures of his campaign committee to several black churches and religious institutions from 1990 to 1993. These expenditures, reported as "donations," ranged from $200 to $5,500.[42]

The Controversy over Church-Based Electoral Activism

The degree to which black churches ought to be involved in electoral politics has been contested within black communities for several generations. While there appears to be a consensus on the importance of church-based networks as a source of information for congregants, African Americans differ on the question of ministers' explicit support of political candidates.

During the interwar period in Chicago, for instance, editorials in black newspapers criticized the practice of political candidates making campaign visits at black churches during Sunday worship services. They also criticized the practice of ministers accepting financial contributions for such visits. As the *Chicago Defender* wrote in the spring of 1920:

> The ministers excuse these things on the grounds that it is their duty to direct their congregations in matters political as well as spiritual. . . . One scarcely, if ever, hears of a white church being used for such purposes. . . . There is generally some sinister reason for this action. The white politicians know how susceptible some of our people are to the urgings of the pulpit. . . . The ministers are aware of this attitude on the part of the political powers and take advantage of it to turn a handy penny for themselves.[43]

More than half a century later and in another city, an editorial in Cleveland's black newspaper, the *Call and Post*, expressed remarkably similar sentiments. Entitled "Churches and Political Prostitution," the 1978 editorial noted that "many black and white politicians have seized every opportunity to use the black church as a base for political operations." Acknowledging the importance of black churches as vehicles for the dissemination of political information and as a means to encourage civic activities, the editorial agreed that ministers should "in their church bulletins, during pastoral comments, through other means, persuade their parishioners to register, vote, and endorse issues." It added that the church should "use its influence, clout, and facilities to educate minorities in the political process." On the other hand, as the editorial argued, involvement in electoral politics should not involve visits by political candidates during worship services:

> The legitimate entry by the church into political affairs has been prostituted to the point that politicians walk in and out of our pulpits on Sundays, allowed to campaign during church services and make vicious attacks on opponents in political races. White politicians in particular have abused this privilege granted to them by some ministers.

Noting that such practices were usually not allowed at white churches or synagogues, the editorial asserted that

> some ministers try to rationalize and justify these abuses by allowing both Democrats and Republicans to appear and thus claim the church is non-partisan. . . . To accept the trivial donations given in the collection plate by these politicians is almost sinful in itself if it is given to influence voting. . . . Religious services should be that and no more.[44]

The direct involvement of black clerics in electoral politics continues today. Candidate or party endorsements by black clerics usually occur during Sunday worship services on the eve of local, state, or national elections. For instance, Bishop David L. Ellis of Detroit's Greater Grace Church overtly endorsed both local candidates and Democratic presidential candidate Bill Clinton the Sunday before the 1992 General Election.[45] During the church's live radio broadcast, Bishop Ellis introduced three local judicial candidates described as "personal friends" and "very fine people," and told the congregation "we are supporting all of them on Tuesday." Bishop Ellis then proclaimed—using the campaign slogan of the Clinton-Gore team—"we are going to vote for a change."

Outspokenly defensive about his public support of these candidates and giving biblical legitimacy to his engagement in political activities, Bishop Ellis defended his endorsements by saying,

> We preachers are highly criticized because we talk like this. . . . Everyone that knows the sound of my voice, you ought to vote for a change. . . . Just pull that Democratic switch. Punch that Democratic button.

As he proclaimed, "I don't know who your candidate is but as of today, your candidate is the Clinton-Gore ticket, the Democratic ticket all the way." Bishop Ellis assured the congregation and the radio audience of his independence: "We ain't being paid a dime to talk about something political." To further legitimize his support of these candidates, Bishop Ellis referred to himself as a "community leader." He also promised transportation to voters who needed assistance on election day. Referencing a 1988 Bush campaign slogan and citing a negative stereotype often leveled against blacks by whites, he insisted:

> I'm just here as a guide and as a leader in this community to tell you it's time for a change. . . . Read my lips—it's time for a change! . . . Let's get our lazy selves up tomorrow morning and get out there. Amen! Get to the polls. If you ain't got a way, call here. . . . We'll send somebody to pick you up. I'll bring the van myself. I'll take you to the poll. Amen! You say, "I can't write." I'll guide your hand. I'm serious about this. Time for a change.

Most clerical candidate and party endorsements are not as direct as that of Bishop Ellis. Earlier that Sunday in Cincinnati, Ohio, presidential candidate Bill Clinton visited the Tryed Stone Missionary Baptist Church.[46] Although Clinton did not speak during the service and the minister did not ask members to vote for him, the service expressed support for the presidential candidate symbolically in other ways. When asking the congregation for contributions to Thanksgiving baskets for poor families in the city during pastoral announcements, Reverend Culbreath told the congregation, "There's a candidate out there that says there needs to be a change, and he speaks that because the economic situation is so grave, we want to give a helping hand again this year."

During the congregational prayer, after reading names of about two
dozen members of the congregation who requested prayer from the minister, Reverend Culbreath announced, "I've got a note here that the governor
would like a spiritual prayer before he leaves." With applause from the
congregation, the minister intoned, "Saints, let's pray." With the choir
singing a gospel standard, "I Don't Feel No Ways Tired," the minister
requested divine assistance in Clinton's behalf.

In return for their endorsements, ministers may urge their views of morality on potential candidates. For instance, during the 1983 mayoral campaign in Chicago, a group of black ministers called Prophets for People
expressed concerns over Harold Washington's views on abortion and homosexuality. Writing to Washington's secretary about an upcoming meeting
between the ministers' group and Washington, Reverend Clarence Hilliard,
the executive director of Prophets for People, noted that the ministers

> are interested in sharing our views and interacting with our future mayor on
> two moral issues that are of grave concern to us. . . . One is the question of homo-
> sexuality or the "Gay Rights Movement," and the other is the question of abortion
> or the "Right to Life" vs. "abortion on demand" controversy. It is our belief that
> we can come to a satisfactory agreement so that as we engage in the serious
> business of this campaign and may not unwittingly prove to be an embarrassment
> to each other.[47]

Reverend Hilliard would later recount how Washington agreed during the
meeting that he would "not do anything to initiate legislation in regard to
Gay rights."[48]

Some ministers, believing that politics and religion should be separate,
abstain altogether from overt support of political candidates, even when
their own congregants express support for such activity. In one example, a
married couple, members of an interracial and multicultural church on
Chicago's northside, wrote to Harold Washington after his victory in the
1983 Democratic mayoral primary:

> In the service immediately following your nomination, our pastor, Al Smith, told
> us that specific demonic powers rule individual cities. . . . In Daniel 10 Gabriel
> has to wrestle for 21 days with the "Prince of Persia" to get a message through
> Daniel. [Our minister] stated that the demonic forces enslaving this city have had
> their physical manifestation in the "Machine" that runs City Hall. Excitedly, he
> shared that your successful breach of the visible "Machine" means that the in-
> visible "Prince of Chicago" has sustained a mortal blow, too.[49]

In a second letter, the same couple invited Washington to address about one
thousand church members at a prayer breakfast, stating that "we're confident that the People of Faith Temple will offer you a very sympathetic
forum."[50] Several days later, however, Faith Tabernacle's minister revoked
the invitation:

I have been informed that a member of our congregation . . . has invited you to address the members of Faith Temple on Sunday . . . and at our Prayer Breakfast. . . . Please be advised that [our member] was not acting on behalf of the leadership of Faith Tabernacle and was not authorized to extend an invitation to you as a candidate or to any other candidate. You are most welcome to attend these functions, but in keeping with our policy of remaining apolitical, you will not be allowed or asked to speak.[51]

Congregants' Attitudes toward Church-Based Activism

Concerns about the influence of clerics over the black electorate may be exaggerated. Although the 1991 Chicago Area Survey showed that among black church members more than half reported candidate visits at their churches, a 1980/NBC associated poll suggests that few ministers, black or white, specifically endorse political candidates. Ninety-seven percent of whites ($N = 2,098$) and 92 percent of blacks ($N = 178$) reported that they had not been asked by a religious leader to vote for a specific candidate in that year's fall election. An overwhelming majority of respondents (more than 80 percent of both blacks and whites) also felt that an endorsement of a candidate by a religious leader would have no effect on their choice of candidates.

On the other hand, both black parishioners and political entrepreneurs view black clerics as indigenous leaders. A 1984 *USA Today* survey asked: "A variety of groups and people occupy leadership roles within the black community. For each person or groups I mention, please tell me how effective you think [they] are as leaders—very effective, somewhat effective, or not very effective?" Figure 12.1 shows the "very effective" responses for six leadership categories mentioned in this order: local black officeholders, national political leaders, the NAACP, the Urban League, black ministers and clergy, and Jesse Jackson. Jesse Jackson, a minister-politician, ranked first (65 percent), and black ministers (40 percent) as a group ranked second to the NAACP (45 percent) as the most effective leaders. Black ministers were perceived to be more effective than national black political leaders (33 percent), local black elected officials (29 percent), and the civil rights organization the National Urban League (26 percent). The clerical leadership category even rivals the oldest and most prominent civil rights organization for African Americans, the NAACP.

Although some commentators criticize the appropriateness of black clerics as representatives of black interests in the American polity,[52] political entrepreneurs certainly woo the activist clergy within black communities as a means to legitimize and garner support for their political goals. Moreover, Lincoln and Mimiya's survey of over two thousand black clergy between 1978 and 1984 reveals that black ministers of the various mainstream black denominations overwhelmingly approve of an activist ministry.[53]

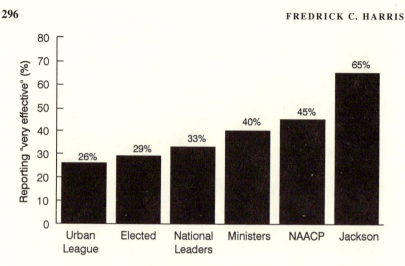

Figure 12.1. Perceived Efficacy of Black Leadership as Community Leaders: Groups and Individuals ($N = 280$)

Lincoln and Mimaya found that over 90 percent of black ministers, independent of age, education, and denominational affiliation, supported clerical involvement in civil rights demonstrations and clerics expressing their views on social and political issues. They also cite a Gallup survey on a similar question in 1968 that showed nonwhites more supportive than whites of ministers speaking out on social and political issues. Finally, they found in a 1986 survey of African Methodist Episcopal Church leaders that nearly 90 percent supported clerical involvement in social issues, while only 3 percent agreed that churches should keep out of political matters altogether. Lincoln and Mamiya conclude from these surveys that "there is broad support and consensus in the black community, both within and without the church, among clergy and laity, for a social prophecy role for black churches. . . . The attitude is pervasive that churches should be involved in and express their views on everyday social and political issues." They further conclude, "It is also clear that black people generally support a much more activist role for their churches than do whites."[54]

Although Lincoln and Mamiya's extensive survey reveals a consensus among black clerics in the post–Civil Rights period, they may overstate the case by extending this consensus to African Americans as a whole. Two surveys at approximately this time measured popular attitudes toward church-based political activism. An NBC/Associated Press survey of 2,400 respondents in October of 1980 asked two questions: "Should the churches and members of the clergy express their views on day-to-day social questions, or should they keep out of social matters?" and "What about politics? Do you think the churches and members of clergy should be involved in politics, like backing a candidate for public office, or don't you think so?"[55] The September 1984 *USA Today* poll of over 1,200 registered

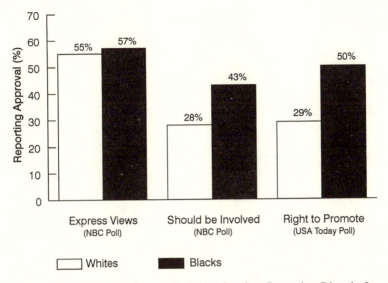

Figure 12.2 Public Opinion on Religious Leaders Becoming Directly Involved in Political Matter, by Race

voters also asked: "In general, do you think it is right or wrong for religious leaders to promote a particular political point of view during religious services?"

Figure 12.2 shows affirmative responses to all three questions by race. Blacks and whites equally approved of churches and clergy expressing their views on social issues, although blacks approved slightly more than whites (57 percent compared to 55 percent, with about a third of both black and white respondents agreeing that churches and clergy should not express their views on social issues). However, blacks and whites differed more dramatically in regard to the explicit involvement of religious institutions in politics. While less than a third of whites thought that churches or clergy should be able to back political candidates (28 percent) and that religious leaders had a right to promote a particular point of view during religious services (29 percent), more than two-fifths (43 percent) of blacks approved of such involvement and half (50 percent) approved of clerics promoting a political point of view during religious services.

The Effects of Church-Based Stimuli on Political Participation

The black-white differences in approval of church-based political activism may simply reflect racial differences in the incidence of that activism. Those differences in approval may also reflect racial differences in the actual effect of church-based stimuli on political participation.

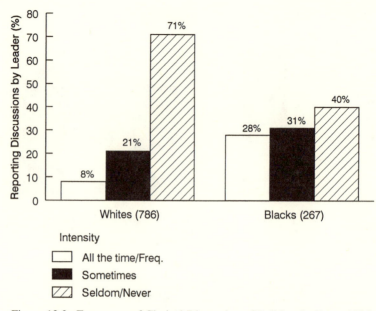

Figure 12.3. Frequency of Clerical Discussion of Politics, by Race, 1984

A 1984 *USA Today* poll of over 1,200 registered voters asked about the frequency of political discussions during religious services: "How often does your (minister/priest/rabbi) discuss political issues as part of the service?" Figure 12.3 reveals striking racial variations. Blacks were three times more likely (28 percent) than whites (8 percent) to report that their religious leaders discussed politics all the time or frequently. They were also more likely than whites (31 percent compared to 21 percent) to report that such discussions took place "sometimes." Nearly three-fourths, or 71 percent, of whites reported that their clerics seldom or never discussed political issues during religious services, compared to only two-fifths (40 percent) of black respondents.

Given the historical importance of black religious institutions in black political mobilization, we might predict from the quantitative data that clerical discussion of politics would have a greater effect on the political participation of blacks than on whites. In fact, the same 1984 *USA Today* survey that showed large racial differences in the frequency of political discussions during religious services also reveals racial differences in the effects of clerical political discussion in church on the political participation of churchgoers. Figure 12.4 displays the average rate of campaign participation by the reported frequencies of clerical political discussion during the service for both blacks and whites. The campaign participation rate is a cumulative index of questions that asked if respondents distributed

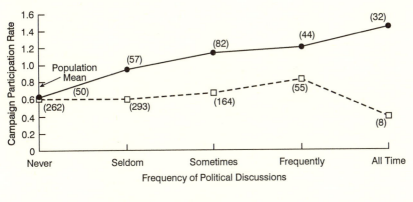

Figure 12.4. Mean Campaign Activity, by Frequency of Clerical Discussion at Place of Worship, Blacks and Whites. Figures in parentheses represent the number of respondents in each category.

literature for a candidate, went to a political meeting or rally, gave money to a candidate, called on the telephone in behalf of a candidate, or helped to register voters.[56]

Among registered voters who reported that their religious leaders never discussed political issues during religious services, the rate of participation in campaign activities is about the same for both blacks and for whites. However, as clerical discussions increase in frequency, the rate of participation diverges between the two groups. Among blacks, the average rate of campaign activity gradually increases as respondents reported that their religious leaders talked "seldom," "sometimes," "frequently," or "all the time" about politics.

Discussion of politics in church also raises the participation rate of whites, but more slowly and not as much. We see no increase between "never" and "seldom," and only a small increase when leaders discuss politics "sometimes" in religious services. The white participation rate does not exceed the population average (0.77) until respondents report that their minister, priest, or rabbi discusses political issues "frequently" as part of the service. The rate of participation returns to below the average level among whites exposed to clerical discussion of politics "all the time," but this decline is probably an artifact of the small number of white respondents in that category.

Among registered black voters, the link between campaign activity and the frequency of clerical discussion of politics is almost linearly positive. As political discussions increase in frequency, so does the level of campaign activity. The average rate of campaign activity is 0.94 for blacks who reported that their leaders "seldom" discussed politics, and jumps to

TABLE 12.1

Effects of Race and Clerical Discussions on Campaign Activism (Ordinary Least Squares Estimates)

	Independent Model		Interactive Model	
	b	(SE)	b	(SE)
Demographic Factors				
Education	.16***	(.03)	.15***	(.04)
Gender (Male)	−.01	(.07)	.02	(.08)
Urban	−.01	(.07)	.02	(.08)
Age	.14***	(.04)	.11**	(.05)
South	.05	(.08)	.02	(.06)
Income	.07*	(.04)	.05	(.05)
Race (Black)	.42***	(.09)	−.67	(.30)
Religious Resources				
Church Attendance	.08**	(.03)	.08*	(.04)
Clerical Discussion	.11***	(.03)	.04	(.04)
Attendance × Black			.02	(.04)
Discussion × Black			.18**	(.07)
Total cases	1,029		1,021	
Adjusted R^2	.08		.09	

Source: 1984 *USA Today* Survey of Registered Voters.

Note: Entries are unstandardized regression coefficients with standard errors in parentheses. *** $p < .001$. ** $p < .01$. * $p < .05$.

1.43 for those blacks who reported that their leaders discussed politics "all the time."

Using the same survey, table 12.1 shows the OLS (ordinary least squares) estimates of the effects of race and the frequency of church-based political discussions on campaign activism. Controlling for demographic factors, one model shows the results of the independent effects of clerical discussion of politics on campaign activity; the second model, the regression model, shows the interactive effects of race and the frequency of clerical discussion of politics. Controlling for SES (socioeconomic status), demographic factors, and the effects of church attendance as a civic-oriented resource for electoral participation,[57] the frequency of clerical discussions has a positive and independent effect on campaign participation.

The impact of clerical discussion of politics ($b = 0.11$, beta = 10) rivaled income ($b = 0.07$, beta = 0.07) and exceeded church attendance ($b = 0.08$, beta = 0.07) as a predictor of campaign activism, although race ($b = 0.42$, beta = 0.16) and education ($b = 0.16$, beta = 0.17) were, among these churchgoers, stronger predictors of campaign activism than clerical discussion of politics. The strong impact of race on campaign activism in 1984 is probably attributable specifically to Jesse Jackson's presidential election campaign in 1984,[58] and generally to the contextual effects of black office seeking and black representation on black mobilization in this period.[59]

As the second OLS model demonstrates, being black and hearing frequent political discussions by one's religious leader diminished the independent effect of clerical discussions on campaign activism. The interactive model suggests that—independent of personal SES and demographic factors—religious institutions were a potent force for black electoral mobilization in 1984. The combined effects of race and the frequency of clerical discussion of politics suggest that black religious institutions were, as several analysts have demonstrated and speculated, critical resources for mobilizing campaign activity during the 1984 elections.

The 1984 *USA Today* survey therefore suggests both that clerical discussion of political matters are relatively infrequent among whites compared to blacks and that such discussions among whites appear not to greatly stimulate political participation. However, church attendance, a religiously based resource for civic participation, positively predicts campaign activity for both blacks and whites ($b = 0.08$, beta = 0.07). For today's African Americans, religious institutions may serve as an indigenous source of political information and stimulation that competes favorably with mainstream sources of political information.

Comparing White and Black Church-Based Political Activism in 1991

Katherine Tate's analysis of black electoral behavior indicates that religious institutions are an important organizational resource for disseminating information about elections, encouraging church members to vote, providing individuals a base from which to work with political campaigns, and allowing individuals to financially contribute to political candidates. Responses to the 1984 National Black Election Study found that these modes of church-based electoral activism varied in intensity, ranging from 60 percent of African Americans reporting that they were encouraged to vote at their place of worship to 10 percent reporting that they worked for a political candidate through religious institutions.[60] Although Tate's findings confirm the enduring significance of religious institutions as a resource base for black electoral mobilization,[61] we cannot judge from the National Black Election Study how these modes of activism compare with those in other ethnic and religious groups.

Questions on church-based political activism from the 1991 Chicago area survey provide a snapshot of various modes of church-based activism

TABLE 12.2
Church-Based Political Activism by Race/Ethnicity In Metro
Chicago (Percentage of Church Members Who Participate)

	Blacks	Whites	Latinos
Discuss politics			
Nearly all the time	6	2	8
Frequently	15	7	10
Sometimes	30	30	18
Rarely	30	42	46
Never	19	20	18
Encourage members to vote			
Yes	65	30	36
No	35	70	64
Host candidate visits			
Frequently	14	2	10
Only sometimes	43	10	19
Basically never	43	88	71
Take up a collection			
Yes	10	1	3
No	90	99	97
Number of cases	145	463	22

Source: Northwestern University, 1991 Chicago Area Survey.

and the ways these modes differ in intensity by race and ethnicity, religious orientation, and social class.[62] Church members were asked how often their religious leaders discussed politics, if their place of worship encouraged members to vote, how often candidates for public office made visits, and whether their place of worship had ever taken up a collection for a political candidate. About 83 percent of the 1,027 respondents reported that they were members of a religious institution. Using this group as a base, table 12.2 reports the frequency of responses from questions measuring church-based activism for African Americans, Anglo-whites, and Latinos.

For each of the four modes of church-based activism, African Americans reported more involvement than did Anglo-whites and Latinos in this survey.[63] The modes of church-based activism varied in intensity for each act. More than a third of all respondents reported being encouraged to vote at their place of worship, 20 percent reported that political candidates visited their place of worship "frequently" or "only sometimes," about 10 percent reported that their religious leader discussed politics during religious services "nearly all the time" or "frequently," and 3 percent stated that their place of worship had taken up a financial collection for a political candidate.

TABLE 12.3

Church-Based Political Activism by Religious Orientation In Metro
Chicago (Percentage Who Participate)

	Catholic	Jewish	Protestant
Discuss politics			
Nearly all the time	0	15	3
Frequently	7	15	11
Sometimes	26	51	30
Rarely	44	18	37
Never	22	0	18
Encourage members to vote			
Yes	25	42	54
No	75	58	46
Host candidate visits			
Frequently	2	3	7
Only sometimes	12	28	24
Basically never	85	69	69
Take up a collection			
Yes	2	0	5
No	98	100	95
Number of cases	333	33	270

Source: Northwestern University, 1991 Chicago Area Survey.

As in the 1984 *USA Today* survey, the intensity of church-based activism varied by race and ethnicity. African Americans were more than twice as likely as Anglo-whites to hear frequent discussions of politics from their clerics and to be encouraged to vote. They were more than twice as likely to receive visits from political candidates and to have had a collection taken up for a candidate at their place of worship. For Latinos, the intensity of church-based activism may be greater than for Anglo-whites but less than for African Americans.

Table 12.3 shows that church-based political activism also varied by religious orientation. Catholics reported less political activism at their place of worship than did either Jews or Protestants. Jewish respondents reported that their leaders discussed politics more than Protestants did; candidate visits at synagogues were reported as frequently as at Protestant churches. On the other hand, Protestants, more than Jews, reported being encouraged to vote and collections being taken for candidates at their place of worship. However, given the small number of Jewish respondents in the 1991 Chicago area survey who reported affiliating with a synagogue ($N = 33$), these estimates should be read with caution.

Like the findings of Verba and his colleagues, results from the Chicago area survey indicate that church-based political activism varies by race/ ethnicity and religious orientation. African Americans are more likely to receive political stimuli at their place of worship than are Anglo-whites and Latinos, and Jews and Protestants are more likely to receive such stimuli than Catholics.

Education and Church-Based Activism

In addition to variations by race and ethnicity, exposure to church-based political stimuli varies considerably by education and religious orientation. Figure 12.5 reports from the 1991 Chicago area survey the average rate of political activism within religious institutions by education for blacks, whites, and for white Protestants and white Catholics. The sample size of Jews and Latinos, as well as of African American Catholics, was too small for a comparison over educational categories.[64]

As the figure demonstrates, the intensity and direction of church-based political activism vary between educational categories of blacks and whites. The average rate of church-based activism for blacks with less than a high school education is about one standard deviation above the mean, while for blacks with a high school education, the average rate of activism is about three-quarters of one standard deviation above the mean. In contrast, blacks with some college and with a full college education are less likely to report political activism at their place of worship than are blacks with less education. The average activism scores of both college-educated groups hovered around one-half of a standard deviation above the mean for the population as a whole. These findings indicate that for African Americans at churches in the Chicago area, church-based political activism may mediate the socioeconomic disadvantages of blacks in the political arena.

For whites, the average rate of church-based activism also changes by education and religious orientation, but in the opposite direction. Whites of all three educational categories are less likely to be exposed to church-based activism than are blacks. Protestant and Catholic whites with less than a high school education and with a high school education receive, on average, fewer political stimuli in church than do their counterparts with some college or more. However, within the two highest educational categories among college-educated whites, there are noticeable differences. While the average rate of activism among white Catholics dips to below one-quarter of a standard deviation below the mean, the average rate for college-educated white Protestants nudges toward the population mean.

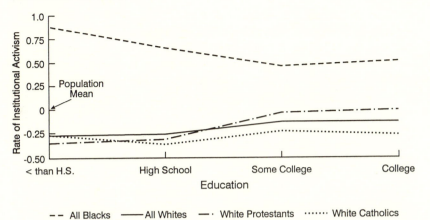

Figure 12.5. Mean Rate of Church-Based Activism by Race/Religious Orientation and Education

Personal Determinants of Institutionally-Based Activism

Table 12.4 shows OLS estimates of personal determinants of church-based political activism in the 1991 Chicago area survey. Demographically, socioeconomic advantages have a negative effect or no effect at all on being exposed to political stimuli at church. The greater one's income, the less likely one is to be exposed to political stimuli at a place of worship ($b = -.12$, Beta $= -.07$). The relationship between being exposed to church-based political stimuli and education is statistically insignificant. In this OLS model, the strongest predictor of being exposed to political stimuli at one's place of worship is race. Being African American is positively related to receiving political stimuli at one's place of worship ($b = 1.15$, Beta $= .28$), while being Latino has no effect (here, as in the rest of this analysis, the small number of Latino cases makes interpretation difficult).

Additionally, the model provides estimates of the effect of one's religious orientation on exposure to church-based political activism. A question on the 1991 Chicago area survey asked respondents who claimed a Protestant affiliation: "Some people have had deep religious experiences which have transformed their lives. These experiences are sometimes described as 'being born again in one's faith' or 'discovering Jesus Christ in one's life.' There are deeply religious people who have not had an experience of this sort. How about you—have *you* had such an experience?" Twenty percent of Protestants in the survey answered positively. I will call this group "born-again" Christians.

TABLE 12.4
Personal Determinants of Church-Based Political Activism (Ordinary Least Squares Estimates)

	b	(SE)
Demographic factors		
Education	.04	(.04)
Gender (male)	−.03	(.14)
Age	−7.04	(8.66)
Income	−.12**	(.06)
African American	1.51***	(.19)
Latino	.42	(.31)
Religious orientation		
Catholic	−.49***	(.18)
Protestant	.01	(.20)
Born-again Protestant	.80***	(.20)
Jewish	.62*	(.35)
Total Cases = 826		
Adjusted R^2 = .16		

Source: Northwestern University, 1991 Chicago Area Survey.
Note: Entries are unstandardized regression coefficients with standard errors in parentheses. *** $p < .001$. ** $p < .01$. * $p < .10$.

Table 12.4 shows that being Jewish ($b = 0.26$, beta = 0.06) or a born-again Christian ($b = 0.80$, beta = 0.13) is positively associated with exposure to political stimuli at one's place of worship. In contrast, being Catholic is negatively associated with exposure to church-based political activism ($b = -0.49$, beta = -0.11). The differences between Catholics and Protestants in 1991 in Chicago are similar to the findings of other researchers on religious institutions and political participation.[65] They provide further evidence on how the internal structure of institutions may promote or undermine civic action.[66] Congregationally organized religious institutions such as Protestant churches seem more likely to promote political action than do hierarchically structured institutions such as Catholic churches.

Conclusion

Religious institutions within African American communities are important resources for black political mobilization. These resources include clerical appeals, candidate contacts at religious services, church-sponsored political forums and rallies, group endorsements by ministers and religious groups, and fund-raising for political candidates. These sources of information and activism have deep historical roots. Black religious institutions also serve as resources for political entrepreneurs by providing campaign funds and workers and a mobilizable source of voters. Although the direct involvement of black religious institutions produces some ambivalence in the black population, by and large black clerics have a strong commitment to political activism, and black churchgoers generally approve of that commitment. Their approval may well be related to the stronger positive effect on black political activism than on white activism. Both quantitative and qualitative data indicate that black religious institutions have a potent effect on black political activism by providing information about politics and by facilitating political mobilization.

Notes

1. Morris 1984. For further discussion of the role of black churches during the Civil Rights movement, see McAdam 1982.
2. A. Reed 1986, 45.
3. Hamilton 1972, 110–45; Berenson, Elifson, and Tollerson 1976; Childs 1980; A. Reed 1986, 41–60; Lincoln and Mamiya 1990.
4. For a further discussion on black clerics supporting and undermining collective black interests, see Reed 1985; Marable 1983; and Harris 1994a. For specific historical episodes, see Meier and Rudwick 1969; Randolph [1929] 1990; Meier and Rudwick 1979; and Clark 1986.
5. Putnam 1993, 173.
6. Verba et al. 1993b.
7. Walker 1982.
8. Ibid.; Washington 1985.
9. Foner 1988, 93; 110. For specific details on the role of the African Methodist Episcopal (AME) Church in Reconstruction politics, see Walker 1982.
10. See Logan 1968; and Franklin 1980, 285.
11. Walton 1972.
12. The Agrarian Revolt of the 1890s saw one brief moment of interracial mobilization where both blacks and poor whites in the South mobilized against the economic domination of Bourbons and northern industrialists. But even in that moment, the Populist Party was organized around racially separate rural organizations. As historian Lawrence Goodwyn notes of black mobilization during the Agrarian Revolt, "White supremacy prevented black farmers from performing the kinds of collective public acts essential to the creation of an authentic movement culture." Goodwyn 1978, 122–23. See also Franklin 1980, 260–63.
13. Frazier [1963] 1974, 48.
14. Mays and Nicholson [1933] 1969, 9.
15. Higginbotham 1993, 17.
16. Gosnell [1935] 1967, 96, 96–97.
17. Critics of the otherworldly perspective of African American religion may have erroneously attributed the lack of black mobilization in the South during the

Jim Crow era to the otherworldly tenets of African American Christianity. As I have argued elsewhere (Harris 1994a), when opportunity structures for participation expanded and sanctions against participation eased, religiously based resources were forged for black political mobilization. These sources of action had their effects even when clerical leadership discouraged political mobilization. The study of black political mobilization during several historical periods would benefit from an analysis of how dominated individuals and groups act strategically under a range of punitive sanctions and opportunity structures. For further insights into how individuals and groups act under systems of domination, see Scott 1985 and 1990. For a perspective on how southern African Americans overtly and subtly resisted Jim Crow see Kelley 1990 and 1993.

18. Bunche 1973, 490, 501.

19. Ibid., 592–93, 599.

20. Johnson 1956, 189.

21. See Johnson 1956, 193. For further historical details, see Harris 1994a.

22. Johnson 1956, 203.

23. Kilson 1971, 171, 17–18.

24. Hamilton 1972, 117. For further details on the organizational structure of black Protestant denominations, see Harris 1994b.

25. Verba et al. 1993b, 477.

26. Ibid., 477, table 4 on 485, 491–92, 491.

27. Bulletin, Second Baptist Church, Evanston, Illinois, February 25, 1990. I would like to thank Miasha Goss for assistance in compiling church bulletins during 1990 and 1991 for this research.

28. Cassette tape, Reverend Dr. Charles G. Adams, "What Do These Stones Mean?" Hartford Memorial Baptist Church, Detroit, Michigan, November 1, 1992. I would like to thank Don R. Weston for providing me with this cassette tape.

29. Letter of Reverend W. L. Upshire of the Prince of Peace M.B. Church to Harold Washington, January 29, 1983, Harold Washington Papers, box 35, Harold Washington Library, Chicago, Illinois. I would like to thank Colin Murry, a curator at the Harold Washington Library in Chicago, for making available these papers and for encouragement during the six days I spent plowing through the Washington Papers.

30. For further details and examples of religious institutions disseminating political information, see Harris 1994b.

31. *Herald*, Progressive Community Center, Chicago, Illinois, October 7, 1990.

32. Participant observation, morning worship service, Mount Vernon Baptist Church, Chicago, Illinois, March 13, 1994.

33. Cavanagh and Foster 1984.

34. E. Troy Fletcher, Park Manor Christian Church, to Harold Washington, February 28, 1983, Harold Washington Papers, box 36.

35. Dr. Royce D. Cornelius, pastor of the Mount Pleasant Missionary Baptist Church, to Harold Washington, February 28, 1983, Harold Washington Papers, box 37.

36. For an itemized list of church and clerical contributions to Harold Washington's 1983 mayoral campaign, see Harris 1994a.

37. For details, see ibid.

38. Rush to clerics in his district, May 11, 1992 (in possession of author).

39. Hofeld to clerics, July 16, 1992 (in possession of author).

40. Bulletin, Abyssinian Baptist Church, New York, New York, March 28, 1993.

41. See Vernon Jarrett's commentary "'Hired' Preachers Don't Always Win Votes,' *Chicago Sun-Times*, December 20, 1988.

42. For details on itemized contributions to churches from the Richard M. Daley campaign committee, see Harris 1994b.

43. Gosnell [1935] 1967, 97.

44. *Call and Post*, September 20, 1978.

45. Cassette tape, Bishop David L. Ellis, Greater Grace Broadcasts, Detroit, Michigan, November 1, 1992, 12:00 P.M. service.

46. Cassette tape, Pastor Anderson Culbreath, "Fear and How to Deal with It," Tryed Stone Missionary Baptist Church, Cincinnati, Ohio, November 1, 1992, 10:00 A.M. service.

47. Reverend Clarence Hilliard, executive director, Prophets for People, to Velma Wilson, January 19, 1983, Harold Washington Papers, box 37.

48. See H. Young 1988 for Reverend Hilliard's comments about Harold Washington's meeting with the black clerical group during the 1983 mayoral campaign (140–43).

49. Paul and Nancy Littleton to Harold Washington, March 1, 1983, Harold Washington Papers, box 37.

50. Paul and Nancy Littleton to Harold Washington, March 10, 1983, ibid.

51. Pastor Al Smith of Faith Tabernacle Church to Harold Washington, March 17, 1983, Harold Washington Papers, box 37.

52. A. Reed 1986.

53. Lincoln and Mimiya 1990, 223.

54. Ibid., table 26 on 225, 226.

55. NBC News/Associated Press national poll, taken October 8–10, 1980. Polling data were provided through Roper Center for Public Opinion Research at the University of Connecticut.

56. The questions for the five indicators of campaign participation had response categories of "yes" and "no." The index has a numeric range of 0 to 5 and was commuted by the positive responses of each question on campaign activity. The index has a population mean of 0.77. The questions asked: "So far this year, have you, yourself, done any of the following things in any one of the political campaigns or primaries, either national or local?"

Distributed literature for a candidate?

Gone to a political meeting or rally?

Given money to a candidate?

Called on the telephone on behalf of a candidate?

Helped to register voters?

57. See Harris 1994b for a discussion of how church attendance functions as a civic-oriented resource for voter participation.

58. Tate 1991 and 1993.

59. Kleppner 1985; Bobo and Gilliam 1990; Tate 1993.

60. Tate 1993, table 4.5.

61. For further readings on religion and black electoral mobilization in the post–Civil Rights era, see Dawson, Brown, and Allen 1990; and Harris 1994b.

62. These survey results are from the 1991 Chicago Area Survey conducted by the Northwestern University Survey Laboratory from April 28 to June 6, 1991. For further details concerning the survey, see Harris 1994a. Results that report findings on Latinos may be biased by their small representation in the survey ($N = 42$) and by the surveying of only English-speaking respondents. Questions 2, 3, and 4 were partially replicated from the 1984 National Black Election Study at the University of Michigan. Exact questions from the survey are as follows:

> **1.** How often does your (minister) (priest) (rabbi) discuss political issues as part of the service? Does this happen nearly all the time, frequently, sometimes, rarely, or never?
>
> **2.** How often do political candidates visit your place of worship during election time? Would you say frequently, only sometimes, or basically never?
>
> **3.** Has your place of worship ever encouraged members to vote in any election?
>
> **4.** Has your place of worship ever taken up a collection for any political candidates during any election?

63. The reported frequencies for Latinos should be read with caution given the small number of Latinos in the population sample ($N = 42$) and even the smaller number who reported being members of a church ($N = 22$). Additionally, interviewers surveyed only English-speaking respondents.

64. To access the educational variations for racial/ethnic religious groups, an institutionally based activism index was constructed from the standardized z-scores that were composed from the four modes of church-based activism. The activism index has a Conbach Alpha reliability coefficient of .50.

65. Verba et al. 1993.

66. See Putnam 1993 for further discussion.

Part IV

ETHNIC DIFFERENCES IN POLITICAL OPINIONS AND PARTICIPATION

13

Race and Voter Registration in the South

JAMES E. ALT

DESCRIBING Sunflower County, in the heart of the Mississippi Delta and the birthplace, in 1954, of White Citizens' Councils, Constance Curry writes

> In the 1950s, Sunflower black people comprised almost 75 per cent of the total population of 56,000, but only 0.3 percent were registered to vote. The number of black registered voters has increased dramatically over the years, but old arrangements and the power of intimidation and violence linger. Even with a majority black population in . . . the county, registered black voters make up only 50 percent of the electorate.
>
> "And just being registered doesn't make the difference," says [longtime African American resident and activist] Mae Bertha Carter. "People don't know how important it is to vote. . . . We need some voter education. People aren't scared anymore, they just aren't in the habit."[1]

This paper describes the evolution of race and voter registration in the South over the years since the passage of the Voting Rights Act in 1965. It serves two related purposes. One is to resolve issues of evidence and measurement that affect a variety of basic but quite specific questions about race and registration. For instance, do black and white registration rates still differ in the South? By how much? What has changed? Why has it? If black rates are still lower, is it a holdover of "old arrangements" and "intimidation," or are blacks just not "in the habit"? How could one tell? Are registration patterns different in counties in which blacks form a majority? Put another way, are the features Carter and Curry point out in Sunflower County true in general, or at least true in general of counties where blacks form majorities?

The second reason for asking broadly about what has happened to race and registration in the South since the Voting Rights Act is to help resolve some continuing controversies about the act itself. Much current debate involves legalistic arguments over whether the act can be used to justify creating electoral district boundaries to guarantee majority status to minority groups.[2] Often submerged by that argument is a related scholarly dispute over how far black registration in the South had and would have advanced without the act, how effective the act was, and why and how quickly its effects were felt. Many of those who oppose the creation of majority-minority districts believe that the act "solved" the problem of black enfranchisement quickly.[3] Others who support the creation of such districts believe that citizens who obtain majority status become more likely to register and vote. In fact, the findings of this chapter offer little support for either of these views. On the one hand, while the Voting Rights Act clearly made a big difference, the route to black enfranchisement, particularly where blacks could form majorities, was neither quick nor easy. On the other, the evidence is that majority-black counties no longer differ much in the registration behavior they display from counties in which blacks are much smaller minorities.

The analysis that follows reveals about half a dozen main findings. First, in the South between 1972 and 1988 (at least where data are available), black registration rates generally increased while white registration rates decreased. Nevertheless, despite the increase in black registration rates, whites even as recently as 1988 were still more likely to register to vote in every state, and often by a significant margin. Whites have a numerical advantage over blacks in the vast majority of counties (and all states) in the South, an advantage that derives partly from the obvious fact that there are more voting-age whites than blacks, and partly from the different registration propensities of the races. However, another important finding of the chapter is that this latter factor—racial differences in registration rates—became less important over the period in maintaining white numerical advantage. Even so, before 1988, there were never many counties where blacks registered at higher rates than whites. There were just about *no* counties in which blacks, while *less* than a majority of the voting-age population, became a majority of the county's electorate by registering at a higher rate than whites. However, I find that in the late 1980s *for the first time* blacks were regularly able to form a majority of the registered electorate in those counties where they formed a majority of the eligible voting-age population.

Interestingly, Mae Carter's feeling that blacks were not in the habit of voting no longer finds expression in any general tendency that differentiates the races, at least in my data. Once whites register, they tend to stay registered. There was a time twenty years ago when this was less true of blacks, but recently it is as true of blacks as of whites. At any rate, there is no longer a statistically detectable difference between races with respect to staying on the rolls, once there. Moreover, white registration rates fluctuate more between presidential and nonpresidential election years than do black registration rates. This might be due to greater geographical mobility among whites.[4] Holding this on-year, off-year cycle constant reveals that the oft-discussed "Jackson surge" in black voter registration in 1984 was on the order of 5–6 percentage points. Apparently, *none* of these findings needs to be qualified in any way to take account of whether blacks form a larger or smaller portion of the eligible electorate, a striking contrast to what was evident two decades earlier.

What the Voting Rights Act Achieved

How much of an effect did the Voting Rights Act have, and how quickly was its effect felt? How great were the racial differences in registration rates in the South that remained after the act? I believe its effects were big (though they varied in size from place to place, in largely explicable ways) and that they were mostly felt quickly, but racial differences in registration rates, smaller than before but still significant, persisted for at least two decades after the act. These answers are based on aggregate, county-by-county figures for voter registration by race.[5]

The Size of the Act's Effects

First, how much of an effect did the Voting Rights Act have on changes in registration differences between whites and blacks? Figure 13.1 gives an answer for each of the states and years for which data exist. Each point represents average white registration advantage within a state: the ratio of white to black county-level registration rates, weighted by county size and averaged over the state. A value of 2 means simply that the white registration rate is twice as high as the black registration rate. That is, it represents the cumulative effect of everything affecting relative registration by race, apart from the advantage whites derived from their larger numbers. Whatever the source of white advantage in registration rates, whether the factors are political, legal, extralegal, social, or economic—everything except just relative numbers in the eligible pool of voters—this variable measures it.[6] Additionally, the vertical axis is in log scale to emphasize the continuing changes taking place after 1972. I plot the states for which there are data individually in the figure; the correspondence among state-specific trends after 1972 is so clear that there is no need to present an average.

Relative to whites, blacks were gaining ground even before the Voting Rights Act, though in an average southern country, registered whites would have had a numerical advantage of about four to one in terms of relative registration rates. The act produced the biggest change between 1960 and 1970, in which this advantage, on average, was about cut in half. Nothing else in the period produced a change of anything like this magnitude.

The effect of the act does vary by state. Relative black gains are evident

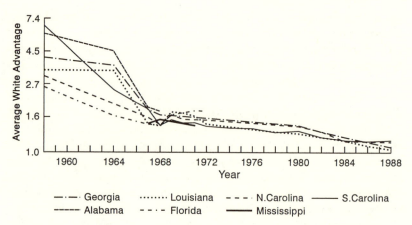

Figure 13.1. White Advantage, 1958–1988 (Average Deviation from Equality).
Y axis is in log scale; zero denotes equal effort by each race.

in Florida and South Carolina before the act, but big relative changes came only after the act in Alabama, Georgia, and Louisiana. Timpone finds that the act had the biggest effect on black registration in Alabama, Louisiana, and Mississippi.[7] The fact that I highlight slightly different patterns in some states is due to the concomitant changes taking place in white registration in the same period, some of which were also due to the act.

Figure 13.1 shows quite simply how striking were the changes in the racial character of southern patterns of registration in the period immediately following the passage of the Voting Rights Act of 1965. Before, an average southern political county unit had white numbers (compared to black) in its electorate that vastly exaggerated the relative numbers of whites in its voting age-population. After, the exaggeration was far smaller, and the transformation happened in a very few years.

The Reason the Act Worked

What the Voting Rights Act did was to break up the legal and institutional foundations of a registration system in the South that was by and large designed to guarantee the election of white candidates. The act was not the only thing to happen in this period, but it was, nevertheless, central. I have elsewhere extensively analyzed and discussed the complex relationships between the legal changes and enforcement provisions of the act and other legal, demographic, and organizational changes taking place at the same time.[8] Basically, my results emphasize the roles of organizational mobilization and legal impediments to registration in the period before the act, and the importance of enforcement by federal registrars in the effect the act had on the emergence of counties in which blacks formed majorities. I present a brief review of my principal quantitative findings.

First and foremost I find that, in the pre-act South, the effects of legal disenfranchising devices and what Matthews and Prothro call white "race organizations"—that is, organizations aimed at keeping blacks in their place—far outweighed socioeconomic factors in explaining (relative) levels of black registration. This is especially clear when it is taken into account that race organizations had greater effects where blacks formed a larger proportion of the population; black organizations stimulated black registration rates, and white organizations retarded them most in the counties with the highest black voting-age population proportions. In the same way, literacy tests had their greatest disenfranchising effect (on blacks relative to whites) in counties with highest black population proportions. Only in counties with very few blacks did literacy tests disadvantage whites relative to blacks. Poll taxes kept many whites as well as blacks off the rolls; indeed, in terms of ultimate registration rates, in counties where over 40 percent of the voting age population was black, the poll tax disadvantaged whites more than blacks. Interestingly, residence requirements, not even covered by the act, disenfranchised whites more than blacks.

After the act was passed, in the late 1960s, a far higher proportion of black majority counties visited by federal registrars achieved black majority electorates than black majority counties not visited by federal registrars. In fact, although in 1967–68 only about a fourth of the majority black (eligible population) counties in Alabama, Georgia, Louisiana, and Mississippi achieved majority-black electorates, every county in these states that did have a majority-black electorate in that period either had received a federal examiner or was geographically adjacent to one or more counties that did. Moreover, the overall impact of federal registrars appeared to wear off over time, in that registration rates in counties not visited by registrars became comparable to the rates in those that were. Nonetheless, black majority counties visited by federal registrars achieved black registration majorities roughly a decade earlier than counties elsewhere in the South. Finally, but equally importantly, the effects of previous disenfranchisement devices also appeared to wear off over time, so that the black-white registration differential is no longer greatest in the most heavily black counties.

White Advantage after the Act

With the legal impediments of the pre-act South swept away, blacks and whites both registered in increasing numbers, as described by Black, Stekler, and others.[9] The numbers of new white registrants meant that blacks remained a minority of the registered electorate. Blacks registered at greater rates than they had before passage of the act, but somewhat at some-what lower rates than whites, other things equal, as figure 13.1 shows.

Particularly from 1972 on, three features of figure 13.1 are clear: differ-ences among states are far smaller than before; white advantage in registra-tion rates declines slowly but steadily; but white advantage never goes away altogether, at least not yet. More importantly, by focusing attention on white and black registration rates simultaneously, figure 13.1 reveals how often they move together. For instance, the much-discussed surge in black registration surrounding Jesse Jackson's 1984 campaign does not show up in figure 13.1. This does not mean that more blacks did not regis-ter, but that the increase in black registration rates that year must have produced a countervailing increase in the registration of whites.[10] In terms of figure 13.1, the year 1984 does not even show up as a blip in the slow, steady downward trend in *relative* white registration advantage.

These estimates are out of step with much of the literature. In part, this reflects a conflict of types of data—aggregate versus survey data. Survey research really did seem to suggest that the problem of racial disparities in registration had been solved, or was on its way to solution. For instance, the National Election Study shows blacks and whites in the South registering at equal rates as early as 1980. The Census Bureau's Current Population Surveys, while not finding equality in racial registration rates in the South until 1984, typically projected interracial differences of 3–6 percentage points from 1972 to 1982.[11] In fact, Engstrom notes that the argument that black and white registration rates were more similar in the South than in the North was often raised by opponents of the 1982 extension and amendment of the Voting Rights Act.[12] In any event, there was little hard data, so schol-ars relied on the surveys.

By contrast, my estimates show that blacks have continued to cut into white advantage, though at a much slower pace, since 1972. White advan-tage has been cut again by about a third since the late 1960s. If present changes continue, white advantage on average might disappear by some time in the 1990s.[13] What this will mean for electoral outcomes, for the election of black officials, and for broader policy outcomes[14]—indeed, as well as whether it will in fact happen—remains to be seen.

Race and Registration since 1972

What exactly are the patterns of racial differences in registration rates that underlie the smooth downward trend of figure 13.1? Following a rapid rise in white registration rates right after the act, the basic trend is a slow de-cline in these rates in most places after 1972. These changes in the white rates are coupled with a rapid rise in black registration rates before and right after the act, followed by their slower, but persistent, increase ever since. Please bear in mind when I write of "the South" that I am using data from the four states that publish official statistics on registration by race—the Carolinas, Georgia, and Louisiana—and one can only conjecture about how patterns might differ in other southern states. I now turn to details of population changes and estimates of registration changes and discuss some points of consistency between my interpretation of these statistics and others' results.

Analysis of Race and Registration Rates

The increase in the number of southern whites from 1964 to 1984 was larger than the corresponding increase among blacks, and so the doubling of the black registration rate from 29 to 60 percent in the 1960s added only as many new black registrants (1.7 million) as the much smaller proportionate increase added among the much larger eligible white population (1.8 million).[15] Nevertheless, these changes in the racial mix in the South—net inmigration by whites and outmigration by blacks—fundamentally altered the racial balance in a large number of political units. The biggest change was the decline in the number of districts in which blacks formed a majority of the population. According to the 1950 census, of the 369 counties in the four states for which we have registration data (again: Georgia, Louisiana, and the Carolinas), about 100 had majority-black voting-age populations; 82 still did at the time of the act. By the 1980 Census, fewer than 50 still did, and the number is probably 40 or fewer today.

Southern white registration rates rose from about 65 percent in 1964 to 76 percent by 1967. States where white registration levels were low, partly as a result of the poll tax, included Texas, Arkansas, and Virginia. In contrast, white registration rates of 90 percent and more were reached in Alabama, Louisiana, and Mississippi by 1967, though these rates have recently been falling. The 76 percent white registration rate recorded by the Civil Rights Commission in 1967 (in the states covered by the act) represented about a 19-point advantage over black registration rates. This difference still existed over a decade later, though the relevant data is not always easy to come by. Stanley mentions census data that show that in 1980, 58 percent of blacks were registered. His data also reveal that whites comprised 80 percent of the eligible population but 84 percent of the actual electorate.[16] These numbers taken together, by a straightforward calculation, imply that the white registration rate must be 76.1 percent. Happily, this is virtually identical to the figure of 77 percent for that year, which Stanley obtains from survey data for white registration. In a moment we shall see

320

TABLE 13.1

Estimated Voter Registration Rates by Race, State, and Year (Percentage of Eligible Population Registered to Vote)

	Black Voting-Age Population			
	1972	1980	1984	1988
Georgia	—	45.8	52.6	52.2
Louisiana	55.3	54.6	59.9	59.1
North Carolina	46.9	46.7	61.1	59.7
South Carolina	49.4	48.7	53.9	46.4
	White Voting-Age Population			
	1972	1980	1984	1988
Georgia	—	69.1	70.4	70.5
Louisiana	83.9	78.0	77.1	70.5
North Carolina	73.2	72.0	75.5	73.8
South Carolina	63.7	60.8	60.9	53.5

Note: Cell entries are the estimated percentage of voting-age eligibles registered to vote in each year and state. See the appendix for data sources and adjustments.

that this difference is very close to what I obtain with different, independent data and calculations.

The four-state counts of voter registration by race can be transformed into registration rates by dividing them by a contemporaneous estimates of white and black voting-age populations. Voting-age data by race are available only from the decennial censuses. Data in intercensus years can be estimated by interpolation. Thus, for the period since 1972, the figures for registered voters in these states derive from official counts, but those for voting-age populations derive from estimates, since the voting-age populations of both races change considerably within decades. Indeed, even though the black population in the South is growing more slowly than the white population—accounting for the decline in black concentration and the number of majority-black counties—it is nevertheless growing. Failure to allow for this growth biases upward many (official) estimates of black registration rates.

Table 13.1 presents the estimated, adjusted registration rates by state and race. For blacks, they are uniformly about 5 percentage points below the Voter Education Project estimates regularly published in the *Statistical Abstract of the United States*. Black registration rates in 1972 apparently ranged around 50 percent, slightly down from 1967–68 but higher than some Civil Rights Commission estimates of registration for 1969, 1970, and 1971 suggest. The increase in 1972 may reflect the effects of political organizations countering white challenges to post-act registration of many blacks.

We can see right away from table 13.1 that the decline in white registration relative to black since 1972 is due to a combination of increases in black registration rates in some states (especially North Carolina and to some extent Georgia) and decreases in white registration rates in others (most notably Louisiana), and decreases in registration rates of both races (but greater among whites) in South Carolina. Table 13.1 apparently reveals no net change in black registration rates between 1972 and 1980. Then there is a jump of 5–7 percentage points in 1984 in three states, and even more in North Carolina, though about a third of that state's change occurred in 1982, amid the stimulus of redistricting and a shift to district-based legislative elections. Black registration rates were then flat to slightly down between 1984 and 1988, except in South Carolina, where they fell more steeply.

Consistency with Other Analyses

After 1970, even though there were hundreds of counties in the South in which blacks formed a potential majority based on numbers alone—let alone many others where they could have formed majorities by expending effort to outregister whites—political and legal attention focused less on registration and more on the effects of other political changes with "dilutive" potential.[17] Of course, dilution could frustrate even aggressive registration campaigns. Such campaigns were also maybe too costly, even in many counties where black majorities could form. Of course, such counties were becoming less common.

Possibly, many people believed the survey results that suggested the black and white registration rates were equal. However, even in the survey data, the awaited equality never quite appeared: Tate, Stanley, and Davison all show that black turnout is recently typically a few percentage points lower than white turnout, except in 1984, when black registration and turnout was stimulated by the Jesse Jackson campaign.[18] Turnout is not the same as registration, but other, more disturbing results ensued.

Following the lead of Abramson and Claggett,[19] Stanley's, Hagen's, and Tate's studies all showed that the survey report of black registration and turnout is often a substantial overestimate. More troubling, the black over-report of black registration in surveys is larger than the white overreport of white registration. Stanley has data that make it clear that black survey responses overestimate black registration rates by something like 10 points. No one has a compelling account of why this happens.[20] The result, however, is that survey findings of no more racial disparity in registration rates were probably inaccurate. When corrections for differential over-reporting are introduced, the surveys confirm the aggregate data showing that white advantage persisted.

Two other important independent studies, neither published, confirm this as well. First Hagen shows in a thorough analysis of the Census Current Population Survey for 1984 (over 90,000 cases) that, even after controlling for a host of socioeconomic, contextual, legal, and political variables, and all their interactions with race, southern blacks apparently registered, on average, at about 92 per cent the rate of southern whites.[21] His regressions are logistic, so this statement holds only around average values of the explanatory variables. However, typical effects of overreporting (even though it is a big data set, this is, after all, survey data) would bias the "92 percent" upward, resulting in an underestimate of racial disparities. Furthermore, any (as I show below, transitory) effects of the Jackson campaign in 1984 will also only make this interracial difference appear smaller. Even without making big adjustments, this suggests interracial differences of 5 to 7 percentage points (say, nearly 10 percent of the typical average rates of 60–70 percent).

Second, Alan Lichtman, in a brief submitted to the Delta Division of the Northern District of Mississippi U.S. District Court, showed how federal jury polls could be used to estimate racial differences in registration.[22] By examining returned questionnaires from potential jurors, which included a question about race—assuming the federal courts had drawn the samples randomly from the registered electorate and correcting for nonresponse, movers, and undeliverable envelopes along the way—Lichtman estimates black registration rates to be about 20 percentage points below white rates. This, holding only for part of Mississippi, could be an upper bound to the sort of racial disparities we are likely to observe.

Putting all this evidence (written between 1986 and 1990) together, it seems to me that the new consensus should be that blacks participate in the South at lower rates than do whites. This does not make the Voting Rights Act a failure, nor does it show that mobilization of blacks could not be self-sustaining, but only that the road to racial parity is a long one. My aggregate data do not really explain where the black disadvantage comes from. Hagen's study is extremely important since it shows that blacks continue to suffer a residual disadvantage even after many other relevant factors are controlled. It is important to point out that the existence of such a residual disadvantage after so many other explanatory factors have been held constant is also not itself sufficient to demonstrate the existence of discrimination,[23] since it does not show that otherwise willing blacks have been coerced or similarly prevented from registering. It does, however, make one want to probe further for the causes of continuing racial disparities.

Persistence and Stability in Black and White Registration

Levels, Cycles, and the "Jackson Surge"

Indeed, there is the possibility that Mae Carter alluded to at the outset, that blacks are "not in the habit" of voting. I interpret this comment empirically as the prediction that blacks will be found to circulate in and out of the registered electorate more than whites, or to have a higher rate of "drop-off" from one election to the next. Indeed, behind the presidential election-year data in table 13.1 lies a regular on-year, off-year cycle in voter registration. As a first step, I consider whether this cycle is greater for blacks than for whites.[24]

Figures for the intervening biennial years reveal that on average, between each pair of presidential election years shown in table 13.1 and the off-year election two years later, black registration rates decline on average by 2.6 percentage points. Black registration rates regain (apart from 1984, on which more in a moment) 2.65 percentage points on average by the next presidential election year, so across a succession of terms, black registration rates are, on average, increasing very, very slowly. Davison finds the same sort of cycle in black turnout.[25] The changes are indeed steady and similar from time to time and place to place: only once did black registration rates rise in the biennium after a presidential election (by 1 point, in South Carolina, in 1982), and only once did they fall in the biennium before a presidential year (by two points, in South Carolina, in 1988).

White registration rates, by contrast, vary more across states and time, and fall almost steadily across the period. The 1972 figures are already several percentage points below those of 1967–68, and the fall continues through 1980 and 1988. Around this steady decline (which slowed in 1984), there is a two-year cycle similar to that in black registration, as average white registration rates drop in off years and rise in presidential election years. However, independent of their steady downward trend, white registration rates on average increase about four percentage points in the biennium before and decrease about four percentage points in the biennium after a presidential election. This swing is about one and one half times the size of the black registration cycle.

This understanding of the cyclical nature of registration rates allows estimation of the magnitude of the Jackson surge in registration in 1984. The actual increase in black registration rates from 1982 to 1984 in the three states for which there are data in both years is 7.4 percentage points. If one expects the usual 2.65 point upswing, this leaves the rest of the increase—the Jackson surge—at about 5 percentage points. This is about half the size of the effect usually reported in surveys, which are probably afflicted by overreporting. The upward response of white registration to the Jackson surge is evident in North Carolina as white registration rates rose (relative to the underlying downward trend) by 3.5 percentage points. Given the subsequent decline of these rates, it is reasonable to believe that white registration rates might also have been lower by similar amounts in Louisiana and South Carolina in 1984, except for the surge in black registration. It appears that the races mobilized and countermobilized in 1984, as more whites registered where more blacks registered.

Persistence of Registration Patterns

Given this observed cycle, I want to probe the data a little further to investigate whether blacks are indeed more likely to circulate in and out of the registered electorate. I think of a system in which many individuals flow in and out of the registered electorate as unstable. By contrast, in a stable system, most individuals, once registered, stay registered, purely random factors apart. This equates stability with retention, which can be measured directly with estimates of the rate at which registrants, once registered, stay registered, random fluctuations apart.

I estimate the stability of registration (for each of the races in the New South) from a number of "ecological" regressions. Each of these regressions has the following structure. For a biennium beginning with an even-numbered year (denoted t) and ending in year $t + 2$, for a county (denoted i), for the variable PBR (the proportion of voting age blacks registered), I estimate the regression of the form

$$PBR_{i,\, t+2} = p^* \, PBR_{i,\, t} + q^* \, (1 - PBR_{i,\, t})$$

with no intercept and where the second explanatory variable is the proportion of voting-age blacks who were not registered to vote at time t. It is a standard interpretation of such regressions that the parameter p is an estimate of the proportion of blacks registered at time t who are still registered two years later.[26] In what I have called a stable system, this estimated proportion would be statistically indistinguishable from unity. Such regressions were run separately for white and black registration rates, within states according to data availability, and the results were then averaged across states according to whether the year $t + 2$ was a presidential year or an off year.

The estimated rates are displayed in figure 13.2. For both races, it appears recently as though almost all those registered in off years are still registered two years later. That is, registration rates in any given county may move up or down, but across counties there was no systematic drop-off in registration among the previously registered in the biennium from an

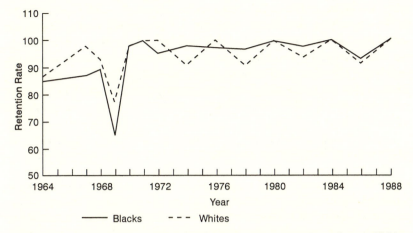

Figure 13.2. Registration Persistence, Whites and Blacks, Four States, 1964–1988.

off year to a presidential year. For whites, in fact, this estimated rate of retention in presidential years of previously registered voters is never significantly different (above or below) from 100 percent.

Retention of registered blacks was a little different earlier in the period. For blacks in 1972 the retention rate was only 95 percent from 1971 (and only 80 percent from 1970), so there appears to have been quite a loss among those previously registered, even though it was offset by a great deal of new registration. Since for whites in 1972 the retention rate was 100 percent, there was nothing especially unstable about that year. More likely, black registration rates may have settled down only after 1972, and this early period may be what Mae Carter was describing.[27] However, for blacks, the estimated retention rate rises to 97 percent in 1976 (that is, the rate of retention from 1974), on to 99 percent in 1980, and to 100 percent thereafter.

The off years are different, both from other years and between the races. Retention from two years before in the off years beginning in 1974 averages 93.3 percent for whites and 95.5 percent for blacks. Moreover, the estimated difference of 2.2 percentage points in the rates of slippage of whites and blacks off the rolls in the two years after presidential elections is (just) statistically significant.[28] This is remarkable, since my initial conjecture was that the *lower* rate of black registration could be due to the lower black retention rate. Far from it: even though relatively fewer blacks register, those who do are, other things equal, at least as likely if not more likely to remain registered.

The lowest rates of retention for each race, respectively 90 and 92 percent, are naturally enough estimated in 1986. That is, after the Jackson surge in registration in 1984, unusually large numbers of registered voters of both races dropped off the rolls. Nevertheless, the difference between races persists. While apparently those who stay registered in the off year are on the whole still registered two years later, regardless of race, post–presidential year drop off is higher among whites.

It is just not clear why this is so. Some of the difference could reflect greater population mobility among whites within and into the South. Net black mobility for much of the period is out of the South. Purging (and indeed local differences in the thoroughness of purging), canvassing, and reregistration could matter, as could different laws governing the convenience of registration. The main difference among the states on which figure 13.2 is based is that South Carolina does not have neighborhood locations for registration (none of the states has deputy registrars or mail registration), and all but North Carolina purge every three or four years.[29] But in any case, why any of these differences would create interracial differences in the magnitude of the cycle and dropoff rate is not clear.

To sum up, while racial differences in registration rates have declined, they have done so recently principally through a higher rate of white dropoff in registration in the two years after presidential elections.[30] These results apparently isolate the timing of the persistent decline in white registration rates across the period. In any case, these results strongly suggest a stable system, at least after 1972. Although it did take nearly a decade after the Voting Rights Act was passed for that equal retention rate to come about, blacks have been at least as able as whites to stay registered once registered, at least for the last ten years of the study.

Black Majorities: Beginning of a New Era?

There is one other important change that my data reveal. A few decades ago, there were hundreds of counties in the South in which blacks were a majority of those eligible to register, though black outmigration and white inmigration reduced the number of such counties in my four-state sample by as much as a quarter just since 1968. Regardless, in such counties, by simply registering at the same rates as whites, blacks could have become a majority of the registered electorate.[31] In the seven states covered by the Voting Rights Act (which include my four), in Matthews and Prothro's data for 1958–60, there were no counties in which blacks formed a majority of the registered electorate. Figure 12.3 shows how blacks have fared more recently at forming electoral majorities in such counties.

Before the act, registration drives had secured two county-level majority-black registered electorates in the states covered by the act. By 1968, this number had risen to thirty-one, nearly 40 percent of the eighty-two

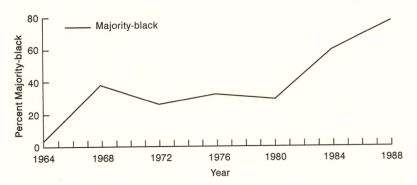

Figure 13.3. Majority-Black Counties, Southern States, 1964–1988. Percentages are based on counties in which blacks are more than 50 percent of eligibles.

counties in which blacks were a majority of eligibles. (I commented above on the role of federal registrars in bringing about this increase.) In the four-state sample, this "success rate" was lower, around 25 percent. This proportion changes only a little in the 1970s: by 1980 there are three fewer counties with a black majority of eligibles and two more counties with a black majority of those registered, so the success rate is about 29 percent. By contrast, the number of counties with more registered blacks than whites nearly doubles between 1980 and 1988, while the number of counties where blacks are a majority of eligibles falls by 20 percent, producing the spectacular increase to a success rate of 75 percent shown in figure 13.3.

It is hard to give a simple explanation of the change, though I think the stimulus of the Jackson campaign in 1984 must have had a role.[32] What mostly happens is that systematic statistical analysis no longer differentiates behavior in these densely black counties from the rest of the South. Econometric analyses show that white registration rates increase where black population concentrations are higher, while black registration rates increase where white registration rates are higher, other things equal.[33] Thus whites registered most (as did blacks, in response) where more blacks lived, and qualitatively this continues to be the case. However, in the 1970s, just a little extra white registration or black nonregistration often left blacks slightly short of a majority; apparently, this is no longer true.

However, a few words of caution are in order about the accuracy of my classification of counties according to whether blacks are a majority of the eligible voting-age population. Statistical analysis like mine requires making assumptions, and it is important to know if the assumptions are borne out. Hence, I repeatedly reported attempts to show that different sorts of data or different methods of analysis involving different assumptions produced the same or consistent results. The question of whether more blacks or whites in a county are registered depends only on the accuracy of the published official counts of registration by race, which are subject to unknown amounts of error. However, even to derive the results described in this section, I had to estimate county voting-age population composition. In most cases, I could treat the racial composition of the population as known, and assume that both races shared a common age distribution. That is probably not quite true, and thus the assumption introduced a small amount of error. Census tables could be used to estimate the difference between the under-eighteen proportions of the black and white populations in these states, but the tables were not readily available.

For the years between 1970 and 1980, I also assumed that the voting-age population of each race within each county changed (grew or shrank) by a constant amount each year in order to interpolate population figures for the intermediate years. That probably did not produce too much error, either. I also assumed that the same rates of change observed through the 1970–80 period continued after 1980, which is more troublesome, especially by the late 1980s, but the only alternative was to do no analysis of post-1980 behavior until the 1990 census was available.

Nevertheless, qualitatively I believe the findings of this section to be robust. There was apparently a large increase in the late 1980s in the proportion of counties in which blacks formed a majority of the registered electorate, based on those counties in which blacks were a majority of eligibles. In 1988 there were still no cases where blacks formed a majority solely by registering at greater rates than whites. There could be a few more or less counties than I estimate where blacks are indeed a majority of the eligibles, or a handful where blacks in fact are not a majority of eligibles but are a majority of those registered. But the basic fact—the big increase in the number of counties where the number of registered blacks is greater than that of whites—is unlikely to be an artifact of the data.

Conclusions

Black registration rates continued to be lower than white registration rates long after the Voting Rights Act, consistent with the estimates of Lichtman, Davison, and Hagen, but inconsistent with the unvalidated results reported in the National Election Study and some other surveys. Moreover, over the last twenty years, white registration rates have declined in some parts of the South while black registration rates there have remained constant, and black rates have risen in other areas while white rates in those areas have remained constant. The result has been a gradual squeezing of the average difference within counties between black and white registration rates.

Some of this squeezing comes from the greater ability of blacks now (compared to two decades ago) to remain registered once registered, and some reflects the greater rate of drop-off among whites after presidential years. Whether the gradual decline of white registration rates, which is reflected in their greater drop-off, also prefigures the long-run depoliticization of racial questions in the South is an interesting speculation for further research. Nevertheless, in spite of the squeeze, and even though blacks increasingly form majorities of the registered electorate where they are a majority of the eligible voting-age population, practically nowhere have blacks registered at rates greater than whites. The continuing erosion of the black share of the population has reduced the number of counties in which equal or less-than-equal effort would secure black electoral majorities. Registration alone is therefore no longer viable as an empowering strategy for southern blacks. Naturally, in consequence, to increase the payoff from black voting, attention has shifted to ways of constructing either interracial coalitions or majority-black districts within counties.

But it is a change to be able to say, pick a county at random in which blacks are a majority of the eligibles and it is very likely that they will also be a majority of the registered electorate. This did not happen immediately after the passage of the Voting Rights Act; indeed, it was certainly not true for a long time afterward. It is also not the case in general that just because blacks could more easily form a majority, they became likelier to mobilize and register. Those who believe that mobilization is a self-sustaining process will have to come to grips with the long-standing white advantage shown in figure 13.1 as well as the loss of momentum for black registration after the withdrawal of federal registrars from those counties where blacks were most numerous in the population. By the same token, the only-recent changes in black-majority status shown in figure 13.3 do not mean that the act was irrelevant. It was a very important act, but big changes take time, and require more than the passing of a law.

Appendix

Pre-1960 county registration and population data, as well as data on legal requirements for registration, were taken from the Matthews and Prothro Southern County data, originally provided on cards courtesy of Jim Prothro. Registration requirements were taken from Smith 1960. Interim data on voter registration for 1964 and 1967 were taken from U.S. Commission on Civil Rights 1968. Subsequent registration data for 1968–71 were provided by the Voter Education Project. These data were collected by Philip Wood at the University of Essex. Population data for 1970 and 1980 were taken from the U.S. Census. Voter registration data for 1972–88 were provided by Election Data Services of Washington, D.C. Confirmatory data for Georgia was provided by Michael Binford.

Matthews and Prothro's data on registration is mainly for 1960, though apparently for some states (at least Georgia), 1958 figures were used. No white registration data were available for 1960, but data for some counties were printed in U.S. Commission on Civil Rights, *Voting* (Washington, D.C., 1971), and were added to the earlier data. These data were also collected by Philip Wood.

For the 1960s and 1970s, changes occurring between census years are assumed to occur at a constant rate, in order to allow interpolation of voting-age population figures for noncensus years. For the 1980s, population changes occurring between 1970 and 1980 are extrapolated forward in time year by year.[34] These results will be (dis)confirmed when 1990 census data become available. The extrapolation probably produces greater measurement error than the interpolation.

Notes

1. Curry 1992, 18.
2. The act has recently been used less to modify registration processes and more to decide the boundaries of districts in order to create districts in which members of minority groups can form electoral majorities, in order, it is argued, to give minorities "a chance of winning."
3. For example, consider Thernstrom's contention that in its first five years, "what the Voting Rights Act accomplished—black enfranchisement—was precisely what it aimed to do" (1987, 18).
4. Moreover, I could not find any registration differences that could be attributed to racial differences in the application of rules for purging the registration lists.
5. The data for the years before 1963 were collected by Matthews and Prothro 1966. I have supplemented their data with statistics for 1964–72 collected by the Voter Education Project and published by the U.S. Commission on Civil Rights (1968 and subsequent years). Such data have been officially reported by South Carolina and, with some gaps, by North Carolina, Georgia, and Louisiana since 1972.
6. I focus on the ratio of white to black registration rates. Many changes take place in the period; some affect whites, some blacks, some both. The relative rates are the key also to discrimination.
7. Timpone 1995.
8. This section summarizes findings reported in Alt 1994.
9. See Black 1976 and Stekler 1983.
10. I give systematic quantitative evidence for this as a general pattern of southern registration politics in Alt 1994.
11. Hagen 1988.

12. Engstrom 1988.

13. At least if the adjustments that were needed to keep changes in voting-age population synchronized with changes in registration are correct. See my discussion in the next section.

14. Button 1989.

15. Stanley 1987, 6; Black and Black 1987, 12–22.

16. Stanley 1987, 97 and 154.

17. These changes, intended to reduce relative black voting strength by changing either district boundaries (per se or through annexation) or method of selection (at-large elections or appointment replacing district elections) produced over 80 percent of the preclearance objections brought by the Justice Department under the act before 1980. By contrast, fewer than 2 percent of the challenges were to changes in registration procedures, reregistration, or purges. See Engstrom 1988.

18. Tate 1988; Stanley 1987, 35–36; and Davison 1986.

19. Abramson and Claggett 1984.

20. Many think that the race of the interviewer is at the heart of this effect, but there are studies that disconfirm this.

21. Based on my calculations from the results reported in Hagen 1988.

22. Lichtman 1986.

23. Blau and Duncan point out how the existence of such a residual disadvantage after alternative causes are controlled for is a necessary but not sufficient consideration for the existence of discrimination in employment. See Blau and Duncan 1967, chap. 6.

24. I do not show the statistical work that was carried out in order to smooth and detrend the various series of race-based registration rates, but a variety of different approaches yield qualitatively identical findings.

25. Davison 1986.

26. Formally, as is well-known, such an estimate is unbiased if $E(p_i \mid PBR_i) = p$. Polynomial regressions and weighted least squares were used to check for possible bias. See Lichtman and Langbein 1978 for further details.

27. In 1972 I switch from data estimated and disseminated by the Voter Education Project to statistics released by the individual states. Changes in the data could also be responsible for the unstable results in the early period.

28. This conclusion is based on the standard errors of the coefficients of the regressions used to estimate dropoff.

29. Moreover, while the standard errors of the underlying regressions were substantially lower (indicating greater predictive success) for whites than for blacks early in the period, there is no longer any difference between races, though Georgia continues to be harder to predict than are the other states.

30. Of course, these results are no stronger than the assumptions of the ecological model. See n. 26.

31. From 1980 to 1988, the proportion of counties in which blacks registered at higher rates than whites increased from about 5 percent to nearly 15 percent. Since until recently there were so few cases where blacks registered at higher rates, it is not surprising that they never achieved majority status through differential registration rates.

32. When blacks registered at greater rates in 1984, the data show that whites did so as well, but the smaller number of whites where blacks are a majority of eligibles means that even this counter mobilization may not produce a white numerical advantage in the registered electorate.

33. Alt 1994.

34. Many of the issues involved in such data adjustments, as well as of other statistical techniques used in this chapter, are discussed in a recent symposium volume edited by Rubinfeld (1991).

14

The Effects of Ethnicity on Political Culture

RODOLFO O. DE LA GARZA

THIS PAPER compares Puerto Rican and Anglo (non-Hispanic whites) support for economic individualism and democratic norms, two values that analysts agree are central to American political culture.[1] Its objective is to determine if there are differences between the two groups regarding these values, and to measure the extent to which ethnic factors explain whatever differences exist.

We focus on Puerto Ricans for two reasons. First, we agree with the judgment that the several Latino national origin groups are distinct populations and should be analyzed as such.[2] Thus, we focus on Puerto Ricans rather than on Hispanics in general. More significant, however, is that because of Puerto Ricans' unique relationship to American society,[3] analysts have argued that they are unlikely to integrate as European immigrants have.[4] More recently, Puerto Ricans have also been described as the exception to an otherwise successful story of Hispanic integration.[5] These assessments suggest that, for reasons that will be described subsequently, Puerto Ricans are the Latino population most likely to fit the national stereotype of Hispanics as unpatriotic and preferring welfare over self-sufficiency.[6] Our purpose is to determine if this is indeed the case, and if so, the extent to which ethnic factors explain these patterns.

Methodology

This paper tests three hypotheses regarding Puerto Rican support of U.S. political values. All recognize that ethnicity is dynamic and evolves in response to changing political, social, and economic circumstances,[7] rather than primordial and essentially immutable.[8] However, one argues that maintaining traditional ethnic characteristics impedes the development of support for American values, the second that Americanization spurs rejection of those values, and a third that Puerto Ricans follow the path of other immigrants and integrate into society over-time.[9]

The first hypothesis is that Puerto Ricans are less supportive than Anglos of core American values. This is because, unlike European immigrants,

Puerto Ricans have refused to abandon their traditional values and to participate fully in in U.S. society.[10] This tendency has been enhanced by programs such as bilingual education and affirmative action, which not only help Puerto Ricans maintain traditional characteristics but also socialize them into a welfare mentality rather than into the nation's ethic of self-sufficiency.[11] We call this the *degenerated culture hypothesis*.

The second hypothesis is that the more Puerto Ricans learn about how U.S. society functions, the less likely they are to support the nation's core values. That is, as they acquire the credentials required for success and then are rebuffed, Puerto Ricans learn that U.S. society denies them their rights and privileges. Thus, like similarly situated minorities in other societies,[12] Puerto Ricans become alienated from rather than committed to society's core values. We label it the *politicized ethnicity hypothesis*.

The third hypothesis is that Puerto Ricans will follow the path of European immigrants.[13] Like European immigrants, the foreign born arrive with their cultural values intact, and they are almost naively hopeful about their future. As succeeding generations Americanize, they remain strongly supportive of U.S. society but become critical of the nation's social and political processes. This is the *immigrant hypothesis*.

While these hypotheses all assume that Puerto Ricans have lower socioeconomic characteristics than Anglos, each makes different assumptions about how other ethnic characteristics are distributed among Puerto Ricans. The politicized ethnicity and the immigrant hypotheses require that the foreign-born Puerto Ricans be more likely than the native-born Puerto Ricans to retain Spanish and to identify racially in non-Latino terms. The degenerated culture perspective is that there is no difference between the foreign and native born on these dimensions. Finally, the politicized ethnicity hypothesis also requires that native-born Puerto Rican economic attainment lag behind that of Anglos despite comparable English-language competence and high educational attainment; the immigrant hypothesis requires the foreign born to do worse than the native-born but assumes little difference between native born Puerto Ricans and Anglos; the degenerated culture formulation assumes Puerto Ricans do much worse than Anglos regardless of nativity.

The analysis begins by dividing the respondents by national origin, that is, Anglo and Puerto Rican. Puerto Ricans are then grouped according to nativity, language competence, and racial self-identification. The socioeconomic characteristics of Puerto Ricans within these four categories are then compared with those of Anglos. The results will indicate the extent to which they satisfy the premises of our three hypotheses. These four ethnic categories are then used to compare Anglo and Puerto Rican support for economic individualism. We then use various regression procedures that incorporate all the sociodemographic and ethnic characteristics to determine the independent effect that each ethnic characteristic has on support for economic individualism. This approach is then used to measure support for democratic norms and political values.

It should be noted that the consequence of using four ethnic indicators to operationalize ethnicity in the regression analysis is to make "national origin" into a residual ethnic category. That is, it suggests the extent to which the "meaning" of being Puerto Rican transcends nativity, language competence, and racial self-identification. In other words, if after controlling for socioeconomic characteristics, nativity, language competence, and racial self-identification, the results of the regression reveal statistically significant differences associated with "national origin," this would mean that Puerto Ricans differ from Anglos because of ethnic characteristics other than those included in the analysis.

The data are from the Latino National Political Survey (LNPS), which interviewed a nationally representative sample of Mexican, Cubans, and Puerto Ricans between August 1989 and February 1990.[14] The survey also interviewed 456 Anglos (non-Hispanic whites) residing in the primary sampling units from which the Latino sample was drawn. LNPS includes 589 Puerto Ricans who are representative of 90.2 percent of all Puerto Ricans eighteen and over residing in the continental United States. A respondent was defined as Puerto Rican if he, one parent, or two grandparents were solely of Puerto Rican ancestry.

The sample was specifically designed to include respondents from across the nation and from across the social spectrum. Seventy-two percent of Puerto Rican respondents reside in the Northeast, 15 percent in Florida, 9 percent in the Midwest,and the remainder are divided between the Southwest including Texas (1 percent) and the West Coast (3 percent). One-fourth of all Puerto Rican respondents come from low-density areas (5–20 percent), 25 percent from areas in which Latino households constitute 20–49 percent of the area, and half reside in majority Latino areas. Additionally, the analysis incorporates population weights so that the sample accurately reflects the demographics of each group. Puerto Rican respondents had the choice of being interviewed in English or Spanish, and 60.4 percent chose Spanish.

The independent variables used in the analysis are divided into socio-demographic and ethnic indicators (see table 14.1). The former includes gender, religious affiliation, household income, education, occupation, and age. The latter include national origin, nativity, self-rated language competence, and racial self-identity.

Ethnicity is a multidimensional and dynamic social construction that combines objective and subjective dimensions that include but transcend national origin.[15] Thus, different individuals from the same national origin group may vary in the extent to which they manifest ethnic characteristics,

TABLE 14.1
Puerto Rican and Anglo Sociodemographic and Ethnic Characteristics (Percentages)

			Puerto Rican	
	Anglo	*Puerto Rican*	*Foreign born*	*Native born*
Nativity				
Foreign born	4.5	65.7	—	—
Native born	95.5	34.3	—	—
Racial identity				
Non-Latino	100.0	62.3	66.8	53.5
White	0.0	0.0	(62.9)	(48.8)
Black	0.0	0.0	(3.9)	(4.7)
Latino referent	0.0	37.7	33.2	46.5
Language ability				
English dominant	100.0	20.7	7.8	45.5
Bilingual	—	45.1	43.3	49.0
Spanish dominant	—	34.2	49.0	5.9
Gender				
Female	52.3	55.6	57.6	51.7
Male	47.7	44.4	60.3	43.9
Age				
18–24	13.2	20.4	10.4	39.5
25–34	22.8	28.8	21.5	43.0
35–50	27.7	31.7	40.6	14.6
51–65	15.6	12.6	19.0	0.3
66+	20.7	6.5	8.6	2.6
Education				
0–8 yrs	1.1	30.1	41.0	9.5
9–12, no degree	24.3	21.8	19.4	26.5
High school diploma or				
GED	54.7	37.0	30.5	49.3
Post-high school educ.	19.9	11.1	9.2	14.7
Work status				
Not in labor force	31.1	37.8	42.1	29.7
Unemployed	5.0	12.1	10.6	15.0
Employed	63.9	50.2	47.3	55.2
Religious affiliation				
Catholic	21.3	65.2	67.9	59.9
Protestant	54.1	22.3	23.1	20.7
Other/no preference	24.7	12.5	9.0	19.4
Homeowner				
No	39.3	86.7	85.0	91.1
Yes	60.7	13.3	15.0	9.9

TABLE 14.1 *(cont.)*

| | Anglo | Puerto Rican | Puerto Rican | |
			Foreign born	Native born
Household size				
One	14.4	9.7	10.7	7.7
Two	40.4	19.1	17.5	22.0
Three	17.7	21.1	20.7	21.8
Four	12.3	19.0	17.2	22.4
Five plus	15.1	31.2	33.8	26.1
Household income				
$0–12,999	20.7	45.5	51.3	34.7
$13,000–19,999	12.1	17.0	15.7	19.4
$20,000–29,999	23.9	17.3	16.1	19.7
$30,000–39,999	15.7	11.5	10.3	13.6
$40,000–49,999	9.9	4.1	3.1	6.0
$50,000+	17.8	4.6	3.5	6.7
N^a	(456)	(589)	(387)	(202)

Note: Responses for individual categories may add up to more or less than 100 percent due to rounding.

[a] Totals for each variable may vary due to nonresponses.

that is, in their ethnicity. Therefore, to understand the social and political significance of ethnicity, it is necessary to operationalize it with measures that reflect these multiple characteristics.

The ethnic indicators used here tap three key objective and one subjective characteristic universally associated with Latino ethnicities. National origin, the most basic of our measures, identifies an individual's ancestral country of origin. Nativity indicates whether or not an indiviudal is an immigrant, a distinction that is central to understanding how ethnicities evolve.[16] Language competence is the cultural characteristic considered most central to ethnic maintenance and reproduction.[17] Here, language competence is measured by combining responses to two questions asking what language is usually spoken at home and what is the respondent's overall ability in the language other than the one in which the interview was conducted. This produced a nine-point scale that was collapsed into three categories: English dominant, bilingual, Spanish dominant.

Racial self-identity is an indicator of ethnicity's subjective dimensions. LNPS operationalized racial identification with the following item: Do you consider yourself white, black, or something else? Those who answered "something else" were asked to indicate what that was. Those who responded referring to Spanish or Latin American origin labels or to "brown" colors were categorized as "Latino referents."

In combination, these ethnic variables suggest the degree to which an individual has been socialized into mainstream U.S. society. At one end of the spectrum are the foreign born, Spanish dominant, and those identifying in non-Latino terms. At the other end are Anglos and Puerto Ricans who are native born, English dominant, and who identify racially with Latino referents.

We associate those Puerto Ricans who identify racially as white or black (non-Latino terms) with maintaining an unincorporated perspective because Puerto Ricans have historically identified in these terms.[18] In contrast, those who prefer a Latino racial identify seem to be taking on a new ethnic identity that differs from what traditional Puerto Rican society has historically produced. Minority group members who take on such new identities are usually well integrated into their host societies but are frustrated by their inability to participate fully in them. That is, they speak the majority language and are educated within the mainstream institutions, but they encounter prejudice and discrimination that prevents them from reaping the rewards of their efforts and achievements.[19] Puerto Ricans who identify racially as Latinos may be following this pattern.

Analysis

Ethnic and Socioeconomic Characteristics

As table 14.1 illustrates, the socioeconomic and ethnic characteristics of native- and foreign-born Puerto Ricans and Anglos best meet the assumptions of the politicized ethnicity hypothesis. That is, while Anglo educational and income attainment is higher than that of Puerto Ricans regardless of how they are classified, the gaps between foreign- and native-born Puerto Ricans are equal to or greater than those between the native born and Anglos. However, the native born do not do as well relative to Anglos as their education and language competence would predict. While approximately 65 percent have at least a high school education, 53 percent have household incomes of less than $20,000. Among Anglos, close to 75 percent have at least a high school degree, but the percentage of those with household incomes below $20,000 drops to almost 32 percent. Also, while native- and foreign-born Puerto Ricans both include a high percentage of bilinguals, the small percentage of native born who are Spanish dominant is matched by the small numbers of English-dominant foreign born. And, almost half of the native born are likely to identify racially as Latinos, while only a third of the foreign born did so.

Economic Individualism

Economic individualism is defined as the willingness to assign to individuals rather than to government the responsiblity for providing housing, income, and jobs. Whether poor or rich, black or white, Americans agree that an individual's success is primarily determined by her own effort, and that the poor are to blame for their poverty. Furthermore, even the poor prefer individual efforts to governmental or other collective initiatives to overcome poverty.[20] Most Americans also resist government-sponsored housing, jobs, and guaranteed income programs because of their belief in economic individualism.[21]

Each of the three hypotheses described previously offers a different prediction regarding Puerto Rican support for these three indicators of economic individualism. If the degenerated culture hypothesis is correct,

> Puerto Ricans, regardless of within group differences in ethnic characteristics, support economic individualism less than Anglos.

According to the politicized ethnic hypothesis,

> Puerto Rican support for economic individualism declines as individuals become more knowledgeable about American society. Thus Puerto Ricans who are native born, English dominant, and Latino identifiers will be less supportive of economic individualism than Anglos and than Puerto Ricans who are foreign born, Spanish dominant, and non-Latino identifiers.

According to the immigrant hypothesis,

> Puerto Ricans per se are supportive of economic individualism, but the native born, English dominant, and Latino identifiers are more so than the foreign born, Spanish dominant, and non-Latino identifiers. Anglos, however, are the most supportive.

To measure support for economic individualism, respondents were asked to indicate where they placed themselves on each of three five-point scales that had the following items as end points:

A. 1. The government should provide jobs for everyone who wants a job.
   5. It's up to each person to get his own job.
B. 1. Individuals should provide their own housing.
   5. The government should provide housing to anyone who needs it.
C. 1. The government should guarantee every person or family a minimum income, even if no one in the family can work.
   5. People should work and earn their own income.

TABLE 14.2

Agent Responsible for Jobs, Housing and Income, by National Origin, Nativity, Racial Identity, and Language Ability (Percentages)

| | National Origin | | Puerto Rican | | | | | | |
| | | | Nativity | | Language | | | Racial Identity | |
	Anglo	Puerto Rican	Foreign Born	Native Born	Spanish Dominant	Bilingual	English Dominant	Latino	Non-Latino
Who should provide jobs?									
1 Government	8.3	30.4	31.9	27.7	38.5	30.6	16.5	30.4	29.7
2	8.1	9.6	8.8	11.1	9.6	10.8	6.7	12.9	8.1
3	31.7	28.4	24.7	35.2	16.8	31.3	40.8	26.5	29.6
4	18.7	4.6	4.2	5.6	4.0	3.3	8.9	2.4	5.3
5 individual	33.3	27.0	30.5	20.4	31.1	23.9	27.1	27.8	27.2
N^a	(442)	(587)	(387)	(202)	(201)	(266)	(122)	(212)	(350)
Who should provide housing?									
1 Government	16.9	45.3	48.7	38.9	57.3	41.7	33.0	47.5	44.0
2	13.9	12.8	12.7	12.8	6.9	14.4	18.8	11.3	13.2
3	38.0	25.8	20.5	35.9	22.0	27.6	28.4	24.1	26.9
4	11.7	4.2	3.3	6.1	4.9	2.4	7.4	4.6	4.0
5 individual	19.4	11.9	14.8	6.2	8.9	13.8	12.3	12.5	11.9
N^a	(444)	(585)	(385)	(202)	(201)	(265)	(122)	(212)	(349)
Who should provide income?									
1 Government	10.5	24.1	25.5	21.2	29.4	25.5	12.2	25.5	23.6
2	9.7	9.8	9.6	10.0	9.9	8.8	11.6	8.1	11.2
3	33.2	31.2	31.0	31.8	28.7	31.5	34.9	29.9	32.5
4	18.9	7.3	5.8	10.0	3.7	8.5	10.3	8.6	7.0
5 individual	27.7	27.6	28.1	27.0	28.3	25.6	31.0	27.8	25.6
N^a	(441)	(585)	(385)	(202)	(200)	(266)	(122)	(212)	(375)

Note: Responses for individual categories may add up to more or less than 100 percent due to rounding.

[a] Totals for each variable may vary due to nonresponses.

As table 14.2 illustrates, Anglos are much more likely to support individual responsibility for each of these measures than are Puerto Ricans, regardless of how they are categorized. Among Puerto Ricans, the patterns associated with ethnic differences are less consistent. Overall, the foreign born, Spanish dominant, and non-Latino racial identifiers are more likely to favor governmental intervention in each of these areas, while the native born, English dominant, and Latino identifiers tend somewhat toward favoring individual responsiblity. These patterns are most obvious when comparing Spanish- and English-dominant respondents.

These patterns are most supportive of the immigrant hypothesis. That is, as Puerto Ricans incorporate into U.S. society, their support for economic individualism increases. Thus, the native born are much less supportive of governmental intervention than are the foreign born, and as respondents move from Spanish to bilingualism to English, their support for governmental intervention declines. However, compared to Anglos, the English dominant are ambivalent about the extent to which individuals should be responsible for these needs. This latter view is compatible with both the immigrant and politicized ethnic arguments.

To determine the independent effect that the ethnic variables have on these attitudes, the dependent variables were regressed on the sociodemographic and ethnic indicators in table 14.1.[22] First, Puerto Ricans were analyzed in isolation from Anglos, and then Puerto Ricans and Anglos were analyzed together.

Whether Puerto Ricans are analyzed separately or together with Anglos, ethnic characteristics do not have statistically significant independent effects on support for economic individualism.[23] The only exception to this is that when Puerto Ricans are analyzed separately, the native born are more supportive than the foreign born of individualism. Contrary to all three hypotheses, these results indicate ethnic characteristics do not affect support for economic individualism.

Democratic Values and Patriotism

Our focus here is on support for democratic values as measured through political tolerance, trust in government, and patriotism. Political tolerance is a tenet of American politics, despite the fact that Americans articulate substantial amounts of intolerance.[24] Trust in government is essential to the functioning of a democratic polity. Furthermore, declines in recent years notwithstanding,[25] Americans have long been characterized by high levels of trust in government. Patriotism is a measure of support for the nation. Because of the nation's heterogeneous cultural foundation, American identity is defined in political terms. To prove their "Americanism," therefore, citizens regularly proclaim their love for and pride in the nation, and a "good American" is expected to be patriotic[26] and to defend the nation against its critics.[27]

Democratic Values and Political Norms

PATRIOTISM

A 1990 National Opinion Research Center (NORC) survey found that Americans perceive "Hispanics" to be the least patriotic of six groups considered.[28] This image is consonant with the rhetoric of the Official English movement and some elected officials that describes Spanish speakers as threatening national unity because of their unwillingness to integrate into mainstream society.[29]

More than any other Latino population, Puerto Ricans have a unique and troubled relationship to the United States.[30] Their country acquired as a territory following the Spanish-American War, Puerto Ricans expected their nation to become independent, as Cuba had. Instead, it remained an American territory. Then in 1917, Puerto Ricans were granted U.S. citizenship even though they did not seek it. This citizenship, however, was of limited significance since those who remained in Puerto Rico could neither elect their own officials nor vote in U.S. elections. Furthermore, Puerto Ricans who came to the mainland also had limited electoral opportunities since they were Spanish speakers, and the franchise could be limited to English speakers. Although Puerto Ricans began electing their own governor in 1948 and drafted a constitution in 1950, the creation of commonwealth status in 1952 perpetuated disenfranchisement; Puerto Ricans who remained in Puerto Rico could not participate in U.S. elections.

There is some debate about how the status of the island affected Puerto Rican political participation in New York, where most Puerto Ricans have historically resided. Although Puerto Ricans developed community organizations and were electorally engaged in local politics early in the century,[31] the Puerto Rican government maintained an active presence in these neighborhoods. This presence, combined with either Puerto Ricans' realistic expectation of returning or their continuous experience of circular migration, dampened Puerto Rican engagement with politics in New York and the nation.[32] Further spurring disengagement was the disdain with which the major parties, especially the Democrats, viewed Puerto Ricans.[33]

Puerto Rican engagement with mainland governmental institutions dramatically increased as the number of mainland and island-born settlers reached a critical mass in the late 1960s. At that point, activist organizations began demanding that U.S. institutions respond to Puerto Rican needs,[34] and this reduced but did not eliminate the role of commonwealth offices in Puerto Rican political life.

The status of Puerto Rico remains unsettled, however, and this gives rise to conflicting loyalties among Puerto Ricans just as it did among the Mexican population in the Southwest after 1848.[35] Then, the Mexican government offered inducements to persuade residents of the lands lost in the war to return to Mexico, and Mexicans had to decide whether they would remain Mexican and return or become Americans and stay. Puerto Ricans face an even more difficult dilemma: not only must they decide whether to stay in the United States or return to the island, they also have to decide the terms that will govern the existence of their homeland—that is, among statehood, independence and commonwealth status.

Puerto Ricans, thus, may not voice strong patriotism. Their deep attachment to the Puerto Rican nation, the lack of political opportunity historically available to Puerto Ricans in the United States, and the fact that even though they are citizens, they have limited political rights as long as they remain in Puerto Rico may prevent Puerto Ricans from developing deep political attachments to the United States. Also, as indicated by the assassination attempt on President Harry Truman, *independistas* consider the United States to be their nation's oppressor and enemy. Although they have long been a small minority,[36] independistas continue to influence Puerto Rican political dialogues.

This history may result in Puerto Ricans of all backgrounds and ideological views expresing less patriotism than Anglos do. Nonethless, ethnic characteristics could exacerbate these sentiments. Thus, the degenerated culture hypothesis is:

Puerto Ricans, especially the foreign born, Spanish, dominant, and non-Latino identifiers, voice less patriotism than do Anglos.

The politicized ethnicty hypothesis is:

Puerto Ricans, especially the native born, English dominant, and Latino identifiers, voice less patriotism than do Anglos.

The immigrant hypothesis is:

Puerto Ricans who are native born, English dominant, and non-Latino identifiers voice patriotism comparable to Anglos, while the foreign born, Spanish dominant, and Latino identifiers voice lower patriotism than do Anglos.

Two items were used to measure patriotism: (1) How strong is your love for the United States: extremely strong, very strong, somewhat strong, or not very strong? (2) How proud are you to be an American: extremely proud, very proud, somewhat proud, or not very proud? The responses were combined into a scale ranging from 1 to 7, as shown in table 14.3.

TABLE 14.3
Patriotism by National Origin, Nativity, Language Ability, and Racial Identity (Percentages)

| | National Origin | | Puerto Rican | | | | | | | |
| | | | Nativity | | Language | | | Racial Identity | |
Patriotism	Anglo	Puerto Rican	Foreign Born	Native Born	Spanish Dominant	Bilingual	English Dominant	Latino	Non-Latino
1 Weak	0.3	1.7	1.7	1.8	3.2	0.7	1.5	1.3	2.1
2	1.5	2.0	2.3	1.5	3.8	1.7	0.0	3.1	0.4
3	2.4	11.5	12.4	9.9	15.4	10.3	8.0	10.2	14.9
4	6.6	14.6	14.9	14.1	13.8	17.8	9.1	11.9	16.5
5	24.8	32.9	36.9	25.6	35.2	34.6	25.9	32.2	34.3
6	19.5	11.3	11.8	10.2	8.4	11.8	14.3	11.3	11.4
7 Strong	44.9	25.9	20.0	36.9	20.2	23.1	41.2	30.1	20.4
N	(442)	(576)	(374)	(303)	(192)	(261)	(122)	(206)	(344)

Note: Responses for individual categories may add up to more or less than 100 percent due to rounding.

Overall, these responses support the immigrant hypothesis. Although Anglos are more likely to express high patriotism than are Puerto Ricans, regardless of how the latter are categorized, patriotism among Puerto Ricans increases as English competence goes up and is much higher among the native born than the foreign born. However, as predicted by the politicized ethnicity hypothesis, non-Latino racial identifiers express higher patriotism than Latino identifiers do.

Further analysis support these findings.[37] That is, nativity and language competence have independent, statistically significant effects on patriotism. Whether Puerto Ricans are analyzed separately or together with Anglos, the native born, non-Latino identifiers and those who know English (English dominant and bilinguals) express higher patriotism at statistically significant levels than do the foreign born, Latino identifiers, and Spanish dominant.

It is especially noteworthy that when Puerto Ricans and Anglos are analyzed together, national origin yields no statistically significant relationship to patriotism. In other words, there is no evidence that any ethnic characteristic other than language ability, nativity, and racial identification explains the difference between Anglos' and Puerto Ricans' patriotism.

These results support the immigrant hypothesis and, to a lesser extent, the politicized ethnicity hypothesis. As the former predicts, Puerto Ricans who learn English and are mainland born are more patriotic. However, even if they have these characteristics, if they identify racially as Latinos, they are likely to express less patriotism than those who identify as either black or white.

TRUST IN GOVERNMENT

It is unclear how Puerto Ricans should respond to question regarding trust in government. Puerto Rico is a democracy where between 80 and 90 percent of the electorate votes. To the extent of its resources, the government of Puerto Rico appears to be accountable and responsive. In the United States, however, Puerto Ricans have been victims of discrimination that was either sponsored or tolerated by government agencies. For example, it was not until the early 1970s that Spanish monolinguals could vote in New York elections. Thus, on the mainland the political process has not reached out to them, they are underrepresented electorally, and government has not provided the public services they need.[38]

These experiences are likely to be reflected in Puerto Rican atitudes toward government. It is not clear how the degenerated culture hypothesis would incorporate their perspectives. According to this hypothesis, reliance on governmental programs such as this view posits could produce high trust in government; conversely, such reliance could generate distrust if it creates unmet expectations.

The politicized ethnicity and immigrant hypotheses are more easily formulated. The former states:

> Puerto Ricans have lower trust of government than do Anglos; the native born, English dominant, and Latino identifiers have lower trust than do the foreign born, Spanish dominant, and non-Latino identifiers.

The immigrant hypotheis is:

> Puerto Ricans who are foreign born, Spanish dominant, and non-Latino identifiers are more trusting of government than are either the native born, English dominant, and non-Latino identifiers or Anglos.

Two items were used to measure trust in government: (1) How much of the time do you think you can trust government officials to do what is right: just about always, most of the time, some of the time, or almost never? (2) Would you say that the government generally is run by a few people looking out for their own interest or is run for the benefit of all? The responses were combined into a five-point scale as illustrated in table 14.4.

The results again tend to support the immigrant hypothesis. Although Puerto Ricans overall voice higher trust in government than Anglos do, this is especially true of the foreign born and Spanish dominant. Differences in racial identity appear to be unrelated to trust in government.

Further analysis reinforces these patterns.[39] Whether analyzed separately or compared with the data on Anglos, the only ethnic characteristic that has a statistically significant, independent effect on trust is language ability—that is, the English dominant are significantly less trusting than the Spanish dominant. Again, it is noteworthy that when we analyze Puerto Ricans and Anglos together, after controlling for language, racial identity, and nativity, we find that differences in national origin have no independent, statistically significant effect on the extent to which an individual trusts government.

POLITICAL TOLERANCE

The American record on political tolerance is mixed. Although the nation is rhetorically committed to it, in practice American politics is replete with examples of intolerance.[40] Puerto Rico, on the other hand, has a history of intense political debates over issues such as the status of Puerto Rico and the official language policy and has very high levels of electoral participation.[41] That these have been conducted without recurring violence suggests that Puerto Ricans have high levels of political tolerance. Puerto Rican society is also more racially tolerant than is U.S. society.[42] Furthermore,

TABLE 14.4

Trust in Government, by National Origin, Nativity, Language Ability, and Racial Identity (Percentages)

| | National Origin | | Puerto Rican | | | | | | | | |
| | | | Nativity | | Language | | | Racial Identity | |
Trust in Government	Anglo	Puerto Rican	Foreign Born	Native Born	Spanish Dominant	Bilingual	English Dominant	Latino	Non-Latino
1 Low	1.2	2.3	2.1	2.9	3.7	2.4	0.0	4.3	1.3
2	24.0	27.5	27.5	27.5	23.4	27.6	34.1	23.3	27.9
3	65.8	48.6	45.7	54.3	44.0	47.5	58.9	50.2	48.9
4	8.0	19.0	21.2	14.7	25.2	19.6	7.0	18.1	19.9
5 High	0.0	2.5	3.5	0.7	3.6	2.9	0.0	4.0	1.9
(N)	(550)	(408)	(361)	(189)	(193)	(240)	(116)	(191)	(333)

Note: Responses for individual categories may add up to more or less than 100 percent due to rounding.

Puerto Ricans have been victims of discrimination, a factor that may enhance their tolerance. That is, they may be inclined to treat others as they would like to be treated.

Political tolerance was measured using the following items developed by Sullivan, Pierson, and Marcus:[43]

> There are many controversial groups in the United States. From the groups that I name and the ones that you think of, select the one group you dislike the most.

> Tell us how strongly you agree or disagree with the following statements: Members of (selected group) (1) should not be allowed to hold elective office in the United States, (2) should be allowed to teach in public schools, (3) should be allowed to hold public rallies in our city.

The responses to items 2 and 3 yielded a scale and were scored in combination; item 1 was scored independently because it did not make up part of that scale.

Again, the degenerated culture hypothesis offers little guidance regarding political tolerance. The politicized ethnicity and immigrant hypotheses are more straightforward. According to the former:

> Puerto Ricans, especially the English speaking, native born, and Latino identifiers, are more politically tolerant than are Anglos.

According to the latter:

> Puerto Ricans, especially the Spanish dominant, foreign born, and non-Latino identifiers, are more tolerant than are Anglos.

"Traditional" Puerto Ricans differ from Americanized Puerto Ricans and Anglos regarding disliked groups. If the Ku Klux Klan and nazis are combined, Anglos and Puerto Ricans who are native born, English dominant, and Latino racial identifiers have very similar dislikes. Gays and communists, however, are the primary concern for the foreign born, Spanish speakers, and non-Latino identifiers (see table 14.5).

Although neither group voices much tolerance, Anglos, contrary to our hypotheses, are more tolerant than are Puerto Ricans. Among Puerto Ricans, the native born, English dominant, and Latino identifiers are more willing to allow groups they disagree with to hold rallies and teach, as the politicized ethnicity hypothesis predicts. The foreign born and Spanish speakers, however, are more likely to allow such groups to hold office, which the immigrant hypothesis predicted (see table 14.6).

Further analysis supports neither hypothesis.[44] When Puerto Ricans are analyzed separately, ethnic characteristics manifest no statistically significant, independent relationship to political tolerance. When Puerto Ricans and Anglos are analyzed together, nativity and racial identification do have

TABLE 14.5
Most Disliked Groups, by National Origin, Nativity, Language Ability, and Racial Identity (Percentages)

| | National Origin | | Puerto Rican | | | | | | | |
| | | | Nativity | | Language | | | Racial Identity | |
Most Disliked Group	Anglo	Puerto Rican	Foreign Born	Native Born	Spanish Dominant	Bilingual	English Dominant	Latino	Non-Latino
Communists	14.9	22.4	27.8	12.0	32.2	17.3	17.4	21.5	23.6
Nazis	31.2	9.9	8.5	12.6	9.1	9.5	12.4	9.7	9.8
KKK	32.8	36.8	24.7	59.7	16.7	43.2	55.9	42.2	32.8
Gays	7.9	21.3	27.7	9.1	27.0	23.6	6.5	19.0	23.6
Black Muslims	2.4	1.2	1.2	1.2	1.9	1.1	0.2	0.3	1.8
English	—	3.2	4.6	0.5	6.2	2.3	0.2	2.7	3.7
Atheist	6.6	3.8	4.3	2.8	5.8	1.6	5.4	2.4	4.4
Other/don't know	4.3	1.4	1.1	2.0	1.1	1.4	2.0	2.2	0.4
(N)	(456)	(589)	(387)	(202)	(201)	(266)	(122)	(212)	(350)

Note: Responses for individual categories may add up to more or less than 100 percent due to roundings.

TABLE 14.6
Political Tolerance, by National Origin, Nativity, Language Ability, and Racial Identity (Percentages)

| | National Origin | | Puerto Rican | | | | | | |
| | | | Nativity | | Language | | | Racial Identity | |
Allow Disliked Group to:	Anglo	Puerto Rican	Foreign Born	Native Born	Spanish Dominant	Bilingual	English Dominant	Latino	Non-Latino
Hold rallies/teach									
1 Low	33.6	32.8	34.1	30.5	31.0	34.0	32.9	29.9	34.5
2	14.1	12.5	11.5	14.3	11.6	13.1	12.6	11.6	12.8
3	24.4	35.4	39.6	27.5	42.3	36.2	22.5	37.1	35.0
4	16.9	11.7	8.8	17.3	8.7	9.9	20.9	10.9	12.1
5	8.8	4.6	4.4	5.0	4.2	3.9	6.7	4.7	4.2
6	1.2	0.6	0.1	1.5	0.2	1.2	0.0	0.9	0.4
7 High	1.0	2.4	1.6	3.9	1.9	1.8	4.4	4.9	1.0
(N)	(438)	(559)	(365)	(195)	(192)	(251)	(116)	(204)	(333)
Hold Office									
1 Strongly agree	56.6	48.9	7.4	4.1	4.9	8.5	3.8	6.7	6.4
2 Agree	24.7	34.6	12.0	7.0	12.4	8.5	10.2	10.9	9.3
3 Disagree	13.7	10.2	37.2	29.7	40.2	34.1	26.8	37.4	33.1
4 Strongly disagree	5.0	7.4	43.4	59.2	42.6	49.0	59.3	44.9	51.2
(N)[a]	(438)	(568)	(369)	(199)	(191)	(257)	(119)	(207)	(338)

Note: Responses for individual categories may add up to more or less than 100 percent due to rounding.
[a] Totals for each variable may vary due to nonresponses.

an independent, statistically significant effect on political tolerance. The native born and Latino racial identifiers express more tolerance regarding the rights of disliked groups to hold rallies and to teach than the foreign born and non-Latino identifiers, which the politicized ethnicity hypothesis predicts.

The pattern concerning tolerance of disliked groups holding public office is different. It is the only instance in which national origin has an independent effect on tolerance. That is, regardless of their nativity, language, racial identity, and socioeconomic characteristics, Puerto Ricans are less willing than Anglos to have members of groups they dislike hold office.

Discussion

Mainstream America perceives "Hispanics" to be unsupportive of the nation's core values. Because Puerto Ricans are the nation's poorest Hispanic population and have the most troubled political relationship to the nation, they are the Latino population most likely to fit this national stereotype. This study evaluated the validity of this image by analyzing Puerto Rican and Anglo support for economic individualism, patriotism, trust in government, and political tolerance.

The results suggest several conclusions. First, Anglos are more supportive of these values than Puerto Ricans are. The exception to this is that Puerto Ricans express higher trust in government than Anglos do. Second, the extent to which ethnic factors shape these differences is neither substantial nor consistent. Third, when ethnic factors do affect support for these values, they do so in ways that parallel the history of European ethnics. That is, support for these values increases as Puerto Ricans incorporate into U.S. society—that is, become native born and learn English. Fourth, racial identity does not consistently or substantially affect support for these values. Fifth, with one minor exception, there is almost no evidence that any ethnic characteristics other than language, nativity, and racial identity affect Puerto Rican support for these values.

This means that Puerto Ricans and Anglos who are similarly situated are equally supportive of core American values. In other words, Anglos and Puerto Ricans who are native born and English dominant have comparable education and income, are equally patriotic, trusting of government, supportive of economic individualism, and willing to allow members of groups they dislike to hold rallies and teach in public schools. Puerto Ricans who express lower support for these values tend to be those who are foreign born and Spanish dominant. As they and their mainland-born children learn English, their support for these values becomes indistinguishable from that of Anglos who find themselves in similar socioeconomic conditions. We hope these findings will help dismiss the stereotype that portrays Puerto Ricans in particular and Latinos in general as unpatriotic, undemocratic, and unsupportive of economic individualism.

Finally, this study makes clear the need to conceptualize and operationalize ethnicity in multidimensional terms that include national origin and other characteristics. Our results suggest that there may be no need to expand beyond the four ethnic indicators used here. Unless such an approach is used, it will be impossible to go beyond stereotypes when attempting to explain how ethnicity affects sociopolitical behavior.

Notes

1. Tocqueville 1945; Fuchs 1991; Lipset 1964; Huntington 1983; Sniderman and Hagen 1985.
2. T. Smith 1990, 3; Bean and Tienda 1988, 2.
3. Moore and Pachon 1985.
4. Glazer and Moynihan 1963.
5. Chavez 1991.
6. T. Smith 1990.
7. A. Smith 1981; Yancy, Ericksen, and Juliani 1976.
8. Isaacs 1989.
9. Although all Puerto Ricans are U.S. citizens by birth, island-born Puerto Ricans share the demographic and cultural characteristics of Latino American immigrants. Therefore, for analytical purposes in this paper, Puerto Ricans born in Puerto Rico are considered as foreign born and are treated as immigrants. Puerto Ricans born in the United States are defined as native born.
10. Glazer and Moynihan 1963.
11. Chavez 1991, 139–59.
12. A. Smith 1981.
13. Fuchs 1991.
14. de la Garza et al., 1992.
15. Barth 1969; A. Smith 1981.
16. Alvarez 1984; Portes 1984.
17. Keefe and Padilla 1987.
18. Rodriguez 1989.
19. Smith 1981.
20. Feldman 1988; Kinder and Sears 1985, 675.
21. Feldman 1983.
22. The dependent variable was dichotomized into support for governmental responsiblity (categories 1 and 2) and support for individual responsiblity (categories 4 and 5). Category 3 was removed from these analyses. Four multiple logistic regressions were run for each dependent variable, two that included only Puerto Ricans, and two that included Puerto Ricans and Anglos. In both cases, because racial identity may derive from the other independent variables, the first regression

included all the independent variables except racial identification, and the second included it and the other independent variables. We report only the results of the second, noting any statistically significant changes that resulted from adding racial identity. The results are available from the author upon request.

23. Statistically significant effects are those with a P-value of equal to or less than 0.05.

24. Sullivan, Pierson, and Marcus 1982, 33–51.

25. Abramson 1983, 193–94.

26. T. Smith 1990.

27. Delameter, Katz, and Kelman 1969.

28. T. Smith 1990.

29. de la Garza and Trujillo 1989; Fuchs 1991, 255.

30. Moore and Pachon 1985, 31.

31. Rodriguez-Morazzani (1991–92); Falcon 1984.

32. Jennings 1988, 69–75; Glazer and Moynhihan 1963, 98–109.

33. Baver 1984, 43–60.

34. Rodriguez-Morazzani 1991–92; Baver 1984; Rivera 1984.

35. Weber 1973.

36. U.S. Commission on Civil Rights 1976, 14–15.

37. The analysis consisted of ordinary least squares regression using the same variables as those used to analyze support for economic individualism. Results are available from the author upon request.

38. Baver 1984; Falcon 1984.

39. See n. 37.

40. Fuchs 1991; Sullivan, Pierson, and Marcus 1982.

41. Jennings, 1988.

42. Rodriguez-Morazzani 1991–1992.

43. Sullivan, Pierson, and Marcus 1982.

44. The analysis of attitudes regarding allowing rallies and teaching consisted of an ordinary least squares regression; logistic regression was used to analyze "holding office." Both equations use the same variables that were used to analyze support for economic individualism. Results are available from the author upon request.

15

Race, Ethnicity, and Political Participation

SIDNEY VERBA, KAY LEHMAN SCHLOZMAN,
AND HENRY BRADY

DEMOCRACY RESTS on the fundamental ideal of the equal consideration of the needs and preferences of each citizen. Political participation is the mechanism by which those needs and preferences are communicated to political decision makers and by which pressure is brought to bear on them to respond. Thus, equality in political participation—embodied in the most obvious principle of equal consideration of citizen preferences: one person, one vote—would seem to be a necessary condition for democracy.

This paper compares the political participation of three groups defined by their race or ethnicity—African Americans, Latinos, and whites[1]—in order to understand from whom and what the government hears. Because Americans have a rich array of participatory alternatives for expressing their concerns to public officials, we construe political participation quite broadly and consider forms of activity that go well beyond the traditional focus on the vote. Since we seek to delineate the actual content of what activists say, we pay particular attention to modes of activity that have the capacity to carry messages to the government so that we can discern the extent to which there are racial and ethnic differences in the issues that animate political participation. Lastly, we shall consider participation in nonpolitical domains, forms of voluntary activity that not only are intrinsically interesting but have political implications.

Participation and Democracy

Of course, in no democracy, including the United States, are all citizens equally active in politics. Whether disparities in participation constitute a violation of the principle of equal protection of interests, however, rests upon two fundamental considerations: the extent to which those who are not involved differ in politically salient ways from those who are and the extent to which their abstention is the result of free and voluntary choice. With respect to the former, if activists are representative of all citizens in terms of their preferences and needs for government action, it would matter little that some citizens take part and others do not; the participants could speak effectively for those who are more quiescent. When it comes to the groups in question here, however, it is well known that African Americans, Latinos, and whites do differ in their attitudes on political matters, partisan affiliations, vote choices, and needs for government policy. Hence, any divergences in their rates of activity are of potential concern, and divergences in those activities which can communicate the most information about citizen preferences and apply the most pressure on the recipients of that communication—activities that have most clout—are of even greater concern.

The second consideration has to do with whether differences in participation reflect free choices. Failure to participate is not always evidence of voluntary abstention. American history is replete with examples of explicit denials of political rights. If equal participation is barred either by law or by informal political obstacles such as discriminatory literacy tests or all-white primaries, then inactivity is not the result of free choice and democracy is compromised. When such barriers are lifted—as they have been, by and large, in the United States—the situation becomes less clear. If some citizens opt not to take part in politics because they prefer to spend their time and money in other ways or because they do not care about public affairs, then there is less reason for concern if their views do not receive proportionate attention from political elites. But if they do not take part because they lack the resources that facilitate political activity, then these departures from the norm of political equality may pose a more serious challenge to democracy. In this case, inactives do not take part because they cannot, rather than because they do not want to. The differential activity levels across racial and ethnic groups that we shall document in this paper have many sources, but one of the prime ones is differential access to the resources that foster participation.[2]

The Citizen Participation Study

Our data come from a large-scale, two-stage survey of the voluntary activity of the American public. The study is unusual in focusing on voluntary activity not simply in politics but also in churches and organizations. In addition, we construed political participation quite broadly, including not only voting and other forms of electoral activity such as working in campaigns and making financial contributions but also contacting public officials, attending protests, and getting involved either formally or informally on local issues.

Ordinary surveys have inadequate numbers of African American or Latino respondents for analysis—especially the more active members of these groups. Our study is not as richly endowed as we would like but has a much larger pool of respondents. The first stage consisted of a 15,000-case random telephone survey of the American public. These short screener interviews provided a profile of political and nonpolitical activity as well as the basic demographic information. This survey produced 1,400 African American and 894 Latino respondents. We then conducted longer, in-person interviews with 2,517 of the original 15,000 respondents, weighting the sample so as to produce a disproportionate number of both activists as well as members of the two minority groups. The follow-up survey included 477 African Americans and 370 Latinos.[3] The data from the follow-up survey presented in this chapter have been weighted to produce an effective random sample.[4]

Who Participates? Political Activity

This chapter focuses on the political participation of three racial/ethnic groups in the United States: African Americans, Latinos, and whites. The first is a disadvantaged internal group that has faced centuries of political, social, and economic discrimination; the second a newer immigrant group facing similar disadvantage. Historically, minority groups in America—especially African Americans, but Latinos as well—have faced many legal and institutional barriers to full participation as citizens. However, the issue today is not one of the extension of the rights of participation to these groups: full citizenship rights have been available to African Americans since the passage of important civil rights legislation—in particular, the Voting Rights Act—during the 1960s, and similar rights accrue to Latinos once they become citizens, a difficult but not insuperable hurdle. Instead, the issue is the use of political rights once achieved, the extent to which these groups seek to and are able to take full advantage of the opportunity to participate in political life.[5]

The contrast between African Americans and Latinos is an intriguing one from the point of view of participation. Among the most significant transformations of American politics in recent decades has been the mobilization of African Americans. During the 1950s rates of activity for African Americans were substantially lower than for whites. Several factors—the lowering of de jure and de facto barriers to activity, mobilization by the Civil Rights movement, and the dramatic increase in the proportion of African Americans with higher levels of education and higher-status occupations—operated together to narrow the gap during the 1960s and early 1970s. Indeed, studies showed that, controlling for socioeconomic status, blacks participated as much as and perhaps more than whites.[6] In addition, the period has witnessed a substantial increase in the number of African

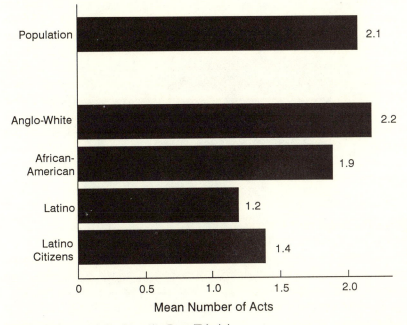

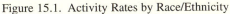

Figure 15.1. Activity Rates by Race/Ethnicity

Americans in political office and an enhanced role for African Americans in other political decision-making arenas.

Americans of Hispanic or Latino origin are among the fastest growing segments of the American population. In some areas of the country, they constitute a major group within the citizenry. There have been significant attempts to mobilize Latinos to political activity, particularly voter turnout drives in the Southwest and California. However, we would expect Latinos to be somewhat behind African Americans in terms of political mobilization. Like other immigrant groups, Latinos face special obstacles of language and legal status, and political movements among Latinos are of more recent vintage than the Civil Rights movement.

How do the three racial/ethnic groups compare in terms of their political activity? Figure 15.1, which shows the average number of political acts for the three groups on an additive scale of political activity,[7] indicates that African Americans and whites are fairly similar in participation. Latinos, in contrast, evince lower levels of overall activity. The difference is fairly large. However, by including all Latino respondents in our sample, the data probably overstate the Latino participatory deficit. In our study, we interviewed respondents regardless of their citizenship status. Twenty-two percent of the Latino respondents in our sample are not citizens. Since they are barred from voting—an activity that appears in the scale—it seems reason-

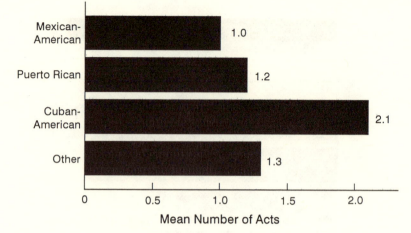

Figure 15.2. Activity Rates by Place of Origin, Latinos

able to look at the activity of Latino citizens separately.[8] Considering citizens only, the mean score for Latinos rises from 1.18 to 1.41. This narrows the gap but, nevertheless, leaves a substantial difference.[9]

Latinos are, of course, a diverse group. Figure 15.2 uses data from our larger screener survey to compare average overall participation scores for the main Latino subgroups—the majority who are of Mexican origin, as well as those whose roots are in Puerto Rico, Cuba, or other parts of Latin America (usually Central America). Americans of Cuban origin, on average, engage in about as many political acts as the national average—indeed, somewhat more. Those from Mexico, Puerto Rico, or other parts of Latin America are well below the national average.[10]

With some interesting variations, the pattern in figure 15.1 is replicated when we consider the various kinds of participation separately. Figure 15.3 compares the three racial/ethnic groups (plus Latino citizens) in terms of their involvement in electoral activity: voting, getting involved in campaigns, and making campaign contributions. For the three activities, the differences between African Americans and whites are small in magnitude and inconsistent in direction. African Americans are somewhat less likely than whites to report voting.[11] When it comes to activity within a campaign, African Americans are more likely to say that have worked in a campaign but less likely to say they have given money.[12] In each case, however, Latinos—even Latino citizens—are less active.

Figure 15.4, in turn, shows the proportion of these three groups engaging in various nonelectoral forms of participation: contacting public officials; attending protests, marches, or demonstrations; getting involved informally on local community issues; serving in an unpaid capacity on a local

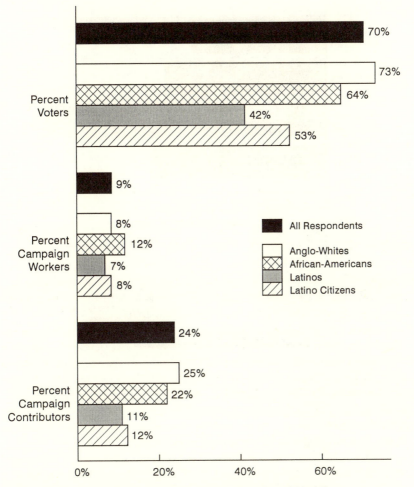

Figure 15.3. Activity Rates in Electoral Politics by Race/Ethnicity

community governing board—for example, a school or zoning board—or attending meetings of such a board; and being affiliated with—that is, being a member of or a contributor to—an organization that takes stands on political issues.[13] African Americans and whites are more or less equally active informally in their communities, with Latinos lagging somewhat. Latinos, however, are slightly more likely than blacks to report membership on a local board. The differences among the three groups with respect to a relatively common form of political participation, affiliation with an organization that takes stands in politics, are much larger: whites are considerably more likely than are African Americans and, especially, Latinos, regardless of citizenship, to be involved in a political organization.

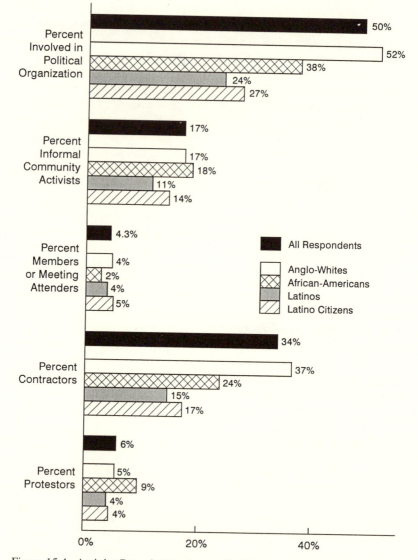

Figure 15.4. Activity Rates in Nonelectoral Politics by Race/Ethnicity

The figures for contacting and protesting bear closer scrutiny. These are both forms of political involvement that permit the communication of clear messages to policy makers; however, they differ in significant ways. While a larger proportion of the public engages in contacting than in protesting, contacting requires a higher level of communications skills than does attending a demonstration, a form of activity that was important to the American Civil Rights movement and that has often been considered to be the weapon of the weak.[14] Compared to protests, contacts with government officials permit the transmission of much more precise messages—including concerns about how policies affect an individual. In addition, while protests may be used as a device to promote minority group solidarity, getting in touch with a public official may require a minority group member to cross a racial or ethnic barrier: only 43 percent of the African American contactors ($N = 65$) reported that the official they contacted was also African American, and 29 percent of the Latino contactors ($N = 40$) reported that the official they contacted was also of Latino origin; in contrast, 94 percent of the whites ($N = 689$) indicated that the official they contacted was white.

The data in figure 15.4, which show a sharp contrast in the patterns for contacting and protesting, are consistent with these considerations, especially in relation to the comparison between African Americans and whites. The former are less likely to contact an official and more likely to protest than are the latter. Since overall levels of activity are quite similar between the two groups, it is interesting to note that the differences are quite substantial. The contrast in choice of activity may reflect the fact that African Americans are as politically mobilized and involved as the white portion of the population but have not received—or do not perceive themselves to have received—full acceptance. As usual, Latinos are the least active group. They are only slightly less likely than members of the white majority to report having protested, but substantially less likely to report having gotten in touch with a government official.[15]

The Volume of Activity

What the government hears depends not only on who is active but on how much they do. Voting is the single activity for which there is mandated equality; each citizen gets one vote. Otherwise, citizens are free to give more or less money and time, to write many or few letters, to attend many or few demonstrations. Table 15.1 shows, for those who are active, the amount of time or money the three groups devote to their activity as well as the average number of contacts or protests for those who engage in these activities. The data show a distinct difference between inputs of time and money. When it comes to giving time, minority activists are not less active than their white counterparts. Indeed, African Americans and Latinos who get involved in electoral campaigns give more hours per week than do the white activists. The situation is entirely different with respect to money. Among contributors, whites—who are, as we saw, slightly more likely than African Americans and considerably more likely than Latinos to make

TABLE 15.1
Voluntary Contributions of Time and Money by Race/Ethnicity

	Whites	African Americans	Latinos	Latino Citizens
Mean hours contributed to political campaigns (among those who give some time)	6.8	11.4	8.9	9.2
Mean dollars contributed to political campaigns (among those who give some money)	$257	$165	$177	$194
Mean number of contacts (among contactors)	1.7	1.7	1.8	1.8
Mean number of protests (among protesters)	2.0	2.3	2.0	1.8

campaign donations—give substantially more than African Americans or Latinos do when they contribute.[16]

When it comes to contacts and protests, Latinos, African Americans, and whites differ relatively little in the amount of their participation, once they have crossed the threshold to some activity. This is especially clear in relation to contacting. Whites are the most likely to have reported getting in touch with a government official. Among contactors, however, there is almost no difference in how frequently they do so. The data for protesting present a similar pattern. In this case, African Americans are more likely than members of the other groups to have reported attendance at a protest, march, or demonstration. Among protesters, they are also the most likely to protest frequently. However, the group differences in the amount of protest activity among protesters are not nearly as pronounced as the group differences in the likelihood of engaging in any protest.

These data show the special nature of making financial contributions in comparison to other activities. When it comes to political activity that demands time, members of disadvantaged groups (whether poor or racial/ ethnic minorities) are less likely than members of advantaged groups to cross the threshold to activity. However, once over the barrier, they are as active as their more advantaged counterparts. In contrast, when it comes to giving money, there is both a threshold effect (with the disadvantaged less likely to give anything at all) and a difference, among donors, in how much they give.[17]

What, then, does the American public look like in racial and ethnic terms if viewed through the lens of participation? In figure 15.5 we show the racial and ethnic composition of the citizenry, and compare that to what the

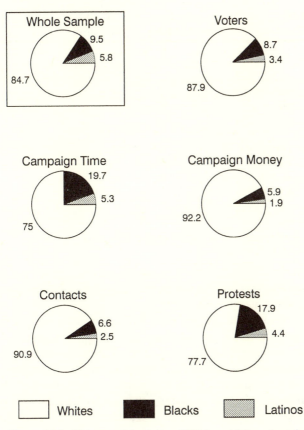

Figure 15.5. Volume of Activity of Whites, African Americans, and Latinos

citizenry would look like if a group's visibility depended on the amount of political activity it produced. The upper-left section of figure 15.5 presents, as a baseline, the distribution of the three racial/ethnic groups within the Citizen Participation Survey.[18] The other circle graphs on figure 15.5 show what the population would look like if the size of each group were proportional to the amount of activity emanating from its members: the number of votes cast; hours worked in campaigns; dollars contributed to candidates, parties, and campaign organizations; contacts with public officials; and protests attended.

Across all the tasks, Latinos are least visible in the activist populations. How visible the three groups are, however, depends upon the mode of activity. The voting population is the closest match in racial/ethnic terms to the population as a whole. African Americans are somewhat less well represented and Latinos substantially less well represented among voters, but the distortion is less than for other activities. Contacts and, especially, campaign dollars show the most pronounced disparities. They come quite unevenly from the three groups.

The patterns for African Americans show considerable variation. With respect to two forms of participatory input—the number of hours devoted to campaigns and the number of protests attended—they are overrepresented.[19] The greater frequency of protest activity may reflect a tradition dating back to the Civil Rights era. The contrast between the political activity of African Americans and Latinos is particularly striking with respect to protests. It is an activity available to those with few resources. However, African Americans use this weapon much more frequently than do Latinos.

Voluntary Activity outside Politics

Information about voluntary activity in the secular and religious domains outside of politics provides a revealing counterpoint to data about political participation. Involvement outside politics can have implications for political activity.[20] First, participation in these spheres—for example, organizing the book fair to raise money for the local PTA or serving on the religious education committee at church—can develop skills that are transferrable to politics even when the activity itself has nothing to do with politics. In addition, these nonpolitical institutions can act as the locus of attempts at political mobilization: church and organization members make social contacts and, thus, become part of networks through which requests for participation in politics are mediated. Moreover, those who take part in religious or organizational activity are exposed to political cues and messages—as when a minister gives a sermon on a political topic or when organization members chat informally about politics at a meeting. For members of groups that have faced constricted opportunities for advancement in the workplace, nonpolitical voluntary activity might assume particular significance in facilitating political involvement.

We begin by considering figure 15.6, which presents data about the involvement of Latinos, African Americans, and whites in nonpolitical organizations and charities.[21] With respect to affiliation with nonpolitical organizations, a familiar pattern emerges: a substantially lower level of activity for Latinos than for African Americans or, especially, whites. Latinos are less likely to be involved with such organizations and, in particular, to be active in or officers of nonpolitical organizations. In contrast, the differences between whites and African Americans are much smaller. A similar, though less pronounced, pattern obtains for charitable involvement.

Because they can work within a particular community, group-based or-

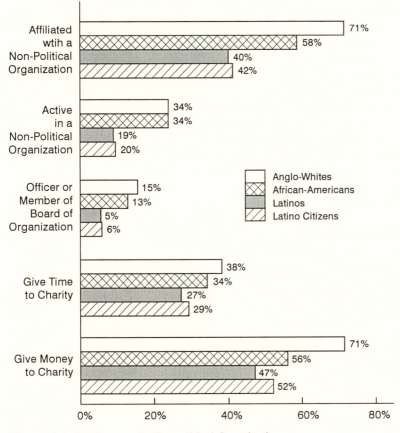

Figure 15.6. Involvement in Nonpolitical Organizations

ganizations can play a significant role for minorities, especially where there are barriers to full and open interaction between the dominant ethnic group and minority groups. Thus, African American or Latino organizations may be particularly significant for the provision of both services and opportunities to develop political skills and consciousness. In this connection, it is important to note that African Americans are more likely to take part in such organizations than are Latinos. Fourteen percent of the African American respondents indicated affiliation with an organization specifically identified with their race or with civil rights. (Nineteen percent of the African Americans affiliated with a nonpolitical organization reported involvement in at least one that has a racial connection.) In contrast, 5 percent of the Latinos (9 percent of those affiliated with a nonpolitical organization) indicated affiliation with a Latino-identified organization.[22]

In short, while whites and African Americans are fairly similar in their secular, nonpolitical participation, Latinos are considerably less active. In comparison to Latinos, African Americans are not only more likely to be involved with nonpolitical organizations, they are more likely to be involved with organizations identified with their own race.

Religious Activity

Religious activity in the United States is more widespread than in other industrialized nations. It is also the least stratified with respect to the representation of income groups. Affluent and poor are equally involved.[23] From the earliest days, the church was the only secondary institution available to African Americans.[24] Since churches can play a significant role not only as spiritual and social institutions but also in generating political involvement, their role for African Americans and Latinos in the United States bears examination.

The data on religious involvement are quite different from those on participation in more secular activities. Figure 15.7 presents data on attendance at church services, time spent on social, educational, or charitable activities within a church, as well as contributions of funds to church. In contrast to most of the other comparisons we have made, whites are not the most active group. By all three measures of religious involvement, African Americans are the most active. The pattern for Latinos is especially interesting. Although they attend church less frequently than do African Americans, their church attendance exceeds that of whites. However, Latinos are the least likely to take part when it comes to church activities beyond attendance at services. The pattern for Latinos is, thus, a puzzling one: a high level of church attendance coupled with a lower level of involvement in auxiliary church activities.

Part of the explanation for this pattern seems to lie in the fact that Latinos are much more likely than African Americans or whites to be Catholic rather than Protestant.[25] Protestant and Catholic churches differ—and Protestant denominations differ among themselves—along several dimensions that would seem to be relevant for the extent of lay participation in church matters: Protestant congregations tend, on average, to be smaller; most Protestant denominations allow for greater lay participation in the liturgy; and most Protestant denominations are organized on a congregational rather than a hierarchical basis. Table 15.2 shows that within all three of the racial/ethnic groups, the average Protestant is not necessarily more likely than the average Catholic to attend church regularly but is much more likely to engage in church-based activities. The relationship holds for all Protestants and Catholics as well as for regular church attenders.[26] Since

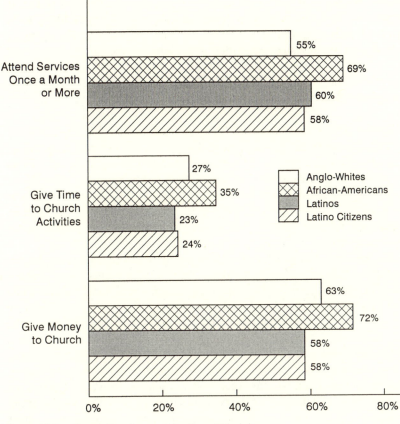

Figure 15.7. Church Involvement by Race/Ethnicity

there are relatively few black Catholics in the follow-up sample (33), we report as well some data from the screener, which had a much larger data base of African American Catholics. The data, shown in the right-hand columns, indicate the number of hours spent each week on educational, social, or charitable activities in the church—beyond attendance at religious services.[27] In all three groups, Protestants are much more active in their churches than are Catholics. On average, the Protestant churchgoer devotes nearly two hours more each week to nonreligious activities in church than does the average Catholic. In short, when viewed in the context of high rates of church attendance among Latinos, the lower level of Latino involvement in educational, charitable, or social activities associated with a church appears to derive from the fact that they are disproportionately Catholic.

TABLE 15.2
Religious Attendance and Activity in Church, by Denomination and Race/Ethnicity

	Percentage Regular Attenders[a] (Screener Data)	Percentage Active[b]		Mean Hours per Week Church Work (Screener Data)	
	All	All	Members	All	Attenders
All					
Protestants	56	35	63	1.7	3.2
Catholics	60	20	32	0.8	1.3
Latinos					
Protestants	68	34	65	2.2	3.2
Catholics	63	19	32	1.0	1.4
African Americans					
Protestants	69	39	59	2.1	3.5
Catholics	53	13	23	0.8	2.4
Whites					
Protestants	53	35	50	1.6	3.2
Catholics	59	21	35	0.8	1.3

[a] Regular church attendance: 2–3 times a month or more
[b] Church activity: 2 hours a month or more

What Do They Say?

As the essays in this volume make clear, questions of representation are fundamental to the politics of race and ethnicity in America. When the discussion is grounded in data, the issue is frequently framed in terms of concerns about descriptive representation, the congruence—or lack thereof—between the demographic characteristics of elected representatives and their constituencies. Information about policy views of these constituencies, especially their politically active members, is much more difficult to acquire. We can extend our analysis, which has concentrated so far on who is active in what ways, an important step further by examining directly the issue basis of citizen activity. Let us now focus on the substantive content of activity by considering what activists actually say.

Political activities differ in their capacity to convey explicit messages to policy makers: votes are limited in their ability to transmit precise information about citizen priorities and preferences—in contrast to, for example, contacts or protests. Forms of participation also vary in the extent to which those who take part bring public policy concerns to their activity. Each time a respondent indicated having engaged in a particular activity, we inquired whether there was any particular issue or problem—"ranging from public policy issues to community, family, and personal concerns"—

that led to the activity. Across the totality of more than thirty-six hundred political acts discussed by our respondents, in 63 percent of cases respondents provided a comprehensible, "codable" answer about the policy concerns that animated the activity.[28] By analyzing the substantive concerns behind what we shall call "issue-based activity," we can characterize more accurately the representativeness of participatory input.

Table 15.3 summarizes the subject matter behind the political activity in which a codable issue concern was expressed and compares the three groups of respondents with respect to the issue concerns that animate their participation. In order to ensure that what is on people's minds is actually communicated to public officials, we focus solely on those activities in which an explicit message can be sent: contacting, protesting, campaign work or contributions accompanied by a communication, informal community activity, or voluntary service on a local board.[29] The issue-based political act is the unit of analysis, and the figures represent the proportion of all issue-based activities for which the respondent mentioned, among other things, a particular set of policy concerns. The figures on table 15.3, thus, represent the proportion of all issue-based activity for which the respondent mentioned, among other things, a particular set of policy concerns.[30]

When we consider the issue bundles behind political activity in table 15.3, what emerges most notably is the diversity of the issues that animate participation. All three groups have an agenda of diverse concerns. In addition, although there are important differences among the groups in terms of the priority given to particular issues, across groups there was a remarkable amount of overlap in the issues mentioned in connection with information-rich activity. White respondents are slightly more likely to have focused on issues of the general health of the economy. They were also more likely to mention social issues—a category for which the overwhelming concern was abortion. In contrast to whites, the two minority groups are more concerned with issues of basic human need, education and youth, and, especially, crime and drugs. Overall, distribution of issue concerns of activist African Americans and Latinos clearly reflects the real circumstances of their lives.

The particular emphasis upon issues of crime, violence, and drugs deserves mention. Among candidates and public officials, these issues have been the traditional bailiwick of white conservatives. In contrast, the minority and white liberal politicians who represent African American and Latino constituencies have often kept issues like drug use and crime at arm's length. It is noteworthy how importantly these issues figure on the agenda of concerns brought to politics by the citizen activists whose communities are most affected by them. Reading the actual comments of those concerned about crime, public safety, and drugs, it is impossible to distinguish the race or ethnicity of the respondent. Within each group, a range of

TABLE 15.3

Motivations for Issue-Based Political Activity, by Race/Ethnicity: Information-Rich Activities Only[a] (Percentages)

	Anglo Whites	African Americans	Latinos
Basic human needs	9	13	13
Taxes	7	3	3
Economic issues (except taxes)	6	2	1
Abortion	9	3	3
Social issues (except abortion)	2	2	2
Education			
Children or youth (except education)	15	26	22
Environment	10	1	9
Crime or drugs	7	25	16
International	3	1	4
Civil rights or minorities	1	6	6
Number of respondents	2,074	233	141

[a] Information-rich acts are those in which an explicit message can be sent to policy makers: contacting, protesting, campaign work or contributions accompanied by a communication, informal community activity, or voluntary service on a local board. The numbers in the cells represent the proportion of such acts having identifiable issue content for which there was a reference to the particular issue.

themes was mentioned. However, more systematic content analysis reveals that blacks and Latinos were somewhat more likely than whites to mention drugs and to refer to their own neighborhoods or communities in discussing these issues. Whites were somewhat more likely to discuss a neighborhood effort to set up a crime watch.

We were also interested in the extent to which the concerns associated with political activity involved civil rights issues. We include under this rubric both general references to "civil rights," "racial issues," or "discrimination" and specific concerns—for example, getting translators for Spanish-speaking prison inmates, hiring more minority teachers in the school system, establishing Martin Luther King's birthday as a state holiday, or opening up the all-Anglo cheerleading squad to Hispanics in a majority–Mexican American high school. Table 15.3 indicates that 6 percent of the information-rich, issue-based activity of both African Americans and Latinos involved reference to such issues. These issues figure in a very small portion, less than 1 percent, of the participation of whites. Because African Americans and Latinos constitute only a fraction of the population, and because African Americans are somewhat, and Latinos are substantially, less likely to participate than are whites, only an extremely small proportion of the messages communicated through the medium of information-rich participation concerns policy matters germane to civil rights or racial or ethnic minorities. Moreover, public officials hear as much about these matters from whites as from African Americans and Latinos combined. In terms of content, since some of references to civil rights issues by whites consisted of negative views of affirmative action, what public officials hear from whites is more mixed than what it hears from either of the other groups.

In addition, for each codable verbatim we noted whether—apart from mention of civil rights or a minority-related *policy* issue—there was a reference to African Americans or Latinos. For example, several respondents—not all of them African American—discussed wanting "to elect New York's first black mayor" in connection with campaign work; a Latino respondent mentioned "Hispanic dropouts" in the context of informal community activity on school issues. When these references are included in the tally, the proportion of codable, information-rich activity that involves reference to minorities or to a particular group is raised to 9 percent for African Americans and 10 percent for Latinos. (For whites, the results are unchanged.)

These data are extremely illuminating, but we must be careful to place them in context. First, what we found about the sets of concerns communicated through the medium of citizen participation reflects the era in which the data were collected. Certain policy issues—for example, concern about economic performance, taxes, or education—are never long absent from the citizen agenda of national or local concerns. In contrast, had we collected the data a few decades earlier, issues like, say, abortion or drugs would, presumably, have carried less weight among the issues animating activity. We likely would have heard more frequent reference to matters of race if the study were conducted during the height of the Civil Rights movement.[31]

A second caveat is simply that the medium of participation is not the only one through which policy makers learn what is on citizens' minds and not the only modality through which citizens can influence what the government does. Public officials can learn about citizen preferences in various ways—for example, through the media, from polls, or from the parties or organized interests. Moreover, other forms of participation that are less effective in communicating explicit policy instructions—most notably, voting—can function as potent weapons of citizen influence over government. In short, information-rich participation is not the whole story of citizen input in American democracy. Still, the sets of messages received through political participation constitute a critical form of input. Although there are industries devoted to the analysis of the content of the media, the results of polls, or the meaning of the vote, we have never before had the raw materials for understanding what is communicated through various forms of citizen participation.

Conclusion

Discussions of citizen activity often focus solely on electoral turnout. In light of the disenfranchisement of blacks in the Jim Crow South, the importance of the vote as a goal to the Civil Rights movement, and the continuing controversies over the Voting Rights Act, the concentration on voting is especially prominent in inquiries about minority politics. Resting on a much broader understanding of what constitutes participation, this chapter has mapped the racial and ethnic demography of from whom, and what, the government hears. What we have found is that generalizations about citizen activity based on what we know about voting do not do justice to the broad array of participatory acts.

Overall, African American are slightly less active and Latinos are considerably less active than whites. However, these participatory inqualities are sharper with respect to an activity that has grown in importance in recent decades but does not figure significantly in discussions of the citizen politics of race and ethnicity: financial contributions. Because the size of donations can vary so dramatically and because the wherewithal to make them is so unevenly distributed, the bias in participatory input is particularly pronounced with respect to money-based activity. The proportion of contacts, protests, hours devoted to campaign work, or, especially, of votes coming from African Americans, Latinos, or whites reflects the demographic composition of the population more accurately than does the proportion of dollars coming from each of these groups. The political implications of this finding bear further exploration.

Interestingly, of the arenas of voluntary activity, politics—the supposedly level playing field on which citizens compete as equals—is the one for which participatory input is most skewed. Activity in the secular and religious domains outside politics is much less biased in the direction of whites. In fact, African Americans are more likely than whites to attend religious services and to be involved in educational, social, or charitable activities associated with their churches. Latinos do attend church but are less active than African Americans or whites with respect to ancillary activities associated with their churches, a function of the fact that they are overwhelmingly Catholic and that Catholics, regardless of race or ethnicity, are less likely to spend time on church-based activity. Even the skewing in financial contributions is less pronounced for charities and churches than it is for politics.

This chapter has also expanded what we know about citizen activity in ways germane to discussions of group representation by considering the subject matter of activity. Using data of a kind that have never before been available, we also delved into what activists actually say when they participate, probing the issues connected with information-rich forms of activity—contacts, protests, campaign activities or contributions accompanied by a communication, informal community activities, and voluntary service on a local governing board. What the government hears on any particular subject is a function of the relative size of the groups involved; the division of opinion within them; their differing levels of activity; and the relative weight carried by the issue in their bundles of issue concerns. These interact in complex ways to influence the amount and the mix of communications on any topic. Concerns about matters having to do with civil rights and the status of minorities figure much more importantly in the activity of Latinos and African Americans than in the activity of whites. However, in comparison to the white majority, these are small groups, and Latinos, in particular, are not especially active. Hence, the net effect is that the messages about civil rights and race are as likely to come from whites as from African Americans or Latinos. Moreover, when they speak on these subjects, white activists convey messages that are much more mixed than do their African American or Latino counterparts. These findings underline a major conclusion: in thinking about participant publics, it is critical not only to inquire about who takes part in what ways and what their views are but also to consider how much they do and what they actually say when they participate.

Notes

1. We refer to *race* and *ethnicity*—and, occasionally, use the term *race/ethnicity*—because African Americans are usually referred to as a racial group and Latinos, who can be of any race, as an ethnic group. The racial/ethnic groups were defined on the basis of self-identifications. In the survey reported here, respondents were asked first whether they considered themselves to be Hispanic or Latino. Then all respondents—regardless of their answer to the first question—were asked their race. The small number who identified themselves both as Latino (or Hispanic or Chicano) and as African American (or black) were asked which they considered themselves mostly, Hispanic or black.

There is no generally accepted nomenclature for the groups to which we refer, and what are the appropriate designations is often a politically volatile question. We use the terms *African Americans* or *blacks* for one of the minority groups and *Latinos* for the other. We use the term "whites" to denote those who described themselves as white but not as Latino or Hispanic.

2. For a fuller discussion of the sources of political activity, see Verba, Schlozman, and Brady 1995.

3. For a further discussion of the identification of the groups and the design of the sample, see Verba, Schlozman, Brady, and Nie 1993a.

4. Where numbers of cases are cited they are unweighted, real cases. This is

standard procedure in work based on survey data. For fuller discussion, see Verba, Schlozman, Brady, and Nie 1993a, appendix A.

5. There is a large literature on the political activity of African Americans and Latinos. For works on African American participation that attempt to describe and explain differential activity rates see, among others, Olsen 1970, 682–97; Verba and Nie 1972, chap. 10; Danigelis 1978; Welch, Comer, and Steinman 1975; Shingles 1981; Guterbock and London 1983; Uhlaner, Cain, and Kiewiet 1987; Bobo and Gilliam 1990. On Latino participation, see de la Garza et al. 1992.

6. See Olsen 1970 and Verba and Nie 1972. Bobo and Gilliam 1990 and Ellison and Gay 1989 argue that while African Americans participated at even higher rates than would have been predicted on the basis of their socioeconomic characteristics during the late 1960s, there has been convergence since then.

7. The components of the additive scale are as follows: voting in national elections; working as a volunteer for a candidate running for national, state, or local office; making a contribution to an individual candidate, a party group, a political action committee, or any other organization that supports candidates in elections; contacting government officials; taking part in a protest, march, or demonstration; working informally with others in the community to deal with some community issue or problem; serving in a voluntary capacity on any local governmental board or council (for example, a school or zoning board) or attending meetings of such a board; and being affiliated with (that is, being a member of or a contributor to) an organization that takes stands in politics.

8. Although it could be argued that, from the perspective of democratic theory, this should be a study of citizens only, we did make a deliberate choice to interview noncitizens. Noncitizens are affected by American laws, and many are permanent residents (legally or illegally). There are a number of philosophical questions as to whether they are appropriately part of the universe for a participation study. Since they may—and do—participate in many ways even though they cannot vote, we decided to include them since they can always be separated in analysis. Garcia and Arce note that "ineligibility from voting does not totally remove the Mexican-born from the electoral process." Garcia and Arce 1988, 147.

9. We might have expected an even larger difference between Latino citizens and noncitizens. It is likely that our sample is biased when it comes to Latino noncitizens, underrepresenting migrant workers or undocumented residents. Hence, those in our sample may well be relatively advantaged in comparison to noncitizen Latinos as a whole.

Our findings about Latino citizens and noncitizens are consistent with those from the National Latino Immigrant Survey as reported by the National Association of Latino Elected and Appointed Officials in "Political Participation among Latino Immigrants," *NLIS Research Notes* 1 (October 1992).

10. The differences among the Latino groups in terms of political activity are consistent with their different socioeconomic profiles, with Cuban Americans more likely to have higher levels of education and higher status occupations. For an overview of social and political data about Latino groups, see de la Garza et al., 1992.

11. Our survey, like all surveys, overestimates voter turnout. Abramson and Claggett 1984 indicate that the gap between self-reported and validated turnout is

especially wide for blacks. We are uncertain as to the applicability of their findings to self-reports of other kinds of political activity.

12. It is interesting to note how many of the African American electoral activists were supporting black candidates. We asked those who had either worked in a campaign or made a contribution about the race of the candidate they supported. Seventy-four percent of the 101 African American campaign activists reported supporting a black candidate. In contrast, only 31 percent of the 24 Latino activists reported supporting a Latino candidate. More than 90 percent of the whites reported supporting a white candidate. Because African Americans were somewhat more likely than other respondents to indicate having been involved in a primary rather than a general election, we suspect that many of the black campaigners were supporting Jesse Jackson in his bid for the Democratic presidential nomination.

Because whites are the overwhelming majority of the population, if citizens supported candidates on a random basis, we would expect a majority of whites, African Americans, and Latinos to support white candidates. Clearly, the process is not random, however: patterns of residential segregation affect the distribution of candidates, and citizens are differentially attracted to candidates who share their race or ethnicity. The bottom line is that all three groups, but especially African Americans, supported candidates from their own group more often than we would expect on the basis of sheer probability.

13. See Schlozman 1994 for an explanation of our measure of organizational affiliation and the definition of a political organization. We consider any organization that takes stands on public issues to be political and support, even passive support, of such an organization to be a form of political activity.

14. The theme of protest as the tactic of the powerless is explored in Lipsky 1970, esp. chaps. 1, 6, 7.

15. Among Latinos, citizens are more likely than noncitizens to contact public officials. Consistent with the notion that protest is an outsider activity, however, Latino noncitizens are slightly more likely than Latino citizens to protest.

16. With respect to the proportion of income contributed, African Americans give a slightly larger percentage of their family income to campaigns (0.11 percent) than do whites (0.09 percent). In contrast, Latinos give a proportion of family income that is about half as large (0.04 percent for all Latino respondents, 0.05 percent for Latino citizens).

17. For data on a similar pattern found in relation to income groups, see Verba, Schlozman, Brady, and Nie 1993a.

18. We present a "population" made up of the three groups we have been considering and omit other ethnic groups such as Asian Americans. Note that, in spite of special efforts to reach African Americans and Latinos, the sample is not a perfect reflection of the racial and ethnic composition of the population.

19. The high volume of African American activity in campaigns may reflect the Jesse Jackson 1988 candidacy and, thus, may be idiosyncratic to the 1988 election.

20. For an exposition of this theme and extensive data demonstrating the way that voluntary activity outside politics leads to political participation, see Verba, Schlozman, and Brady 1995, chap. 12.

21. There are many studies of minority, especially African American, affiliation with voluntary associations and a long-standing debate within sociology as to

whether high levels of African American organizational activity represent "over-compensation." See, for example, Babchuk and Thompson 1962; Orum 1966; Williams, Babchuk, and Johnson 1973; and McPherson 1977. On organizational involvement among Mexican Americans, see Garcia and Arce 1988.

22. Among the more detailed questions we asked was an item about the racial or ethnic composition of the membership of the single organization with which respondents are most involved. A similar pattern emerges in relation to this question: 41 percent of the African Americans report that the membership of their most important organization is mostly or all black; only 18 percent of the Latinos say that their organization is mostly or all Latino in membership.

23. For data and discussion, see Verba, Schlozman, and Brady 1995.

24. There is extensive literature on the history of the black churches. For a discussion and bibliographical references, see Wills 1990. Although some dispute the role of the black churches, arguing that their otherworldliness reduces political engagement, most agree that they are a powerful political force among blacks. See Nelsen and Nelsen 1975, 1. For the role of the black church under slavery, see Franklin 1969, 199, 310, 404–5.

25. In our sample, 25 percent of the Latino respondents are Protestant, and 66 percent are Catholic; 85 percent of the African American are Protestant, and 7 percent are Catholic; 62 percent of the white respondents are Protestant, and 26 percent are Catholic. Interestingly, while Latinos are more likely than whites to attend church services frequently, they are slightly less likely than whites to be a member of a local church (or to attend services in the same congregation or parish). However, this is true for Latino Catholics only. Among Latinos, 74 percent of the Protestants, as opposed to 67 percent of the Catholics, belong to a local church. For whites, this slight relationship is reversed: 73 percent of the Protestants and 77 percent of the Catholics are members of a local church. Church membership for the small number of African American Catholics (76 percent) is analogous to that for white Catholics. African American Protestants, 82 percent of whom belong to a local church, have the highest levels of church membership. These data suggest that there may be some substance to the stereotype that the Catholic Church in America relates less well to the most recent Catholic immigrants than it does to more established Catholic groups.

26. The differences between Protestant and Catholic congregations were probably even more pronounced a generation ago. Although Catholic parishes remain, on average, substantially larger than Protestant congregations, among the important consequences of Vatican II has been increased lay participation both in the liturgy and in parish governance through parish councils. The effects of Vatican II have, presumably, been reinforced by enhanced educational levels among Catholic parishioners and the decrease in priestly vocations. See Gremillion and Leege 1989. Whether the unambiguous distinction between churchgoing Protestants and Catholics with respect to the number of hours they spend on other activities associated with their churches will disappear in the future, we cannot speculate.

27. We did not ask about membership in a local church on the short screener. Hence, we report the data for regular church attenders (those who attend once a month or more).

28. Only 47 percent of voters—in contrast to 84 percent of those active in their

communities, 87 percent of contactors, and 95 percent of protesters—cited at least one identifiable public policy issue as the basis of their activity.

29. Thus, we omit voting, attending meetings of a local board on a regular basis, and campaigning for or contributing to a candidate or electoral organization when the activity is not accompanied by an explicit message.

30. Thus, the act rather than the respondent is the unit of analysis. In coding the open-ended responses, we created over sixty relatively narrow categories. In analyzing the data, we have combined these narrow categories in various ways. The components of the categories in table 15.3 are as follows:

Basic human needs: various government benefits (welfare, AFDC, Food Stamps, housing subsidies, Social Security, Medicare, and Medicaid); unemployment (either as an economic issue or in terms of the respondent's own circumstances); housing or homelessness; health or health care; poverty or hunger; aid to the handicapped or handicapped rights

Taxes: all references to taxes at any governmental level

Economic issues: local or national economic performance; inflation; budget issues or the budget deficit; government spending; other economic issues

Social issues: traditional morality; pornography; family planning, teenage pregnancy, sex education, or contraception; school prayer; gay rights or homosexuality

Abortion: all references to abortion, whether pro-choice, pro-life, or ambiguous

Education: educational issues (school reform, school voucher plans, etc.); problems or issues related to schooling of family members; guaranteed student loans

Environment: specific environmental issues (e.g., clean air, toxic wastes) or environmental concerns in general; wildlife preservation; animal rights

Crime or drugs: crime; gangs; safety in the streets; drugs

Foreign policy: relations with particular nations or foreign policy in general; defense policy or defense spending; peace, arms control, or international human rights issues

Note that many of the categories encompass respondents with quite different issue positions. For example, the social issues category includes many respondents who are not social conservatives, such as those who are concerned about making contraceptives more easily available to teenagers. It should be noted that the categories in table 15.3 are not exhaustive. Issue concerns ranging from gun control to local economic development have been omitted from the table. If the universe of issue concerns had been included, the figures in each column would add to more than 100 percent. A single political act is often inspired by more than one issue concern. The contactor who expressed concern about "public housing, teenage pregnancy, and the child care bill" would have been coded as mentioning three separate issues.

31. We undertook an analogous analysis for the issue concerns discussed in connection with voting. In certain respects, the pattern of responses for voting, summarized below, differs from what we saw in table 15.3, where we considered information-rich activities. First, when voters mentioned issues, they tended to list more of them than did those who undertook other kinds of activity. This is quite reason-

able: one might bring an array of concerns to the polls; in contrast, a letter to a public
official is less likely to be about a laundry list of policy issues. In addition, across
groups, voters are more likely than other kinds of activists to have mentioned economic issues in conjunction with their participation. In terms of group differences,
however, the pattern is parallel to that for information-rich activities. However, the
group differences in the extent to which activity is animated by concern about issues
of basic human need are especially pronounced when it comes to voting.

Issues Voters Mentioned as Concerns (Percentages)

	Whites	African Americans	Latinos
Basic human needs	8	39	19
Economic issues (except taxes)	20	18	14
Taxes	32	25	21
Abortion	18	8	8
Social issues (except abortion)	1	2	2
Environment	10	3	9
Crime or drugs	5	26	21
Foreign policy	16	10	12
Children or youth (except education)	1	1	1
Education	30	17	20
Civil rights or minorities	1	7	6

References _____

Abrams, Kathryn. 1988. "Raising Politics Up." *New York University Law Review* 63:449–531.

Abramson, Paul. 1983. *Political Attitudes in American: Formation and Change.* San Francisco: W. H. Freeman and Co.

Abramson, Paul R., and William Claggett. 1984. "Race-Related Differences in Self-Reported and Validated Turnout." *Journal of Politics* 46:719–38.

Alford, Robert R., and Eugene C. Lee. 1968. "Voting Turnout in American Cities." *American Political Science Review* 62:776–813.

Allen, Howard W., and Kay Warren Allen. 1981. "Vote Fraud and Data Validity." In Jerome M. Clubb, William H. Flanigan, and Nancy H. Zingale, eds., *Analyzing Electoral History: A Guide to the Study of American Voter Behavior.* Beverly Hills: Sage.

Allen, Howard W., Aage R. Clausen, and Jerome M. Clubb. 1971. "Political Reform and Negro Rights in the Senate, 1909–1915." *Journal of Southern History* 37:191–212.

Allen, Richard L., Michael C. Dawson, and Ronald E. Brown. 1989. "A Schema-Based Approach to Modeling an African-American Racial Belief System." *American Political Science Review* 83:421–41.

Allen v. State Board of Elections, 393 U.S. 544 (1969).

Alston, Lee J., and Joseph P. Ferrie. 1985a. "Labor Costs, Paternalism, and Loyalty in Southern Agriculture: A Constraint on the Growth of the Welfare State." *Journal of Economic History* 45:95–117.

————. 1985b. "Resisting the Welfare State: Southern Opposition to the Farm Security Administration." In Robert Higgs, ed., *The Emergence of the Modern Political Economy.* Greenwich, Conn.: JAI Press.

Alt, J. 1994. "The Impact of the Voting Rights Act on Black and White Voter Registration." In Chandler Davidson and Bernard Grofman, eds., *Quiet Revolution in the South: The Impact of the Voting Rights Act, 1965–1990.* Princeton: Princeton University Press.

Altmeyer, Arthur F. 1966. *The Formative Years of Social Security.* Madison: University of Wisconsin Press.

Alvarez, Rodolfo. 1984. "The Psycho-historical and Socioeconomic Development of the Chicano Community in the United States." In R. de la Garza, F. Bean, C. Bonjean, and R. Alvarez, eds., *The Mexican American Experience.* Austin: University of Texas Press.

Amenta, Edwin, and Theda Skocpol. 1988. "Redefining the New Deal: World War II and the Development of Social Provision in the United States." In Margaret Weir, Ann Shola Orloff, and Theda Skocpol, eds., *The Politics of Social Policy in the United States.* Princeton: Princeton University Press.

Amenta, Edwin, and Theda Skocpol. 1989. "Taking Exception: Explaining the Distinctiveness of American Public Policies in the Last Century." In Francis G. Castles, ed., *The Comparative History of Public Policies*. London: Polity Press.

Amenta, Edwin, and Yvonne Zylan. 1991. "It Happened Here: Political Opportunity, the New Institutionalism, and the Townsend Movement." *American Sociological Review* 56:250–65.

Amy, Douglas J. 1993. *Real Choices/New Voices: The Case for Proportional Representation Elections in the United States*. New York: Columbia University Press.

Anderson, Eric. 1981. *Race and Politics in North Carolina, 1872–1901: The Black Second*. Baton Rouge: Louisiana State University Press.

Anderson, Mary. 1936. "The Plight of Negro Domestic Labor." *Journal of Negro Education* 5:66–72.

Anderson v. Celebrezze, 460 U.S. 780 (1983).

Apple, R. W., Jr. 1992. "Steady Local Gains by Women Fuel More Runs for High Office." *New York Times*, May 24, sec. 4.

Applebome, Peter. 1994. "Suit Challenging Redrawn Districts that Help Blacks." *New York Times*, February 14.

Armour v. Ohio, 775 F. Supp. 1044 (1990).

Autes, Michel. 1992. "Le RMI: Une politique de fortune." *Sociétés contemporaines* 9:11–26.

Ayers, Edward L. 1992. *The Promise of the New South: Life after Reconstruction*. New York: Oxford University Press.

Babchuk, Nicholas, and Ralph V. Thompson. 1962. "The Voluntary Associations of Negroes." *American Sociological Review* 27:647–55.

Bacote, Clarence Albert. 1955. "The Negro in Georgia Politics 1880–1908." Ph.D. diss., University of Chicago.

Baker, Paula. 1984. "The Domestication of Politics: Women and American Political Society, 1780–1920." *American Historical Review* 89(3): 620–47.

Baker v. Carr, 369 U.S. 186 (1962).

Baldwin, James. 1984. "Many Thousands Gone." In *Notes of a Native Son*. Boston: Beacon Press.

Banfield, Edward C., and James Q. Wilson. 1967. *City Politics*. Cambridge: Harvard University Press.

Barth, Frederick, ed. 1969. *Ethnic Groups and Boundaries*. New York: Little, Brown.

Baver, Sherrie. 1984. "Puerto Rican Politics in New York City: The Post–World War II Period." In James Jennings and Monte Rivera, eds., *Puerto Rican Politics in Urban America*. Westwood, Conn.: Greenwood.

Bean, Frank, and Marta Tienda. 1988. *The Hispanic Population of the United States*. New York: Russell Sage Foundation.

Beer v. United States, 425 U.S. 130 (1976).

Benedict, Michael Les. 1978. "Preserving Federalism: Reconstruction and the Waite Court." *Supreme Court Review* 39:39–79.

Bensel, Richard Franklin. 1984. *Sectionalism and American Political Development, 1880–1980*. Madison: University of Wisconsin Press.

Berenson, William W., Kirk W. Elifson, and Tandy Tollerson III. 1976. "Preachers in Politics: A Study of Political Activism among the Black Ministry." *Journal of Black Studies* 6:373–92.

Bergman, Peter M. 1969. *The Chronological History of the Negro in America.* New York: Harper and Row.

Bernard, Philippe. 1993. "L'intervention dans les quartiers n'a pas enrayé l'aggravation de phénomènes d'exclusion." *Le monde,* January 16.

Bernier, Lynne Louise. 1991. "Decentralizing the French State: Implications for Policy." *Journal of Urban Affairs* 13:21–32.

Bernier, Lynne Louise, and M. Black. 1987. *Politics and Society in the South.* Cambridge: Harvard University Press.

Berry, Jeffrey M., Kent E. Portney, and Ken Thomson. 1993. *The Rebirth of Urban Democracy.* Washington, D.C.: Brookings Institution.

Black, E. 1976. *Southern Governors and Civil Rights.* Cambridge: Harvard University Press.

Black, Earl, and Merle Black. 1987. *Politics and Society in the South.* Cambridge: Harvard University Press.

Black Elected Officials: A National Register. 1990. Washington, D.C.: Joint Center for Political and Economic Studies.

Blair, George S. 1960. *Cumulative Voting.* Urbana: University of Illnois Press.

Blau, P., and O. Duncan. 1967. *The American Occupational Structure.* New York: Wiley.

Bledsoe, Timothy. 1986. "A Research Note on the Impact of District/At-Large Elections on Black Political Efficacy." *Urban Affairs Quarterly* 22(1): 166–74.

Bobo, Lawrence D. 1983. "Whites' Opposition to Busing: Symbolic Racism or Realistic Group Conflict?" *Journal of Personality and Social Psychology,* 45(6):1196–1210.

Bobo, Lawrence, and Franklin D. Gilliam, Jr. 1990. "Race, Sociopolitical Participation and Black Empowerment." *American Political Science Review* 84: 379–93.

Borges, Jesse Rafael. 1993. "Beyond Deracialization: Toward a Comprehensive Theory of Black Electoral Success." Paper presented at the Workshop on Race, Ethnicity, Representation, and Governance, January 21–22, Harvard University, Cambridge, Massachusetts.

Brams, Steven J. 1975. *Game Theory and Politics.* New York: Free Press.

Brewer v. Ham, 876 F. 2d 448 (5th Cir. 1989).

Briffault, Richard. 1990. "Our Localism: Part I—The Structure of Local Government Law." *Columbia Law Review* 90 (January): 72–85.

Brinkley, Alan. 1984. "The New Deal and Southern Politics." In James C. Cobb and Michael V. Namorato, eds., *The New Deal and the South.* Jackson: University of Mississippi Press.

Brown, J. Douglas. 1972. *An American Philosophy of Social Security: Evolution and Issues.* Princeton: Princeton University Press.

Brown, Michael K. 1988. "The Segmented Welfare System: Distributive Conflict and Retrenchment in the United States, 1968–1984." In Michael K. Brown, ed., *Rethinking the Welfare State: Retrenchment and Social Policy in America and Europe.* Philadelphia: Temple University Press.

Brown, Michael K., and Steven P. Erie. 1981. "Blacks and the Legacy of the Great Society: The Economic and Political Impact of Federal Social Policy." *Public Policy* 29(3):299–330.

Brown v. Thompson, 462 U.S. 835 (1983).

Browning, Rufus P., Dale Rogers Marshall, and David H. Tabb. 1979. "Minorities and Urban Electoral Change: A Longitudinal Study." *Urban Affairs Quarterly* 15:206–28.

———. 1984. *Protest Is Not Enough.* Berkeley and Los Angeles: University of California Press.

———. *Racial Politics in American Cities.* New York: Longman.

Brownstein, Ronald, 1991. "Minority Quotas in Elections?" *Los Angeles Times,* August 28, p. A1.

Buck, Nick, and Norman Fainstein. 1992. "A Comparative History, 1880–1973." In Susan S. Fainstein, Ian Gordon, and Michael Harloe, eds. *Divided Cities: New York and London in the Contemporary World.* Oxford: Blackwell Publishers.

Buckanaga v. Sisseton Independent School District, 804 F. 2d 469 (8th Cir. 1986).

Bullock, Charles S., III. 1984. "Racial Crossover Voting and the Election of Black Officials." *Journal of Politics* 46:238–51.

Bullock, Charles S., III, and Susan A. MacManus. 1987. "Staggered Terms and Black Representation." *Journal of Politics* 49 (2):543–52.

Bunche, Ralph J. 1973. *The Political Status of the Negro in the Age of FDR.* Edited by Dewey W. Grantham. Chicago: University of Chicago Press.

Burke, Albie. 1968. "Federal Regulation of Congressional Elections in Northern Cities, 1871–1894." Ph.D. diss., University of Chicago.

Button, J. W. 1989. *Blacks and Social Change.* Princeton: Princeton University Press.

Cain, Bruce. 1992. "Voting Rights and Democratic Theory: Toward a Color-Blind Society?" In Bernard Grofman and Chandler Davidson, eds. *Controversies in Minority Voting.* Washington, D.C.: Brookings Institution.

California Political Almanac. 1990. Santa Barbara: Pacific Data Resources.

Calvert, Randall. 1985. "Robustness of the Multidimensional Voting Model: Candidate Motivations, Uncertainty, and Convergence." *American Journal of Political Science* 29:69–95.

Caraley, Demetrios. 1976. "Congressional Politics and Urban Aid." *Political Science Quarterly* 91:19–45.

———. 1992. "Washington Abandons the Cities." *Political Science Quarterly* 107: 1–30.

Carmines, Edward G., and James A. Stimson. 1989. *Issue Evolution: Race and the Transformation of American Politics.* Princeton: Princeton University Press.

Carrollton Branch of NAACP v. Stallings, 829 F. 2d 1547 (11th Cir. 1987); cert. denied 485 U.S. 936 (1988).

Castellan M., M. Marpsat, and M. F. Goldberger. 1992. "Les quartiers prioritaires de la politique de la ville." *Insee premiere*, no. 234 (December).

Cates, Jerry. 1983. *Insuring Inequality: Administrative Leadership in Social Security, 1935–1954.* Ann Arbor: University of Michigan Press.

Cavanagh, Thomas E., and Lorn S. Foster. 1984. *Jesse Jackson's Campaign: Primaries and Caucuses.* Washington, D.C.: Joint Center for Political Studies.

Centre for Local Development Strategies. 1992. *Social Regeneration: Directions for Urban Policies in the 1990s.* Manchester, Eng.: Centre for Local Development Strategies.

Chavez, Linda. 1991. *Out of the Barrio*. New York: Basic Books.

Childs, John Brown. 1980. *The Political Black Minister: A Study in Afro-American Politics and Religion*. Boston: G. K. Hall and Co.

Cisneros, Henry G., ed. 1993. *Interwoven Destinies: Cities and the Nation*. New York: W. W. Norton and Co.

Citizens for a Better Gretna v. City of Gretna, 834 F. 2d 496 (1987).

City of Mobile v. Bolden, 466 U.S. 55 (1980).

Clark, Septima. 1986. *Ready from Within: Septima Clark and the Civil Rights Movement*. Edited by Cynthia Stokes Brown. Navarro, Calif.: Wild Trees Press.

Clinton, Governor Bill, and Senator Al Gore. 1992. *Putting People First: How We Can All Change America*. New York: Random House, Time Books.

Cohen, Wilbur J. 1985. "The Social Security Act of 1935: Reflections Fifty Years Later." In *The Report of the Committee on Economic Security*. Washington, D.C.: National Conference on Social Welfare.

Colby, D. 1986. "The Voting Rights Act and Black Voter Registration in Mississippi." *Publius* 16:123–37.

Collins, Patricia Hill. 1991. "We Don't Need Another Dr. King." *New York Times*, January 19, A31.

Collins v. City of Norfolk, 605 F. Supp. 377 (E.D. Va. 1984); 768 F. 2d 572 (4th Cir. 1985); 816 F. 2d 932 (4th Cir. 1987); 679 F. Supp. 557 (E.D. Va. 1988); 883 F. 2d 1232 (4th Cir. 1989).

Congressional Information Service. 1985. *CIS US Congressional Committee Hearings Index Part 1, 23rd Congress–64th Congress, Dec. 1883–Mar. 1917, Reference Bibliography, H1–1-(63–3) S. Doc. v. 7 n.981*. Bethesda, Md.: Congressional Information Service.

Cooper, William J. 1968. *The Conservative Regime: South Carolina, 1877–1900*. Baltimore: Johns Hopkins University Press.

Congressional Record. 1935. 74th Cong., 1st sess. Vol. 79.

Cornish, Dudley Taylor. 1956. *The Sable Arm: Negro Troops in the Union Army, 1861–1865*. New York: Longmans, Green.

Cornwell, Elmer E., Jr. 1964. "Bosses, Machines, and Ethnic Groups." *Annals of the American Academy of the Political and Social Sciences* 353 (May):27–39.

Cossolotto, Matthew. 1991. *The Almanac of Transatlantic Politics*. Washington, D.C.: Brassey's.

Cotter, Cornelius P., James L. Gibson, John F. Bibby, and Robert J. Huckshorn. 1984. *Party Organization in American Politics*. New York: Praeger.

Covotsos, Louis J. 1976. "Child Welfare and Social Progress: A History of the United States Children's Bureau, 1912–1935." Ph.D. diss., University of Chicago.

Cox, Gary W., 1984. "Electoral Equilibrium in Double Member Districts." *Public Choice* 44:443–53.

———. 1987. "Electoral Equilibrium under Alternative Voting Institutions." *American Journal of Political Science* 31:82–109.

———. 1990. "Centripetal and Centrifugal Incentives in Voting Systems." *American Journal of Political Science* 34:903–36.

— 1991. "SNTV and d'Hondt are 'Equivalent.'" *Electoral Studies* 10:118–32.

Cox, Gary W., and Michael C. Munger. 1989. "Closeness, Expenditures, and Turnout in the 1982 U.S. House Elections." *American Political Science Review* 83:217–31.

Curry, C. 1992. "A Right to Be There." *Southern Changes* (August/September).

Dahl, Robert A. 1956. *A Preface to Democratic Theory.* Chicago: University of Chicago Press.

———. 1961. *Who Governs?* New Haven: Yale University Press.

Danielson, Michael N. 1976. *The Politics of Exclusion.* New York: Columbia University Press.

Danigelis, Nicholas L. 1978. "Black Political Participation in the United States: Some Recent Evidence." *American Sociological Review* 43:756–71.

Darkly, R. and Charles D. Hadley. 1988. "Black Women in Politics: The Puzzle of Success." *Social Science Quarterly* 69:3 (September):629–45.

Davidson, Chandler. 1992. "The Voting Rights Act: A Brief History." In Bernard Grofman and Chandler Davidson, eds. *Controversies in Minority Voting.* Washington, D.C.: Brookings Institution.

———. 1984. *Minority Vote Dilution.* Washington, D. C.: Joint Center for Political Studies.

———, ed. *Minority Vote Dilution.* 1989. Washington, D.C: Howard University Press.

Davidson, Chandler, and George Korbel. 1981. "At-Large Elections and Minority-Group Representation: A Re-Examination of Historical and Contemporary Evidence." *Journal of Politics* 43 (November): 982–1005.

Davis, Marilyn, and Alex Willingham. 1993. "Andrew Young and the Georgia State Elections of 1990." In Georgia A. Persons, ed. *Dilemmas of Black Politics.* New York: Harper Collins.

Davis v. Bandemer, 478 U.S. 109 (1986).

Davison, D. 1986. *An Ecological Regression Method to Estimate the Political Consequences of the Voting Rights Act of 1965.* University of Central Florida. Mimeo.

Dawson, Michael C., Ronald E. Brown, and Richard Allen. 1990. "Racial Belief Systems, Religious Guidance, and African-American Political Participation." *National Political Science Review* 2:22–44.

Degler, Carl N. 1974. *The Other South: Southern Dissenters in the Nineteenth Century.* New York: Harper and Row.

de la Garza, Rodolfo O., Louis DeSipio, Angelo Falcon, F. Chris Garcia, and John Garcia. 1992. *Latino Voices: Mexican, Puerto Rican and Cuban Perspectives on American Politics.* Boulder, Colo.: Westview Press.

de la Garza, Rodolfo, and Armando Trujillo. 1989. "Latinos and the Official English Debate: Language Is Not the Issue." In David Schniederman, ed., *Language and the State: The Law and Politics of Identify.* Quebec: Les Editions Yvon Blais.

Delameter, J., D. Katz, and H. Kelman. 1969. "On the Nature of National Involvement: A Preliminary Study." *Journal of Conflict Resolution* 12 (3):320–57.

Derthick, Martha. 1979. *Policymaking for Social Security.* Washington, D.C.: Brookings Institution.

DeSantis, Vincent P. 1982. "Rutherford B. Hayes and the Removal of the Troops and the End of Reconstruction." In J. Morgan Kousser and James M. McPherson, eds. *Region, Race, and Reconstruction: Essays in Honor of C. Vann Woodward.* New York: Oxford University Press.

Dodson, Debra L., and Susan J. Carroll. 1991. Rutgers University. Center for the American Woman and Politics, "Reshaping the Agenda: Women in State Legislatures." Typescript.

Doenecke, Justus D. 1981. *The Presidencies of James A. Garfield and Chester A. Arthur.* Lawrence: The Regents Press of Kansas.

"Doté de 5 Milliard de Francs le 'Plan d'urgence pour la ville' Renforce l'intervention de l'etat dans les quartiers en crise." 1993. *Le monde,* 30 July, 8–9.

Downs, Anthony. 1957. *An Economic Theory of Voting.* New York: Harper and Row.

Dreier, Peter, and Bruce Ehrlich. 1991. "Downtown Development and Urban Reform: The Politics of Boston's Linkage Policy," *Urban Affairs Quarterly* 26 (3):354–75.

Du Bois, W. E. B. [1935] 1992. *Black Reconstruction in America, 1860–1880.* New York: Atheneum.

Dunleavy, Patrick. 1981. *The Politics of Mass Housing in Britain, 1945–1975.* Oxford: Clarendon Press.

Eaton, B. C., and R. Lipsey. 1975. "The Principle of Minimum Differentiation Reconsidered: Some New Developments in the Theory of Spatial Competition." *Review of Economic Studies* 42:27–49.

Edsall, Thomas Byrne, with Mary D. Edsall. 1991a. "Race." *Atlantic Monthly,* May, 84.

———. 1991b. *Chain Reaction: The Impact of Race, Rights, and Taxes on American Politics.* New York: W. W. Norton.

Eisinger, Peter K. 1980. *The Politics of Displacement.* New York: Academic Press.

Elliott, Frank. 1992. "Alabama County Trying It." *Winston-Salem Journal* February 2, A13.

Ellison, Christopher G., and David Gay. 1989. "Black Political Participation Revisited: A Test of Compensatory, Ethnic Community, and Public Arena Models." *Social Science Quarterly* 70:101–19.

Engstrom, Richard L. 1985. "Racial Vote Dilution: The Concept and the Court." In Lorn S. Foster, ed., *The Voting Rights Act: Consequences and Implications.* New York: Praeger.

———. 1988. "Black Politics and the Voting Rights Act." In James Lea, ed., *Contemporary Southern Politics.* Baton Rouge: Louisiana State University Press.

Engstrom Richard L., and Charles J. Barilleaux. 1991. "Native Americans and Cumulative Voting: The Sisseton-Wahpeton Sioux." *Social Science Quarterly* 72:388–94.

Engstrom, Richard L., Delbert A. Taebel, and Richard L. Cole. 1989. "Cumulative Voting as a Remedy for Minority Vote Dilution: The Case of Alamagordo, New Mexico." *Journal of Law and Politics* 5:469–97.

Erie, Steven P. 1988. *Rainbow's End.* Berkeley and Los Angeles: University of California Press.

Europa World Yearbook. 1992. Vols. 1 and 2. London: Europa Publications.

Faberon, Jean-Yves. 1991. "Les principes de la loi d'orientation pour la ville." *La revue administrative* 44 (November–December): 510–16.

Falcon, Angelo. 1984. "A History of Puerto Rican Politics in New York City, 1860s to 1945." In James Jennings and Monte Rivera, eds., *Puerto Rican Politics in Urban America.* Westport, Conn: Greenwood Press.

Farley, Reynolds. 1984. *Blacks and Whites: Narrowing the Gap?* Cambridge: Harvard University Press.

———. 1991. "Residential Segregation of Social and Economic Groups among Blacks, 1970–1980." In Christopher Jencks and Paul E. Peterson, eds., *The Urban Underclass*. Washington, D.C.: Brookings Institution.

Featherman, Sandra A. 1992. "Barriers to Representing Woman and Blacks in Pennsylvania: The Impacts of Demography, Culture, and Structure." In Wilma Rule and Joseph P. Zimmerman, eds. *United States Electoral Systems: Their Impact on Women and Minorities*. New York: Greenwood Press.

Feddersen, Timothy J. 1993. "A Voting Model Implying Duverger's Law and Positive Turnout." *American Journal of Political Science* 36:938–62.

Feddersen, Timothy J., Itai Sened, and Stephen G. Wright. 1990. "Rational Voting and Candidate Entry under Plurality Rule." *American Journal of Political Science* 34:1005–17.

Feldman, Stanley. 1983. "Structure and Consistency in Public Opinion: The Role of Core Beliefs and Values." *American Journal of Political Science* 32:416–40.

———. 1988. "Economic Individualism and American Public Opinion." *American Political Quarterly* 11:3–29.

Felsenthal, Dan. 1990. *Topics in Social Choice: Sophisticated Voting, Efficacy, and Proportional Representation*. New York: Praeger.

Finegold, Kenneth. 1988. "Agriculture and the Politics of U.S. Social Provision." In Margaret Weir, Ann Shola Orloff, and Theda Skocpol, eds., *The Politics of Social Policy in the United States*. Princeton: Princeton University Press.

Fiorina, Morris. 1992. *Divided Government*. New York: Macmillan.

Flanigan, Nancy H. Zingale. n.d. Beverly Hills, Calif.: Sage Publications.

Foner, Eric. 1988. *Reconstruction: America's Unfinished Revolution, 1863–1877*. New York: Harper and Row.

Forrester, Andrew, Stewart Lansley, and Robin Pauley. 1985. *Beyond Our Ken: A Guide to the Battle for London*. Fourth Estate.

Fossett, Mark A., and K. Jill Kiecolt. 1989. "The Relative Size of Minority Populations and White Racial Attitudes." *Social Science Quarterly* 70(4):820–35.

Franklin, John Hope. 1969. *From Slavery to Freedom: A History of Negro Americans*. 3d ed. New York: Vintage Books.

———. 1980. *From Slavery to Freedom: A History of Negro Americans*. 5th ed. New York: Alfred A. Knopf.

Frazier, E. Franklin. [1963] 1974. *The Negro Church in America*. New York: Alfred A. Knopf.

Freidel, Frank. 1965. *F.D.R. and the South*. Baton Rouge: Louisiana State University Press.

Fuchs, Lawrence H. 1991. *The American Kaleidoscope: Race, Ethnicity and the Civic Culture* Hanover, N.H.: University Press of New England.

Gaffney v. Cummings, 412 U.S. 735 (1973).

Garcia, John A., and Carlos Arce. 1988. "Political Orientations and Behaviors of Chicanos: Trying to Make Sense Out of Attitudes and Participation." In F. Chris Garcia, ed., *Latinos and the Political System*. Notre Dame, Ind.: University of Notre Dame Press.

Garfinkel, Irwin. 1992. *Assuring Child Support: An Extension of Social Security*. New York: Russell Sage Foundation.

Garreau, Joel. 1991. *Edge City: Life on the New Frontier*. New York: Anchor Books.

Garza v. Los Angeles County Board of Supervisors, Slip opinion no. CV 88–5143 KN, 918 F. 2d 763 (9th Cir. 1990).

Garza v. United States, 918 F. 2d 763 (1991).

Gay, Anthony E. 1993. "Congressional Term Limits: Good Government or Minority Vote Dilution?" *University of Pennsylvania Law Review* 141: 2311–2369.

Gelfand, Mark. 1975. *A Nation of Cities: The Federal Government and Urban America, 1933–1965*. New York: Oxford University Press.

Gelman, Andrew, and Gary King. 1994a. "Enhancing Democracy through Legislative Redistricting." *American Political Science Review* 88 (3):1–19.

———. 1994b. "A Unified Method of Evaluating Electoral Systems and Redistricting Plans," *American Journal of Political Science* 38 (2).

Glaser, James M. 1994. "Back to the Black Belt: Racial Environment and White Racial Attitudes in the South." *Journal of Politics* 56 (1):21–41.

Glazer, Amihai, Debra G. Glazer, and Bernard Grofman. 1984. "Cumulative Voting in Corporate Elections: Introducing Strategy into the Equation." *South Carolina Law Review* 35:295–309.

Glazer, Nathan, and Daniel P. Moynihan. 1963. *Beyond the Melting Pot*. Cambridge: MIT Press.

Glendon, Mary Ann. 1993. "What's Wrong with the Elite Law Schools?" *Wall Street Journal*, June 8, A16.

Goldman, Robert Michael. 1976. "A Free Ballot and a Fair Count: The Department of Justice and the Enforcement of Voting Rights in the South, 1877–1893." Ph.D. diss., Michigan State University.

Gomez v. City of Watsonville, 863 F. 2d 1407 (9th Cir. 1988); 489 U.S. 1080 (1989).

Goodwyn, Lawrence. 1978. *The Populist Movement: A Short History of the Agrarian Revolt in America*. Oxford: Oxford University Press.

Gordon, Linda. 1991. "Black and White Visions of Welfare: Women's Welfare Activism, 1890–1945." *Journal of American History* 78(2):559–90.

Gordon v. Lance, 403 U.S. 1, 6 (1971).

Gosnell, Harold F. [1935] 1967. *Negro Politicians: The Rise of Negro Politics in Chicago*. Chicago: University of Chicago Press.

Green, Paul M. 1982 "Legislative Redistricting in Illinois, 1871–1982: A Study of Geo-Political Survival." In Anna J. Merritt., ed., *Redistricting: An Exercise in Prophecy*. Institute of Government and Public Affairs and the Department of Journalism, University of Illinois.

Greene, Lorenzo, and Carter G. Woodson. 1930. *The Negro Wage Earner*. Washington, D.C.: Association for the Study of Negro Life and History.

Greenstone, J. David 1993. *The Lincoln Persuasion: Remaking American Liberalism*. Princeton: Princeton University Press.

Greenstone, J. David, and Paul E. Peterson. 1973. *Race and Authority in Urban Politics*. New York: Russell Sage Foundation.

Gremillion, Joseph, and David E. Leege. 1989. "Post–Vatican II Parish Life in the United States: Review and Preview." *Notre Dame Study of Catholic Parish Life* (report no. 15).

Grémion, Catherine. 1991. "Décentralisation an X." *French Society and Politics* 9 (3–4): 32–42.

Grimshaw, William J. 1992. *Bitter Fruit: Black Politics and the Chicago Machine.* Chicago: University of Chicago Press.

Grofman, Bernard. 1983. "Measures of Bias and Proportionality in Seats-Votes Relationships." *Political Methodology* 9 (3):295–327.

———. 1992. "Expert Witness Testimony and the Evolution of Voting Rights Case Law." In Bernard Grofman and Chandler Davidson, eds., *Controversies in Minority Voting.* Washington, D.C.: Brookings Institution.

———. 1993. "Throwing Darts at Double Regression—and Missing the Target: A Comment on Wildgen's 'Social Alchemy in the Courtroom.'" *Social Science Quarterly* 74:480–88.

Grofman, Bernard, and Chandler Davidson. 1992. "Postscript: What Is the Best Way to a Color-Blind Society?" In Bernard Grofman and Chandler Davidson, eds., *Controversies in Minority Voting: The Voting Rights Act in Perspective.* Washington, D.C.: Brookings Institution.

Grofman, Bernard, and Lisa Handley. 1989. "Minority Population Proportion and Black and Hispanic Congressional Success in the 1970s and 1980s." *American Politics Quarterly* 17:436–45.

———. 1991. "The Impact of the Voting Rights Act on Black Representation in Southern State Legislatures." *Legislative Studies Quarterly* 16:111–28.

———. 1992. "Preconditions for Black and Hispanic Congressional Success." In Wilma Rule and Joseph P. Zimmerman, eds., *United States Electoral Systems: Their Impact on Women and Minorities.* New York: Greenwood.

Grofman, Bernard, Lisa Handley, and Richard G. Niemi. 1992. *Minority Representation and the Quest for Voting Equality.* New York: Cambridge University Press.

Grofman, Bernard, and Arend Lijphart, eds. 1986. *Electoral Laws and Their Political Consequences.* New York: Agathon Press.

Grofman, Bernard, Michael Migalski, and Nicholas Noviello. 1986. "Effects of Multi-member Districts on Black Representation in State Legislatures." *Review of Black Political Economy* 14(4):51–63.

Gross, Jane. 1992. "Indifference and Disgust Are Leading in California." *New York Times*, May 22, A18.

Guinier, Lani. 1991a. "No Two Seats: The Elusive Quest For Political Equality." *Virginia Law Review* 77 (8): 1412–1514.

———. 1991b. "The Triumph of Tokenism: The Voting Rights Act and the Theory of Black Electoral Success." *Michigan Law Review* 89:1077–1154.

———. 1992. "Voting Rights and Democratic Theory: Where Do We Go from Here?" In Bernard Grofman and Chandler Davidson, eds., *Controversies in Minority Voting.* Washington, D.C.: Brookings Institution.

———. 1993. "Groups, Representation, and Race Conscious Districting: The Case of the Emperor's Clothes." *Texas Law Review* 71:1589–1642.

———. 1994a. *The Tyranny of the Majority: Fundamental Fairness in Representative Democracy.* New York: Free Press.

———. 1994b. "[E]racing Democracy: The Voting Rights Cases." *Harvard Law Review* 108:109–37.

Guterbock, Thomas M., and Bruce London. 1983. "Race, Political Orientation, and Participation: An Empirical Test of Four Competing Theories." *American Sociological Review* 48:439–53.

Gutman, Herbert G. 1976. *The Black Family in Slavery and Freedom, 1750–1925.* New York: Pantheon Books.

Hacker, Andrew. 1992. *Two Nations: Black and White, Separate, Hostile, Unequal.* New York: Charles Scribner's Sons.

Hagen, Michael G. 1988. *Racial Differences in Voter Registration and Turnout.* Mimeo.

———. 1993. "The Salience of Racial Issues." Center for American Political Studies Occasional Paper #93–11, Harvard University.

Hamilton, Charles V. 1972. *The Black Preacher In America.* New York: William Morrow.

Hamilton, Dona Cooper, and Charles V. Hamilton. 1992. "The Dual Agenda of African American Organizations since the New Deal: Social Welfare Policies and Civil Rights." *Political Science Quarterly* 107:435–52.

Harris, Fredrick C. 1994a. "'Rock in a Weary Land': Religious Institutions and African-American Political Mobilization." Paper presented at the fourth session of the Workshop on Race, Ethnicity, Representation, and Governance, Center for American Political Studies, Department of Government, Harvard University, Cambridge, Mass., June 23–24. 1994.

Harris, Fredrick C. 1994b. "Something Within: Religion as a Mobilizer of African-American Political Activism." *Journal of Politics* 56 (1): 42–68.

Hayes v. Louisiana. U.S. District Court, Western District of Louisiana, Shreveport Division, no. 92-CV-1522.

Higginbotham, Evelyn Brooks. 1993. *Righteous Discontent: The Women's Movement in the Black Baptist Church, 1880–1920.* Cambridge: Harvard University Press.

Hirsch, Arnold R. 1983. *Making the Second Ghetto: Race and Housing in Chicago, 1940–1960.* New York: Cambridge University Press.

Holt Civic Club v. City of Tuscaloosa 439 U.S. 60 (1978).

Horowitz, Donald L. 1989. "Incentives and Behavior in the Ethnic Politics of Sri Lanka and Malaysia." *Third World Quarterly* 10 (4): 18–35.

———. 1991. *A Democratic South Africa? Constitutional Engineering in a Divided Society.* Berkeley and Los Angeles: University of California Press.

Hotelling, Harold. 1929. "Stability in Competition." *Economic Journal* 39:41–57.

House Committee on Ways and Means. 1935. *Economic Security Act.* 74th Cong., 1st sess.

Houston v. Haley, 859 F. 2d 341 (5th Cir. 1988); 869 F. 2d 807 per curium (5th Cir. 1989).

Hout, Michael. 1984. "Occupational Mobility of Black Men, 1962–1973." *American Sociological Review* 49 (3):308–22.

Howard, Alan, and Bruce Howard. 1983. "The Dilemma of the Voting Rights Act: Recognizing the Emerging Political Equality Norm." *Columbia Law Review* 83:1615–33.

Howard, Christopher. 1992. "Sowing the Seeds of 'Welfare': The Transformation of Mothers' Pensions, 1900–1940." *Journal of Policy History* 4 (2):188–227.

Huckfeldt, Robert, and Carol Weitzel Kohfeld. 1989. *Race and the Decline of Class in American Politics.* Urbana: University of Illinois Press.

Huckfeldt, Robert, and John Sprague. 1992. "Political Parties and Electoral Mobilization: Political Structure, Social Structure and the Party Canvass." *American Political Science Review* 86:70–87.

Huntington, Samuel P. 1983. *American Politics: The Politics of Disharmony.* Cambridge: Harvard University Press, Belknap Press.

Ifill, Gwen. 1991. "Female Lawmakers Wrestle with New Public Attitudes on 'Women's Issues.'" *New York Times*, November 18, B7.

Illinois Board of Elections v. Socialist Workers Party, 440 U.S. 173 (1978).

Isaacs, Harold R. 1989. *Idols of the Tribe: Group Identity and Political Change.* Cambridge: Harvard University Press.

Jackson, Kenneth T. 1985. *Crabgrass Frontier: The Suburbanization of the United States.* New York: Oxford University Press.

Jackson, Peter M., Justin Meadows, and Andy P. Taylor. 1982. "Urban Fiscal Decay in UK Cities," *Local Government Studies* 8 (September–October): 23–43.

Jacobs, Jane. 1961. *The Death and Life of Great American Cities.* New York: Vintage.

Jacobson, Gary C., and Samuel Kernell. 1983. *Strategy and Choice in Congressional Settings.* New Haven: Yale University Press.

Jacobson, Louis. 1994. "Grimmer Lives in the Doughnut's Hole." *National Journal*, May, 1194–95.

Jeffers v. Clinton, 730 F. Supp. 196 (E.D. Ark. 1989).

Jencks, Christopher. 1992. *Rethinking Social Policy: Race, Poverty and the Underclass* Cambridge: Harvard University Press.

Jennings, James. 1989. "The Puerto Rican Community: Its Political Background." In F. Chris Garcia, ed., *Latinos and the Political System.* Notre Dame, Ind.: University of Notre Dame Press.

Jennings, James, and Monte Rivera, *Puerto Rican Politics in Urban America.* Westport, Conn.: Greenwood Press.

Johnson, Donald Bruce, and Kirk H. Porter. 1966. *National Party Platforms, 1840–1964.* Urbana: University of Illinois Press.

Johnson, Ruby Funchess. 1956. *The Religion of Negro Protestants: Changing Religious Attitudes and Practices.* New York: Philosophical Library.

Johnston, Ronald. "Negro Preachers Take Sides." 1971. In Hart M. Nelson and Raytha L. Yokley, eds., *The Black Church in America.* New York: Basic Books.

Jones v. City of Lubbock, 727 F. 2d 364 (5th Cir. 1984).

Karlan, Pamela S. 1993. "The Rights to Vote: Some Pessimism about Formalism." *Texas Law Review* 71:1705–40.

Karnig, Albert K. 1983. "Decline in Municipal Voter Turnout: A Function of Changing Structure." *American Politics Quarterly* 11 (4): 491–505.

Karnig, Albert K., and B. Oliver Walter. 1993. "Municipal Voter Turnout during the 1980s: The Case of Continued Decline." In Harry A. Bailey, Jr., and Jay M. Shafritz, eds., *State and Local Government and Politics: Essential Readings.* Itasca, Ill.: F. E. Peacock, Publishers.

Karnig, Albert K., and Susan Welch. 1980. *Black Representation and Urban Policy.* Chicago: University of Chicago Press.

———. 1982. "Electoral Structure and Black Representation on City Councils." *Social Science Quarterly* 63 (1): 99–114.

Kasarda, John D., and Jurgen Friedrichs. 1986. "Economic Transformation, Minorities, and Urban Demographic-Employment Mismatch in the U.S. and West Germany." In Hans-Jurgen Ewers, John B. Goddard, and Horst Matzerath, eds., *The Future of the Metropolis: Berlin, London, Paris, New York.* Berlin and New York: Walter de Gruyter.

Katz, Michael B. 1986. *In the Shadow of the Poorhouse: A Social History of Welfare in America.* New York: Basic Books.

———, ed. 1993. *The "Underclass" Debate: Views from History.* Princeton: Princeton University Press.

Katznelson, Ira. 1976. *Black Men, White Cities.* Chicago: University of Chicago Press.

Katznelson, Ira, Kim Geiger, and Daniel Kryder. 1993. "Limiting Liberalism: The Southern Veto in Congress, 1933–1950." *Political Science Quarterly* 108: 283–306.

Keefe, Susan E., and Amado Padilla. 1987. *Chicano Ethnicity.* Albuquerque: University of New Mexico Press.

Keiser, Richard A. 1990. "The Rise of a Biracial Coalition in Philadelphia." In Rufus P. Browning, Dale Rogers Marshall, and David H. Tabb, eds., *Racial Politics in American Cities.* White Plains, N.Y.: Longman.

Keller, Bill. 1993. "South Africa: To End Oppression Peacefully, A Compromise with Oppressors." *New York Times,* February 21, E2.

Kelley, Robin D. G. 1990. *Hammer and Hoe: Alabama Communists during the Great Depression.* Chapel Hill: University of North Carolina Press.

———. 1993. "'We Are Not What We Seem': Rethinking Black Working-Class Opposition in the Jim Crow South." *Journal of American History* 80:75–112.

Key, V. O., Jr. 1937. *The Administration of Federal Grants to the States.* Chicago: Public Administration Service.

———. 1949. *Southern Politics in State and Nation.* New York: Alfred A. Knopf.

Kilson, Martin. 1971. "Political Change in the Negro Ghetto, 1900–1940s." In Nathan I. Huggins, Martin Kilson, and Daniel M. Fox, eds., *Key Issues in the Afro-American Experience.* New York: Harcourt Brace Jovanovich.

Kinder, Donald R., and David O. Sears. 1981. "Prejudice and Politics: Symbolic Racism versus Racial Threats to the Good Life." *Journal of Personality and Social Psychology* 40:414–31.

———. 1985. "Public Opinion and Political Action." In Jeanne N. Knutson, ed., *Handbook of Political Psychology.* San Francisco: Jossey-Bass.

King, Desmond. 1993. "Government beyond Whitehall: Local Government and Urban Politics." In Patrick Dunleavy, Andrew Gamble, Gillian Peele, and Iain Holiday, eds., *Developments in British Politics 4* London: Macmillan.

King, Gary, and Robert X. Browning. 1987. "Democratic Representation and Partisan Bias in Congressional Elections." *American Political Science Review* 81:1251–76.

King, Gary, and Andrew Gelman. 1991. "Systemic Consequences of Incumbency Advantage in the U.S. House." *American Journal of Political Science.* 35(1): 110–38.

Kirby, John B. 1980. *Blacks in the Roosevelt Era: Liberalism and Race.* Knoxville: University of Tennessee Press.

Kirkpatrick v. Preisler, 394 U.S. 526 (1969).

Kleppner, Paul. 1981. *Who Voted: The Dynamics of Electoral Turnout, 1870–1980.* New York: Praeger.

———. 1985. *Chicago Divided: The Making of a Black Mayor.* DeKalb: Northern Illinois University Press.

Knoles, George Harmon. 1942. *The Presidential Campaign and Election of 1892.* Stanford, Calif.: Stanford University Press.

Kolbert, Elizabeth. 1991. "Albany, Squeezed, Puts Pressure on Local Governments." *New York Times,* March 31.

———. 1992a. "Campaign in California: Little but Commercials." *New York Times,* May 22, A1.

———. 1992b. "Senate Races Marked by Vivid Images." *New York Times,* May 27, A18.

Kousser, J. Morgan. 1974. *The Shaping of Southern Politics: Suffrage Restriction and the Establishment of the One-Party South, 1880–1910.* New Haven: Yale University Press.

———. 1984. "The Undermining of the First Reconstruction: Lessons for the Second." In Chandler Davidson, ed., *Minority Vote Dilution.* Washington, D.C.: Howard University Press.

———. 1992. "The Voting Rights Act and the Two Reconstructions." In Bernard Grofman and Chandler Davidson, eds., *Controversies in Minority Voting: The Voting Rights Act in Perspective.* Washington, D.C.: Brookings Institution.

———. 1993. "Beyond *Gingles*: Influence Districts and the Pragmatic Tradition in Voting Rights Law." California Institute of Technology Social Science Working Paper no. 831.

Krauss, Clifford. 1972. "Senate Passes Bill to Force States to Make Voter Registration Easier." *New York Times,* 21 May, B11.

Laquain, Aprodicio. 1992. "Poor and Rich in the Metropolis." *World Press Review* 39: (July): 21–23.

Latimer, Margaret K. 1979. "Black Political Representation in Southern Cities: Election Systems and Other Causal Variables." *Urban Affairs Quarterly* 15(1):65–86.

Lawless, P. 1991. "Urban Policy in the Thatcher Decade: English Inner-City Policy, 1979–90." *Environment and Planning* 9:15–30.

Lichtman, A. 1986. "Analysis of Racial Distinctions in Voter Registration Rates: State of Mississippi." Report in DC 84–35-WK-0, *Mississippi State Chapter Operation Push v. William Allain.*

Lichtman, A., and L. Langbein. 1978. *Ecological Regression.* Beverly Hills, Calif.: Sage.

Lieberman, Robert C. 1993. "The Structural Politics of Race: Toward a New Approach to the Study of Race and Politics." Paper presented to the American Political Science Association, Chicago.

———. 1994. "Race and the Development of the American Welfare State, from the New Deal to the Great Society." Ph.D. diss., Harvard University.

———. 1995. "Social Construction (continued)." *American Political Science Review* 89 (June): 437–41.

Lijphart, Arend. 1977. *Democracy in Plural Societies: A Comparative Explanation.* New Haven: Yale University Press.

———. 1984. *Democracies: Patterns of Majoritarian and Consensus Government in Twenty-One Countries.* New Haven: Yale University Press.

———. 1985. *Power-Sharing in South Africa.* Berkeley: University of California Institute of International Studies.

———. 1990. "The Politial Consequences of Electoral Laws, 1945–1985." *American Political Science Review* 84:481–97.

Lijphart, Arend, et al. n.d. "Separation of Powers and the Management of Political Cleavages." Manuscript on file with the author.

Lijphart, Arend, and Bernard Grofman, eds. 1984. *Choosing an Electoral System: Issues and Alternatives.* New York: Praeger.

Lijphart, Arend, Rafael Lopez Pintor, and Yasunori Sone. 1986. "The Limited Vote and the Single-Nontransferable Vote: Lessons from the Japanese and Spanish Examples." In Bernard Grofman and Arend Lijphart, eds., *Electoral Laws and Their Political Consequences.* New York: Agathon Press.

Lincoln, C. Eric, and Lawrence H. Mamiya. 1990. *The Black Church in the African American Experience.* Durham, N.C.: Duke University Press.

Lipset, Seymour M. 1964. *The First New Nation.* New York: Basic Books.

Lipsky, Michael. 1970. *Protest in City Politics.* Chicago: Rand McNally.

LoFrisco v. Schaffer, 341 F. Supp. 743 (1972).

Logan, Rayford W. 1968. *The Betrayal of the Negro: From Rutherford B. Hayes to Woodrow Wilson.* New York: Collier Books.

Lowenstein, Daniel H., and Jonathan Steinberg. 1985. "The Quest for Legislative Redistricting in the Public Interest: Elusive or Illusory?" *UCLA Law Review* 33 (October): 1–76.

Lublin, David I. 1994. "Gerrymander for Justice? Racial Redistricting and Black and Latino Representation." Ph.D. diss., Department of Government, Harvard University.

Lubove, Roy. 1986. *The Struggle for Social Security, 1900–1935.* Pittsburgh: University of Pittsburgh Press.

Lucas v. Colorado, 377 U.S. 713 (1964).

LULAC v. Midland Independent School District, 812 F. 2d 1494 (5th Cir. 1987), vacated; 829 F. 2d 546 (5th Cir., en banc, 1987).

MacManus, Susan A. 1987. "Constituency Size and Minority Representation." *State and Local Government Review* 19 (winter): 3–7.

MacManus, Susan A., and Charles S. Bullock III. 1988. "Minorities and Women 'Do' Win At-Large!" *National Civic Review* 77(3): 231–44.

Magrath, C. Peter. 1963. *Morrison R. Waite: The Triumph of Character.* New York: Macmillan.

Mahan v. Howell, 404 U.S. 1201 (1971).

Marable, Manning. 1983. *How Capitalism Underdeveloped Black America*. Boston: South End.

March, James G., and Johan P. Olsen. 1989. *Rediscovering Institutions: The Organizational Basis of Politics*. New York: Free Press.

Martis, Kenneth, et al. 1989. *The Historical Atlas of Political Parties in the United States Congress, 1789–1989*. New York: Macmillan.

Martis, Kenneth, and Gregory A. Elmes. 1993. *The Historical Atlas of State Power in Congress, 1790–1990*. Washington, D.C.: Congressional Quarterly.

Massachusetts Political Almanac. 1990. Vol 1., *Legislative Branch*. Boston: Almanac Research Services.

Matthews, Donald R. 1960. *U.S. Senators and Their World*. New York: Vintage.

Matthews, Donald R., and J. M. Prothro. 1966. *Negroes and the New Southern Politics*. New York: Harcourt, Brace and World.

Mayhew, David. 1986. *Placing Parties in American Politics*. Princeton: Princeton University Press.

Mays, Benjamin E., and Joseph W. Nicholson. [1933] 1969. *The Negroes' Church*. New York: Russell and Russell.

McAdam, Doug. 1982. *Political Process and the Development of Black Insurgency, 1930–1970*. Chicago: University of Chicago Press.

McCorkle, Mach. 1991. "Gantt versus Helms: Toward the New Progressive Era?" *Reconstruction* 1 (3): 18–24.

McCormick, Joseph, II, and Charles E. Jones. 1993. "The Conceptualization of Deracialization: Thinking through the Dilemma." In Georgia A. Persons, ed., *Dilemmas of Black Politics*. New York: HarperCollins.

McCullough, David. 1992. *Truman*. New York: Simon and Schuster.

McCurdy, Charles W. 1986. "Waite Court." *Society* 24:40–45.

McDonald, Laughlin. 1992. "The 1982 Amendments of Section 2 and Minority Representation." In Bernard Grofman and Chandler Davidson, eds. *Controversies in Minority Voting Behavior: The Voting Rights Act in Perspective*. Washington, D.C.: Brookings Institution.

McGregor, James. 1993. "How Electoral Laws Shape Eastern Europe's Parliaments." *RFE/RL Research Report* 2(4):11–18.

McKinley, Charles, and Robert W. Frase. 1970. *Launching Social Security: A Capture-and-Record Account*. Madison: University of Wisconsin Press.

McMillan v. Escambia County, 748 F. 2d 1037 (1984).

McMurry, Donald. 1922. "The Political Significance of the Pension Question, 1885–1897." *Mississippi Valley Historical Review* 9:19–36.

McNeil v. Springfield Park District, 851 F. 2d 937 (7th Cir. 1988).

McPherson, Miller J. 1977. "Correlates of Social Participation: A Comparison of the Ethnic Community and Compensatory Theories." *Sociological Quarterly* 18:197–208.

Mead, Lawrence M. 1992. *The New Politics of Poverty: The Nonworking Poor in America*. New York: Basic Books.

Meckel, Richard A. 1990. *Save the Babies: American Public Health Reform and the Prevention of Infant Mortality, 1850–1929*. Baltimore: Johns Hopkins University Press.

Meier, August, and Elliot Rudwick. 1969. "The Boycott Movement Against Jim Crow Street Cars in the South, 1900–1906." *Journal of American History* 55:756–75.

———. 1979. *Black Detroit and the Rise of the UAW.* Oxford: Oxford University Press.

Mény, Yves. 1992. "La république des fiefs." *Pouvoirs* 60 (January): 17–24.

Michelman, Frank I. 1989. "Conceptions of Democracy in American Constitutional Argument: Voting Rights." *Florida Law Review* 41:443–90.

Mills, Edwin S. 1987. "Nonurban Policies as Urban Policies." *Urban Studies* 24:561–69.

Minow, Martha. 1991. "From Class Actions to Miss Saigon: The Concept of Representation in the Law." *Cleveland State Law Review* 39:269–300.

Moe, Terry M. 1989. "The Politics of Bureaucratic Structure." In John E. Chubb and Paul E. Peterson, eds., *Can the Government Govern?* Washington, D.C.: Brookings Institution.

Mollenkopf, John Hull. 1992. *A Phoenix in the Ashes: The Rise and Fall of the Koch Coalition in New York City Politics.* Princeton: Princeton University Press.

Monroe v. City of Woodville, 819 F. 2d 507 (5th Cir. 1987); 881 F. 2d 1327 (5th Cir. 1989); rehearing denied, 897 F. 2d 763 (5th Cir. 1989).

Moore, Joan, and Harry Pachon. 1985. *Hispanics in the United States.* Englewood Cliffs, N.J.: Prentice-Hall.

Moreland, L. W., R. P. Steed, and T. A. Baker, eds. 1986. *Blacks in Southern Politics.* New York: Praeger.

Morin, Richard. 1988. "Largest Downtowns Eluded Bush's Grasp." *Washington Post,* November 25, A29–30.

Morris, Aldon D. 1984. *The Origins of the Civil Rights Movement: Black Communities Organizing for Change.* New York: Free Press.

Mukenge, Ida Rousseau. 1983. *The Black Church in Urban America: A Case Study in Political Economy.* Lanham, Md.: University Press of America.

Mulderink, Earl F. 1988. "'We Want a Country': New Bedford's Irish-American and Afro-American Communities during the Civil War Era." Paper presented at the 1988 Annual Meeting of the American Studies Association.

Munro v. Socialist Workers Party, 479 U.S. 189 (1986).

Myers, David. 1992. "A Social Recession Grips the Nation." *Philadelphia Inquirer,* May 22, A19.

Myrdal, Gunnar. 1944. *An American Dilemma: The Negro Problem and Modern Democracy.* New York: Harper and Brothers.

Nagel, Jack. 1993. "Lessons of the Impending Electoral Reform in New Zealand." *Newsletter of PEGS* 3:11–13.

National Archives. Files of the Social Security Administration. Record group 47.

National Association of Latino Elected and Appointed Officials. 1992. "Political Participation among Latino Immigrants." *NLIS Research Notes* 1 (October).

Nelsen, Hart M., and Anne Kusener Nelsen. 1975. *Black Church in the Sixties.* Lexington: University of Kentucky Press.

Nelson, William E., and Philip J. Meranto. 1977. *Electing Black Mayors.* Columbus: Ohio State University Press.

Nieman, Donald G. 1991. *Promises to Keep: African Americans and the Constitutional Order, 1776 to the Present*. New York: Oxford University Press.

Niemi, Richard G., and Patrick Fett. 1986. "The Swing Ratio: An Explanation and an Assessment." *Legislative Studies Quarterly* 11:75–90.

O'Loughlin, John. 1979. "Black Representation Growth and the Seat-Vote Relationship." *Social Science Quarterly* 60(1): 72–86.

Olsen, Marvin. 1970. "Social and Political Participation of Blacks." *American Sociological Review* 35:682–97.

Olzak, Susan. 1990. "The Political Context of Competition: Lynching and Urban Racial Violence, 1882–1914." *Social Forces* 69:395–422.

Orfield, Gary, Sara Schley, Diane Glass, and Sean Reardon. 1993. "The Growth of Segregation in American Schools: Changing Patterns of Separation and Poverty since 1968." Publication of the National School Board Association, Council of Urban Boards of Education.

Orloff, Ann Shola. 1988. "The Politics of America's Belated Welfare State." In Margaret Weir, Ann Shola Orloff, and Theda Skocpol, eds., *The Politics of Social Policy in the United States*. Princeton: Princeton University Press.

O'Rourke, Timothy G. 1992. "The 1982 Amendments and the Voting Rights Paradox." In Bernard Grofman and Chandler Davidson, eds., *Controversies in Minority Voting Behavior: The Voting Rights Act in Perspective*. Washington, D.C.: Brookings Institution.

Orum, Anthony M. 1966. "A Reappraisal of the Social and Political Participation of Negroes." *American Journal of Sociology* 72:32–46.

Ostrom, Elinor. 1983. "The Social Stratification–Government Inequality Thesis Explored." *Urban Affairs Quarterly* 19 (September): 91–112.

Palfrey, Thomas. 1989. "A Mathematical Proof of Duverger's Law." In Peter Ordeshook, ed., *Models of Strategic Choice in Politics*. Ann Arbor: University of Michigan Press.

Parenti, Michael. 1967. "Ethnic Politics and the Persistence of Ethnic Identification." *American Political Science Review* 67:717–26.

Parker, Frank R. 1984. "Racial Gerrymandering and Legislative Reapportionment." In Chandler Davidson, ed., *Minority Vote Dilution*. Washington, D.C.: Joint Center for Political Studies.

———. 1990. *Black Votes Count: Political Empowerment in Mississippi after 1965*. Chapel Hill: University of North Carolina Press.

Parkinson, Michael. 1985. *Liverpool on the Brink*. Cambridge: Policy Journals.

Parsons, Stanley B., William W. Beach, and Michael J. Dubin. 1986. *United States Congressional Districts and Data, 1843 to 1883*. Westport, Conn.: Greenwood Press.

Patterson, James T. 1967. *Congressional Conservatism and the New Deal: The Growth of a Conservative Coalition in Congress, 1933–1939*. Lexington: University of Kentucky Press.

———. 1969. *The New Deal and the States: Federalism in Transition*. Princeton: Princeton University Press.

———. 1981. *America's Struggle against Poverty, 1900–1980*. Cambridge: Harvard University Press.

Patterson, Samuel C., and Gregory A. Caldeira. 1983. "Getting Out the Vote: Participation in Gubernatorial Elections." *American Political Science Review* 77:675–89.

Payne, Wardell J., ed. 1991. *Directory of African American Religious Bodies*. Washington, D.C.: Howard University Press.

Peach, Ceri. 1987. "Immigration and Segregation in Western Europe since 1945." In Gunther Glebe and John O'Loughlin, eds., *Foreign Minorities in Continental European Cities*. Stuttgart: Franz Steiner Verlag Wiesbaden GMBH.

Peirce, Neal R. 1993. "The GOP Senators' Pork in a Poke." *National Journal*, April 24, 1006.

Perkins, Frances. 1946. *The Roosevelt I Knew*. New York: Viking.

Peterson, Paul E., ed. 1985. *The New Urban Reality*. Washington, D.C.: Brookings Institution.

Pettigrew, Thomas. 1972. "When a Black Candidate Runs for Mayor: Race and Voting Behavior." In Harlan Hahn, ed., *People and Politics in Urban Society*, vol. 6. Beverly Hills, Calif.: Sage Publications.

Phillips, Peggy A. 1987. *Modern France: Theories and Realities of Urban Planning*. Lanham, Md.: University Press of America.

Pickvance, Chris. 1991. "The Difficulty of Control and the Ease of Structural Reform: British Local Government in the 1980s." In Chris Pickvance and Edmond Preteceille, eds., *State Restructuring and Local Power: A Comparative Perspective*. London and New York: Pinter Publishers.

Pinderhughes, Dianne. 1987. *Race and Ethnicity in Chicago Politics*. Urbana: University of Illinois Press.

Pitkin, Hanna. 1967. *The Concept of Representation*. Berkeley and Los Angeles: University of California Press.

Piven, Frances Fox, and Richard A. Cloward. 1988. *Why Americans Don't Vote*. New York: Pantheon Books.

Plotkin, Sidney. 1987. *Keep Out: The Struggle for Land Use Control*. Berkeley and Los Angeles: University of California Press.

Polsby, Nelson W. 1968. "The Institutionalization of the House of Representatives." *American Political Science Review* 62:144–68.

Potter, David M. 1972. *The South and the Concurrent Majority*. Edited by Don E. Fehrenbacher and Carl N. Degler. Baton Rouge: Louisiana State University Press.

Portes, Alejandro. 1984. "The Rise of Ethnicity: Determinants of Ethnic Perceptions among Cuban Exiles in Miami." *American Sociological Review* 49:383–97.

Powell, G. Bingham, Jr. 1986. "American Voter Turnout in Comparative Perspective." *American Political Science Review* 80:17–43.

Presley v. Etowah County, 112 S. Ct. 820 (1992).

Preston, Michael B. 1987. "The Election of Harold Washington: An Examination of the SES Model in the 1983 Chicago Mayoral Election." In Michael B. Preston, Lenneal J. Henderson, Jr., and Paul Puryear, eds., *The New Black Politics*, 2d ed. New York: Longman.

———. 1990. "Symposium: Big-City Black Mayors. Have They Made a Difference?" In Lucius J. Barker, ed., National Political Science Review, vol. 2. New Brunswick, N.J.: Transaction Publishers.

Preteceille, Edmond. 1991. "From Centralization to Decentralization: Social Restructuring and French Local Government." In Chris Pickvance and Edmond Pre-teceille, eds., *State Restructuring and Local Power: A Comparative Perspective.* London and New York: Pinter Publishers.

Price, Douglas. 1977. "Careers and Committees in the American Congress." In William O. Aydelotte, ed., *The History of Parliamentary Behavior.* Princeton: Princeton University Press.

Purdum, Todd S. 1992. "In Carving Up of Districts, Some Share the Leftovers." *New York Times,* June 5, A1.

Putnam, Robert D. 1993. *Making Democracy Work: Civic Traditions in Modern Italy.* Princeton: Princeton University Press.

Quadagno, Jill. 1988a. "From Old-Age Assistance to Supplemental Security Income: The Political Economy of Relief in the South, 1935–1972." In Margaret Weir, Ann Shola Orloff, and Theda Skocpol, eds., *The Politics of Social Policy in the United States.* Princeton: Princeton University Press. Pp. 235–63.

———. 1988b. *The Transformation of Old Age Security: Class and Politics in the American Welfare State.* Chicago: University of Chicago Press.

Rae, Douglas W. 1967. *The Political Consequences of Electoral Laws.* New Haven: Yale University Press.

Ralph, James. 1993. *Northern Protest: Martin Luther King, Jr., Chicago, and the Civil Rights Movement,* Cambridge: Harvard University Press.

Randolph, Phillip A. [1929] 1990. "Negro Labor and the Church." In Herbert Aptheker, ed., *A Documentary History of the Negro People in the United States.* Vol. 3. New York: First Carol Publishing Group.

Ranney, Austin. 1972. "Turnout and Representation in Presidential Primary Elections." *American Political Science Review* 12:224–38.

Ransom, Bruce. 1987. "Black Independent Electoral Politics in Philadelphia: The Election of Mayor W. Wilson Goode." In Michael Preston, Lenneal B. Henderson, Jr., and Paul L. Puryear, *The New Black Politics.* 2d ed. New York: Longman.

Reed, Adolph, Jr. 1986. *The Jesse Jackson Phenomenon: The Crisis of Purpose In Afro-American Politics.* New Haven: Yale University Press.

———. 1988. "The Black Urban Regime: Structural Origins and Constraints." In Michael Peter Smith, ed., *Power, Community, and the City.* Vol. 1. New Brunswick, N.J.: Transaction Press.

Reed, Judith. 1992. "Of Boroughs, Boundaries and Bullwinkles: The Limitations of Single-Member Districts in a Multiracial Context." *Fordham Urban Law Journal* 19:759–80.

Regents of the University of California v. Bakke, 438 *U.S.* 265 (1978). Reprinted in Malcolm M. Feeley and Samuel Krislov, eds. 1985. *Constitutional Law.* Boston: Little Brown.

Reinhold, Robert. 1992. "Chasing Votes from Big Cities to the Suburbs," *New York Times,* June 6, 1.

Rex, John. 1988. *The Ghetto and the Underclass: Essays on Race and Social Policy.* Aldershot: Gower.

Reynolds v. Sims, 377 U.S. 533 (1971).

Rich, Wilbur C. 1989. *Coleman Young and Detroit Politics.* Detroit: Wayne State University Press.

Riker, William H. 1962. *The Theory of Political Coalitions*. New Haven: Yale University Press.

———. 1982. "The Two-Party System and Duverger's Law: An Essay on the History of Political Science." *American Political Science Review* 76:753–66.

Rivera, Monte. 1984. Organizational Politics of the East Harlem Barrio in the 1970s." In James Jennings and Monte Rivera, *Puerto Rican Politics in Urban America*. Westport, Conn.: Greenwood Press.

Robertson, Mrs. G. Harris. 1912. "The State's Duty to Fatherless Children." *Child-Welfare Magazine* 6(5): 156–60.

Rodriguez-Morazzani, Roberto P. 1991–92. "Puerto Rican Political Generations in New York: Pioneros, Young Turks and Radicals." *Centro* 4 (1): 96–116.

Rogers v. Lodge, 458 U.S. 613 (1982).

Rohde, David W. 1991. "Something's Happening Here; What It Is Ain't Exactly Clear: Southern Democrats in the House of Representatives." In Morris P. Fiorina and David W. Rohde, eds., *Home Style and Washington Work*. Ann Arbor: University of Michigan Press.

Rohter, Larry. 1992a. "A Black-Hispanic Struggle over Florida Redistricting." *New York Times*, May 30, A6.

———. 1992b. "Florida Is Rethinking the Way Presidents Are Elected." *New York Times*, June 7, A25.

Roosevelt, Franklin D. 1938. "Message to the Congress Reviewing the Broad Objectives and Accomplishments of the Administration, June 8, 1934." In Samuel I. Rosenman, ed., *The Public Papers and Addresses of Franklin D. Roosevelt*. Vol. 3. New York: Random House.

Romero v. City of Pomona, 883 F. 2d 1418 (9th Cir. 1989).

Rosenberg, Gerald N. 1991. *The Hollow Hope: Can Courts Bring about Social Change?* Chicago: University of Chicago Press.

Rosenstone, Steven J., and John Mark Hansen. 1993. *Mobilization, Participation, and Democracy in America*. New York: Macmillan.

Rosenstone, Steven J. and R. Wolfinger. 1978. "The Effect of Registration Laws on Voter Turnout." *American Political Science Review* 72(1): 22–45.

Rubinfeld, D., ed. 1991. "Statistical and Demographic Issues Underlying Voting Rights Cases." *Evaluation Review* 15:659–815.

Rueschemeyer, Dietrich, Evelyne Huber Stephens, and John D. Stephens. 1992. *Capitalist Development and Democracy*. Chicago: University of Chicago Press.

Rusk, David. 1992. "America's Urban Apartheid." *New York Times*, May 21, A29.

Rusk, Jerrold G., and John Stucker. 1978. "The Effect of the Southern System of Election Laws on Voting Participation." In Joel H. Silbey, Allan G. Bogue, and William H. Flanigan, eds., *The History of American Electoral Behavior*. Princeton: Princeton University Press.

Rust v. Sullivan, 111 S. Ct. 1759 (1991).

Sack, Kevin. 1992. "Albany Legislators Agree on Plan for Revised Congressional Lines." *New York Times*, June 4, A1.

Sailors v. Board of Education, 387 U.S. 105 (1967).

Salyer Land Co. v. Tulare Lake Basin Water Storage District 410 U.S. 719 (1973).

Sanchez v. Bond, 875 F. 2d 1488 (10th Cir. 1989).

Sanders, Heywood T. 1980. "Paying for the 'Bloody Shirt': The Politics of Civil War Pensions." In Barry S. Rundquist, ed., *Political Benefits*. Lexington, Mass.: Lexington Books, D.C. Heath.

Sassen, Saskia. 1991. *The Global City: New York, London, Tokyo.* Princeton: Princeton University Press.

Savitch, H. V. 1988. *Post-Industrial Cities: Politics and Planning in New York, Paris, and London.* Princeton : Princeton University Press.

Sawyer, Jack, and Duncan MacRae, Jr. 1962. "Game Theory and Cumulative Voting in Illinois, 1902–1954." *American Political Science Review* 56:936–46.

Schelling, Thomas C. 1978. *Micromotives and Macrobehavior.* New York: W. W. Norton.

Schlesinger, Arthur M., Jr. 1960. *The Age of Roosevelt: The Politics of Upheaval.* Boston: Houghton Mifflin.

Schlozman, Kay Lehman. 1994. "Voluntary Associations in Politics: Who Gets Involved?" In William Crotty, Mildred A. Schwartz, and John C. Green, eds. *Representing Interests and Interest Group Representation.* Lanham, Md.: University Press of America.

Schmalz, Jeffrey. 1992. "Clinton Carves Wide and Deep Path through the Heart of Reagan Country." *New York Times*, November 4, B1.

Schmidt, Vivian. 1990. *Democratizing France: The Political and Administrative History of Decentralization* Cambridge: Cambridge University Press.

Schmidt, William E. 1994. "This Blessed Plot, This Glitzy Mall, This England." *New York Times*, May 9, E16.

Schneider, William. 1992. "The Suburban Century Begins." *Atlantic Monthly* (July): 33–44.

Schrodt, Philip A. 1981. "A Statistical Study of the Cube Law in Five Electoral Systems." *Political Methodology* 7:31–53.

Schuman, Howard, Charlotte Steeh, and Lawrence Bobo. 1985. *Racial Attitudes in America: Trends and Interpretations.* Cambridge: Harvard University Press.

Schuman, Tony. 1985. "Housing Abroad: Social Housing in France." *Journal of Housing* 42 (July–August): 142–44.

Schwartz, Bernard, ed. 1970. *Statutory History of the United States: Civil Rights, Part 1.* New York: McGraw-Hill, Chelsea House.

Scott, James C. 1985. *Weapons of the Weak.* New Haven: Yale University Press.

———. 1990. *Domination and the Arts of Resistance.* New Haven: Yale University Press.

Sears, David O., and Donald R. Kinder. 1985. "Whites' Opposition to Busing: On Conceptualizing and Operationalizing Group Conflict." *Journal of Personality and Social Psychology*, 48:1141–47.

Senate Committee on Finance. 1935. *Economic Security Act*, 74th Cong., 1st sess.

Shaw v. Reno, 1993 U.S. Lexis 4406.

Shepsle, Kenneth A. 1989. "The Changing Textbook Congress." In John E. Chubb and Paul E. Peterson, eds., *Can the Government Govern?* Washington, D.C.: Brookings Institution.

———. 1991. *Models of Multiparty Electoral Competition.* New York: Harwood Academic Publishers.

Sherman, Richard B. 1973. *The Republican Party and Black America from McKinley to Hoover, 1896–1933.* Charlottesville: University Press of Virginia.

Shingles, Richard D. 1981. "Black Consciousness and Political Participation: The Missing Link." *American Political Science Review*. 75:76–91.

Shockley, Evelyn E. 1991. "Voting Rights Act Section 2: Racially Polarized Voting and the Minority Community's Representative of Choice." *Michigan Law Review* 89 (February): 1038–67.

Silver, Hilary. 1991. "The Privatization of Housing in Great Britain." In William Gormley, ed., *Privatization and Its Alternatives*. Madison: University of Wisconsin Press.

———. 1993. "National Conceptions of the New Urban Poverty: Social Structural Change in Britain, France and the United States." *International Journal of Urban and Regional Research* 17(3): 336–54.

Sitkoff, Harvard. 1978. *A New Deal for Blacks: The Emergence of Civil Rights as a National Issue*. Volume 1: The Depression Decade. New York: Oxford University Press.

Skocpol, Theda. 1991. "Targeting within Universalism: Politically Viable Policies to Combat Poverty in the United States." In Christopher Jencks and Paul E. Peterson, eds. *The Urban Underclass*. Washington D.C.: Brookings Institution.

———. 1992. *Protecting Soldiers and Mothers: The Political Origins of Social Policy in the United States*. Cambridge: Harvard University Press, Belknap Press.

Skocpol, Theda, and Edwin Amenta. 1985. "Did Capitalists Shape Social Security?" *American Sociological Review* 50 (4): 572–75.

Skocpol, Theda, Christopher Howard, Susan Goodrich Lehmann, and Marjorie Abend-Wein. 1993. "Women's Associations and the Enactment of Mother's Pensions in the United States." *American Political Science Review* 87: 686–701.

Skowronek, Stephen. 1982. *Building a New American State: The Expansion of National Administrative Capacities, 1877–1920*. Cambridge and New York: Cambridge University Press.

Smith, Anthony. 1981. *The Ethnic Revival in the Modern World*. Cambridge: Cambridge University Press.

Smith, Constance E. 1960. *Voting and Election Laws: Laws for Voters*. New York: Oceana Publications.

Smith, Robert C. 1981. "Black Power and the Transformation from Protest to Politics." *Political Science Quarterly* 96 (3): 1–43.

———. 1990. "Recent Elections and Black Politics: The Maturation or the Death of Black Politics?" *Political Science and Politics* 23 (2): 160–62.

Smith, Rogers M. 1993. "Beyond Tocqueville, Myrdal, and Hartz: The Multiple Traditions in America." *American Political Science Review* 87:549–66.

Smith, Tom. 1990. "Ethnic Survey." In *General Social Survey Topical Report No. 19*. Chicago: National Opinion Research Center, University of Chicago.

Smothers, Ronald. 1992. "After 115 Years, A Black Will Represent Alabama." *New York Times*, May 23, A8.

———. 1994. "Jackson Tours to Tell Blacks of New Threat." *New York Times*, June 5, 24.

Sniderman, Paul M., and Michael Gray Hagen. 1985. *Race and Inequality: A Study in American Values*. Chatham, N.J.: Chatham House Publishers.

Socolofsky, Homer E., and Allan B. Spetter. 1987. *The Presidency of Benjamin Harrison*. Lawrence: University Press of Kansas.

Sonenshein, Raphael. 1993. *Politics in Black and White*. Princeton: Princeton University Press.

Soni, Sushma. 1990. "Defining the Minority-Preferred Candidate under Section 2." *Yale Law Journal* 99 (2): 1651–68.

South Carolina v. Katzenbach, 383 U.S. 301 (1966).

Specter, Michael. 1991. "States vs. Cities." *Washington Post*, March 24.

Squires, James. 1992. "When You See Perot, You See Perot." *New York Times*, June 5, A20.

Stanback, Thomas M., Jr. 1991. *The New Suburbanization: Challenge to the Central City*. Boulder, Colo.: Westview Press.

Stanley, Harold W. 1987. *Voter Mobilization and the Politics of Race*. New York: Praeger.

Stanley, Harold W., and Richard G. Niemi. 1992. *Vital Statistics on American Politics*. 3d ed. Washington, D.C.: CQ Press.

Steiner, Gilbert Y. 1966. *Social Insecurity: The Politics of Welfare*. Chicago: Rand McNally.

Stekler, P. 1983. "Black Politics in the New South: An Investigation of Change at Various Levels." Ph.D. diss., Harvard University.

Sterner, Richard. 1943. *The Negro's Share: A Study of Income, Consumption, Housing, and Public Assistance*. New York: Harper and Brothers.

Stewart, Charles H., III. 1991. "Lessons from the Post–Civil War Era." In Gary W. Cox and Samuel Kernell, eds., *The Politics of Divided Government*. Boulder, Colo.: Westview Press.

Stewart, Charles H., III, and Barry R. Weingast. 1992. "Stacking the Senate, Changing the Nation: Republican Rotten Boroughs, Statehood Politics, and American Political Development." *Studies in American Political Development* 6:223–71.

Still, Edward. 1984. "Alternatives to Single-Member Districts." In Chandler Davidson, ed., *Minority Vote Dilution*. Washington, D.C: Howard University Press.

Stinchcombe, Arthur L. 1968. *Constructing Social Theories*. New York: Harcourt, Brace and World.

Sugden, Robert. 1984. "Free Association and the Theory of Proportional Representation." *American Political Science Review* 78:31–44.

Sullivan, John L., James Pierson, and George E. Marcus. 1982. *Political Tolerance and American Democracy*. Chicago: University of Chicago Press.

Suro, Robert. 1992. "Texas G.O.P. Wins on Redistricting." *New York Times*, January 17, A15.

Swain, Carol M. 1993. *Black Faces, Black Interests: The Representation of African-Americans in Congress*. Cambridge: Harvard University Press.

Taagepera, Rein, and Matthew Soberg Shugart. 1989. *Seats and Votes: The Effects and Determinants of Electoral Systems*. New Haven: Yale University Press.

Tashjian v. Republican Party of Connecticut, 470 U.S. 208 (1986).

Tate, Katherine 1988. "Protest to Politics: The New Black Voters in American Elections." Harvard University. Mimeo.

———. 1991. "Black Political Participation in the 1984 and 1988 Presidential Elections." *American Political Science Review* 85 (4): 1159–76.

———. 1993. *From Protest to Politics: The New Black Voters in American Elections*. Cambridge: Harvard University Press.

Teasley, C. E., III. 1987. "Minority Vote Dilution: The Impact of Election System and Past Discrimination on Minority Representation." *State and Local Government* 19 (3): 95–100.

Terry v. Adams, 345 U.S. 461, 484 (1953).

Thernstrom, Abigail M. 1987. *Whose Votes Count? Affirmative Action and Minority Voting.* Cambridge: Harvard University Press.

Thornburg v. Gingles, 478 U.S. 30, 50 n.17 (1986).

Tiebout, Charles M. 1956. "A Pure Theory of Local Expenditures." *Journal of Political Economy* 64:416–24.

Timpone, R. 1995. "Mass Mobilization or Government Intervention? The Growth of Black Registration in the South." *Journal of Politics* 57 (2): 425–43.

Tindall, George. 1949. "The Campaign for the Disfranchisement of Negroes in South Carolina." *Journal of Southern History* 15:212–34.

Tocqueville, Alexis de. 1945. *Democracy in America.* Vols. 1 and 2. New York: Knopf.

Toner, Robin. 1992. "Anxious Days for Bush's Campaign as G.O.P. Heads into a 3-Way Race." *New York Times*, May 21, A22.

Tufte, Edward. 1973. "The Relationship between Seats and Votes in Two-Party Systems." *American Political Science Review* 67 (June): 540–54.

Turner, James P. 1992. "A Case-Specific Approach to Implementing the Voting Rights Act." In Bernard Grofman and Chandler Davidson, eds., *Controversies in Minority Voting.* Washington, D.C.: Brookings Institution.

Uhlaner, Carole J., Bruce E. Cain, and D. Roderick Kiewiet. 1987. "Political Participation of Ethnic Minorities in the 1980s." Social Science Working Paper, California Institute of Technology.

United Jewish Organizations of Williamsburgh v. Carey, 430 U.S. 144.

United States v. Dallas County Commission, 739 F. 2d 1529 (1984).

Upham v. Seamon, 456 U.S. 37 (1982).

Urwin, D. W., and W. E. Paterson, eds. 1990. *Politics in Western Europe Today.* Singapore: Longman Group.

U.S. Bureau of the Census. 1931. *Fifteenth Census of the United States: 1930, Population.* Washington, D.C.: Government Printing Office.

————. 1991. *Poverty in the United States, 1990.* Current Population Reports, series P-60, no. 175. Washington: Government Printing Office.

U.S. Commission on Civil Rights. 1968. *Political Participation.* Washington, D.C.: Government Printing Office.

————. 1971. *Voting.* Washington, D.C.: Government Printing Office.

————. 1976. *Puerto Ricans in the Continental United States: An Uncertain Future.* Washington, D.C.: Government Printing Office.

U.S. Committee on Economic Security. 1985. *The Report of the Committee on Economic Security.* Washington, D.C.: National Conference on Social Welfare.

U.S. Congress. 1935. *Congressional Directory.* 74th Cong., 1st sess., 2d. ed. Washington, D.C.: Government Printing Office.

————. 1989. *Biographical Directory of the United States Congress, 1774–1989.* Washington, D.C.: Government Printing Office.

U.S. National Commission on Urban Problems. 1968. *Building the American City.*

91st Cong., 1st sess. House Document no. 91–34. Washington, D.C.: Government Printing Office.

U.S. Social Security Board. 1937. *Social Security in America: The Factual Background of the Social Security Act as Summarized from Staff Reports to the Committee on Economic Security.* Social Security Board Publication no. 20. Washington, D.C.: Government Printing Office.

Uzee, Philip D. 1950. "Republican Politics in Louisiana, 1877–1900." Ph.D. diss., Louisiana State University.

Valelly, Richard M. 1993. "Party, Coercion, and Inclusion: The Two Reconstructions of the South's Electoral Politics." *Politics and Society* 21:37–67.

Verba, Sidney, and Norman H. Nie. 1972. *Participation in America.* Chicago: University of Chicago Press.

Verba, Sidney, Kay Lehman Schlozman, and Henry E. Brady. 1995. *Voice and Equality: Civic Voluntarism in American Politics.* Cambridge: Harvard University Press.

Verba, Sidney, Kay Lehman Schlozman, Henry Brady, and Norman Nie. 1993a. "Citizen Activity: Who Participates? What Do they Say?" *American Political Science Review* 97:303–18.

———. 1993b. "Race, Ethnicity and Political Resources: Participation in the United States." *British Journal of Political Science* 23:453–97.

Verhovek, Sam Howe. 1992a. "Congressional District Plan Unveiled." *New York Times,* May 27, B1.

———. 1992b. "Redistricting Plan Spurs Lawmakers' Criticism." *New York Times,* May 28, B1.

Voinovich v. Quilter, 794 F. Supp. 695 (1992).

Wacquant, Loic J. D. 1995. "The Comparative Structure and Experience of Social Exclusion: 'Race,' Class, and Space in Chicago and Paris." In Katherine McFate, Roger Lawson, and William J. Wilson, eds., *Poverty, Inequality, and the Future of Social Policy: Western States in the New World Order.* New York: Russell Sage.

Waldron, Jeremy. 1990. "Right and Majorities: Rousseau Revisited." In John W. Chapman and Alan Wertheimer, eds., *Majorities and Minorities* Nomos, vol. 23. New York: New York University Press.

Walker, Clarence E. 1982. *A Rock in a Weary Land: The African Methodist Episcopal Church during the Civil War and Reconstruction.* Baton Rouge: Louisiana State University Press.

Walters, Ronald W. 1994. "Correspondence." *Reconstruction* 2 (3): 190–91.

Walton, Hanes, Jr. 1972. *Black Political Parties: An Historical and Political Analysis.* New York: Free Press.

Wang, Xi. 1993. "Black Suffrage and Northern Republicans, 1865–1891." Ph.D. diss., Columbia University.

Washington, James M. 1985. *Frustrated Fellowship: The Black Baptist Quest for Social Power.* Macon, Ga.: Mercer University Press.

Weatherford, M. Stephen. 1992. "Measuring Political Legitimacy." *American Political Science Review* 86:149–67.

Weaver, Leon. 1984. "Semi-proportional and Proportional Representation Systems in the United States." In Arend Lijphart and Bernard Grofman, eds., *Choosing an Electoral System: Issues and Alternatives*. New York: Praeger.

―――. 1986. "The Rise, Decline, and Resurrection of Proportional Representation in Local Governments in the United States." In Bernard Grofman and Arend Lijphart, eds., *Electoral Laws and Their Political Consequences*. New York: Agathon Press.

Weber, David J. 1973. *Foreigners in the Native Land: Historical Roots of the Mexican Americans*. Albuquerque: University of New Mexico Press.

Weiher, Gregory R. 1991. *The Fractured Metropolis: Political Fragmentation and Metropolitan Segregation*. Albany: State University of New York Press.

Weir, Margaret. 1992. *Politics and Jobs: The Boundaries of Employment Policy in the United States*. Princeton: Princeton University Press.

Weir, Margaret, and Theda Skocpol. 1985. "State Structures and Possibilities for 'Keynesian' Responses to the Great Depression in Sweden, Britain, and the United States." In Peter B. Evans, Dietrich Rueschemeyer, and Theda Skocpol, eds., *Bringing the State Back In*. Cambridge and New York: Cambridge University Press.

Weiss, Nancy J. 1983. *Farewell to the Party of Lincoln: Black Politics in the Age of FDR*. Princeton: Princeton University Press.

Welch, Susan. 1990. "The Impact of At-large Elections on the Representation of Blacks and Hispanics." *Journal of Politics* 52 (4): 1050–76.

Welch, Susan, and Timothy Bledsoe. 1988. *Urban Reform and Its Consequences*. Chicago: University of Chicago Press.

Welch, Susan, John Comer, and Michael Steinman. 1975. "Ethnic Differences in Political and Social Participation: A Comparison of Some Anglos and Mexican-Americans." *Pacific Sociological Review* 18:361–82.

Welch, Susan, and John R. Hibbing. 1984. "Hispanic Representation in the U.S. Congress." *Social Science Quarterly* 65 (2): 328–35.

Wells, David. 1982. "Against Affirmative Gerrymandering." In Bernard Grofman, Arend Lijphart, Robert B. McKay, and Howard A. Scarrow, eds. *Representation and Redistricting Issues*. Lexington, Mass.: Lexington Books.

Wharton, Vernon Lane. 1965. *The Negro in Mississippi, 1865–1890*. New York: Harper Torchbooks.

Whitcomb v. Chavis, 403 U.S. 124, 159 (1971).

White, Walter. 1948. *A Man Called White: The Autobiography of Walter White*. New York: Viking.

White v. Daniel, no. 88–0568 (E.D. Va. Aug. 31. 1989); 909 F. 2d 99 (4th Cir. 1990).

Wiecek, William W. 1988. *Liberty under Law: The Supreme Court in American Life*. Baltimore: Johns Hopkins University Press.

Williams, Alan J., Nicholas Babchuk, and David R. Johnson. 1973. "Voluntary Associations and Minority Status: A Comparative Analysis of Anglo, Black, and Mexican Americans." *American Sociological Review* 38.

Williams, Linda. 1989. "White/Black Perceptions of the Electability of Black Political Candidates." *National Political Science Review* 2:45–64.

Williams v. Rhodes, 393 U.S. 23, 32 (1968).

Willmott, Peter, and Alan Murie. 1988. *Polarisation and Social Housing: The British and French Experience*. London: Policy Studies Institute.

Wills, David. W. 1990. "Beyond Commonality and Plurality: Persistent Racial Polarity in American Religion and Politics." In Mark A. Noll, ed., *Religion and American Politics.* New York: Oxford University Press.

Wills, Garry. 1992. *Lincoln at Gettysburg: The Words that Remade America.* New York: Simon and Schuster.

Wilson, James Q. 1989. *Bureaucracy: What Government Agencies Do and Why They Do It.* New York: Basic Books.

Wilson, William Julius. 1987. *The Truly Disadvantaged: The Inner City, the Underclass, and Public Policy.* Chicago: University of Chicago Press.

——. 1990. "Race-Neutral Policies and the Democratic Coalition." *The American Prospect* 1:74–81.

Wines, Michael. 1992. "Bush's Campaign Tries Madison Ave." *New York Times,* May 27, A18.

Witte, Edwin E. 1962. *The Development of the Social Security Act.* Madison: University of Wisconsin Press.

Wolfinger, Raymond E.. 1965. "The Development and Persistence of Ethnic Voting." *American Political Science Review* 59:896–906.

——. 1974. *The Politics of Progress.* Englewood Cliffs, N.J.: Prentice-Hall.

Wolfinger, Raymond E., and Stephen J. Rosenstone. 1980 *Who Votes?* New Haven: Yale University Press.

Wolters, Raymond. 1970. *Negroes and the Great Depression: The Problem of Economic Recovery.* Westport, Conn.: Greenwood Press.

Wood, Robert C. 1960. "The Impotent Suburban Vote" *Nation,* March 26, 272–73.

Woodward, C. Vann. 1974. *The Strange Career of Jim Crow.* 3d rev. ed., New York: Oxford University Press.

Yancy, William, Eugene P. Ericksen, and Richard N. Juliani. 1976. "Emergent Ethnicity: A Review and Reformulation." *American Sociological Review* 41:391–403.

Yanos, Alexander Athan. 1993. "Reconciling the Right to Vote with the Voting Rights Act." *Columbia Law Review* 92:1810–66.

Yick Wo v. Hopkins, 118 U.S. 356, 370 (1886).

Young, Henry J., ed. 1988. *The Black Church and the Harold Washington Story.* Bristol, Ind.: Wyndham Hall Press.

Young, Ken, and John Kramer. 1978. *Strategy and Conflict in Metropolitan Housing: Suburbia versus the Greater London Council, 1965–1975.* London: Heinemann.

Young, Iris, Justice. 1990. "Democracy and Group Difference" Paper presented at the American Political Science Association Annual Meeting.

Zax, Jeffrey S. 1990. "Election Methods and Black and Hispanic Council Membership." *Social Science Quarterly* 77 (2): 339–55.

Zikmund, Joseph, II. 1968. "Suburban Voting in Presidential Elections, 1948–1964." *Midwest Journal of Political Science* 12:239–58.

Zimmerman, Joseph F. 1992. "Enhancing Representation Equity in Cities." Wilma Rule and Joseph F. Zimmerman, eds., *United States Electoral Systems: Their Impact on Women and Minorities.* Westport, Conn.: Greenwood Press.

Contributors

JAMES E. ALT is Professor of Government and Codirector of the Program in Political Economy at Harvard University.

KENNETH BENOIT is a Ph.D. candidate, Department of Government, Harvard University.

HENRY E. BRADY is Professor of Political Science and Public Policy and Director of UC Data at the University of California, Berkeley.

JOHN M. BRUCE is Assistant Professor of Government at Georgetown University.

RODOLFO O. DE LA GARZA is Mike Hogg Professor of Community Affairs in the Department of Government at the University of Texas at Austin and Vice-President of the Tomas Rivera Center, a Latino Policy Institute.

ANDREW GELMAN is Assistant Professor of Statistics at the University of California at Berkeley.

LANI GUINIER is Professor of Law at the University of Pennsylvania. She is the author of *The Tyranny of the Majority: Fundamental Fairness in Representative Democracy.*

FREDRICK C. HARRIS is Assistant Professor of Political Science and a member of the Frederick Douglas Institute for African-American Studies at the University of Rochester.

GARY KING is Professor of Government and Director of the Harvard Data Center at Harvard University. He is currently finishing a book entitled *A Solution to the Ecological Inference Problem.*

ROBERT C. LIEBERMAN is Assistant Professor of Political Science and Public Affairs at Columbia University.

DAVID IAN LUBLIN is Assistant Professor in the Department of Government and International Studies at the University of South Carolina.

DAVID HAYWOOD METZ graduated summa cum laude with a B.A. in Government from Harvard College. He is currently a budget and management analyst for the City of Milwaukee.

PAUL E. PETERSON is the Henry Lee Shattuck Professor of Government and the Director of the Center for American Political Studies at Harvard University.

KAY LEHMAN SCHLOZMAN is Professor of Political Science at Boston College.

KENNETH A. SHEPSLE is Professor of Government and Director of the Program in Political Economy at Harvard University.

THEDA SKOCPOL is Professor of Government and Sociology at Harvard University.

KATHERINE TATE is an Associate Professor of Political Science at The Ohio State University.

RICHARD M. VALELLY is Associate Professor of Political Science at Swarthmore College.

SIDNEY VERBA is the Carl H. Pforzheimer University Professor at Harvard University and President of the American Political Science Association.

MARGARET WEIR is a Senior Fellow in the Governmental Studies Program at the Brookings Institution.

Index

Abram, Kathryn, 30
Abramson, Paul R., 321
Accountability: political process and, 23, 24, 30; racial and minority groups, 29, 30, 37–38; voting rights and, 31–32; winner-take-all, 43
Activism: church-based, 278, 283–84, 286–87, 291–307, 375n.21, 376n.26; concerns and issues of, 368–71, 373, 376n.28, 377nn.30 and 31; contacting and protesting, 360–61, 362; level of activity, 361–64, 372; participation and democracy, 354–61, 372, 374n.7; racial factors, 376n.22
Adams, Charles, 287
ADC (Aid to Dependent Children). *See also* Social Security Act of 1935
Administrative institutions, 158–59
AFDC. *See* Aid to Families with Dependent Children
Affirmative action: public opinion on, 7–8, 276n.12 quotas and, 6–8; redistricting and, 87
African Americans: advancement of African American policy interests, 114–22; districts and, 11, 21, 35, 37–41, 76*t*, 114–15; elections and elected officials, 87–88, 106–7, 110n.24, 112–14, 115, 124, 125n.5, 189, 210, 211, 251, 255–59, 262–74; employment of, 141, 142–43, 159–60, 163; as an interest group, 25; mathematical models of representation, 94–105; political activism of, 356–64, 368–73, 374n.6, 375n.12; political fairness for, 23, 28, 31, 94–105; political parties and, 11–13, 195, 246–47, 280–81; political power of, 257, 280, 307n.12; presidential elections, 13; public housing for, 224; racial bloc voting, 13–14; Reaganism and, 148; Reconstruction and, 194, 280; redistricting and, 75, 113, 114–25; single parent families, 179; social policies and, 4, 135–49, 151, 152–53; socioeconomic issues, 129, 135–36, 137, 141–42, 177–78; standards of racial fairness for, 86–94; upward mobility of, 146; urban issues of, 5, 225, 228, 229,

246, 247–50; volunteer and religious activism of, 364–68, 372, 375n.21; voting by, 73, 247–50, 253–55; women's clubs, 140. *See also* Black electoral success theory; Minorities; Race and racism; Religious institutions, African American; Social policies
African Methodist Episcopal Church (AME), 280, 296
Agrarian Revolt, 307n.12
Agricultural workers. *See* Employment issues
Aid to Dependent Children (ADC). *See* Social Security Act of 1935
Aid to Families with Dependent Children (AFDC), 134, 148–49
Alabama: African American population in, 249–50; African American workers in, 174; cumulative voting in, 72, 73; elections in, 32, 88, 252, 258, 273; electoral regulations, 212; limited voting in, 73; redistricting in, 37, 116–18, 122; restrictions on suffrage, 203–4; social programs, 139; voter registration in, 316, 317, 319
Alternative vote (AV). *See* Voting
Altmeyer, Arthur J., 166
American Dilemma (Myrdal), 283
Arizona, 140
Arkansas, 200–201, 319
Arrington, Richard, 273
Arthur (Chester) administration, 200, 201, 202, 204, 210, 212
Asian Americans, 276n.22
Australia, 74
Australian ballot. *See* Secret ballot
Austria, 71*f*, 76

Bachus, Spencer, 118
Baker v. Carr (1962), 25
Bakke, Allen. See *Regents of the University of California v. Bakke*
Baldwin, James, 156
Balladur, Edouard, 238
Baptist church, 280
Beer v. United States (1976), 91